# Understanding SAP™ APO

AF737994

Wolfgang Eddigehausen

ISBN Number: 0-615-11500-4

This book is dedicated to:

My wife, Desirée, who encouraged me to continue throughout all the months.

My parents who laid the foundation for my professional career.

Without my family I would not be what I am today.

# Foreword

The last decade of the $20^{th}$ century saw the large-scale advent of packaged software. In the previous decades scores of expensive programmers treaded water, barely keeping non-core Information Technology systems such as General Ledgers, Accounts Payable Ledgers and Logistics systems alive. This allowed no opportunity for IT to really add value to business in areas such as customer interfaces and supply chain management. During the 1990's many large and medium sized organizations rectified this waste of resources through the implementation of packaged software. "ERP" became a conventional wisdom and a whole industry was created to implement it.

In a number of instances the obvious advantages of packaged software were overshadowed by failures. Large complex implementations tried to achieve in months, what IT had not achieved in decades before. The industry around ERP created its own hype; competition was fierce, and there were huge temptations to sell quick fix "diet pill" solutions. Corporations were promised the equivalent of the Charles Atlas campaigns of the 1950's. As with the visual images of Charles Atlas, and the reality of the effort required to get to such corporate fitness, there were expectations that were not met. Yet the implementation of an ERP foundation is the necessary investment in infrastructure that, on its own, does not yield immediate and dramatic results, but provides the foundation for the real value achievable from Information Technology.

The SAP supply chain solution is the natural extension of the basis built by integrated, reliable and functional package software, to start addressing the matters that really matter to business, and where the benefits will be much more obvious and costs easier to justify, often yielding benefits that are multiples of the cost of implementation within the first year.

During the ERP days, the shortage of experienced internal staff resulted in consultants often putting large and expensive teams on the client projects. Amongst other side effects, it created a false consulting industry where "consultants" added no value other than knowing how to find their way through the configuration screens of the software. Those days are over, and the true consultant is re-emerging; an individual who has done it before several times, and has real business advice and solutions to offer.

This book supports our philosophy that the client personnel should be empowered with enough knowledge to get maximum benefit from the experienced consultant in the minimum time, and at a reasonable cost. From the consultant's viewpoint, this allows for the satisfaction of more creative and productive work where real issues are tackled instead of doing the same old configuration process that was done on the previous three projects.

Hans Visser
CEO, CSIPER Consulting

www.csiper.com

# About the Author

Wolfgang Eddigehausen was born and grew up in Germany. He studied at the Technical University in Darmstadt where he earned a degree in Mechanical Engineering, Finance and Accounting.

After completing his degree, he started to work for a large German multi national company in 1986. Based on the subjects studied, it was a natural progression getting involved in the Supply Chain Management. He gained a wealth of knowledge in the warehousing and distribution areas as a project member in various countries such as France, Great Britain, and South Africa. In 1992 he took up an offer as a project manager for the SAP R/2 implementation of the Material Management and Production Planning modules in South Africa. From there it was a small step to get involved in SAP R/3, which he did when joining a local South African consulting house in 1994. He is currently still working with the same company, specializing on the SAP R/3 Logistics Modules, and lately on the SAP New Dimension Product, APO.

He is a certified SAP consultant in Material Management (MM), Production Planning (PP), and Accelerated SAP (ASAP). During the last years he was involved in various activities and projects in Europe, South Africa, Singapore, Australia, and the USA. Currently residing in the USA, he is fully dedicated towards the Supply Chain Management area and the use of SAP APO in particular. His area of expertise includes not only the general Supply Chain Management area, but also a very detailed knowledge of the APO package. Knowing the problems accompanied with getting started on a new platform like APO, he decided to write this book to the benefit of all who need to gain an in-depth knowledge of APO.

# 1 Preface

It all started in August 1997 when SAP announced APO as part of their Supply Chain Management Initiative called SCOPE (Supply Chain Optimization, Planning and Execution). I had already been working with various clients in this area and found that often something was missing in the SAP R/3 environment which was exactly that, an integrated supply chain management planning and optimization tool. More than once clients decided to overcome this shortage by implementing additional software packages. This strategy, although the only feasible solution at this time, proved to offer various traps. A considerable amount of time and money was spent on developing interfaces from and to SAP R/3. This promised to deliver the desired result, but it was clear up-front that this would slow down the on-line R/3 system and degrade the responsiveness. Batch interfaces, once they are working require not only patience from the user but also need to be monitored daily. Software is never error free and why should the batch interface, quickly developed by an implementation team with limited understanding of the two packages in question, be different? This statement is not meant to degrade the implementation teams, which are doing their best to get the desired results. It is just a fact that companies like SAP spent thousands of hours to develop software packages with highly complex data structures and interdependencies. It is therefore virtually impossible to "quickly" interface core functions. Only very few people would buy a car from one manufacturer and implant another manufacturer's engine because it is more powerful. On top of that, I doubt that they will be happy about this decision in the long run. While the task of interfacing R/3 is not easy, often it is underestimated. As a result the developed interfaces are scaled down versions of what is required, are based on currently applied business processes and the current organizational structure. What does this mean?

- Scaled Down Interface
  Functionality required by the business is not implemented due to the high cost and the time required for delivering. As a result, the solution delivered to the business is not well accepted and not utilizing the real functionality of either

R/3 or the other interfaced software package. The interface acts like an applied handbrake while at the same time functionality paid for in R/3 is not utilized.

- Current Process Orientation
  Time constraints and sometimes missing business vision lead to a situation where interfaces focus solely on current business processes. Companies all over the world face constant changes and only those that can react fast can survive. Systems by nature are not always flexible and SAP has done a lot to keep R/3 as flexible as possible. Interfaces focussed on current processes are counterproductive and expensive to maintain although cheaper in the beginning.
- Current Organizational Structure Orientation
  Similar to above in motivation and effect, it is unfortunately sort of common practice to focus on the current organizational structure. Trying to break out, or worse add new entities, requires change of the interfaces again. It is surprising that in a time of mergers and mega mergers this practice can still be found.

The answer to these problems is not to be a perfectionist when developing interfaces, but to avoid them as far as possible. This can be achieved by checking the following:

- What is the real value I get?
  A critical look at the added value a supplementary software package (or custom system) can deliver is required. Do not compare what the two could do, but rather what they will do for your business after the implementation is complete. Consider the cost caused by the interfaces. It is not only the development cost, which is important, but also the running cost. As said above, interfaces often limit the co-operation of the two systems and limit the achieved value considerably.
- Are there solutions within R/3?
  They might not be as elegant or sophisticated, but they work without extra development. I know of cases where highly sophisticated systems are interfaced to R/3 but the extra cost is in no way justifiable when compared to the added value they deliver.

- Can I use vendor-supplied interfaces?
  SAP is opening R/3 for other systems by means of standard interfaces (e.g. BAPI). APO from SAP is only one of these systems. But be aware that system vendors might claim to work with these interfaces but make you pay for the development. Keep your hands away if the source code of an interface has to be adapted to suit your business.

Coming back to SAP APO, I was obviously highly interested in this new development. It took another few months before SAP released their Advanced Planner and Optimizer (APO), which was then part of a whole family of other products called New Dimension Products. I went through every document I could get and read more than a thousand pages before I finally had the opportunity to get hands-on experience. The documents I had proved to be either too high level or too detailed. While viewing a nice colorful presentation, I could not see how the things are supposed to work. And then I had these hands-on oriented documents which explain the how but not the concept behind the low-level task.

This book is aimed to bridge this gap. It starts with an overview of the technical environment in which APO runs. This includes an overview of the hardware landscape. Then follows a detailed description of the APO modules, the business processes covered, and the flow of data within APO. Anybody interested in APO must read these sections to understand the concepts.

I hope this book will be an efficient way to gather all the information required for building up understanding about APO as well as to support the daily work with APO. Whether it is as a user or as a project member responsible to implement APO.

Somebody who is truly working with an APO system and knows what it requires to set up such a system successfully wrote this book. It is therefore based on real experience in the Supply Chain Management discipline rather than on generic knowledge. Should you have any further question regarding Supply Chain Management issues, APO in general, or this book in particular, I would be more than happy to help as much as possible. I can be contacted using the following e-mail address:

apo@fast.net.au

It is my intention to complement this book with another edition that will cover all new functionality of the upcoming releases. Providing me with your feedback will allow me to concentrate even more on topics of general interest. I encourage you to do so to help me giving the APO community with the most valuable information possible.

This book is not meant to be a replacement for qualified training.

# 2 Introduction

## 2.1 Supply Chain Management

In a highly competitive market, efficient Supply Chain Management is no longer just a way to improve the overall profitability of an enterprise, but it becomes more and more a prerequisite for those companies that want to remain in the market. Up to some years ago, the majority of enterprises focussed on the optimization of internal processes. While this possibly provided an optimum for the specific entity, the overall efficiency of the supply chain starting at the vendor and going right through to the customer was not considered and in the worst case was even negatively affected by these activities. Optimizing one element of the supply chain certainly reduced the element's overall cost but sometimes increased the overall cost of the entire supply chain. The reason for this striving for local optima was quite often the only possibility as powerful software and hardware was either not available or out of reach from a financial point of view. Reduced cost for both and an increased awareness for this problem resulted in the advent of powerful yet more affordable solutions. Supply Chain Management Optimization right now is one of the fastest growing areas within the area of standard software and with increasing demand the cost will further decrease. This self-accelerating process is predicted to last for the foreseeable future. Technologies like the Internet support efficient Supply Chain Management and at the same time force companies to go this way. Consumers demand nowadays more customized products with lower lead times. The time where everybody drove the same type of car is over; consumers want their "personalized" car and that within a short lead-time. The challenge is to minimize all non-value added waiting time and to synchronize all activities within the supply chain. This leads to a responsive and highly adaptable environment where not only the consumer satisfaction is ensured, but where, at the same time, intermediate stock holding levels and stock obsolescence are minimized.

Efficient Supply Chain management breaks traditional "Planning Kingdoms". Companies are still responsible for efficient shop floor planning. But when it comes to the optimization of the entire supply network, collaboration across multiple companies is not an option but a prerequisite. This is a cultural issue that will have by far more of an impact on a company than the implementation of a new ERP system, whether this is SAP or another package. The introduction of Supply Chain Management solutions must go hand in hand with intensive Change Management activities.

The first wave of streamlining the logistical process focussed on the optimization of internal processes for the supplier, manufacturer, or customer. This approach lead to savings within the three entities, but, at the same time often, increased costs on the other level. In a second wave, the entities were linked and exchanged information via Electronic Data Interchange (EDI) for example. This again reduced cost due to faster response time.

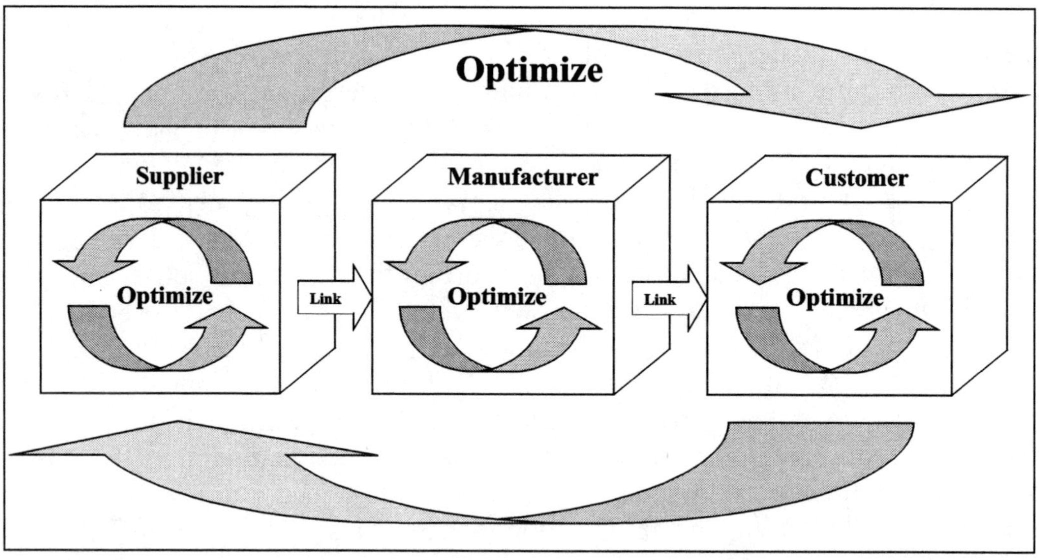


**Graphic 1 – Supply Chain Optimization**

Currently, with the Supply Chain Management approach the whole chain from component supply through to consumer consumption is seen as a chain that needs to be optimized across all levels. Supply Chain Management requires powerful systems that are open to exchange data with various other systems, thus optimizing the entire supply chain.

Supply Chain Management is an approach where data from various entities is collected processed, and presented in a form that supports the decision-making process. More and better information leads to faster response time and lower stock levels thus improving customer satisfaction and reducing the overall supply chain cost.

## 2.2 Introduction to APO

APO offers various planning tools to aid an efficient Supply Chain Management. Its task is solely the planning of these activities. APO is geared towards the optimization of the entire supply chain. Execution and process control takes place in an On Line Transaction Process (OLTP) system. SAP R/3 is one of them and certainly the preferred one as all required interfaces are supported. Each of the 3 planning modules within APO is aimed at a certain planning horizon as depicted in the diagram below.

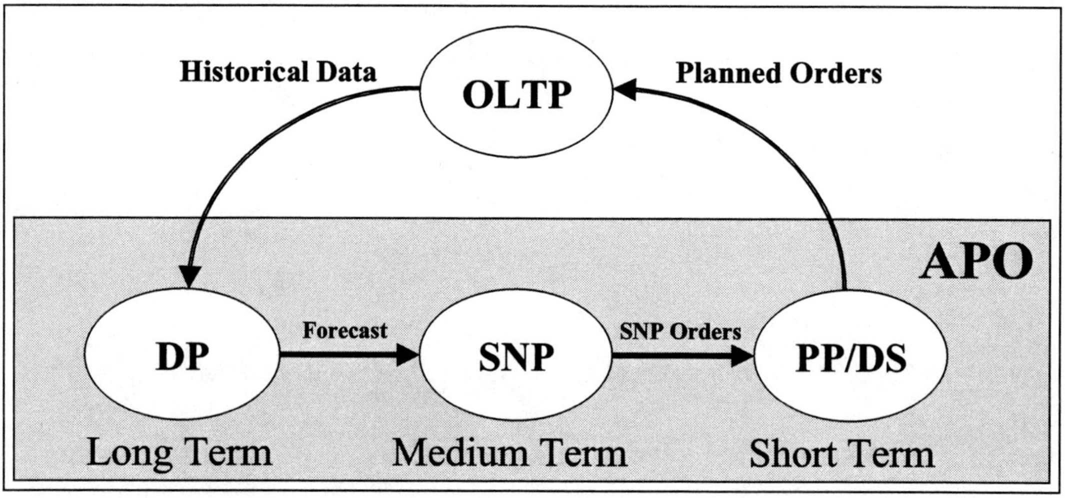


**Graphic 2 – Planning Horizon**

DP — is aimed at the long-term demand planning, and the output is an unconstrained demand plan. A monthly planning horizon for one to two years is common for this task.

SNP — follows up on this plan and matches demand with supply in the medium term. Optimization can be carried out. Planning horizons commonly used are 3 months in 4 weekly and 2 monthly buckets. Infinite scheduling is carried out.

| | |
|---|---|
| PP/DS | only comes into action at manufacturing sites and offers finite scheduling. A two-to-four week planning horizon is common for this task. Optimization of production including sequencing is carried out. |
| Deployment | plans the distribution of products within the supply chain network. This is usually carried out with a one-to-two week horizon. Deployment is part of the SNP module. |
| TLB | (Transport Load Builder) is combining loads with the same destination and ensures an economical use of transport resources. It is not optimizing route planning! The planning horizon is similar to deployment and in the region of up to one week. TLB is part of the SNP module. |
| TP/VS | supports the distribution of products within the entire supply chain. Once it will be available in release 3.0, it will to some extent replace functionality of TLB. The transportation component is more orientated towards medium to long term planning. The vehicle scheduling is a short term planning and optimization tool based on the deployment results. |
| Global ATP | supports ERP system by providing product availability data across plants and systems. It can not only support various plants in one R/3 system, but also various R/3 installations, and even heterogeneous environments with SAP R/3 and other systems. |

The DP and SNP modules are also used for strategic planning and simulations (what if analysis). Another new module that comes with APO deals specifically with situations where multiple plants exist and/or multiple systems are used.

## 2.3 Planning with APO and R/3

When starting to work with APO a lot of functions look very familiar, although there is a whole lot of new terminology. In fact looking at R/3 release 4.5 (or higher) shows plenty of commonality. We will discuss in this chapter that APO is a planning tool at the planning process and compare it with the functionality offered in R/3.

R/3 planning starts with the long-term Sales and Operations Plan (SOP), which is an unconstrained demand (sales) plan. It is also called the forecast. This plan is usually carried out in monthly or weekly buckets. The data R/3 is using is stored in Information Structures, which are fed by the core R/3 transactions. The database used is not the transactional one where one would find for example all sales orders. The Information Structure provides an accumulated view on data and is customizable according to individual needs.

Once the unconstrained demand plan is finalized, Independent Requirements are created. These Independent Requirements are broken down into daily buckets and constitute the exact production and/or transportation demand. Rough Cut Capacity Planning and Infinite Scheduling is possible after the Independent Requirements have been picked up by the Master Production Schedule (MPS) run, which creates planned orders. Only a subset of all materials is planned using the MPS run. The MPS run creates a constrained plan as it takes resource capacities into account or at least highlights possible resource problems. The planner then adjusts the MPS plan to make it feasible.

The last step in this process is the Material Requirements Planning (MRP) run with the subsequent Scheduling or Capacity Requirements Planning (CRP). This step involves all materials that require planning. Capacity Requirements Planning (CRP) is also referred to as Finite Scheduling.

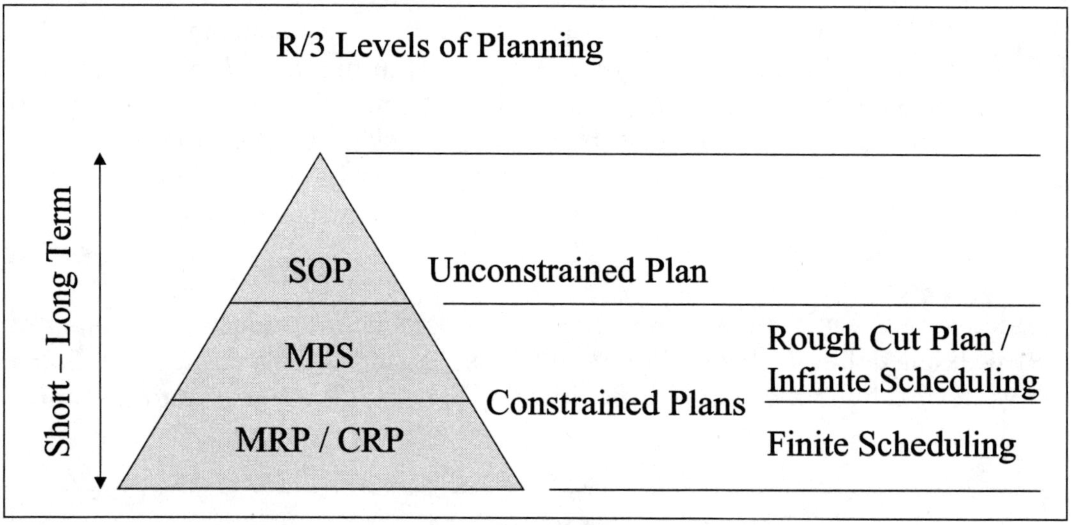


**Graphic 3 – Planning with R/3**

If we have a look at APO, not too much is different. At least at the first glance. The long term unconstrained plan is generated in an environment called Demand Planning (DP). Data storage for historical data as well as the forecast is in the InfoCube. The InfoCube is very similar in function to the Information Structures in R/3 and data is also accumulated according to individual needs. What is different, is the comfort with which tasks are performed, the much more user-friendly graphical user interface, and last but not least there is lots of additional functionality not available currently in R/3. The output is again an unconstrained plan as it was with R/3.

In the next step, the unconstrained plan is released from DP to Supply Network Planning (SNP) for further processing. SAP calls the input to SNP Forecast, although the word Independent Requirements is also used sometimes. In essence it is the same. SNP picks up these forecasts like MPS the Independent Requirements and creates a constrained plan in the SNP run. The big difference is that APO does not just load resources assuming an infinite capacity as R/3 does, but it can create feasible plans and optimize them when using the SNP Optimizer. A non-optimizing version called the Heuristics does pretty much the same as the R/3 MPS does. Again the difference is how. Furthermore APO is really a network-planning tool, planning for the entire network in one run and taking into considerations production and distribution. This is really a huge difference! SNP also offers Transportation Planning and Deployment (with possible optimization). Transportation Optimization will come with a future release. Usually not all products will be planned in SNP.

The last step is again Finite Scheduling, which is done in Production Planning & Detailed Scheduling (PP/DS). PP/DS offers sophisticated tools far above R/3 and allows for example the optimization of the planned order sequence to minimize setup and tear down times.

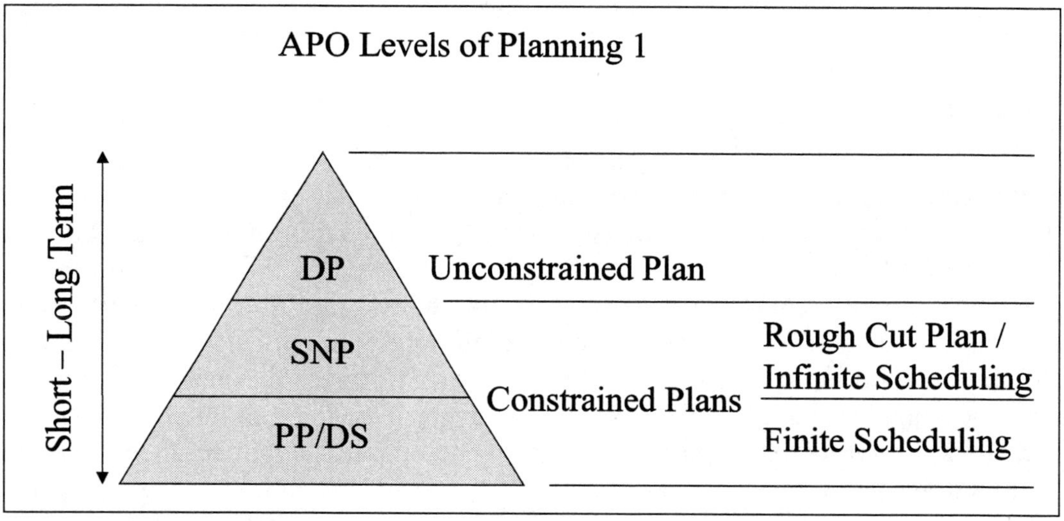


**Graphic 4 – Planning with APO 1**

In addition to the above-described functionality, APO offers the Capable-to-Match (CTM) functionality. CTM is a hybrid between the SNP run and the Finite Scheduling in PP/DS. CTM can create a finite scheduled feasible plan that requires no further refinement. PP/DS sequence optimization might still be carried out. SNP could still be carried out, but is actually not necessary.

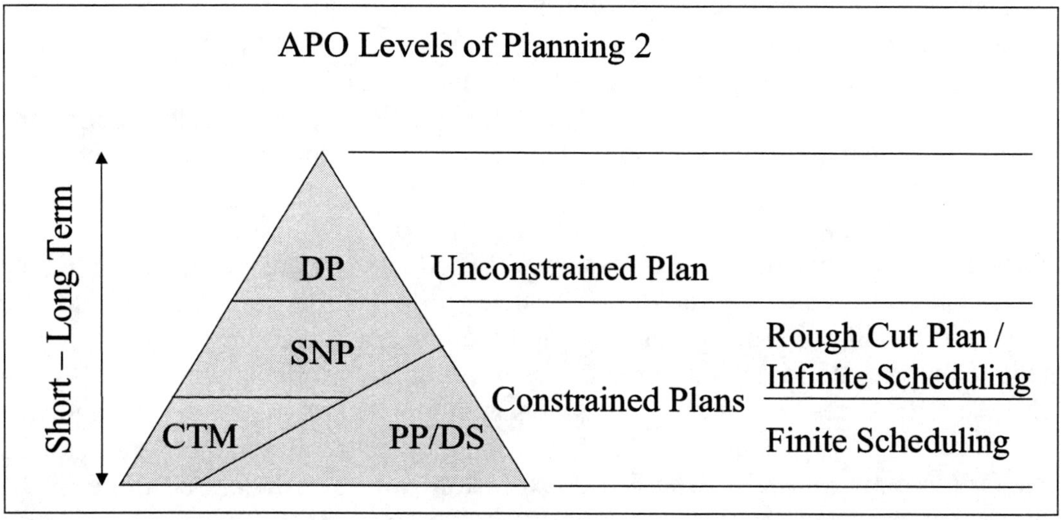


**Graphic 5 – Planning with APO 2**

As we have seen above, APO replaces the MPS and MRP run usually carried out in the OLTP system. Based on this there is no need to perform these activities anymore in the OLTP system. This assumption is right and wrong as it depends on whether you plan all or only some products in APO.

Most companies run MPS for all strategic products or other products that require special attention during planning. These might be all products manufactured on bottleneck resources. It is good practice to plan such products that were part of the MPS run using APO. For the remaining products, two options are feasible.

1. All products planned in APO
   If all remaining (non-MPS) products are also planned in APO no other planning activities need to take place in the OLTP system. This might be the

most elegant solution as only one system is used to perform all planning activities. For this scenario one must consider the additional load on APO as the number of planning objects increases rapidly when adding the non-MPS products. It is also required to use production process models that include all components, which will certainly slow down not only the SNP planning, but also the detailed scheduling in PP/DS.

2. Some products planned in R/3, some in APO
   Should some of the products not be planned in APO, it is required to plan them separately in the OLTP system. This solution might be rather confusing for the planner, as the question will always be where the product/component is planned, in APO or the OLTP system. If the intention is to use APO for strategic products/components only, this is the option to go for.

In the above comparison the expression "all products" means products for which dependent requirements should be created. Products or components that are replenished using re-order point procedures or forecast-based procedures do not need to be planned in APO at all. The assumption, for products planned with one of these procedures, is that there is always enough stock available when required. Individual BOM explosion with determination of exact requirements is not carried out for planning purposes. The BOM explosion can nevertheless be done in the OLTP system to generate the shop floor control papers.

APO has its own Production Process Models that contain the Bill of Material and Routing data, usually held in R/3. If a product is planned in APO, there is no need to store the bill of material and routing data anymore in R/3. At least for the production planning purposes. If the PPM in APO contains all data required for the execution of the planned production order in R/3, then this area also does not need anymore the bill of material and routing to be in R/3. The problem is that we still need this data for Costing purposes. First of all, the standard cost of the product needs to be established (Costing with Quantity Structure). To do so, the system, which is R/3, needs the bill of material (product and component quantities) and the routing (resource consumption). During the execution of the production order in R/3, this data is needed again to compare planned and actual consumption to derive the deviations.

As a result, PPM information stored in APO must be duplicated in R/3 in the form of the BOM and routing, as otherwise product costing will not be possible. This is the case as long as these data objects are not properly integrated and accessible from both systems. In my mind, the PPM data object needs to be enriched by costing information and be made available to both, APO and R/3. Where the PPM is stored physically is of no functional importance and must be decided based on access considerations.

## 2.4 The APO Planning Hierarchy

APO offers various planning tools that can be characterized by planning horizon, planning area, and planning object. Each of these tools support one of the classical planing tasks that need to be carried out in order to efficiently manage a supply network. The following table gives an overview of a possible network of planners. This is not meant to be the solution for any business using APO, it merely gives an idea of the complexity of a planning hierarchy.

| Planning Area | Planning Horizon | Planning Object | Function | APO Module (*) |
|---|---|---|---|---|
| Supply Chain | | | | |
| | Long-term Strategic | Network | Network Designer | ND |
| | Mid-term | Network | Supply Chain Planner | SNP |
| | Short-term | Network | Supply Chain Manager | SNP |
| Transportation | | | | |
| | Long-term | Fleet | Fleet Planner | DP & SNP |
| | Mid-term | Order | Transportation Planner | TP |
| | Short-term | Load | Transportation Manager | VS |
| Production | | | | |
| | Long-term | Resource | Resource Planner | DP & SNP |
| | Mid-term | Order | Production Planner | PP |
| | Short-term | Activity | Shop Floor Supervisor | DS |

| Planning Area / Planning Horizon | | Planning Object | Function | APO Module (*) |
|---|---|---|---|---|
| Strategic Sourcing / Purchasing | | | | |
| | Long-term | Contract | Procurement Planner | DP & SNP |
| | Mid-term | Order | Buyer | SNP |
| | Short-term | Requisition | Controller | PP |
| Demand | | | | |
| | Long-term | Global Forecast | Demand Planner | DP |
| | Mid-term | Customer Forecast | Key Account Manager | DP |
| | Mid-term | Promotion | Marketing Manager | DP |
| | Short-term | Forecast | Demand Manager | DP |
| | Short-term | Order | Sales Representative | DP |

**Table 1 – Planning Tasks**

(*) The modules Network Design (ND) and Transportation Planning and Vehicle Scheduling (TP/VS) are in development and will be available as part of the release 3.0 functionality.

## 2.5 The System Environment

APO is a completely new software package. Unlike other offerings in the Supply Chain Market, it is one application and not a mix of bought software applications that were adapted to somehow fit together. The benefit is a clear, easy to understand and, most of all, consistent layout of all functions. It also often looks and feels like R/3 but is not part of it. The target market obviously is the existing R/3 customer base, but it can, at the same time, run in conjunction with any other non-SAP system. The APO interfaces are supported by R/3 (release 3.1 upward), but not by R/2. At least one site running R/2 is also using APO with custom written interfaces.

### 2.5.1 Software

Most of the APO system is written in ABAP, the proprietary language used as well for R/3. Any programmer will feel familiar as key elements like the data dictionary or the editor is used the same way as in R/3. Some modules were taken over from ILOG, a company that works extensively in the data optimization and visualization segment of programming.

The integration of ILOG delivered functions is totally seamless to the user. There is never a moment where the user thinks to work with something that does not feel like APO. The table below gives an overview of ILOG components that complement APO.

The ILOG modules are not written in ABAP, but in other languages like C++. The cooperation of SAP and ILOG is intended to expand, and the next joined development is the Optimization Extension Workbench. With this workbench it will be possible to plug in special optimization routines into APO. These optimization routines can be either special developments from ILOG for a specific business or proprietary developments from customers who wish to use own specialized optimization rules.

| APO | ILOG Module | Usage |
|---|---|---|
| Supply Chain Cockpit and Supply Chain Engineer | Views | Visualization if the supply chain model |
| Supply Network Planning | Planner | Optimization of the supply network plan |
| Production Planning / Detailed Scheduling | Scheduler | Capacity planning and optimization |
| Capable-to-Match | Scheduler | Capacity planning and optimization |
| Transportation Planning | Dispatcher | Deployment of transportation capacities |

**Table 2 – ILOG Modules**

The commonality between R/3 and APO includes the Graphical User Interface (GUI). It is the same as the one used for R/3 (any version 4.5 and up will do). Once the GUI is installed on the user's PC, access to APO is as easy as it is with R/3. After starting the GUI, the user will type in the APO system name instead of the R/3 system name. The logon procedure is therefore identical and, once logged in the system, looks very familiar. Help, System tools and Office is at the same place, obviously the name of the various APO specific drop-down boxes and tree structures are different. A surprise will come up once the Supply Chain Cockpit is launched. This interactive screen, which supports all main daily tasks to be performed by the planner, definitely is something new. It makes work much easier and supports plenty of graphical aids. For a detailed description of the Supply Chain Cockpit refer to the appropriate chapter.

## 2.5.2 liveCache

APO uses a technology called liveCache to enable a fast response for most of the transactions. liveCache is a technology where the majority of master and transaction data is stored in memory and not in a database stored on disks. liveCache is written in C++ and not in ABAP. It can be seen as a memory resident database. All SNP and PP/DS orders are stored in it together with various time series. This allows APO programs to read and write data into fast memory instead of using slower disks. Important entities in liveCache are the ATP Time Series that store all demands and supplies aggregated per day. The PP/DS planning table where planned orders can be rescheduled "on the fly" also benefits extremely from liveCache. Optimization routines without using liveCache would be very time-consuming if not impractical. The liveCache concept is the reason for the high requirements in terms of system memory. This must not be seen as a disadvantage compared to competitive products, as those products can obviously not provide the responsiveness of the APO liveCache.

| | InfoCube | Tables | liveCache |
|---|---|---|---|
| DP | | | *1 |
| SNP | | | |
| PPDS | | | |
| GATP | *2 | | |

**Table 3 – Data Storage Concept**

*1 At a later stage, liveCache technology will also be used to store data used in Demand Planning. We will see to which extent it is feasible to store entire InfoCubes in liveCache.

*2 Global ATP uses InfoCubes to initially store and maintain Product Allocations. They are copied into liveCache before being used in Global ATP.

Currently, the liveCache in APO contains the following data:

- Master Data
  The storage of master data takes place in conventional table structures and in liveCache. This is transparent to the user. Deletion of master data deletes the entries in liveCache at the same time.
- Order Network Data
  The Order Network Data is the information about all orders in APO. Orders can either originate in APO itself (e.g. newly created planned production orders) or be transmitted from an OLTP system (e.g. sales orders). Order data remain in liveCache as long as the order is "active".
- Time Series Data
  For each product the Time Series Data stipulates all demands and supplies. Global ATP for example uses this data to determine product availability.

### 2.5.3 Hardware and Network

The APO hardware configuration and network requirements depend very much on the user's requirements. APO is very modular and several hardware units can be used simultaneously, each dedicated to a certain task. On the other hand one piece of hardware can run everything. APO is, like R/3, based on the client-server architecture. The following table lists all APO components of the client server network.

- Presentation Server
  The client workstation, or presentation server, is the PC the user is working on. It can be running under Windows NT, 95 or 98. On this PC the Graphical User Interface must be loaded (see next chapter). The presentation server can also be used to run the optimizing programs if that is not done on either the optimization server(s) or on the application server.
- Database Server
  The database server is the repository of all data except such information that is stored in liveCache. It is also used to store liveCache data if the system is shut down. It can be run using various operating systems. APO was initially developed to run under Windows NT with an Oracle database. As of release

2.0 the Microsoft SQL server is also supported. UNIX operating systems (HP-UX, IBM AIX, Sun Solaris, etc.) are supported with release 2.0 to work together with an Oracle database. As in R/3, exactly one database server is required.

- Application Server
  The application server is the place where all applications are running. Optimization programs can also run on dedicated optimization servers, thus taking a lot of strain off the application server. The application server and the database server can be the same machine. Global ATP functionality is also executed on the application server. Various applications servers can be clustered around one database server. For possible operating systems, see the database server explanation above.
- liveCache Server
  The liveCache server requires a reasonably sized main memory (RAM). Depending on the requirements, the memory should start at 2Gb. The liveCache server can run only under Windows NT and not under any UNIX operating system.
- Optimization Server – Supply Network Planning
  The SNP optimization server must be a high performance PC that runs under Windows NT. The constraint is the CPU speed. There are no specifically high requirements for either disk capacity or main memory. The optimization server and presentation server can be the same machine. Care needs to be taken in a multi-user environment if the optimization is carried out on a presentation server, as this PC must probably be available to other users as well. The allocation of optimization servers is done via customizing (or transaction SM59) and can therefore easily be changed even while the system is running.
- Optimization Server – Capable-to-Match
  For the CTM optimization server, the same restrictions apply as for the SNP optimization server. See above notes for the SNP server.
- Optimization Server – Detailed Production Scheduling
  For the PP/DS optimization server, the same restrictions as for the SNP optimization server apply. See above notes for the SNP server.
- Global ATP Server

Currently Global ATP functionality is carried out mainly in the liveCache and application server. Future plans in this area include the introduction of a dedicated Global ATP server.

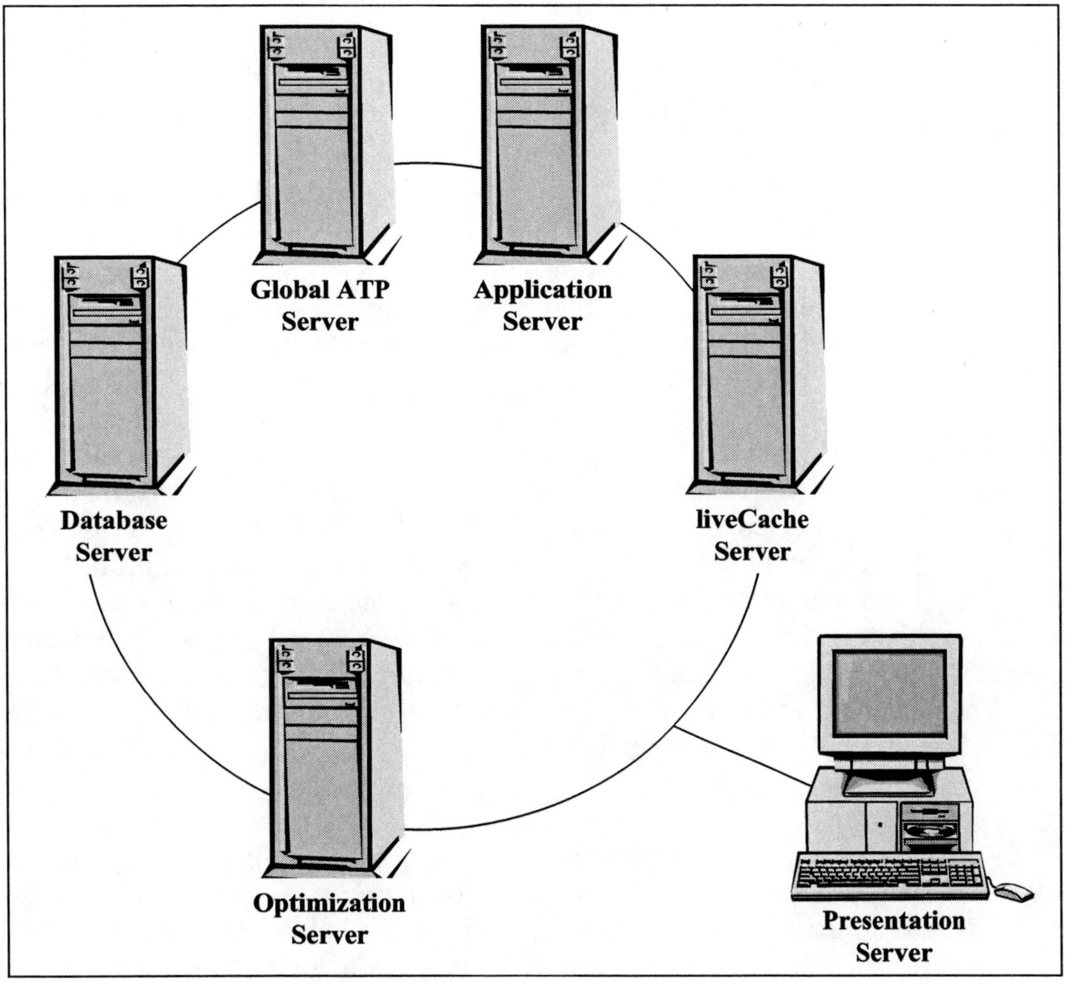


**Graphic 6 – APO Large System Landscape**

The graphic above shows a large system setup where all activities are handled on separate units as far as possible. Small evaluation or test systems can consist of a single Windows NT based server with PC workstations as required. It is not possible in this case to run any UNIX operating system at the moment as some of the components only run under Windows NT.

## 2.5.4 Graphical User Interface

The Graphical User Interface (GUI) of APO is that of R/3. The SAP GUI is downwards compatible for both APO and R/3. Release numbers distinguish the various levels APO and R/3 software. In the case of the GUI it is version numbers. A GUI version with a certain number supports the same or lower R/3 release number. This does not work this easily with APO. APO release 1.1 is the equivalent to R/3 release 4.5, and APO release 2.0 corresponds to R/3 release 4.6.

In order to run APO release 1.1 or lower, it was necessary to install the GUI that was delivered with APO. This GUI came with some extensions specifically added for APO. This GUI is released for Windows 95, 98, and NT. Windows 95 or 98 is supported but causes problems. Even with Windows 98 Second Edition, when using APO for a longer time, some elements on the screen are not displayed anymore although they are still there and accessible (as long as you know where the are). I decided to live with this problem avoiding the installation of Windows NT. The nice thing with the APO GUI is that one can use the same GUI for both R/3 and APO. The only difference is the system ID specified in the GUI's Logon Pad.

With APO release 2.0, a new GUI based on the "SAP Enjoy" initiative is available. It is also released for all Windows operating systems. When installing the GUI, it is necessary to select the installations of the APO add-on's. Other than that no differences exist between the GUI installation for R/3 and APO. Once installed, any APO and/or R/3 system can be used. I have been running the version 4.6 GUI with both, release 1.1 and 2.0 of APO on a Windows 98 Second Edition based system with the problems described further down.

The main problem I found with this new GUI is that the minimize, maximize, and close buttons are not at the right top position of the screen, but a bit to the left of it. This as such is not an issue, but they are now exactly behind the Microsoft Office buttons and thus not accessible. This is really annoying, and the only way around is to run the GUI in a smaller window. The new 4.6 GUI allows extended customizing of its appearance. It can even be set to a mode that makes it operate like the older version GUI. This improves the responsiveness of the screen tremendously and overcomes the problem described above. Any disadvantage? No SAP Enjoy GUI anymore, but therefore a GUI that I enjoy much more.

## 2.6 APO and the Internet

Some people might wonder what a Supply Chain Management tool like APO has got to do with the Internet. At first glance, it looks as if APO is a system used by large companies to optimize their supply chain. That is right, but not the whole story by far.

First of all, when dealing with various partners (the members of the supply chain), it is nice to have a network that works without any big hassles when setting up. The other question is, whether every partner in the supply chain has a sophisticated hardware/software system (if any) and access to dedicated networks. Lots of partners in the supply chain are indeed smaller entities. This could be the subcontractor who needs to be instructed and informed about the production schedule or the supermarket around the corner with which a Vendor Managed Inventory (VMI) agreement exists. These are typically the partners that need a possibility to communicate with the manufacturer and its APO system. Another application is the collaboration with carriers to enable them to plan for upcoming transportation requirements. In order to access the APO system one can use any point-to-point network or the Internet. When using the Internet, there are three possibilities.

1. Internet enabled APO Communication
2. Internet enabled Data Transfer for APO
3. APO to support Internet Activities

The graphic below provides an overview of these 3 groups. The numbers in the graphic depict the information flow path according to the numbering of the groups and options outlined above. The options are described in detail just after the graphic.

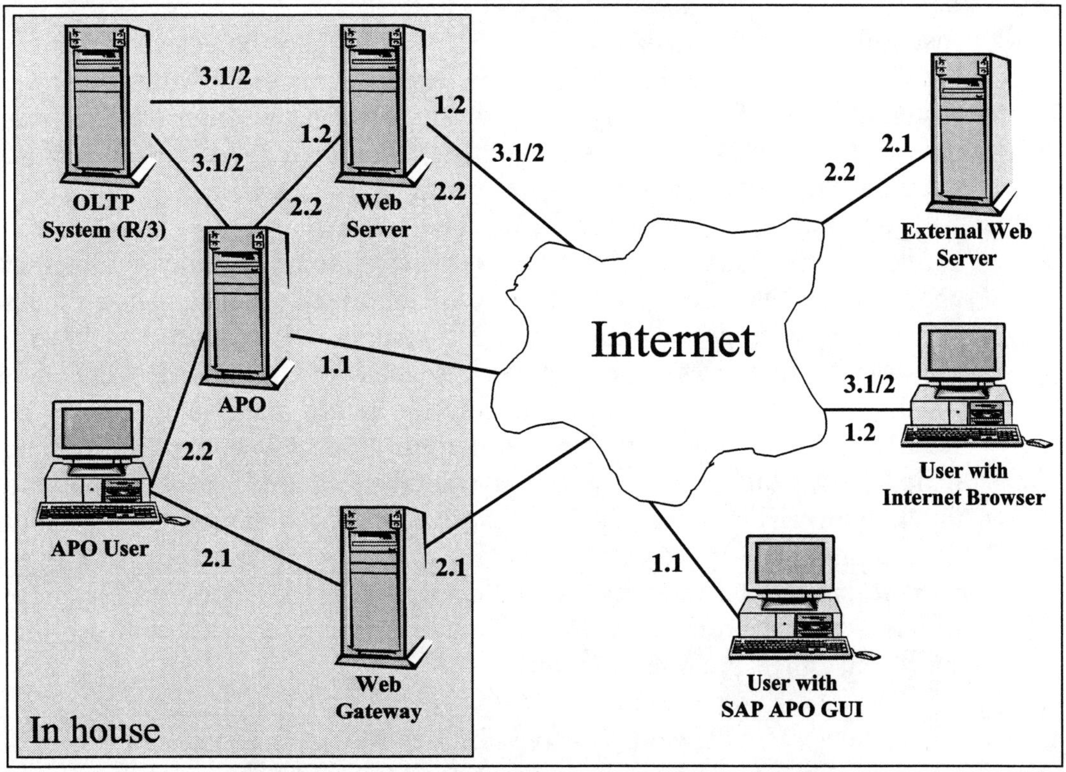


**Graphic 7 – APO and the Internet**

## 1. Internet enabled APO Communication

1.1. APO and Internet - Direct Access of APO

In this scenario, the APO server must be made accessible through the Internet via its TCP/IP address. This is a rather easy task, but has some disadvantages. First of all the security of this approach is questionable, as the whole system on which APO is loaded is sort of "open" for anybody. The normal APO built-in security with logon ID and password is obviously still active. It is also required to install the SAP APO GUI on the user's PC. This leads to the next problem. I cannot imagine that a casual user of APO will find his or her way around the system. There is nothing wrong with the GUI, but it is designed for users who access the system as part of their daily job and only after a thorough training was provided. The beauty of this solution is its simplicity, as absolutely no extra development is required to access any part of APO.

1.2. APO and Internet - APO Access via Web Server
Unlike the option discussed above, it is required to have dedicated Internet applications that generate HTML pages. Authorized users can access these pages via a web server. On the user site, it is only required to have a standard Internet browser, and there is no need for a local SAP APO GUI. As the user accesses only specific selected pages via a web server, the security issue is much smaller. Furthermore special web pages can be scaled down offering only the absolutely required information and functionality. This in turn ensures that inexperienced casual users without prior training can use these pages. This is the only feasible possibility to provide Internet users access to an APO system. Collaborative Planning, which is due to be released in the middle of the year 2000 will use this approach. Others are due to follow.

In both cases we were investigating the possibilities for external partners to access an APO system. One could also think about an APO user who needs to access information available on the Internet or to post information on other Internet sites. This leads to a third scenario.

## 2. Internet enabled Data Transfer for APO

2.1. APO and Internet - Information Retrieval on the Internet
Depending on the user's tasks, it might be helpful to easily access information that is available on the Internet while working in APO. In order to achieve this, the APO system must be able to connect through a web gateway to the Internet. Special transactions can then retrieve information on the web and post them directly into the APO system as if it was own data. The integration is seamless, as the user does not even need to see where the information originates. An example is the tracking of goods that were shipped with a carrier. Besides the shipment date and number (APO based information), the carrier's web page could be

accessed in the background using the Internet to obtain up-to-date tracking information.

2.2. Internet-enabled Procurement

Lots has been said and written about Business to Business (B2B) procurement, and this business area really seems to be the hottest topic in a long while. Software vendors predict phenomenal savings and returns on investment. While this is certainly true for the purchasing of consumables, one must be more careful when talking about the procurement of production supplies. True, B2B can speed up and facilitate any procurement activity, but it only hooks into the procurement process after the decision to buy was made. I am not questioning the potential savings of B2B initiatives, but a properly run APO system ensures that the right product (component) is bought at the right time. B2B might reduce 50% of the purchasing cost, but APO might show that the business does not need to purchase at all, thus reducing the purchasing cost by 100% and on top of that not incurring any expenditure at all.

The question is not B2B or APO. They both belong together and need to be implemented together to really provide the business with sustainable savings and efficiency improvements.

Two other possible ways an APO system can work together or use the Internet are still left. They are described in the following chapters.

## 3. APO to support Internet Activities

3.1. APO and Internet - APO as ATP Backbone

Another area where APO can deliver excellent results is as an ATP backbone for Internet shopping. Many companies, and well-known ones, offer Internet shopping nowadays, some making this their sole business. The annoying fact is that lots of them have a nice front-end, their web page. But behind this web page is yesterday's technology. Whoever accessed one of these sites must have seen messages like "ships usually within 3 days". If you ask me, that is not good enough. I am not interested what usually happens. I want to know when exactly the item can be shipped to me, even if it is Saturday night. These companies would do well with an ATP server. It does not have to be APO, but some of them surely could improve their customer service by offering on-line information based on an APO Global ATP check. In this case APO acts as a backbone for Internet Shopping and the ATP check performed uses the same information as the users sitting in the company's office. Obviously, one would set up different rules for orders coming from the Internet compared to such entered from a company employee. The access to the APO system is performed from the company's OLTP system.

3.2. APO and Internet - APO as Product Configuration Engine

In the same line is another excellent opportunity for APO. High-tech products offered on the Internet nowadays are often configurable, and the user selects the components he or she wants. I tried this and was disappointed to see messages like "this component might require....". As a customer I want the system to tell me whether my selection is feasible or not. Again the front-end looks great, but behind the scene is an outdated or at least user-unfriendly system. What is missing here to stop guesswork is a dynamic BOM explosion based on my selections. This can be accomplished by linking APO to the OLTP system to exactly perform this task. And on top of this, the company could provide the user with an accurate ATP check and precise delivery information since the configuration is feasible and all components checked. In this case the access to the APO server is done as well from the company's OLTP system.

## 2.7 The APO Components

APO has three main components:

- Demand Planning
- Supply Network Planning and Deployment
- Production Planning & Detailed Scheduling

The "component" Supply Chain Cockpit and the accompanying Supply Chain Engineer with the Alert Monitor are no functional components as the other four are. The Supply Chain Cockpit is the graphical presentation of the functionality of the four components, which enables--together with the Supply Chain Engineer--an easy to use intuitive communication with APO.
Some of these components are further broken down, and I will explain them one by one in the following chapters. The emphasis is on a functional overview, rather than providing a "How To" guide. APO in its current version has solutions aimed mainly at the Consumer Packaged Goods (CPG) and Hi-Tech industry. The current release is 2.0. This is the release this book is based on.

Each of the following chapters provides an introduction and overview of the respective module. This is followed by an explanation of the data environment. A methodology section that provides the background understanding needed to implement and run an APO system comes next. Following this is an explanation of the main transactions. At the end of each section is a guide that helps to carry out some tasks that usually prove to be difficult to carry out.

# 3 Demand Planning

## 3.1 Introduction

The aim of APO Demand Planning is to create a forecast (demand plan), which will then be used as a driver for Supply Network Planning. Demand Planning offers a set of powerful forecasting models and tools exceeding those in R/3. Forecast models include the well-known Trend, Seasonal and Trend-Seasonal models, Exponential Smoothing models, and new ones like Causal models and Composite Forecasting. In the following chapters, I shall explain all concepts and activities required setting up an APO Demand Planning system, followed by the various forecast models offered by APO. It must be understood that using two different models will lead to having two different results, and it is vital for the one selecting the forecast model to fully understand the respective limitations and benefits of a certain forecast model.

Demand Planning offers planning and forecasting at any level of the supply chain, independent of the "On Line Transaction Processing" (OLTP) system. Obviously SAP R/3 is the preferred partner of an APO system as interfaces from and to R/3 and APO are delivered with the software. But this does not exclude the possibility of APO being linked to any other system. In this context R/2 must be seen as just another OLTP system as no standard interfaces in R/2 exist. R/3 systems supporting APO are those with release level 3.1H or higher. For these systems the APO core interface (CIF) is available. CIF has to be loaded onto the R/3 system and allows the configuration of the interfaces between APO and R/3.

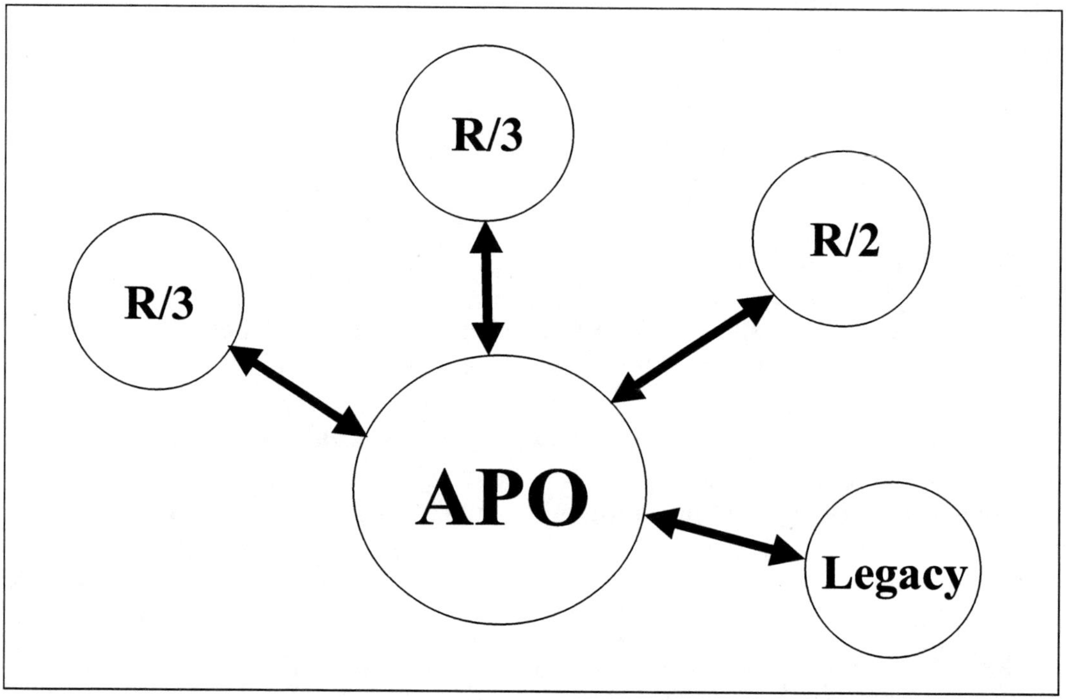


**Graphic 8 – OLTP Satellite Systems**

APO Demand Planning is supply chain-driven. This means the emphasis in APO is not to plan single entities such as a plant but the whole process of buying, making, moving, and selling, which is the Supply Chain. R/3 on the other hand is an "Enterprise Resource Planning" (ERP) system that focuses primarily on the control and execution of processes within one company (enterprise or plant thereof). Anybody who has worked with R/3 knows how much all activities, controls, and planning are around an R/3 plant. This is required to optimally deploy a manufacturing process, but is hindering a global planning approach based on the concepts of Supply Chain Management. Within limits SAP tried to integrate a more global planning approach. Flexible Planning within the Sales and Operations Planning environment allows forecasting independent of plants. It is basically this concept, which is the foundation for APO Demand Planning. On top of this, APO DP offers easy planning integration of customers, new forecasting models, and a totally new, more appealing, user interface. While going through Demand Planning, we shall see that the differences in concept between R/3 and APO are not enormous. The real differences will be revealed later in Supply Network Planning and Production Planning & Detailed Scheduling.

Somebody with good working knowledge of the R/3 forecasting tools and methodologies will feel "at home" within a short time span. What is left is to get used to a new user interface and to some new forecasting tools. To see the impact on using different forecast models for the same product and historical data, it is a good exercise to run several forecasts (or planning scenarios) for the same product and storing them for subsequent comparison. APO also offers various tools to validate usability of the different models. We shall come to this a bit later.

There is another similarity between APO and R/3. Flexible Planning reads data of the Information Systems within R/3, and APO uses the new "Business Information Warehouse" (BW) to do so. Again the concept is the same; what is different is how things are done on a detailed level. This does not imply that APO DP is a copy of R/3; it is just a logical continuation and further development. APO has a dedicated task, the optimization of the Supply Chain Network, and it does this without limitations, which would be imminent if it had to run as a module within R/3.

## 3.2 Overview

Nothing is black and white in forecasting, and no model does really explain and predict future requirements with certainty. The idea is to come as close as possible to a stable and reliable demand plan. It is imperative to understand interdependencies of consumption with factors leading to the usage (sales) of a product. Although very similar, the task to forecast sales and internal consumption is different. Internal consumption might be caused by production and dependant requirements of sold products, maintenance of assets with a predicted service part usage, or any other item required to run the business like consumables. Dependant requirements of production or maintenance orders do not need to be forecasted as this is done for the higher-level product in which the components are used. Unplanned consumption in production on the other hand can be subject to forecasting.

Forecasting is not a mandatory task, and a company might well be very successful without performing any forecast. How can this be? First of all, there is the possibility to use re-order point procedures instead of forecasts. This will work well in a world of stable demand with or without growth and where the supply of products or components is secure in terms of lead-time stability. In other cases, the demand might be not predictable but the supply side is characterized by short lead times with a multitude of possible vendors. Thirdly and that is true only for time series-based and causal models, the higher the amount of markets served and the respective market penetration, the easier the forecast job will be. Lower sales (or product usage) in Asia might be compensated by higher ones in Europe and vice versa. This leads to the situation described first. Never forget that forecasting (except judgmental models) is applied statistics, and the higher the number of data elements, the more reliable the results are.

Another aspect worth thinking about is that, in a typical manufacturing environment, only a fraction of the products are subject to forecasting. These are the products to be sold. After the forecasting is carried out, APO will generate dependant requirements based on the Production Process Model (PPM) or when closer to production based on the Production Bill of Material (BOM) or the PPM.

In this step, scrap values or yield factors are also taken into account. In R/3 the MRP type of the BOM's top-level item could be for example Forecast Based (VV), the subordinate components can have one of several MRP types available. In APO all products in the InfoCube are subject to forecast.

In some companies one finds products that have both dependant requirements as a result of a BOM or PPM explosion and independent requirements. This is the case if the same product is used as a component (or semi finished) and as a product ready for sale. A good example is the Automotive Industry where the same product can be used to manufacture a car (in which case dependant requirements were created) and can be sold as a spare part (where forecasting might be carried out which results in independent requirements). Special care has to be taken here as to not mix up these requirements. In APO the same product can have more than one requirements strategy, which allows planning separately per requirements strategy.

The open nature of APO allows collaborating on forecasts with interested parties, internal and external. Forecasts can be shared with customers and vendors long before the execution in terms of purchase orders or sales orders takes place. Multi level planning is carried out using a top down, middle through, or bottom up approach. Planning is consistent and supported by aggregation factors. Version Management allows the maintenance of various planning versions by means of copying and deleting versions.

APO did away with a lot of limitations, which can be found in R/3. Forecasting can be done on several levels such as product groups or products (multilevel vertical flexibility), and it can be done on virtually any organizational structure as long as it is defined in APO (multi-organizational horizontal level). New is as well the possibility to plan for Sales Promotions. Here, an entire sales campaign for a product or a product range can be planned individually, which adds Market Intelligence to the forecast. Effects like cross product cannibalization and deferred consumer purchases can be taken into account.

### 3.2.1 The DP Planning Steps

Various steps are carried out within the DP process. They are listed below.

- Prepare Forecasting
    - Set up InfoCube
    - Define DP Profiles and Parameters
    - Define Master Data
- Carry Out Forecast
    - Apply Forecast Model
    - Create and Revise Forecast
    - Fine Tune Forecast Results
    - Apply Promotions
    - Accept Final Forecast
- Interact with SNP
    - Release Forecast to SNP
    - Receive SNP Plan

### 3.2.2 The DP Planning Environment

The DP environment is made up of three main building blocks that enable the user to perform the forecasting and promotional planning task. They can be described as follows:

- InfoCube
  The InfoCube is the main data repository of DP. It stores all historical data as well as the generated forecasts. It provides the data that can be used.
- Profiles
  The Profiles allow setting defaults that define how the standard forecasting tools are used within the specific users' environment. They provide standardized rules on how to use the data provided by the InfoCube.
- Planning Book
  The Planning Book is the interface between the system and the user. It is configurable to allow concentrating on the data the user really needs. Custom

specific rules (Macros) can be defined here as well. It provides the definitions of what data is visible and which macros are used.

All these definitions come together in the Interactive Planning screen and the Interactive Promotion Planning screen. This is depicted in the picture below.

In the following chapters we shall go through all of these objects one by one and gain an understanding on how they work together and what the interdependencies are.



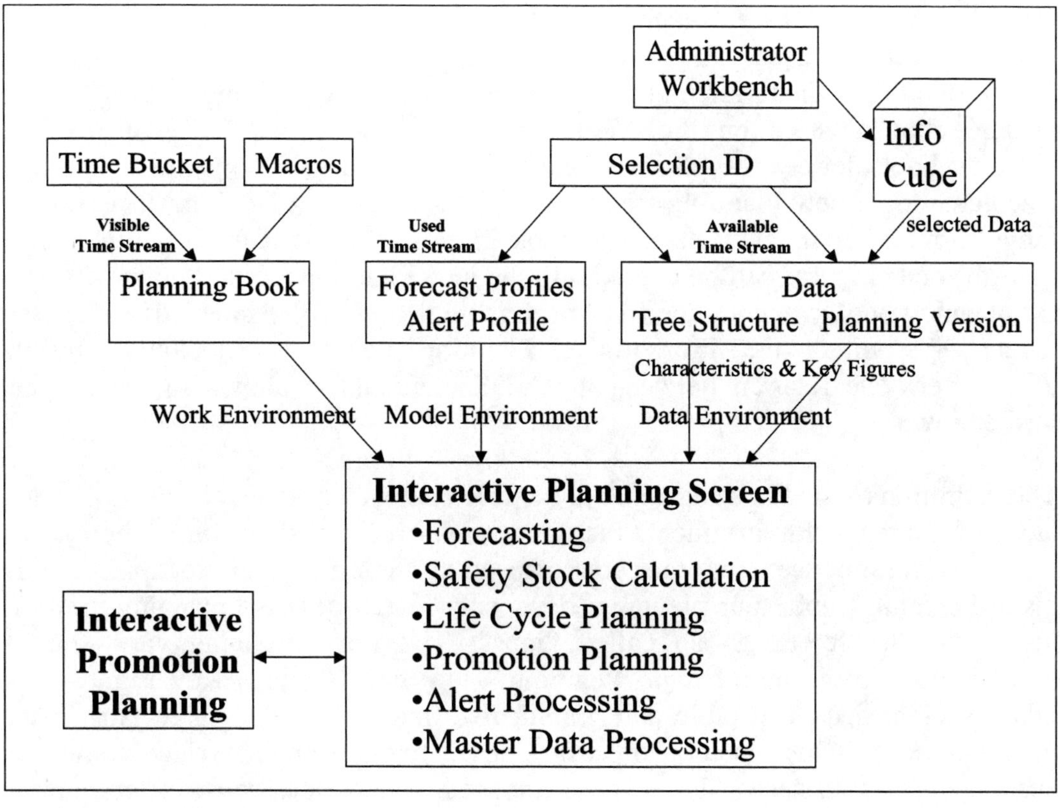


**Graphic 9 – DP Overview**

# 3.3 The DP Methodology

## 3.3.1 Planning Book

The Planning Book defines amongst other parameters the layout of the Interactive Planning Screen, which is the heart of the APO DP module. Per InfoCube several planning books can be defined, but a planning book can be linked to only one InfoCube. With any given planning book, several planning versions of the same InfoCube can be used. APO comes standard with a planning book named "APO_BOOK1". This planning book can be used when creating your new own planning books based on the APO demo InfoCube called DP_REFER. The planning book defines the planning methods available to the planner. Note that when creating a new Planning Book, the referred Planning Book must be for the same InfoCube as the new Planning Book. In this case the Row Structure and/or the Advanced Macros can be copied into the new Planning Book. In opposition to the planning book, which is the freely definable layout of the Interactive Planning Screen, the Interactive Promotional Planning Screen is not customizable whatsoever. The relation between these DP elements is shown in the graphic further down.

The definition of the Planning Book is flexible and each planner can set up his/her Demand Planning Environment. Planning books for the same InfoCube can be created with reference to another one to speed up the process of creation. For any given Planning Book, four planning views exist. Each of these planning views is visible on the screen as so called "tabs". The only planning view that is customizable is the initial main Planning View that displays Key Figures and other calculated data in table and graphical format. The other three tabs in the Planning Book, which is the Forecast, Causal, and Composite view, cannot be customized (at this stage). These views are used to provide specific information in their respective areas (General Forecasts, Causal Forecasts, and Composite Forecasts). All rows in the Main Planning View can be labeled individually as required. Any of the rows that are used in the Main Planning View and any of the other views carry the same labeling throughout all views. The column header appearance can be adjusted as well. Rows and columns can be swapped if desired.

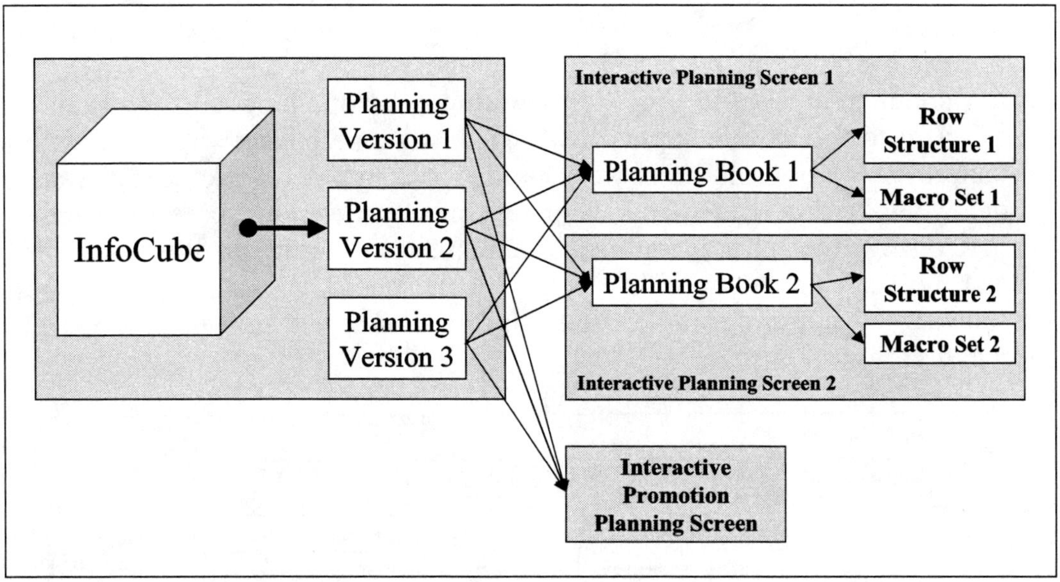


**Graphic 10 – Planning Book & Version**

### 3.3.1.1 Time Buckets

Time Buckets in APO represent the exact duration of time (or time characteristics) to which the key value or forecast applies. Possible time buckets within APO DP can be a week or a month. Time characteristics defined in the planning book must also be available in the Info Cube. If for example the time bucket is defined in weekly buckets, the InfoCube must also provide information in weekly buckets. In order to transfer the unconstrained plan from DP to SNP it is necessary to define a time bucket profile with daily buckets. For further information regarding the transfer to SNP please refer to the appropriate chapter.

The time bucket profile contains the following information:

- Number of buckets
  The number of buckets represents the number of periods (see above) used in this profile.
- Sequence within time bucket
  It is common practice to plan short term in weeks, and long term in months. If we want to follow this approach we need two time bucket sequences within the profile. One would be in weeks with for example 4 weeks, and the other one would be for 11 months to complete one year, which is the total planning horizon. We then allocate the sequence number "1" to the first time sequence, and the sequence number "2" to the second one. Underneath is a diagram showing this approach where also the historical data is displayed in weeks and months.

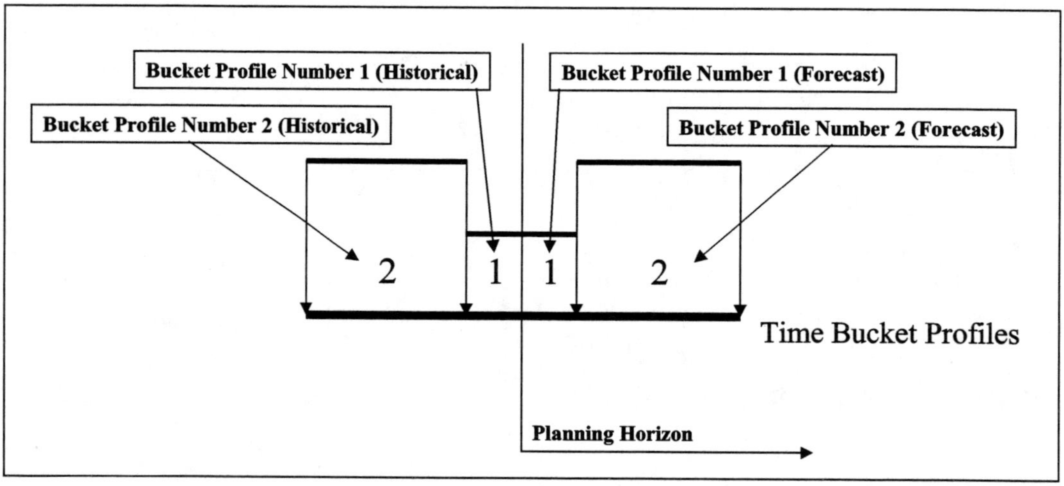


**Graphic 11 – DP Time Buckets 1**

Time buckets are not only defined for the Planning Book in DP. The forecast profile also contains information regarding the forecast and the historical horizon. The forecast horizon in the forecast profile defines the period for which a forecast has to be carried out. The historical horizon defines the period on which the forecast is based on if Time Series Based, Causal, or Composite forecast models are deployed. The system requires that both, the historical and the forecast horizon be defined at least with the same number of periods as stipulated in the forecast profile. Whether or not historical data is available from the Info Cube is immaterial. The following graph shows these dependencies.

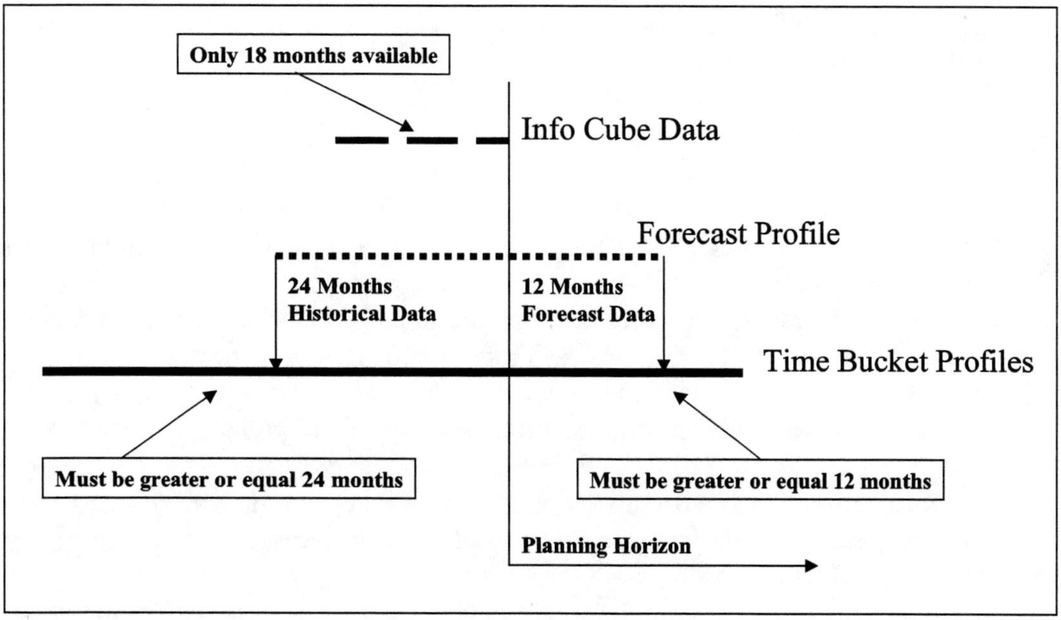


**Graphic 12 – DP Time Buckets 2**

The number of months in the above graphic is an example.

Note for planning using weekly buckets:

- The first day of the week is Monday by default. This cannot be changed.
- The planning horizon start date will be set to the Monday of the week, if the defined planning horizon date does not represent a Monday.

Note for planning using weekly and monthly buckets:

Planning with weekly and monthly buckets reveals an adherent problem of our calendar. The relation between weeks and months is neither the same from month to month nor is the number of weeks in a month a natural number. As a result of this, in daily life we work with an approximation of 4.25 weeks per month. This is not good enough for a sophisticated planning system like APO. The shortest month in our calendar has 20 workdays (assuming a five-day week) and the maximum number of workdays is 23 in any month. Within APO the concept of "Transitional Days" is used.

Example:
We plan using 13 weekly buckets and after that 9 monthly buckets which completes one year's cycle. The forecast horizon starts on July 1, 1999. First of all APO will reset the forecast starting date to the previous Monday, which is June 28, 1999. From there onwards 13 weekly buckets will be displayed. The last weekly bucket represents the week from September 20, 1999 onwards. After that APO will show the total for the 4 Transitional Days (Monday 27 through Thursday 30) in a column with the header "September". After that the 9 monthly buckets from October 1999 through to June 2000 are displayed.

The different amount of workdays per month is accounted for by the system through the usage of an average of workdays per period and a subsequent correction when forecasting.

### 3.3.2 Advanced Macros

Macros are used to read data in the planning view spread sheets (grids), and to subsequently process the input data according to user-defined calculations, conditions and rules. They are similar to calculations, which are carried out in conventional spreadsheets, but specialized for the forecasting application. Macros are defined per planning book, which has as a consequence that they can only work within a given planning book. Within DP, macros are used amongst others in the following areas:

- Aggregation and Distribution

APO predefined macros are used to apply proportional factors and do not need to be developed.

- Consensus Based Forecast
  In a Consensus meeting commonly agreed macros could be defined which will subsequently be applied to a whole range of products.
- General Forecasting
  A macro could even be used to create an entire forecast in a case where none of the standard models deliver the expected result.
- Data Evaluation
  Historical data or forecast results can be evaluated efficiently by setting up macros. The result of such an evaluation could be an alert (see below) or the automatic update of such data based on even complex conditions.
- Promotion Planning
  As an alternative to using the Interactive Promotion Planning screen, macros can be used to calculate promotions based on the forecast.
- Alert Monitor
  DP is the only APO module where planners can define their own alerts by means of setting up macros, which react to predefined conditions.

The execution of macros is event driven. Possible events are:

- Start
  The macro runs every time the planning view is called up and shown on the screen. It will not be executed again irrespective of activities performed during the planning session.
- Exit
  The macro runs every time the planning data is saved. The macro can be run repeatedly by saving the planning table. Therefore the condition is actually not "Exit" but "Save".
- Default
  Every time the planning view is called up (same as in "Start"), the <Enter> key is pressed, or the planning data is saved (same as in "Exit") the macro is run.

If multiple macros are defined, then they are executed in the sequence as they appear in the tree structure of the planning screen. Any macro can also be executed interactively if not explicitly excluded.

Macros are also used for alert processing. Unlike all other APO areas, there are no predefined alerts in Demand Planning. Alerts can be created using macros that are executed just like any other macro. See also the chapter "Alert Monitor".

#### 3.3.2.1 Macro Builder

Macros are created in a special transaction called the Macro Builder. It can be called from the tree structure or from within the Planning Book Design transaction. In the Macro Builder transaction macros are created for the use in a specific planning book. Macros are InfoCube specific, as the planning book view is linked to a specific planning book and this planning book to a specific InfoCube. The Macro Builder allows a graphically oriented, intuitive creation of macros. Macros can be compared to a 4th generation programming language. There are an enormous amount of operators available that should satisfy all business requirements. Macros are single or multi-step calculations and consist of:

- Control Instructions
  Controls are logical conditions such as "if" and "else".
- Arguments
  This is the data input of the calculation. It is residing in a cell or is a constant. A macro can also easily be set up to perform the same calculation based on a whole row, column, or area.
- Operators
  An operator logically joins arguments. Examples are "+", "-", ">" or more complex ones that are used to round results or calculate square roots.
- Conditions
  A condition consists of an argument and operators.
- Functions
  You use functions to trigger a calculation based on a whole range within a grid. An example would be to calculate the maximum of 12 monthly forecast figures for both, the univariate and the MLR forecast. The result would provide the absolute highest forecasted quantity irrespective of the forecast model used.
- Results

The result of a macro is either a value to be written into a cell, row, column, or an area, or it can be the trigger for an alert.

After the creation of a macro, it will be checked for logical consistency. This avoids the creation of macros that are not conclusive and could therefore not be carried out. When opening the Macro Builder, the following five sections appear on the screen:

- Elements — This is the elements repository that can be used to create a macro. From here the elements are dragged to the Macros section.
- Planning Table — This section provides an overview of the InfoCube structure as used in the planning book.
- Macros — The Macro section is the construction section where macros are defined. Drop here the elements selected in the Elements section.
- Events — The events section displays all macros for the particular planning book and how they are executed.
- Clipboard — Any element that is deleted during a macro builder work session is put there. It is also possible to manually put elements there. All elements can be dragged and dropped back to the macro section as and when required.

### 3.3.3 Planning Approach

Common to all forecast techniques is the deployment of a bottom up, middle through or top down planning approach. APO stores data consistently, not disproportional, over all levels using aggregation and distribution factors. This ensures that the sum (or average) of all forecast values in one level of the hierarchy is equal to the figure found on the next hierarchy level. Distribution is carried out by means of Proportional Factors or using the Pro Rata approach. This is true in the case of Top Down Planning and in the down stream of Middle Through Planning.

#### 3.3.3.1 Aggregation and Distribution

In the case where Totals are created, aggregation is simply an addition of all values of a given level where the result is stored on the higher level. Another possibility is to store the average of all elements of the subordinate level on the superior level. Distribution takes place according to Proportional Factors or using a Pro Rata method. Proportional Factors are derived from historical data before the first forecast is carried out. Different proportional factors (one per Key Figure) can be calculated for the same characteristic. This enables distribution according to various key figures.

Aggregation and distribution happens automatically in the background while creating or editing forecast values. Aggregation and Distribution rules are defined per InfoCube. The calculation of aggregated and distributed figures is obviously resource intensive and care must be taken when defining the data to be aggregated or distributed. Proportional Factors are defined as decimal values ranging from Zero to 1 with the total being 1. The following aggregation and distribution rules can be set up:

| Aggregation Type | Rule Description | Example | Comment |
|---|---|---|---|
| Average | Calculate mean average of subordinate values and display in superior level | 1 | E.g. average price of product group |
| Total | Calculate total of subordinate values and display in superior level | 2 | E.g. total forecast of product group |
| None | No Aggregation is carried out | 3 | Set this option at least for all text fields |

**Table 4 – Aggregation Types**

| Distribution Type | Rule Description | Example | Comment |
|---|---|---|---|
| Pro Rata with Aggregation Type "Average" | Create Mode: Superior level Average is copied into subordinate value (4.1)<br>Change Mode: Maintain same proportions after editing as they were before (4.2) | 4 | Must be selected if Aggregation Type "Average" is defined |
| Pro Rata with Aggregation Type "Total" | Create Mode:<br>use Proportional Factors if defined (5.1)<br>or Even Distribution (5.2)<br>Create Mode and Change in same Planning Session:<br>maintain proportions (5.3)<br>Change in new Planning Session:<br>maintain proportions (5.3) | 5 | |
| Proportional Factor of current row | Distribute according to Fixed Proportional Factor of current row | 6 | |
| Proportional Factor of alternate row | Distribute according to Fixed Proportional Factor of alternate row | 7 | |
| None | No Distribution is carried out | 8 | Must be selected if Aggregation Type "None" is defined |

**Table 5 – Distribution Types**

Examples:

1 Aggregation Type Average

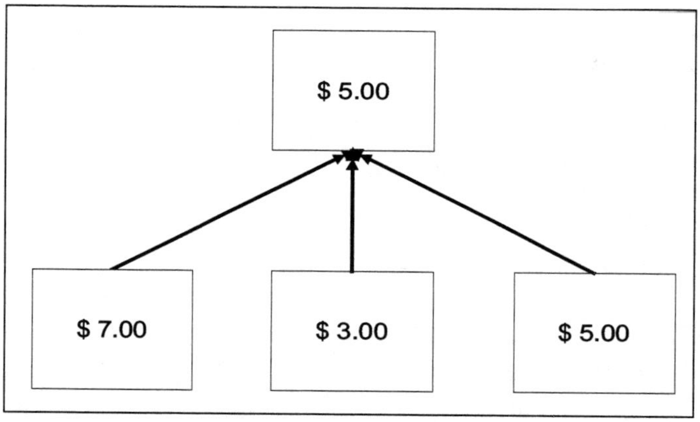


**Graphic 13 – Proportional Factors: Type 1**

2 Aggregation Type Total

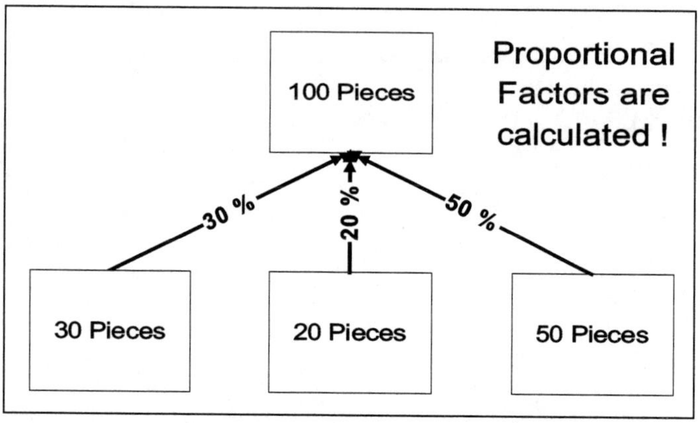


**Graphic 14 – Proportional Factors: Type 2**

3 Aggregation Type None

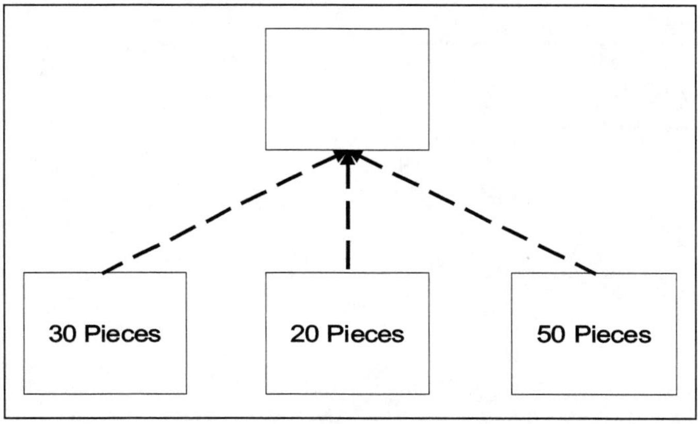


**Graphic 15 – Proportional Factors: Type 3**

4.1 Distribution Type Pro Rata in conjunction with Aggregation Type Average – Create

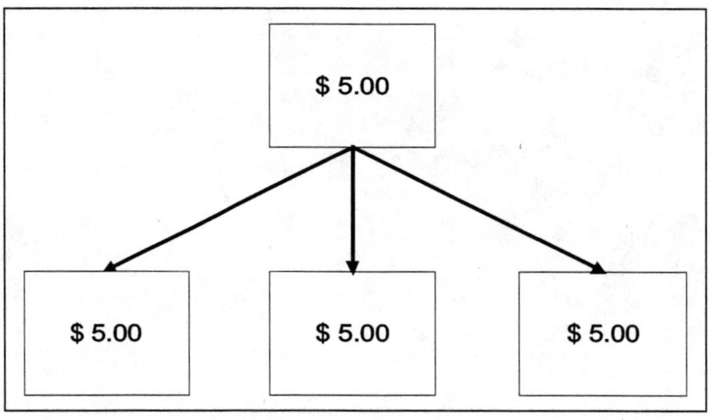


**Graphic 16 – Proportional Factors: Type 4.1**

4.2 Distribution Type Pro Rata in conjunction with Aggregation Type Average – Change

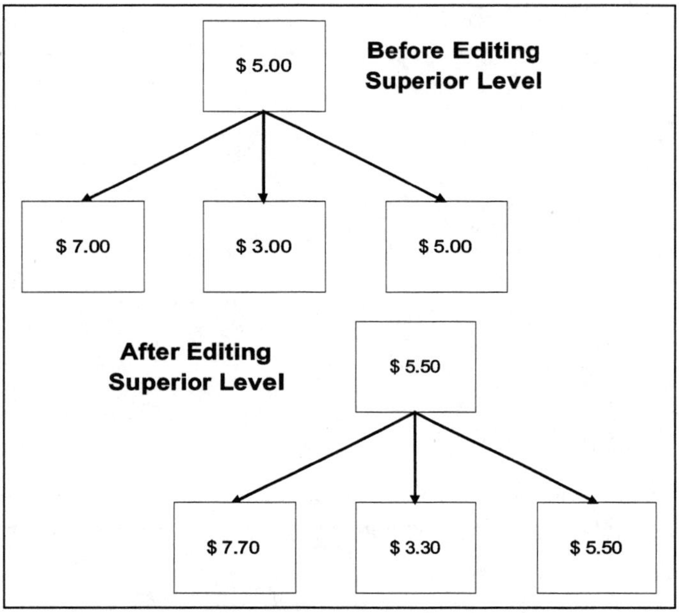


**Graphic 17 – Proportional Factors: Type 4.2**

5.1 Distribution Type Pro Rata in conjunction with Aggregation Type Total – Create – PF

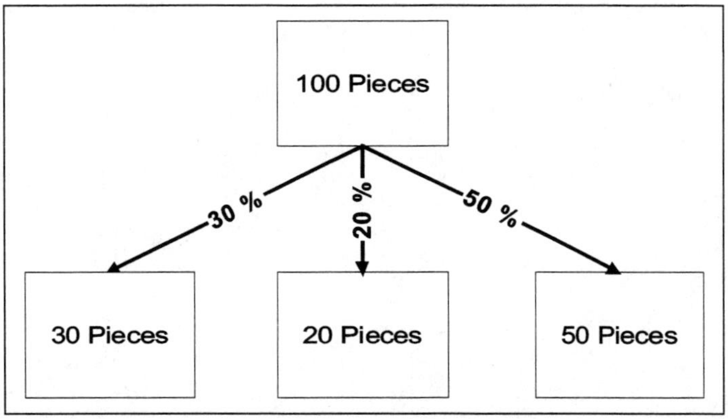


**Graphic 18 – Proportional Factors: Type 5.1**

5.2 Distribution Type Pro Rata in conjunction with Aggregation Type Total – Create – ED

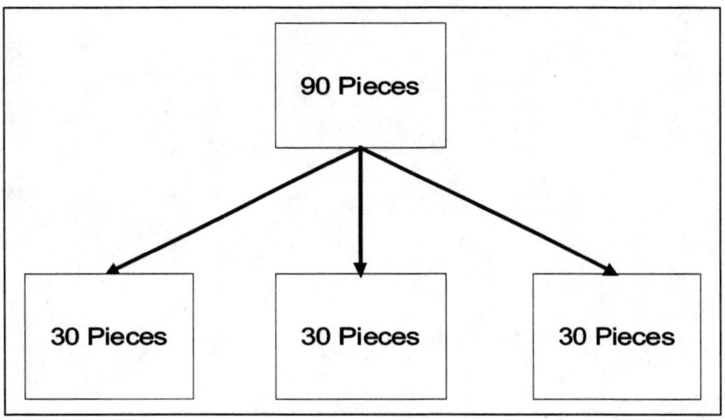


**Graphic 19 – Proportional Factors: Type 5.2**

DP

5.3 Distribution Type Pro Rata in conjunction with Aggregation Type Total – Change

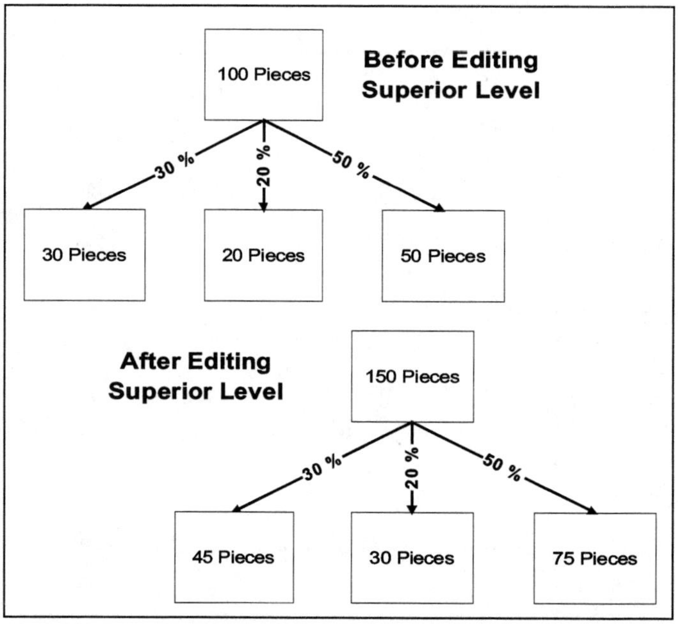


**Graphic 20 – Proportional Factors: Type 5.3**

6 Distribution Type Proportional Factor of current row

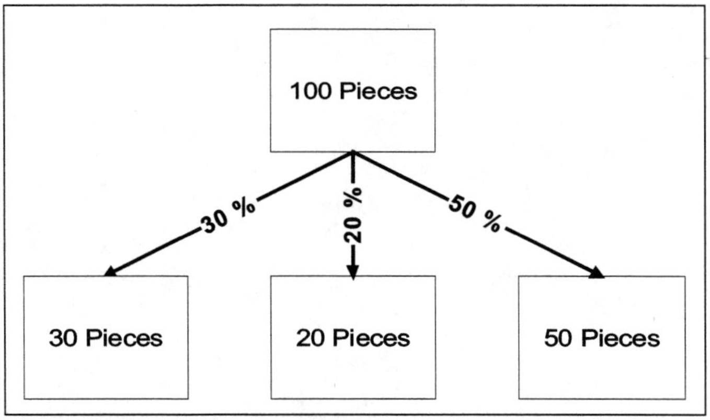


**Graphic 21 – Proportional Factors: Type 6**

7 Distribution Type Proportional Factor of alternate row

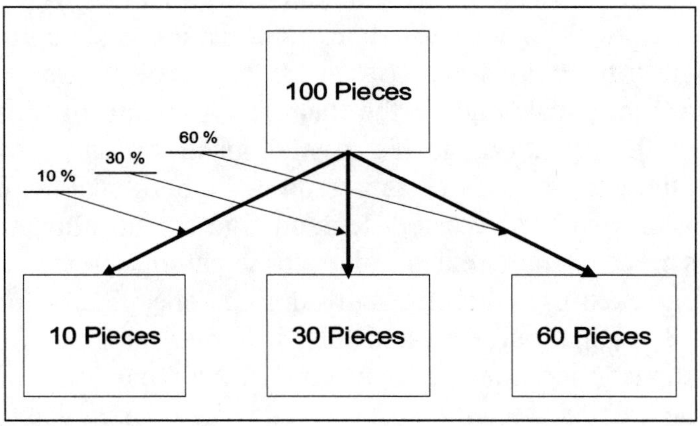


**Graphic 22 – Proportional Factors: Type 7**

8 Distribution Type None

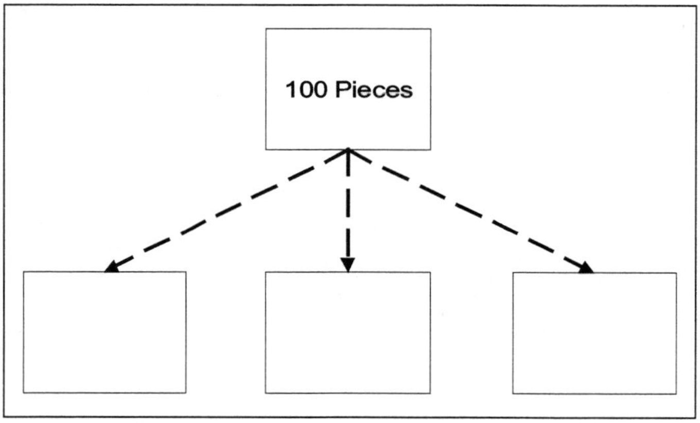


**Graphic 23 – Proportional Factors: Type 8**

When using Proportional Factors, great care must be taken in the following scenario. Based on historical demand Proportional Factors are calculated. After this calculation is carried out, a new characteristics value combination is set up in the system. This new combination obviously carries a Proportional Factor of Zero, as it was not defined while calculating the factors. A rerun of this calculation would not change the situation, as the past demand for the new characteristics value combination is Zero. Forecasting on a higher level with subsequent automatic distribution of the forecasted demand figures will allocate no forecasted demand to this new characteristics value combination. Worse, it will possibly even overwrite an existing value manually defined specifically for this new characteristics value combination. To avoid this, it is mandatory to fix the forecast value so that the distribution does not overwrite it. A regeneration of Proportional Factors should be carried out afterwards to not carry forward this problem. See also the chapter “Fixing of Values”.

The enabling technology for aggregation and distribution is the macro. Macros are defined calculation procedures to manipulate data in a Planning Book and its rows, columns, and cells. The aggregation and distribution macros are predefined and therefore only need to be applied, rather than being developed and applied.

For further information regarding macros see the chapter "Advanced Macros". The Aggregation and Distribution type of a key figure is defined in the InfoCube parameters.

### 3.3.3.2 Fixing of Values

Fixing of values is a technique where one or multiple values on a subordinate level in the planning hierarchy are fixed. Fixed values do not get changed during the distribution of data from a superior level to the subordinate level. Fixing of values works the same way, irrespective of whether the Pro Rata method is used or Proportional Factors. This technique is extremely useful when adding new characteristics value combinations. Fixing of Values has no impact on the aggregation as all data values on the subordinate level are used to aggregate according to the average or total principle.
Fixing or unfixing of values is initiated by activating the context sensitive menu on the cell (of the forecast or any other value) which should be fixed, and selecting "Fix/Unfix Value".

Example:
The following example is based on the Distribution Type Pro Rata in conjunction with Aggregation Type Total – Change (model 5.3, see above).

The system carries out the following calculation:

| | | |
|---|---|---|
| Step 1 | Calculate quantity to be distributed | $150-30=120$ |
| Step 2 | Calculate factor for product B | $20/(20+50)=29\%$ |
| Step 3 | Calculate factor for product C | $50/(20+50)=71\%$ |
| Step 4 | Calculate quantity for product B | $29\%*120=34$ |
| Step 5 | Calculate quantity for product C | $71\%*120=86$ |

In order to store fixed values for a key figure, it is required to define a second key figure that contains the fixed values. This second key figure must have the suffix "F". If for example the used key figure is called "ABC01", then the key figure to store the fixed value must be named "ABC01F". The fixing of a value can be performed on-line irrespective of whether this second key figure exists or not. The problem is that without the second key figure being defined the fixed value cannot be stored separately.

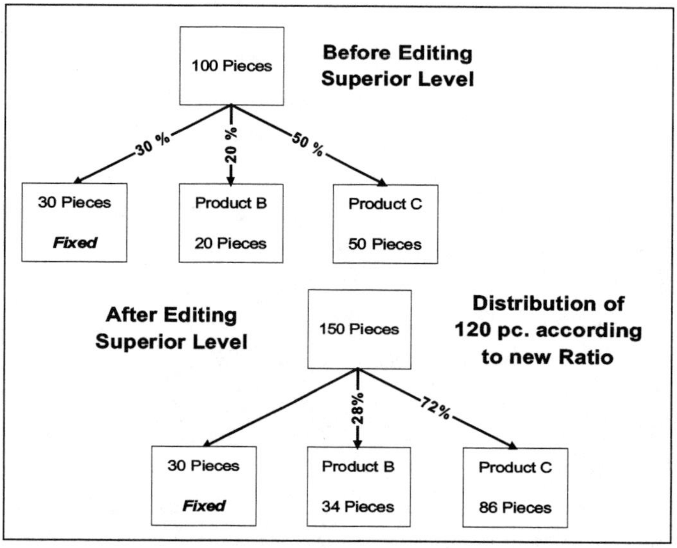


**Graphic 24 – Proportional Factors: Fixing**

### 3.3.3.3 Top-Down Planning

Top-Down Planning starts at the highest level of the hierarchy and uses Proportional Factors or the Pro Rata Method, which will distribute the forecasted quantities to all subordinate levels down to the lowest level according to a key figure. The advantage of a Top-Down Planning approach is that only one value on a high level is forecasted and all dependant values are updated automatically by DP. Proportional Factors can be defined to be either valid for a certain period or for the entire planning horizon. The definition of proportional factors is based on historical data, on the planner's input, or on both. It is a disadvantage of this planning approach that data on the lower levels is subject to higher deviations. The key is the quality and reliability of the proportional factor.

Example:
A canned food manufacturer might define as the top level of the planning hierarchy the product group of "Canned Vegetables." One level down could find a breakdown according to the "Vegetable Type" (e.g. beans, tomatoes, and carrots). Finally, on the third level, the distinguishing characteristic is the "Location" which is defined per vegetable type. There are two locations "Denver" and "Atlanta". Before forecasting is carried out, the planner will generate all proportional factors from level one to level two and then from level two to three. This task is carried out either by calculating proportional factors based on historical data or is captured by the planner. This approach with the corresponding factors is shown below. It is assumed that the 3 sets of proportional factors on level one are valid only within the given periods. On level two (locations) the proportional factors are the same for the whole planning horizon.

Data Table:

| **Month / Quarter** | **Proportional Factors** | |
|---|---|---|
| | Level One | Level Two |
| 07/99 | 20 / 40 / 40 % | |
| 08/99 | 25 / 40 / 35 % | |
| 09/99 | 25 / 45 / 30 % | |
| III/99 | | 40 / 60 % |

**Table 6 – Proportional Factors Example 1**

The total forecasted demand for the quarter III/99 is 10.000 cans per month or 30.000 for the whole quarter. The resulting distributed demands can be seen in the illustration below. The Model applied in this example is of type 5.1.

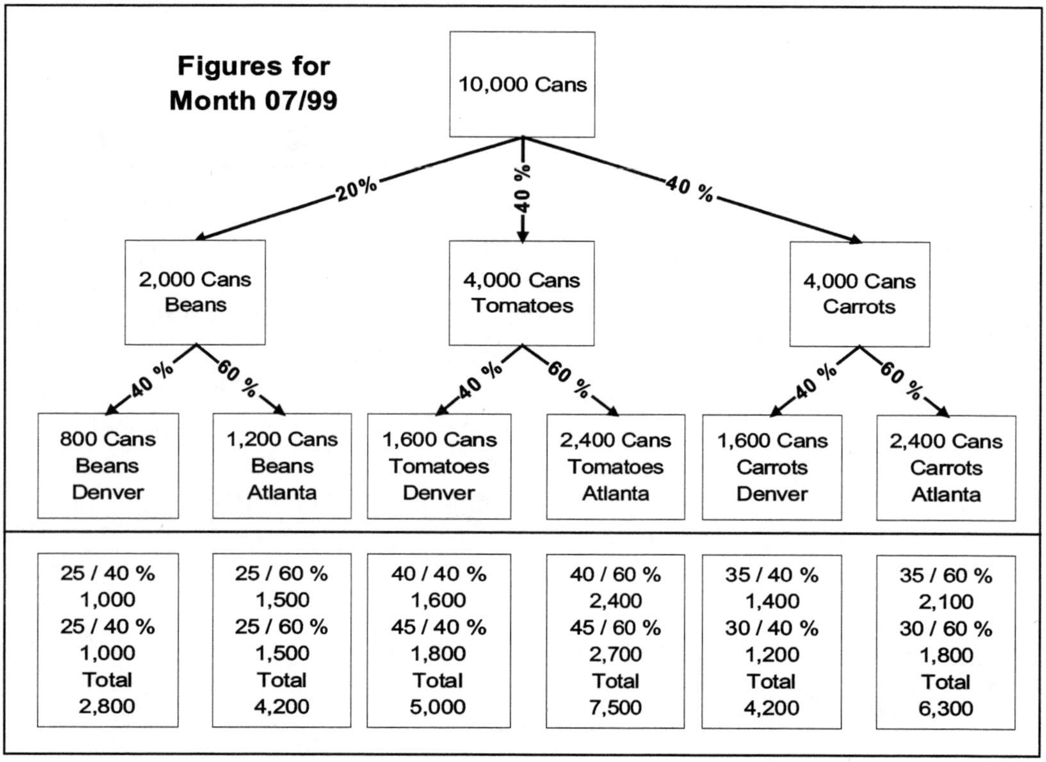


**Graphic 25 – Proportional Factors Example**

The blocks under the bold line in the graphic show the values for the other two months 08/99 and 09/99 as well as the total for the quarter. Each block provides the following information:

Line 1: Share in % of level 2 from upper level 1 and of level 3 from upper level 2 (month 08/99).

Line 2: Absolute quantity after applying the percentages through both levels (month 08/99).

Line 3: Share in % of level 2 from upper level 1 and of level 3 from upper level 2 (month 09/99).

Line 4: Absolute quantity after applying the percentages through both levels (month 09/99).

Line 6: Total absolute demand for quarter III/99

Any change in forecasted quantity of the product group "Canned Vegetables" leads to an update of the "Vegetable Type" and the "Location" forecast quantity. This approach can be used if the proportions between the various vegetables and the respective locations are stable and a change in demand applies to all products in the same way. That means if more beans are sold the demand for carrots also goes up, and at the same time the production split over the different locations remains the same.

Although not specified above, another distribution rule was incorporated in our model. It is the rule that demand of a quarter can be distributed evenly over the three months. Any change on the lowest level would automatically update the two superior levels and recalculate the proportional factors according to aggregation model 2.

### 3.3.3.4 Bottom-Up Planning

Bottom-Up Planning is an approach where forecasts are carried out at the lowest level. From there the system aggregates forecast data automatically to the superior levels.

The advantage of a Bottom-Up Planning approach is the creation of a very detailed forecast on the lowest level with high quality data being passed to the next level. This approach can be used when combining forecasts from various sources as it is the case with "Vendor Managed Inventories" (VMI).

Example:
Let us look at the previous example of the canned food manufacturer. Using the same environment the following data has to be determined to derive the consolidated demand plan.

Data Table:

| Can Size per Month | | Product | | |
|---|---|---|---|---|
| | | Beans | Tomatoes | Carrots |
| Denver | 07/99 | 800 | 1,600 | 1,600 |
| Denver | 08/99 | 1,000 | 1,600 | 1,400 |
| Denver | 09/99 | 1,000 | 1,800 | 1,200 |
| Atlanta | 07/99 | 1,200 | 2,400 | 2,400 |
| Atlanta | 08/99 | 1,500 | 2,400 | 2,100 |
| Atlanta | 09/99 | 1,500 | 2,700 | 1,800 |

**Table 7 – Proportional Factors Example 2**

The result obviously will be the same as in the previous example, a demand of 10,000 per month and 30,000 for the quarter. For this reason there is no graphical presentation of the aggregation of the forecast. The emphasis is to understand that the Bottom-Up planning requires more input-data compared to the Top-Down approach.

#### 3.3.3.5 Middle-Through Planning

Middle-Through Planning is a combination of the Top-Down and Bottom-Up planning approach. It is used where the Top-Down approach using proportional factors does not provide the required accuracy on the lower levels, but where at the same time the lowest level approach of the Bottom-Up approach is either not required or not possible. Another situation might be one in which a VMI customer provides forecasts on product group level only, and the manufacturer breaks this demand down into products using proportional factors. As long as the proportional factors are the same for all VMI customers of the manufacturer and are the same over the time, this approach will work well.

Example:
We shall again follow up on our previous example. The data required to generate the demand plan is somehow in the middle between the Bottom-Up and the Top-Down approach.

Data Tables:

| Quarter | Proportional Factors |
|---|---|
| III/99 | 40 / 60 % |

**Table 8 – Proportional Factors Example 3**

| Cans per Month | Product | | |
|---|---|---|---|
| | Beans | Tomatoes | Carrots |
| 07/99 | 2,000 | 4,000 | 4,000 |
| 08/99 | 2,500 | 4,000 | 3,500 |
| 09/99 | 2,500 | 4,500 | 3,000 |

**Table 9 – Proportional Factors Example 4**

We now require the proportional factors to distribute the demand of cans into the subordinate level to derive the demand per location. The aggregation, which again is of type 2, provides the totals per month and quarter.

### 3.3.3.6 Comparison of Planning Approaches

Each of the planning approaches described above requires an estimation of demand (the forecast) to be carried out. The difference, as we have seen, is the direction in which forecast data is either consolidated or distributed. Data required at any level will be estimated using any of the forecast models and techniques described later. It is important to understand that using the same historical data, the three planning approaches can lead to substantially different results. The following example illustrates this effect.

Example:
We are investigating the demand for two products, Orange and Pineapple Juice. They are the only members of a product group Juices. The historical demand per product as well as the accumulated product group demand can be seen in the following table.

| | Month | | | | | | Total |
|---|---|---|---|---|---|---|---|
| Product | 01/99 | 02/99 | 03/99 | 04/99 | 05/99 | 06/99 | |
| Orange Juice | 100 | 120 | 140 | 160 | 180 | 200 | 900 |
| Pineapple Juice | 150 | 140 | 130 | 120 | 110 | 100 | 450 |
| Group | | | | | | | |
| Juices | 250 | 260 | 270 | 280 | 290 | 300 | 1350 |

**Table 10 – Proportional Factors Example 5**

We now investigate the results of the forecast based on the two planning approaches Bottom Up and Top Down. The third planning approach, Middle Through as a combination of the two aforementioned would react the same way, depending on the direction you plan.

Bottom-Up Planning
We can see easily that Orange Juice is on the incline. Sales increase month by month steadily by 20. In opposition to this, the Pineapple juice is not doing well and sales are declining every month by 10. Based on a univariate-forecast model, the result would be a trend upwards for the Orange Juice and a trend downwards for the Pineapple Juice. On the product group level the total demand appears to be inclining. It is calculated by means of aggregation type "Total". The first forecast result is as follows:

| | Month | | | | | | Total |
|---|---|---|---|---|---|---|---|
| Product | 07/99 | 08/99 | 09/99 | 10/99 | 11/99 | 12/99 | |
| Orange Juice | 220 | 240 | 260 | 280 | 300 | 320 | 1620 |
| Pineapple Juice | 90 | 80 | 70 | 60 | 50 | 40 | 390 |
| Group | | | | | | | |
| Juices | 310 | 320 | 330 | 340 | 350 | 360 | 2010 |

**Table 11 – Proportional Factors Example 6**

Top-Down Planning

With this planning approach and when applying the univariate forecast, the planning will be carried out on product group level first. In a consequent calculation the forecasted demand will be distributed using either an even distribution or, if defined, a proportional factor. In our example we assume a proportional factor with the value 66.6% for Orange Juice and 33.4% for Pineapple Juice. The second forecast result is as follows:

| | Month | | | | | | Total |
|---|---|---|---|---|---|---|---|
| Product | 07/99 | 08/99 | 09/99 | 10/99 | 11/99 | 12/99 | |
| Orange Juice | 207 | 213 | 220 | 227 | 233 | 240 | 1620 |
| Pineapple Juice | 103 | 107 | 110 | 113 | 117 | 120 | 390 |
| Group | | | | | | | |
| Juices | 310 | 320 | 330 | 340 | 350 | 360 | 2010 |

**Table 12 – Proportional Factors Example 7**

Comparison of Results

Bottom Up planning indicates an even stronger demand for Orange Juice in the future. Using the Top Down planning approach we have an estimated moderate

increase for both juices! This is obviously a simplified example, but the principle is clear. If a planning group (in our case the Juice) has members with opposite trends (Orange and Pineapple Juice), then the planning result using a Top Down approach will give wrong results.
We could overcome the latter problem by calculating time dependant proportional factors per month. But then we get into the area of forecasting proportional factors, which in the long run might be even more complicated and less transparent than carrying out the forecast on product level in the first place.

### 3.3.4 Planning Example

The following practical example joins the aspects of Characteristics Value Combination creation, the calculation of Proportional Factors, and the Fixing of Values. We start of with a table that gives us the historical demands per product, customer, and location for the last three months. The last column shows the Proportional Factors, which were calculated based on the total demand in these periods. To simplify the example, a constant model is used.

| Product | Customer | Location | Demand 1 | Demand 2 | Demand 3 | Prop. Factor |
|---|---|---|---|---|---|---|
| Needles | Brown | Denver | 200 | 200 | 200 | 10 |
| Needles | Brown | Atlanta | 400 | 400 | 400 | 20 |
| Needles | Smith | Denver | 100 | 100 | 100 | 5 |
| Needles | Smith | Atlanta | 300 | 300 | 300 | 15 |
| Pins | Brown | Denver | 300 | 300 | 300 | 15 |
| Pins | Brown | Atlanta | 200 | 200 | 200 | 10 |
| Pins | Smith | Denver | 500 | 500 | 500 | 25 |

**Table 13 – Proportional Factors Example 8**

There are no sales of the product Pins to customer Brown from our location Atlanta. This is depicted in the table below.

| Product | Customer | Location | Demand 1 | Demand 2 | Demand 3 | Prop. Factor |
|---|---|---|---|---|---|---|
| Pins | Smith | Atlanta | 0 | 0 | 0 | 0 |

**Table 14 – Proportional Factors Example 9**

Characteristic Value Combinations are now defined for all those combinations where demand existed in the past. This is done using the Mass Generation function. Additionally we define a Characteristic Value Combination for the new combination as shown in the second table. In a bottom-up approach, we forecast the demand for the new Characteristic Value Combination "Pins – Smith – Atlanta" to be 1000. Additionally we fix this value! In a top-down approach, the demand per product is forecasted to be 2000 for Needles and 3000 for Pins.

| Product | Customer | Location | Forecast | Prop. Factor | |
|---|---|---|---|---|---|
| | | | | Old | New |
| Needles | Brown | Denver | 400 | 10 | 6.7 |
| Needles | Brown | Atlanta | 800 | 20 | 13.3 |
| Needles | Smith | Denver | 200 | 5 | 3.3 |
| Needles | Smith | Atlanta | 600 | 15 | 10.0 |
| Pins | Brown | Denver | 900 | 15 | 15.0 |
| Pins | Brown | Atlanta | 600 | 10 | 10.0 |
| Pins | Smith | Denver | 1500 | 25 | 25.0 |
| Pins | Smith | Atlanta | 1000 **Fixed** | 0 | 16.7 |

**Table 15 – Proportional Factors Example 10**

Note that the forecasted demand for the product Pins is not distributed over the fixed value. In the last column the new Proportional Factor including the new Characteristic Value Combination is depicted. It was calculated after all planning was carried out. The overall total new forecasted demand is now 6000 and the Fixing can be released.

### 3.3.5 Forecast Overview

There are various primary forecasting techniques available within APO. They can be broken down into the three basic areas of

- Time Series Based,
- Causal, and
- Judgmental models.

Primary forecasting techniques are carried out first in time. Furthermore there are some secondary techniques that are optional and can be used as a follow up activity after any of the basic forecast techniques were applied. They are

- Composite Forecasting, and
- Consensus Based Forecasting.

To support an efficient forecasting process some other tools are available within APO. They are described under the header of Forecast Support Tools and comprise:

- Life Cycle Management,
- Like Modeling,
- Outlier Correction,
- Workday Correction,
- Safety Stock Calculation, and
- Forecast Valuation.

Not all of these tools can be applied to all of the forecasting models. In some cases, although technically possible, the result might be meaningless. Followed by the forecasting tools overview is an introduction to functionality new to APO. It is

- Promotional Planning.

The last chapters of Demand Planning deal with approaches common to all forecasting techniques.

## 3.3.6 Primary Forecasting Techniques

Time Series Based Models are based on the assumption that the future demand pattern can be described with reasonable quality by extrapolating the consumption pattern found in the past. That is why these models as the first step require a thorough investigation of past consumption patterns. The investigation includes the elimination of any outliers as well as the workday correction. Once this step has been carried out, the forecast as such is a simple extrapolation of the past consumption pattern. There is a magnitude of time series-based models strategies. This type is the most commonly used way to perform a forecast. Univariate forecast methods, which we shall further explore in the following chapters, are based on a single set of data, the time series. In APO they are also called Time Series Based or Statistical Forecasts.

⇒ **Statistical method to extrapolate historical data, which does not require logical relations to other external variables.**

Causal Models explain past demand based on coefficients and forecast the future demand based on the equation developed in the first step. A coefficient is an independent variable (indicator), which is used to describe the change of the dependent variable (the sales demand). Causal models can have one or multiple independent variables, which influence the dependant variable according to fixed or variable relations. Furthermore, it might be possible that an independent variable has a significant influence only within a certain interval. The idea of Causal Models is to explain the consumption of a specific product by using global and easier to predict parameters.
Let me give an example. In our simplified model, the consumption of petrol for passenger cars is depending on the number of cars (independent variable $x_1$) and the price per liter (independent variable $x_2$). Both will influence the consumption (dependent variable y). We now assume that the variable $x_1$ explains the model for any number of passenger cars from Zero to indefinite. Variable $x_2$ is only valid

for petrol prices between a defined lower level $x_{2\ min}$ and an upper level $x_{2\ max}$. This is valid due to the fact that people will not exceed a certain mileage per year even if the price falls below a level $x_{2\ min}$. On the other hand, they will do a minimum mileage per year even if the petrol price exceeds the upper level $x_{2\ max}$. Once we know the relation between petrol price and number of cars, on the one hand, and the petrol consumption on the other hand, we can easily extrapolate and predict the petrol consumption.

⇒ **Method based on historical data and its relationship to consumption in the past, which is then carried forward.**

Judgmental Models are no mathematical models like the other two explained above. This model builds on people's expertise and experience. The input is market knowledge and maybe even intuition and ideas of what is likely to happen in the future. Various methodologies are known. Some literature also talks of applying of "Market Intelligence" emphasizing on the fact that an individual's knowledge or intelligence is used to create a forecast. Any system must support these forecasting activities by providing complete and structured information. This is achieved by the use of the Business Information Warehouse (BW) with its highly configurable and open approach. Furthermore it is required to have an easy way to capture and view forecasts derived. This can be done using the APO Demand Planning functionality.

⇒ **Subjective assessment of probable future consumption carried out by individuals or groups.**

After explaining the three primary forecasting techniques, it must be stressed that in real life usually none of them are deployed in their purest form. Planners will for example run a time series-based model but change a few figures, as they "know" (judgmental) that in a certain month the sales will be different. After gaining an understanding for the primary forecasting techniques, we shall learn in the next step how these differently derived forecasts can be combined and further refined by applying any of the secondary forecasting techniques.

### 3.3.6.1 Time Series Based Forecasting

To this group, which should be well known to any R/3 user, belong some very basic methods that, although simple in concept and fast in processing, might well do the job. All univariate forecasts are based on a past time series.

- Constant Model
  This model is characterized by a stable demand with little-to-no fluctuation over time. Products following this pattern can usually be found in saturated markets. Constant models assume that the demand or consumption of a product will be the same in the forecasted period in comparison to the past periods used to derive the forecast. This does not imply at all that these models do not react to changes in consumption; they just do not anticipate a change. If for example the actual demand in the month of August differs from the forecasted demand for this month, all constant models will forecast a new changed forecast for the month of September. The difference of the various strategies offered within this model is that they adapt faster or slower to such a change.
  Example:
  Products in the midst of their life cycle, where sales patterns are independent of external factors and which at the same time are not subject to increased competition. An example would be the sales pattern of fire matches in the supermarket or the usage of service parts for a fleet of cars with a stable number of units and average age.
- Trend Model
  In this model, a stable, but growing (or shrinking) demand is assumed. The result of the forecast is a quantity, which changes from period to period by exactly the same absolute figure. There is only a subtle difference between the Constant and the Trend Model. The latter examines trends in consumption and anticipates changes to it. This is a proactive approach unlike the Constant Model, which is reactive. The Trend Model pattern could also easily be explained using a causal model if the cause (originator) of the change is known.
  Example:
  This pattern also applies most to products at the midst of their life cycle. Unlike the above there is a certain change (stable increase or decrease) per period, which usually is based on an external factor that cannot be influenced.

Examples are the sales of basic groceries (e.g. salt) where the usage is not dependent on external factors besides the population.

- Seasonal Model
  The seasonal model assumes consumption changes based on one or multiple seasons per group of periods (e.g. per year). The season is finished after the seasonal effect (increase or decrease of demand) is over and the demand is back to its usual value. The season may consist of an increase or a decrease of demand, or both. A seasonal pattern can be caused by certain events (Christmas or New Year), by the average temperature (summer or winter), or weather conditions (rainy season). Event-driven seasons are rather easy to handle, as the time of the occurrence is predictable. Seasons based on weather are difficult to predict for known reasons. Furthermore, the overlay of two independent seasonal effects is complicated, and in this case the usage of a causal model might be more appropriate.
  Example:
  We all know the standard example for seasonal behavior, the ice cream consumption during summer. But there are others, which are not so obvious. Wind screen wiper blades shortly after the start of the rainy season, chocolate before Easter and slimming agents after Christmas and Easter.
- Seasonal Trend Model
  This again is a combination of two effects, the seasonal usage combined with a growing or shrinking number of sales. The seasonal factors (or indices) calculated per period are adjusted by the growth factor. Otherwise the calculation follows the principle of the Seasonal Model.
  Example:
  All the examples above are valid again; the difference is an overlay of an increasing or decreasing market pattern caused by an external factor.
- Intermittent Model
  Irregular demand is the nightmare of any planner. Nothing is predictable and consumption comes and goes without obeying any rule (or at least we don't know the rule). As nothing is predictable, the only chance is to have a higher safety stock and hope to cope with peaks. I would rather suggest using a re-order point procedure instead.
  Example:
  Any product could be an example for this pattern; it really depends on the actual market position the company is in.

- No Forecast
  Following the idea that even no forecast is a forecast, we just copy last year's results and assume we shall use or sell the product the same way we did last year. Using this method we actually do not bother about patterns and dependencies, and as a result any of the above models might apply. The system copies the last year's pattern period-by-period onto the new year.
  Example:
  Again, there is no typical example of product that would follow this principle.

One rule is valid for all the forecasting methods described above. The more good data, that is data which is correct and reliable, you have to run a forecast, the better it is. In cases where historical data is not reliable, it might be the better choice to not use it. This is quite often the case when a new system like APO is implemented, and the data coming from the old system is either not complete, incorrect, or was stored with a different organizational structure in mind.

Model Initialization

Before the first forecast can be carried out, it is required to perform a model initialization. During this process, basic values (model parameters), which are dependent on the model chosen, are calculated. To do this step, it is obviously necessary to have a minimum amount of historical data, and again the amount of data is dependent on the model. The amount of required data is purely a mathematical minimum and does not imply whatsoever that the result is meaningful.
The minimum number of historical data values required to perform the model initialization per forecast model is shown in the following table. The table also shows the parameters calculated for the respective forecast models.

The Ex-Post Forecast always starts after the required number of historical data sets are read. The number of required periods is shown in the table above. The forecast models described above are the basis for what SAP calls the forecast strategy. For almost all of these models, various strategies are available that allow the planner to forecast demand as precisely as the data and his or her knowledge allow. It must be stressed again that forecasting is an interactive task between the planner and the system. A good planner needs to fully understand the concept behind each and every strategy to make the right decisions. The system will only provide feedback, give data quality measurements, and help to cope with huge amounts of data. It will not replace sound business knowledge and experience!

| Model | Number of Historical Data Values | Calculated Model Parameters |
|---|---|---|
| Constant model | 1 | Basic Value |
| Trend model | 3 | Basic Value, Trend Value |
| Seasonal model | 1 season | Basic Value, Seasonal Indices |
| Seasonal trend model | 1 season + 3 | Basic Value, Trend Value, Seasonal Index |
| Intermittent Demand | N/A | N/A |
| No Forecast | N/A | N/A |

**Table 16 – Model Initialization**

All forecast strategies in the number range from 10 to 49 require the planner defining which model is to be used for calculating the forecast. This also applies to strategy 60 and 80. APO offers other strategies that suggest the model with the best fit if the planner does not know which model and strategy is the best. The strategies with automatic model selection should only be used as an exception or when the planner assumes a significant change in the time series pattern. This is due to the fact that their run time is longer than those of other strategies, as the selection process is resource intensive. Strategies in the range 50 to 59 offer this automatic detection of patterns.

Some of the forecast strategies work with default values for required parameters. They are based on the definitions in the univariate and master forecast profiles. When defining the univariate and master forecast profile, a “Default” button allows copying into the profile what is commonly accepted to be a good proposition. The planner might want to alter them to achieve a more acceptable result or just to see the impact on a change. Again it makes sense to do this to get familiar with the APO forecasting capabilities and to store the results in different planning versions for easy comparison of results.

The following table provides an overview of the APO forecast strategies. Note that the numbering is in accordance with numbers that can be found in the Univariate Forecast Profile when defining the default strategy for forecasts. In this profile it is possible to define either a strategy group or a strategy as the default. Should a group be used as the default, the system takes the first strategy within the group when running the forecast.

| Name | Group | Strategies | Trend Dampening Profile |
|---|---|---|---|
| Constant Models | 10 | 11, 12, 13, 14 | |
| Trend Models | 20 | 21, 22, 23 | Optional |
| Seasonal Models | 30 | 31 | |
| Seasonal Trend Models | 40 | 41 | Optional |
| Automatic Model Selection 1 | 50 | 51, 52, 53, 54, 55 | |
| Automatic Model Selection 2 | 50 | 56 | |
| Past History | 60 | 60 | |
| Croston Method | 80 | 80 | |
| Multiple Linear Regression | 90 | 94 | |
| External Model | 99 | 99 | |

**Table 17 – Forecast Strategies**

The following variables are used to depict the mathematical rules.

Actual Value of Period: $A_{(t)}$

Forecast Value of Period: $F_{(t)}$

Weighting Factor of Period: $W_{(t)}$

Period $t$

Number of Periods $n$

The most recent historical data (actuals of current period) is defined as period $t_0$ with preceding periods shown as $t_{-1}$, $t_{-2}$ and so on. The first forecasted period is defined as $t_1$.

The following chapters provide an introduction to forecasting strategies available in APO. Forecasting Strategies in APO have a numeric identifier that is used to select a strategy. This identifier can be seen in the header of each chapter referring to a strategy. For all Constant Models the mathematical formula used to derive the forecast is introduced. These formulas are added to gain some basic knowledge about the calculation and to also develop an idea about the complexity of these calculations. For models other than the Constant Models, no formulas are added, as it is not the core emphasis of this book to provide the theoretical background and all formulas required for statistical forecasting. An abundance of literature is available for this topic.

#### 3.3.6.1.1 Constant Models

Constant Models can be found in Strategy Group 10.

**Strategy 11 - 1st Order Exponential Smoothing**

1st Order Exponential Smoothing is also known as Single Exponential Smoothing abbreviated SES. Like the weighted moving average, this strategy is also based on the principle that, the older the historical data, the less impact it has on the forecast. In addition to this, the previous period's forecast error is taken into account. Weighting is achieved by using the so-called Alpha ($\alpha$) factor and the basic formula for the 1st Order Exponential Smoothing is the following:

$$F_{(t=1)} = \alpha A_{t=0} + (1-\alpha)F_{t=0}$$

This means that the forecast for the coming period is based on the current period's actuals multiplied with the alpha factor plus the previous period's forecast value multiplied with 1 minus alpha. We can now substitute the previous period's forecast as follows:

$$F_{(t=0)} = \alpha A_{t=-1} + (1-\alpha)F_{t=-1}$$

Combining these two equations leads to a new formula for $F_{(t=1)}$:

$$F_{(t=1)} = \alpha A_{t=0} + (1-\alpha) * (\alpha A_{t=-1} + (1-\alpha)F_{t=-1})$$

If we repeat this step 12 times, representing 12 periods under observation, the formula will finally look like this:

$$F_{(t=1)} = \alpha A_{t=0} + \alpha(1-\alpha)A_{t=-1} + \alpha(1-\alpha)^2 A_{t=-2} + \ldots$$
$$\ldots. + \alpha(1-\alpha)^{10} A_{t=-10} + (1-\alpha)^{11} F_{t=-11}$$

The greater the Alpha factor, the more weight is put on the most recent consumption data and vice versa. Note that when using an Alpha Factor of Zero with this strategy, the forecast for the following period equals the forecast of the very first period under observation (which might be a year old)! The other extreme with Alpha equal to 1 results in the forecast for the coming period to be equal to the last period's consumption. Common values for alpha are in the range of 0.3 to 0.5. The weights based on the alpha factor applied to all past data sum up to approximately 1. The impact of historical data decreases exponentially. The following table gives the weight per period for the three alpha factors 0.3, 0.4, and 0.5 based on a 12 period observation frame. The results are always rounded to four digits.

DP

| Alpha | 0.3 | 0.4 | 0.5 |
|---|---|---|---|
| Period t | | | |
| 0 | 0.3 | 0.4 | 0.5 |
| 1 | 0.21 | 0.24 | 0.25 |
| 2 | 0.147 | 0.1440 | 0.125 |
| 3 | 0.1029 | 0.0864 | 0.0625 |
| 4 | 0.0720 | 0.0518 | 0.0313 |
| 5 | 0.0504 | 0.0311 | 0.0156 |
| 6 | 0.0353 | 0.0187 | 0.0078 |
| 7 | 0.0247 | 0.0112 | 0.0039 |
| 8 | 0.0173 | 0.0067 | 0.0020 |
| 9 | 0.0121 | 0.0040 | 0.0010 |
| 10 | 0.0085 | 0.0024 | 0.0005 |
| 11 | 0.0059 | 0.0015 | 0.0002 |

**Table 18 – Alpha Smoothing Factors**

It is easily visible that the impact of historical data diminishes faster with greater alpha values and vice versa. When applying high alpha values, the number of periods under observation can be easily reduced without having a significant loss in forecast quality.

**Strategy 12 - Automatic Alpha Optimization (1$^{st}$ order)**

The Constant Model with Automatic Alpha Optimization (1$^{st}$ order) optimizes the Alpha factor while calculating the forecast values. Other than that there are no differences compared to the strategy explained above. In order to optimize the alpha factor, the system has to carry out the forecast applying various alpha factors. In a consequent step the calculated forecasts are compared using the error values explained in the following chapters. Most common for this technique is the usage of the Mean Square Error (MSE) or the Mean Absolute Percentage Error (MAPE). Unfortunately SAP has not published which approach they take.

## Strategy 13 - Moving Average

The Moving Average model is also referred to as Moving Average Forecast abbreviated MA $_{(n)}$ whereby n depicts the number of periods used. The system calculates the average over the historical time pattern and carries forward this average as the new demand for the following periods of the forecast horizon. All past periods are added up with the same weight. If as an example the forecast horizon is twelve months, all 12 months will have the same impact on the forecasted value, which is the average of the past periods. The forecast for period 2 of the forecast horizon is calculated using the forecasted quantity for period 1 of the forecast horizon plus n-1 periods of the history. All periods have the same weighting, and for this reason the model adapts to changes only very slowly. This strategy is suitable for products with a stable constant demand although it will adapt to changes over time. It requires storing the consumption values of n periods. The higher the number of periods used, the more stable the result on one hand and less responsive to changes on the other hand.

$$F_{(t=1)} = \frac{1}{n} \sum_{t=0}^{1-n} A_{(t)}$$

Unlike the Forecast with Constant model, the number of periods (n) in this equation remains constant.

## Strategy 14 - Weighted Moving Average

Strategy 14 is a derivation of strategy 13. As with the strategy explained above, the system calculates the average over a specified period and carries forward this result as the forecast. Unlike the above strategy, each historical value is multiplied with a factor as specified in the Weighting Group. The total of all weighting factors used is 1. Based on the assumption that the weights decrease over time, this model results in a situation where the most recent historical data has a greater impact than older data.

$$F_{(t=1)} = \frac{1}{n}\left(\sum_{t=0}^{1-n} A_{(t)} * W_{(t)}\right)$$

$$\sum_{t=0}^{1-n} W_{(t)} = 1$$

### 3.3.6.1.2 Trend Models

Trend Models can be found in Strategy Group 20.

Trend Models are very similar to the constant models. The main difference is that all constant models assume a consumption that is stable over time, with no up or downward trend. In other words, a constant model has a Zero Trend. For this reason constant models can be seen as a special form of trend models. The result of a trend model forecast with perfectly constant historical data will therefore be the same as it would be when applying the constant model directly. The general notation for a trend model is depicted below.

$$Y_t = a + bX_t$$

In this formula the time independent basic value “a”, the slope multiplier “b”, and the time dependent observation value $X_t$ explain the forecast value $Y_t$. The sign of the multiplier “b” indicates the relation between the forecast value $Y_t$ and the observation value $X_t$. In case of a positive sign, the forecast value $Y_t$ rises (falls) with a rising (falling) observation value $X_t$ and, in case of a negative sign, the forecast value $Y_t$ rises (falls) with a falling (rising) observation value $X_t$.

APO provides the Trend Dampening Profile as an optional entry for all trend models. A trend dampening profile is used in situations where the identified trend in the past is likely to decrease (flatten out). Mathematically spoken the slope as identified in the formula above decreases from period to period as specified in the trend dampening profile. When attaching a trend dampening profile to a product, the slope "b" will be adjusted as specified when calculating the forecast.

## Strategy 21 - 1st Order Exponential Smoothing

As it is the case with 1st Order Exponential Smoothing for constant models, using this strategy, more weight is put on more recent data. The weight of historical data decreases exponentially over time. 1st Order Exponential Smoothing uses the Alpha Factor, which determines the decrease of the weight factor used per historical data point. Alpha Factors range from Zero to 1. The higher the Alpha Factor, the more weight is put on recent historical data and vice versa. High Alpha values lead to forecasts that are very responsive towards changes. At the same time, they tend to overreact in situations where extraordinary sales were encountered.

Also see the above chapter "Strategy 11 - 1st Order Exponential Smoothing " for further information on the Alpha Factor.

## Strategy 22 - 2nd Order Exponential Smoothing

1st Order Exponential Smoothing is a rather weak strategy to use when trends are imminent. The forecast results trail behind by several periods depending on the Alpha Factor. 2nd Order Exponential Smoothing, which is also called the Holt's Linear Method, overcomes this problem by specifically recognizing trends and incorporating them into the forecast. With this method two smoothing constants, named Alpha and Beta, are used. Both run between Zero and 1. It is important to choose the Alpha and Beta factors in such a way that the error of the forecast is minimized. A method to do so would be to compare the Mean Square Error (MSE) for various Alpha/Beta combinations. The lowest MSE indicates the best-fit Alpha/Beta combination.

The MSE is explained further down in the chapter Forecast Accuracy Analysis.

**Strategy 23 - Automatic Alpha Optimization (2nd order)**

As seen in strategy 22, it can be a rather laborious task to determine the best-fit Alpha/Beta combination. Using the Strategy 23 - Trend Model with Automatic Alpha Optimization (2nd order) the system will perform this optimization for the planner and use automatically the best combination.

#### 3.3.6.1.3 Seasonal Models

Seasonal Models can be found in Strategy Group 30.

A periodical increase and decrease of consumption characterize seasonal models. Typical examples are the sales of ice cream, which peak in summer and the increased energy consumption of private households during winter. In order for such models to work, it is required to define the number of periods per season. Seasonal models cannot be used if the seasonality varies too much. The underlying forecast after the elimination of the seasonal effect is a constant model. The system calculates an average for the periods in questions and then a seasonal factor per period ranging from "Zero" (no sales) to "One" (average sales) to "Greater One" (above average sales).

**Strategy 31 - Seasonal Model based on Winter's method**

All methods discussed above can cope with historical data that shows a constant and/or trend pattern. They would be totally inadequate for situations where a seasonal pattern is detected. Specifically for this type of historical data pattern Winter developed a method that is also known as the Holt-Winter's method. The Holt-Winter's method is an extension of the original Holt's method, which is used for trend models. The Holt-Winter method is implemented in APO as strategy 31.

Holt's model can deal with seasonal and trend patterns and is using in such cases the three parameters Alpha, Beta, and Gamma. In APO this model is used only in connection with seasonal models without a trend and therefore does not require the Beta parameter. The quality of the forecast is dependent on the right combination of the Alpha and Gamma parameter. Using strategy 31, the planner must optimize them manually. To do so it is appropriate to run various forecasts using different sets of the Alpha and Gamma factor and monitor the forecast error (e.g. the Mean Square Error , MSE). This is obviously a rather laborious task and it might be advisable to instead use one of the strategies with automatic model selection.

#### 3.3.6.1.4 Seasonal Trend Models

Seasonal Trend Models can be found in Strategy Group 40.

Seasonal Trend Models are the combination of a trend with a seasonal model. Due to this it is mandatory to define the periods per season. As it is the case with trend models, the usage of a Trend Dampening Profile is possible (see above chapters for more information).

**Strategy 41 - 1st Order Exponential Smoothing**

The model used for historical data that follows a seasonal trend pattern is similar to the one described above. In addition to the Alpha and Gamma factor introduced in the last chapter, a new parameter called Beta is required. The Alpha parameter is used for smoothing of the basic value, the Beta parameter is used for smoothing of the trend value, and the Gamma parameter is used for smoothing of the seasonal index.

### 3.3.6.1.5 Automatic Model Selection Procedure

Automatic Model Selection Procedures can be found in Strategy Group 50.

Up to now all strategies we discussed required the planner deciding which strategy the system should use when carrying out the forecast. Specifically, when dealing with a large number of products or in cases where the pattern is not easily recognizable by the planner, this tends to be a challenge. The answer to this problem is the usage of Automatic Model Selection strategies, which will be introduced in the following chapters. Automatic Model Selection strategies are not entirely new strategies. The system evaluates the historical data and carries out various forecasts. The strategy with the best fit is then used to carry out the forecast. Automatic Model Selection is resource intensive and should therefore not be used as the default strategy. On the other hand the usage of Automatic Model Selection ensures that products where the underlying model has changed are forecasted more accurately. APO provides feedback as to which model was chosen. This allows setting the chosen model as the default model for future forecast runs.

**Strategy 51 - Test for Trend**

With this strategy the system tests by means of a regression analysis for a trend pattern. The forecast will be based on the constant model if no significant trend is detected.

**Strategy 52 - Test for Season**

In a first step, any trend values are eliminated form the historical data. Then an Auto-Correlation test is carried out (see the chapter "Model Fit Analysis for Causal Forecast"). Should the Auto-Correlation test indicate correlation, the trend model is applied. Otherwise the constant model is used.

## Strategy 53 - Test for Trend and Season

Strategy 53 is a combination of the strategies 51 and 52. In an initial step, the system tests by means of a regression analysis for a trend pattern. Then any trend values are eliminated form the historical data, which is followed by an Auto-Correlation test. Depending on the results, a Trend, Seasonal, or Seasonal Trend model will be applied. Should none of these models clearly apply to the historical data, the product will be forecasted using the constant model. Required entry is the periods per season.

## Strategy 54 - Seasonal Model and Test for Trend

When using manual model selection strategies, the planner must provide some input. By doing so the number of possibilities is limited which reduces the overall runtime of the model selection. The two strategies explained in this and the next chapter, follow this principle. They are very similar to the strategies 51 and 52 discussed above.

Based on the assumption that a seasonal model applies to the historical data, the system tests with the strategy 54 for a trend pattern by means of a regression analysis. If the test is successful, the forecast will be based on a seasonal trend model, otherwise a seasonal model is used.

## Strategy 55 - Trend Model and Test for Seasonal Pattern

This test assumes that a trend model applies to the historical data. In a first step, the trend values are eliminated from the historical data. Then an Auto-Correlation test is carried out (see the chapter "Model Fit Analysis for Causal Forecast"). Should the Auto-Correlation test indicate correlation, the seasonal trend model is applied; otherwise the trend model is used.

**Strategy 56 - Forecast with Model Selection Procedure 2**

According to SAP the selection procedure 2 is more precise than the selection procedure 1 used by the strategies discussed earlier, but has longer running times. With strategy 56, the system tests for:

- Constant
- Trend
- Season
- Seasonal Trend

It deploys various combinations of Alpha ($\alpha$), Beta ($\beta$), and Gamma ($\gamma$) factors to determine the optimum result, which is determined by the lowest Mean Absolute Deviation (MAD). Should none of these models clearly apply to the historical data, the product will be forecasted using the constant model. Required entry is the periods per season.

### 3.3.6.1.6 Copy History

The strategy group 60 consists of one strategy only. Using this strategy with the same number as the group, last year's historical data is simply copied and used as the next year's forecast.

### 3.3.6.1.7 Croston Method

The strategy group 80 consists of one strategy only. The strategy has the same number as the group. One of the most difficult tasks in forecasting is to deal with intermittent or lumpy demand. Such cases are characterized by having no dominant pattern, periods without any consumption, and unpredictable consumption in other periods. Croston developed a model specifically for such demand. It works best if a high number of historical data sets of the forecasted product are available.

### 3.3.6.1.8 External Forecast

The strategy group 99 consists of one strategy only. The strategy has the same number as the group. The strategy group 99 is reserved for individual customer-specific forecast routines. This user exit allows the integration of custom-developed forecasting calculations in cases where none of the forecast models offered by APO are sufficient in a particular business environment. A custom-developed forecast model is fully integrated in all other DP transactions and can be used seamlessly.

### 3.3.6.2 Causal Forecasting

All forecast models explained so far had one assumption in common. That is that future consumption can be seen as a function of time. Causal models follow a different approach, which is an explanatory method. The future consumption is determined not in relation to the time but rather to another parameter, the cause of the demand change. Causal forecasts are not necessarily time-dependant although the influencing factor could be time (as in the time-based forecasting techniques). The driver of the forecast, that is the value which influences the forecast, is called the independent variable. Simple Linear Regression explains the behavior of the dependent variable in relation to one independent variable. Multiple Linear Regression (MLR) uses two or more independent variables to explain the dependent variable. APO offers Multiple Linear Regression, which includes Simple Linear Regression if only one independent variable is used. The general formula for Multiple Linear Regression is shown below.

$$Y = a + bX_1 + cX_2 + dX_3......$$

| | |
|---|---|
| Y | represents the Dependent Variable (that is the value, which is forecasted). |
| X | values represent the Independent Variables (these are the values that cause changes in the forecasted quantity). |

a, b, c, d,.... are the Coefficients (these are multipliers of the independent variables or the basic value – intercept - in the case of coefficient "a").

The formula for the Simple Linear Regression is shown below.

$$Y = a + bX_1$$

For both models the sign of the coefficient indicates the relation between the Dependent and Independent Variable. In case of a positive sign, the dependent variable rises (falls) with a rising (falling) independent variable and in case of a negative sign the dependent variable rises (falls) with a falling (rising) independent variable. High coefficient values denote independent variables with a big influence on the dependent variable and vice versa. Both Linear Regression models assume a linear relation between the independent and dependent variables. Non-linear relations cannot be projected using these techniques. During the forecast, the system estimates the values of the coefficients "a" and "b" in the case of Simple Linear Regression and additionally the values of "c", "d", and so on for Multiple Linear Regression.

The calculation of the coefficients in Single Linear Regression can be understood without requiring an in-depth knowledge of mathematical functions or statistical models. We shall therefore go through the basics of Single Linear Regressions but omit the theoretical background and formulas for the Multiple Linear Regression. For those interested in this topic, I suggest reading one of the many available books regarding forecasting techniques.

Below are the formulas used in Simple Linear Regression for the slope "b" and the intercept "a".

$$b = \frac{\sum_{t=1}^{n} (X_t - \overline{X})(Y_t - \overline{Y})}{\sum_{t=1}^{n} (X_t - \overline{X})^2}$$

$a = \overline{Y} - b\overline{X}$

The fit of formula, that is how good the found equation explains the real consumption, can be assessed using the correlation between the X and Y data points. The Correlation Coefficient symbolized $r_{xy}$ ranges from –1 to +1. For more information please refer to the chapter "Model Fit Analysis for Causal Forecast".

The task of the planner is to clearly identify the independent variable that is causing the dependent variable to react. The problem is that a high correlation between two variables does not necessarily mean that there is a causal relation between the two.

The Independent Variable needs to be stored to be available for on-line and batch processing. Two possibilities exist.

1. Variables can be key figures and are stored in the InfoCube together with the other forecast related information. At least one key figure (in the case of Simple Linear Regression) or multiple key figures (in the case of Multiple Linear Regression) need to be defined. This data is stored per period just like any other consumption or forecast data.
2. The second possibility is to store time series variables. Time series variables are not stored in the InfoCube and require the definition in the MLR profile. The minimum number of time series entries is the total of historical and forecast periods as defined in the forecast master profile. The time series data is related to a start date that is specified in the MLR profile. The use of time series is adequate in cases where one does not want to load the independent variable into the InfoCube. It has the disadvantage that it has to be edited every time a forecast is carried out in a new time period.

Should an independent variable for a given period only effect the dependent variable with a time lag, a transformation value can be defined. This transformation value acts as a time offset in MLR. An example would be that the selling price of a product (independent variable) affects the sales volume (dependent variable) only 2 months later. The transformation factor is then 2 months. The Transformation parameter can only be specified when using a key figure as an independent variable.

When performing an MLR based forecast in interactive mode, the system switches over to the "Causal" tab. This tab displays various control parameters (see the chapter "Model Fit Analysis for Causal Forecast") as well as the used independent variables.

MLR based forecasts in APO have the strategy identifier 94.

#### 3.3.6.3 Judgmental Forecasting

Judgmental Forecasting is a manual task where various specialists within a given interest group come together to develop a demand plan. The input they provide is based on their respective knowledge and experience. No formalized input media can be defined. During such a session, a joined demand plan will be worked out and captured into APO. This can be done using the Interactive Planning Screen.

### 3.3.7 Forecast Support Tools

Forecast Support Tools can be classified according to the following criteria:

- Forecast Preparation: Correction or adjustment of historical data before the forecast as well as forecast adjustment during the forecast calculation
    - Outlier Correction
    - Workday Correction
    - Life Cycle Management
- Forecast Evaluation: Calculation of error or quality assessment values after the forecast
    - Error Value Calculation for Univariate Forecast
    - Error Value Calculation for Causal Forecast

In opposition to this, promotional planning is carried out after the forecast has been created. The Promotion Plan can be created and maintained before the forecast run, but will be activated only after the forecast has been carried out. A regeneration of the forecast might require updating the promotional plan.

### 3.3.7.1 Forecast Preparation

In some instances historical data should be adjusted before the forecast is carried out. Reasons might be the quality of data (outlier correction), period adjustment (workday correction), or the requirement to consider the products' life cycles (life cycle management). Workday correction also effects the calculation of forecast figures.

#### Outlier Correction

By definition an outlier is a value, which lies out of the demand pattern and will disable the detection of this pattern or at least have a negative influence on the mathematical correct explanation of the demand pattern. In graphical format, outliers can be easily seen and eliminated by the planner. Again, this is an intuitive approach where the planner's experience is very important. Outliers are not wrong data; they are just an occurrence, which was untypical and will not be repeated. An example would be an export sale in an environment where otherwise only domestic sales take place. In this case the sales data of this period should be corrected so that only the domestic sales remain. This is a logical approach to correcting an outlier. Although precise, this is not feasible in an automated system controlled process. Here mathematical algorithms have to be applied. APO offers such an approach in the form of Outlier Correction.
Outliers are identified as such if they lie outside of a "tolerance lane" which is dependant on the results of the Ex-Post Forecast, the Mean Absolute Deviation (MAD) and a user definable value called Sigma. The planner's task is to define Sigma in a way that the tolerance is neither too wide nor too narrow. Default Sigma is set to 1.25. The tolerance formula is as follows:

$$TL(t) = EP(t) \pm \sigma * MAD$$

Abbreviations used:

| | |
|---|---|
| Tolerance Lane point at time t | $TL(t)$ |
| Ex Post Forecast value at time t | $EP(t)$ |
| User definable value Sigma | $\sigma$ |
| Mean Absolute Deviation | $MAD$ |

Should a historical value be identified as an outlier, then it will be replaced by the corresponding value of the ex post forecast. Outlier Correction functionality works only in connection with Time-Based Forecasting. It can be activated in the Univariate Forecast Profile.

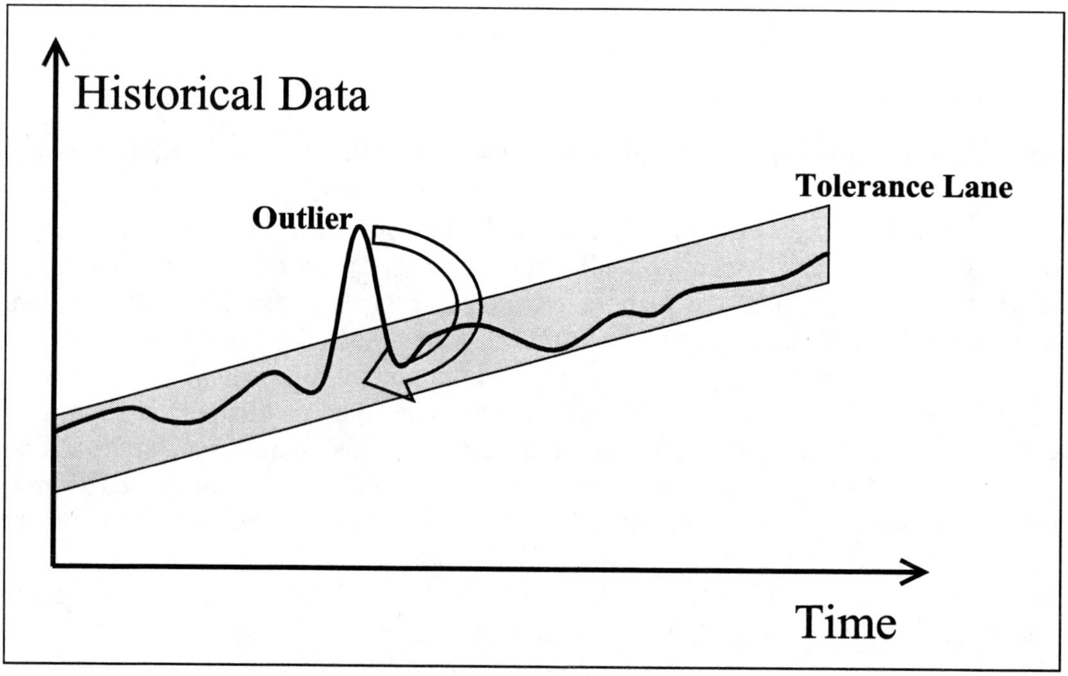


**Graphic 26 – Outlier Correction**

## Workday Correction

Workday Correction is used to compensate for the fact that months have different numbers of workdays. The system first corrects the history according to the actual workdays in the past period. Then in the next step, the forecast is adjusted according to the actual workdays in the forecasted period. Data is stored internally using an average number of workdays. Workdays are defined according to the valid factory calendar of the InfoCube.

The following is an example for this correction based on a trend model with a base demand of 100, a monthly increase of 10, and an average 20 workdays during the year 1999. In this example a factory calendar with no public holidays was used. Results are rounded with no decimals.

| Month | 01 | 02 | 03 | 04 | 05 | 06 | 07 | 08 | 09 | 10 | 11 | 12 |
|---|---|---|---|---|---|---|---|---|---|---|---|---|
| History | 100 | 110 | 120 | 130 | 140 | 150 | 160 | 170 | 180 | 190 | 200 | 210 |
| Workdays | 21 | 20 | 23 | 21 | 21 | 21 | 22 | 22 | 22 | 21 | 22 | 23 |
| Corrected History | 95 | 110 | 104 | 124 | 133 | 143 | 145 | 155 | 164 | 181 | 182 | 183 |

**Table 19 – Workday Correction**

Workday Correction functionality works only in connection with Time-Based Forecasting. When calculating the Corrected History ($H_C$) the system corrects the Original History ($H_O$) according to the following calculation:

$$H_C = H_O * WD_{AV} / WD_{AC}$$

When calculating the Forecast Value (F) the system adjusts the temporarily-stored Forecast ($F_T$) as follows:

$$F = F_T * WD_{AC} / WD_{AV}$$

Actual Workdays ($WD_{AC}$) are taken from the Factory Calendar, the Average Number of Workdays ($WD_{AV}$) is defined in the Univariate Forecast Profile. The average number of workdays needs to be aligned with the period defined in the profile. Workday Correction "normalizes" the forecast result and adjusts the history before using it.

## Life Cycle Management

Another new area, which can be found in APO, is Life Cycle Management. A model can be set up to determine the demand pattern for a product throughout its whole life cycle while taking into consideration factors like product switching or cannibalization, market penetration, and market fatigue to name a few.
Any new product requires some time to gain general acceptance. This phase in period is different for each product and requires careful planning in order to avoid initial oversupply. After a while the product will fall into its normal demand pattern, whether that be a constant, trend, seasonal or any combination thereof. Towards the end of the product's life cycle, a slowdown of demand can usually be seen which is either due to market saturation or the expectation of the new successive product. This period called phase out requires accurate planning, as it is usually very difficult to sell the product after a certain point in time.

Within APO tools for the creation of "Phase in" and "Phase out" profiles as well as "Like Modeling" profiles exist. Life Cycle Management profiles do not work in conjunction with Multiple Linear Regression or Composite Forecasts.

The three profiles for phase in, phase out and like modeling are defined per product irrespective of the location. Any product can have a phase in profile, and/or a phase out profile, and/or a like profile. The definition of these profiles can be done only from within the product master maintenance program. Starting from the Phase In/Phase Out tab of the product master, the three profiles can be created and maintained. The same profile can be attached to multiple products. The maintenance of this product tab is the only area where DP requires a product master. Also refer to the chapter "Master Data Environment" within the SNP section.

Life Cycle Management is product specific. This means that phase in and phase out definitions have to be carried out on the product level. In a future release, DP will also support Life Cycle Management on higher levels (e.g. phase out for an entire product group).

## Phase In Process

The planner defines a percentage value for the phase in period, and per period, of the product. This percentage is the relation between this period's consumption and the "normal" or "mature" consumption that will be achieved after the product's phase in period is over. The percentage increases therefore from period to period (e.g. month to month), up to the time where it reaches 100%. This indicates that the phase in period is at its end.

Example:

A new product will be launched. The phase in period is estimated to last 4 months starting in January 99 and to finish in April 99, after which the normal consumption is reached. At the end of the phase in period, a constant model will explain the demand figures. The estimated demand figures for the new product are shown in the following table. The "Estimated Sales (%)" is the relation between the month's sales forecast and the mature demand, which will be reached in May 99.

| | **Month** | | | | | |
|---|---|---|---|---|---|---|
| | 01/99 | 02/99 | 03/99 | 04/99 | 05/99 | 06/99 |
| Estimated Sales (Pieces) | 7,500 | 12,500 | 15,000 | 20,000 | 25,000 | 25,000 |
| Estimated Sales (%) | 30 | 50 | 60 | 80 | 100 | 100 |

**Table 20 – Phase In Process Example 1**

All that needs to be done when setting up the new product's phase in profile is defining the four percentages (30, 50, 60, and 80) for the phase in period and the constant sales of 25,000 pieces per month. If we are now running the forecast for

April 99, either interactively or in batch mode, the system will correct the historical data and estimate the future sales as follows:

| | Month | | | | | |
|---|---|---|---|---|---|---|
| | 01/99 | 02/99 | 03/99 | 04/99 | 05/99 | 06/99 |
| Original History (Pieces) | 25,000 | 25,000 | 25,000 | | | |
| Corrected History (Pieces) | 25,000 | 25,000 | 25,000 | | | |
| Estimated Sales (Pieces) | | | | 20,000 | 25,000 | 25,000 |

**Table 21 – Phase In Process Example 2**

What happened? To make it easier let's assume that forecasted sales and actual sales for the months January to March 99 are identical. The original sales figure for January, as an example, is 7,500. The phase in percentage is 30%. The system now divides 7,500 pieces by 30% to receive the "normal" sales of 25,000. This step is repeated for all months in the phase in period up to the current date. As we can see easily, the consumption is according to a constant model and in return the forecasted sales for May and June 99 is 25,000 as well. In April, which belongs to the phase in period, the estimated sales have to be adjusted in accordance with the phase in profile (80% of 25,000).

Please note that APO writes the newly calculated historical values into the key figures "Original History" and "Corrected History". All monthly percentages are stored in a table and not in the InfoCube. The estimated sales during the phase in period are not stored at all.

No doubt, this process can be much more complex when planning products, which are assumed to have a seasonal trend pattern! But the principle and the steps involved are the same.

The Phase In Profile is a tool to correctly predict sales based on the planner's knowledge regarding the phase in behavior of a product. APO firstly corrects the demand in the phase in period as if there is no phase in period, secondly it forecasts demand according to a model, and then thirdly adjusts forecasts if the period in question is still within the phase in period. The periods used are in accordance with the planning periods and do not have to be months (as in our example) necessarily.

## Phase Out Process

The planner defines per period a percentage value for the phase out period of the product. This percentage is the relation between this period's consumption and the "normal" or "mature" consumption that was usually achieved. The percentage decreases therefore from period to period (month to month), up to the time where it reaches Zero.

Example:

A product is about to be discontinued. The phase out period is estimated to last 4 months starting in March 99 and to finish in June 99, after which no demand will exist anymore. At the moment a constant model explains the demand figures. The estimated demand figures for the product are shown in the following table. The "Estimated Sales (%)" is the relation between the month's sales forecast and the mature demand that exists up to February 99.

| | Month | | | | | |
|---|---|---|---|---|---|---|
| | 01/99 | 02/99 | 03/99 | 04/99 | 05/99 | 06/99 |
| Estimated Sales (Pieces) | 25,000 | 25,000 | 20,000 | 12,500 | 5,000 | 2,500 |
| Estimated Sales (%) | 100 | 100 | 80 | 50 | 20 | 10 |

**Table 22 – Phase Out Process Example 1**

All that needs to be done when setting up the discontinued product's phase out profile is defining the four percentages (80, 50, 20, and 10) for the phase out period. If we are now running the forecast for April 99, either interactively or in batch mode, the system will correct the historical data and estimate the future sales as follows:

| | Month | | | | | |
|---|---|---|---|---|---|---|
| | 01/99 | 02/99 | 03/99 | 04/99 | 05/99 | 06/99 |
| Original History (Pieces) | 25,000 | 25,000 | 25,000 | | | |
| Corr. History (Pieces) | 25,000 | 25,000 | 25,000 | | | |
| Estimated Sales (Pieces) | | | | 12,500 | 5,000 | 2,500 |

**Table 23 – Phase Out Process Example 2**

What happened this time? We again assume that forecasted sales and actual sales for the months January to March 99 are identical. The system calculates a demand of 25,000 pieces per month for the three months of April through to June. It then applies the phase out percentages, which provides as an example, the final result of 12,500 pieces for the month of April 99.

Please note that APO writes the newly calculated historical values into the key figures "Original History" and "Corrected History". All monthly percentages are stored in a table and not in the InfoCube. The estimated sales during the phase out period are not stored at all.

The Phase Out Profile is a tool to correctly predict sales based on the planner's knowledge regarding the phase out behavior of a product. APO adjusts forecasts if the period in question is within the phase out period according to a planner-defined percentage. The periods used are in accordance with the planning periods and do not have to be months (like in our example) necessarily.

**Like Modeling**

Like Modeling is used in a case where for a product

- No historical data exists

- Not sufficient historical data exists
- Only unreliable historical data exists

It is a basic method where the historical data of one or multiple "like" products are used for the destination product. In the case where the Like profile refers to multiple products, it is possible to define either to sum up or average the referred products' demands. After this definition has taken place, forecasting takes place the normal way. To enable Like Modeling it is necessary to define the Like Product(s) in a Like Profile that is then attached to the product to be planned.

The option to use the average of various products can improve the planning quality in cases where a product behaves similar to a number of products. This is even more the case in situations where the Like Products have a somewhat erratic demand. Summing up the demand of various products is used when a new product replaces a number of old products.

APO always reads the key figure "Original History" of the "like" product and copies the values into the key figures "Original History" and "Corrected History".

### 3.3.7.2 Forecast Evaluation

DP offers several tools that allow the evaluation of univariate (or time series-based) forecasts as well as Causal Analysis. The evaluation result gives the planner a good idea how usable and reliable the forecast will be. Error values are calculated automatically and can be seen on the Interactive Planning Screen. In the following paragraphs, we shall go through all of the error evaluation methods.

**Forecast Accuracy Analysis**

The calculation of all evaluation error values is based on a comparison of forecasted past demand with actual past demand. The higher the deviation is, the higher the error value will be. Monitoring these forecast errors provides a good indication of the accuracy of the forecast. Which error value is best suited to point out a bad forecast model depends on the forecast model and the business environment. Within APO the term "Ex Post Forecast" is used for this technique. During the Ex Post Forecast the following steps are carried out:

- Define the Initialization and the Ex Post Forecast periods by dividing the historical data into two groups.
- Calculate as required the basic value, trend value, and seasonal indices as well as the Mean Absolute Deviation (MAD).
- Calculate the difference between the actual and the forecasted consumption to derive the Total Error.

For the Initialization and the Ex Post Period, historical data is available. The forecast is carried out for the Ex Post Period and the future. The following graph shows the principles of the Ex Post Forecast.

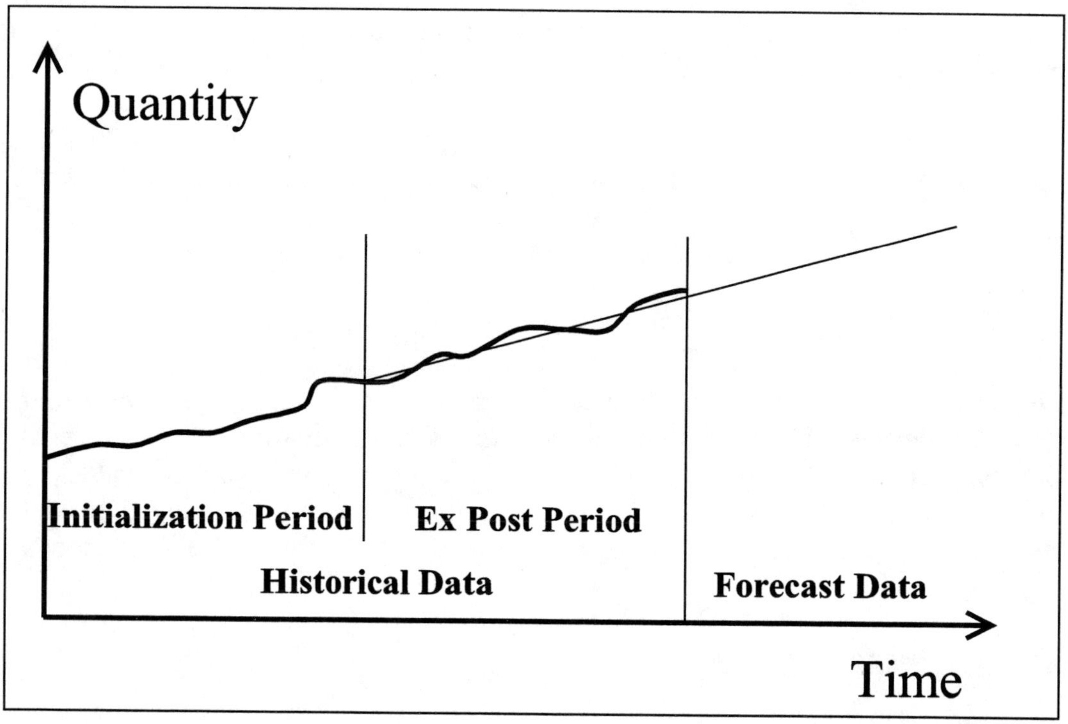


**Graphic 27 – Ex Post Forecast**

Special care must be taken if only very little data is available. In order to carry out an ex post forecast, only a few data points (historical demands) are required. The existence of a low forecast error value specifically in this case does not necessarily mean that the forecast model selected and the demand predicted are reliable.

The six different principles available in APO for calculating forecast error values and determining the forecast accuracy are listed below.

Following abbreviations are used:

| | |
|---|---|
| Actual Value per Period: | $A(t)$ |
| Forecast Value per Period: | $F(t)$ |
| Number of Periods | $n$ |
| Period | $t$ |
| Factor | $\delta$ |

- MAD Mean Absolute Deviation for Forecast Initialization

$$MAD = \frac{1}{n}\sum_{t=1}^{n}\left|A(t) - F(t)\right|$$

The mean absolute deviation represents the sum of all deviations of the forecast from the actual demand. With this calculation method, over and under estimation of actual sales do not cancel each other out. The result is the absolute average deviation per period.

Possible Values: Zero to indefinite

- MAD Mean Absolute Deviation for Ex Post Forecast

$$MAD(t) = (1-\delta)*\left|A(t-1) - F(t-1)\right| + \delta*\left|A(t) - F(t)\right|$$

Possible Values: Zero to indefinite

- ET Error Total

$$ET = \sum_{t=1}^{n} A(t) - F(t)$$

The total error represents the sum of all deviations of the forecast from the actual demand. Using the Error Total, over and under estimation of actual sales cancel each other out. High absolute figures lead automatically to high total errors as this method uses absolute and not relative figures. Furthermore the result is not averaged but accumulated over time.

Possible Values: Zero to indefinite (positive or negative)

- MPE Mean Percentage Error

$$MPE = \frac{1}{n}\sum_{t=1}^{n}\left(\frac{A(t) - F(t)}{A(t)} * 100\right)$$

The mean percentage error adds up the relative deviation of the forecast and provides an average result for the period in question. Over and under estimation of actual sales cancel each other out using this calculation.

Possible Values: Zero to 100% (positive or negative)

- MAPE Mean Absolute Percentage Error

$$MAPE = \frac{1}{n}\sum_{t=1}^{n}\left|\frac{A(t) - F(t)}{A(t)} * 100\right|$$

The mean absolute percentage error adds up the relative deviation of the forecast and provides an average result for the period in question. With this calculation method, over and under estimation of actual sales do not cancel each other out.

Possible Values: Zero to 100%

- MSE Mean Squared Error

$$MPE = \frac{1}{n}\sum_{t=1}^{n}\left(\frac{A(t)-F(t)}{A(t)}\right)^2$$

The mean squared error adds up the absolute deviation of the forecast and provides an average result for the period in question. With this calculation method, over and under estimation of actual sales do not cancel each other out, as the deviation is always squared and therefore positive.

Possible Values: Zero to indefinite

- RMSE Root of the Mean Squared Error

$$MPE = \sqrt{\frac{1}{n}\sum_{t=1}^{n}\left(\frac{A(t)-F(t)}{A(t)}\right)^2}$$

Same as the mean squared error, but providing lower figures due to the fact that the square root of the summation result is calculated.

Possible Values: Zero to indefinite

## Forecast Accuracy Report

The quality of the forecast can be reviewed as well using a function called "Determination of Forecast Accuracy". In order for this program to execute the product master must be defined at all locations for which a forecast exists. Unfortunately the initial screen is rather user-unfriendly, as it is required to stipulate the key figures, which represent the forecast and the historical data. The data generated is helpful to evaluate the forecast quality. A good point is that one can use either corrected or initial historical data, and compare it with either the corrected or initial forecast. The report can be limited to selected products and/or locations. The second screen with the evaluation results shows per product and location the two time series for the forecast and historical data as well as the MAD and ET forecast evaluation key figures.

## Model Fit Analysis for Causal Forecast

APO can perform various tests to determine the quality of an MLR result. These tests provide the planner with information that allows judging whether and how reliable the forecast based on the MLR run will be. As I said before, forecasting is based on probabilities, and even if all tests provide a "perfect' fit, care has to be taken as the result is always based on assumptions that most probably will also be valid in the future – but only "most probably." The challenge is to forecast as precisely as possible but to expect at the same time the unforeseeable.

The analytical measurements in APO can be grouped into the first group that measures the quality (or usability of the entire MLR based forecast) and a second group that provides information about a specific independent variable. Group one comprises the Goodness to Fit measurements R square and adjusted R square, the Auto Correlation Test according to Durbin-Watson, and the Mean Absolute Percentage Error (MAPE). Within the group two we find the Mean Elasticity Test, which tests the influence of a specific independent variable, the Auto Correlation t-test, and the Durbin-h Auto Correlation test.

On the MLR tab of the Interactive Planning screen, the four values that belong to group one are displayed in the top row. Underneath, one can find the other three values of the second group. As these values are calculated per independent variable, they are shown in separate rows and per individual variable. In addition the coefficient for each independent variable is shown in these rows as well as the Constant (a) of the MLR regression formula.

- Goodness to Fit
  The first question when examining the result of an MLR run is how well the independent variable(s) explain the dependent variable. During the MLR run a

linear formula is calculated (see above). In the "Goodness to Fit" test, the deviation between each known historical value (observation) is compared with the value calculated based on the formula. The difference between these two values is used to determine the quality of the formula. Two methods are supported by APO.

1. R square
   Calculation of R square, which is shown as "R**2" on the Causal tab in Interactive Planning, is done according to the following formula.

   $$R^2 = \sum_{t=1}^{n} e_t^2$$

   e denotes the individual error for each observation.

   R square values range from –1 to +1. A value of +1 (-1) indicates a perfect (inverse) effect of the independent variable on the dependent variable. Values close to Zero indicate that the MLR model does not explain the behavior of the dependent variable. A good fit can be assumed for R square values higher than 0.75 (positive or negative). It must be noted that the R square value tends to rise with the number of observations, putting the planner under the possibly false impression that the MLR model provides a good fit.
2. Adjusted R square
   The calculation of the adjusted R square value which is shown as "Corr. R**2" on the Causal tab in Interactive Planning overcomes the problem mentioned above. The following formula is used.

   $$\overline{R}^2 = 1 - (1 - R^2)\frac{n-1}{n-k-1}$$

   k denotes the number of independent variables used in the model.

   It is commonly accepted that this method provides a more reliable goodness to fit result.

- Influence of Independent Variables

  Once a MLR model is found with a reasonable low R square and/or adjusted R square, it is of importance to find out how strong the influence of the independent variable(s) is on the dependent variable. This is done using the Elasticity Test. The Elasticity Test measures the effect of a one- percent change of an independent variable on the dependent variable. The effect on the dependent variable is usually different for each observation point. The Mean Elasticity, which is shown as "M elasticity" on the Causal tab in Interactive Planning shows the average percentage of deviation of the dependent variable caused by the one-percent change of the independent variable. High values for the Mean Elasticity propose a highly responsive dependent variable.

- Correlation Test

  The MLR model should contain only such independent variables as are truly independent from the dependent variable. Otherwise the model would be recursive and cannot provide reliable forecast data. The t-test, which is shown as "t-test" on the Causal tab in Interactive Planning, provides information about this independence. Correlation is the opposite of Independence and needs to be avoided. The correlation test does not provide any information regarding the significance of the independent variable; this is measured using, for example, the Elasticity described above. SAP recommends leaving all independent variables in the MLR model that show a t-test value of greater than 1.4 (positive or negative).

- Auto-Correlation Test

  Another way to test for Correlation is the Durbin-Watson test. It measures Auto-Correlation in time series where no time lag is specified. Its range is from Zero to 4 with 2 as the median indicating the non-existence of Auto-Correlation. Positive Auto-Correlation is depicted by values between Zero and 2; values from 2 to 4 mean negative Auto-Correlation. Acceptable values for this test are in the range of 1.5 to 2.5. The Durbin-Watson test is shown as "Durbin-Watson" on the Causal tab in Interactive Planning. It provides information with respect to all used independent variables. When using time series with lags, the Durbin-Watson test becomes unreliable and should therefore not be used.

Specifically for time series with defined lags, the Durbin-h test provides useful information for a single independent variable. It is suitable only for MLR models with a large number of observations (greater than 100). Auto-Correlation exists for Durbin-h tests with values greater than 1.96. The Durbin-h test is shown as "Durbin h " on the Causal tab in Interactive Planning.

- Mean Absolute Percentage Error
  The Mean Absolute Percentage Error adds up the relative deviation of the forecast and provides an average result for the period in question. With this calculation method, over and under estimation of actual sales do not cancel each other out. The following formula is used:

$$MAPE = \frac{1}{n}\sum_{t=1}^{n}\left|\frac{A(t)-F(t)}{A(t)} * 100\right|$$

  Possible values range from Zero to 100%.

For some of the tests explained above, limits can be defined in a Diagnosis Group that is linked to the MLR Profile. Should a measured value exceed a limit, an alert can be generated. The alert will be displayed in the Alert Monitor and indicated in the Supply Chain Cockpit along with any other possible alerts. The following limits can be defined:

- R square lower limit
- Durbin-Watson lower limit
- Durbin-Watson upper limit
- Durbin h upper limit
- t-test lower limit
- MAPE upper limit

Any value that exceeds the limit is displayed with a red background on the MLR tab of the Interactive Planning Screen.

## 3.3.8 Safety Stock Calculation

The discussions regarding safety stock are never ending. Companies usually keep safety stock as a type of insurance to avoid situations where they could not deliver in time without having it. Then secondly, after the safety stock is built up, no one is really allowed to touch it, which then in turn raises the question why we have it in the first place. I shall not get into this discussion here. We shall just have a look at how APO is calculating the safety stock level.

It is important to understand that safety stock is kept for three reasons: to buffer peaks in demand, for late delivery from a supplier or the owner's production facilities or when the forecasted and actual demand differ significantly. The drivers for the safety stock level as calculated by APO are:

- Desired Service Level

  The desired service level is the main driver for the safety stock level. It is defined as a percentage ranging (in theory) from Zero to 100%. It is important to understand that a service level of 80% does not mean that 80% of the demand is guaranteed to be satisfied. It means that, with a probability of 80%, all demands can be satisfied as and when requested. A service level factor is allocated to each service level percentage (see table below). This table assumes a statistical normal distribution of demand. It is evident that this assumption is true most of the time, but not always. That is why there is always a chance of running out of stock irrespective of the level of safety stock. In theory a 100% service level requires an endless stock! The graph below shows the impact of the desired service level on the safety stock factor. Have a look. In order to increase our service level from 80% to 95%, we need to nearly double the safety stock (2.06/1.05 = 1.96). And it gets worse if you want to climb further up. The safety stock level defined up to now is independent of the forecast accuracy.

- Product Replenishment Lead Time

  A by far smaller impact has the replenishment lead-time of the product. This applies to the production, stock transfer, and purchasing lead-time. In the model used by APO, only the length of the lead-time has an impact, not the deviation of the actual lead-time around the average lead-time. The assumption is that the longer the lead-time is, the longer it takes to cope with suddenly increased demand. But be aware that a long lead time supplier with good delivery standards actually requires less safety stock than a short lead time supplier with bad delivery service.

- Forecast Error
  The method to calculate the forecast accuracy (or its error) is "Mean Absolute Deviation" (MAD). It runs from Zero upwards and increases with the deviation of forecasted and actual demand. The MAD does not have an upper limit. The principle behind the usage of the MAD is that if we have a good forecast, we need less safety stock. The MAD is independent of desired service levels.

The formula used to calculate the Safety Stock is the following:

$$SS = SF * \sqrt{LT * 1.25 * MAD}$$

Abbreviations used:

| | |
|---|---|
| SS | Safety Stock |
| SF | Safety Factor, which is a function of the desired Service Level |
| LT | Lead Time of the product in days consisting of the planned delivery time plus the GR time |
| MAD | Mean Absolute Deviation as calculated during the forecast run |

As discussed above it is important to understand that the safety stock as calculated by APO is oriented towards the changes in demand rather than the deviations in supply. The safety stock can be calculated using the "Safety Stock" function that can be accessed from the DP menu under option Reporting. In order for this program to execute, the product master must be defined at all locations for which the safety stock has to be calculated. The initial screen is rather user-unfriendly, as it is required to stipulate the key figures, which represent the forecast and the historical data. Using the F4 key offers all key figures instead of the really applicable ones. The program will update the Safety Stock field in the product master view Lot Size. Note that it is a prerequisite to maintain the Service Level and the Calculation of TSL fields prior to running the safety stock calculation program.

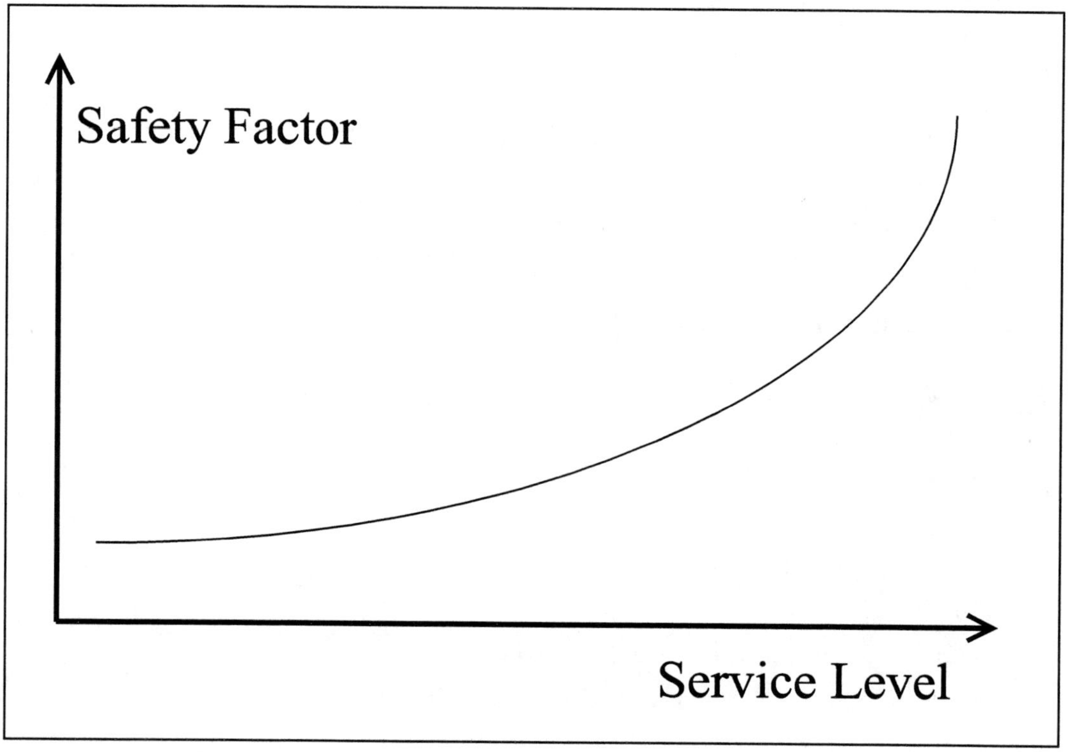


**Graphic 28 – Service Level Graph**

As explained above, the Safety Factor is a function of the desired Service Level. The Safety Factor increases exponentially with an increasing Service Level. This is depicted in the graphic above.

### 3.3.9 Secondary Forecasting Techniques

Secondary Forecasting is a method where various forecast results are joined together to form a new forecast. Composite forecasts are usually generated automatically based on the result of mathematically derived forecasts such as univariate and/or causal forecasts. A composite forecast represents the view of a certain interest group (e.g. the sales department). In opposition to this, the consensus-based forecast is the result of a consensus meeting where various interest groups (e.g. the sales and the marketing department) jointly formulate a common forecast. Input to the consensus-based forecast can be any type of forecast, univariate, causal, judgmental, or composite.

#### 3.3.9.1 Composite Forecast

Composite Forecasting is an approach where various alternate forecasts using different forecasting models are combined into one forecast. The benefit is that the forecasts using different models (time series based and causal) with different strengths and weaknesses are combined into one forecast and, by doing so, overcome the individual models' weaknesses. Composite forecasts are a combination of different models from a planner with a given business goal or view (e.g. the long-term sales forecast view). Composite forecasts are known for their excellent quality and reliability provided the composition rules are defined with care.

The composition is carried out according to mathematical rules such as average of, greatest of all, or others. The rules and the weighting of the forecasts that provide input to the Composite Forecast are defined in the Composite Forecast Profile. Within APO the Composite Forecast has two or more components, time series based forecasts and causal forecasts. Its parameters are defined in the Composite Forecast Profile. The composition of the forecasts can be defined as a time-dependent parameter. Note that macros are used in Consensus Based Forecasts, but not for Composite Forecasts.

#### 3.3.9.2 Consensus-Based Forecast

Consensus Based Forecasting, although it might sound like it, is not another forecast model or composition of forecasts. It is an approach that describes the process where various parties involved in the final forecast meet and agree on an

overall forecast. Different interest groups represented in such a consensus-based forecast meeting are, for example, the long term strategic planning group, the medium term tactical sales group, the short term marketing group, and the medium to short term operations (supply chain management) group. APO provides on-line display of forecasts in absolute and relative numbers, as well as graphical displays with easily adjustable forecast figures. By doing so it supports the process of Consensus Based Forecasting. APO refers to this as well as "Collaborative Forecasting". The difference in the judgmental model is that here the stakeholders (interest groups) from different business areas find a consensus; whereby in the judgmental model one or multiple people from the same business area develop a forecast.
The task of a "Consensus Meeting" could also be the development of an advanced macro, which will then subsequently be applied to a whole range of products. The creation and execution of macros is dealt with in a separate chapter.

### 3.3.10 Promotion Planning

Promotion Planning allows planning of entire sales campaigns for a product or a product range which adds Market Intelligence to the forecast developed initially. The planning of promotions is a complex task, which often is not carried out properly due to missing or inadequate system support. APO offers tools to cope with effects like cross product cannibalization and deferred consumer purchases to name only two of the most common challenges when planning and evaluating a promotion. Let me give an example.

**Example:**
We are planning a promotion for a washing detergent (promoted product) where a fabric softener (banded product) is attached free of charge. Obviously there are several effects that have to be taken into account. First, consumers will buy this special instead of other manufacturers' products, which is the idea. But there are also various side effects:

- The consumer purchases the special instead of our own other product; we cannibalize this other product and have to reduce its forecast.

- The consumer would have bought the regular product in either case and just buys more and/or earlier, this leads to a dip in the sales in the future.
- The banded product will probably see lower sales as the consumer gets it free with the promoted product and does not need to buy it separately.
- Alternatively the consumer might like the banded product after trying it and purchases it later on its own. This again is a desired effect.

All these effects need to be planned carefully, and APO here allows reference to past promotions as an aid.

Promotional Planning has two purposes:

- Plan future promotion – the purpose here is to plan an upcoming promotion, which will ensure the right stock levels are maintained to cope with the promotional demand.
- Exclude past promotional effects on history – the purpose here is to correct past demand, which was caused by a previous promotion. This ensures the right stock levels to cope with the normal demand in future periods.

APO offers tools that ensure a strict separation of forecasts derived from historical data or other methods on the one side, and promotional planning on the other. This separation also allows carrying out forecasting and promotional planning in separate steps and by different planners. Promotion plans are stored separated from the forecast. It is therefore possible to subtract the promotion plan from the actual sales to correct the sales history. By doing so, time-based forecasts provide more reliable results. Promotion plans can be defined for the whole supply network or portions thereof. The time bucket used for the promotion plan does not have to coincide with that of the forecast as long as the time bucket used is defined for the InfoCube. Promotions can be viewed by product (which might show several promotions) or by promotion (which might show several products).

Promotional Planning in APO offers the definition of the Promotional Plan

- In absolute figures
- In relative figures
- Based on past promotions

Promotional Planning is carried out using the Promotional Planning Screen and not the Interactive Planning Screen. The Promotional Planning Screen appears very similar to the Interactive Planning Screen and the working techniques are identical. The results of the promotional planning activities are visible in the Interactive Planning Screen. Basic promotion plans could also be defined in the Interactive Planning Screen using custom developed macros. This approach is helpful for small and uncomplicated promotion plans. In this case it is still required to define specific key figures for the promotional values into which the macro writes the data. While doing so, it is also possible to pick up promotional plans that are in the past. The history on which the forecast is based can then be corrected.

Once a promotion has been defined, its pattern can be used to create a pattern profile. This pattern profile can then subsequently be used to create other promotions without the need to specify all promotional values per period. The promotional patterns are stored together with the revenue factor and promotion cost patterns in the model catalog. The model catalog can be accessed from the Promotional Planning Interactive screen via the tree structure selection.

The following example is based on the promotion described above. The promotion runs from week 1 through to week 4. We shall be planning the promoted product, the banded product, and a cannibalized product. The planning of the promoted product is done in relative figures, which will be then used by the system to calculate absolute figures. The absolute figures of the promoted product are used to calculate the additional demand of the banded product. The assumption here is that half of the additional demand of the banded product is additional demand, the other half results in lost sales of the banded product. This is true only for the period of the promotion (week 1 to 4).

| **Promoted Product** | **Week** | | | | | | |
|---|---|---|---|---|---|---|---|
| | **1** | **2** | **3** | **4** | **5** | **6** | **7** |
| Baseline Forecast | 400 | 400 | 400 | 400 | 400 | 400 | 400 |
| Promotion (%) | 10 | 20 | 10 | 5 | -5 | | |
| Promotion (absolute) | 40 | 80 | 40 | 20 | -20 | | |

**Table 24 – Promotion Planning Example 1**

| Banded Product | Week | | | | | | |
|---|---|---|---|---|---|---|---|
| | 1 | 2 | 3 | 4 | 5 | 6 | 7 |
| Baseline Forecast | 100 | 100 | 100 | 100 | 100 | 100 | 100 |
| Promotion (%) | -20 | -40 | -20 | -10 | | | |
| Promotion (absolute) | -20 | -40 | -20 | -10 | | | |

**Table 25 – Promotion Planning Example 2**

We also have a cannibalized product, which is similar to the promoted product. Its sales will drop with a rate of 20% of the increase we achieve on the promoted product the week before (decrease of sales of the promoted product have no influence). This effect lasts throughout the promotion. All products have a baseline forecast based on a constant model.

| Cannibalized Product | Week | | | | | | |
|---|---|---|---|---|---|---|---|
| | 1 | 2 | 3 | 4 | 5 | 6 | 7 |
| Baseline Forecast | 200 | 200 | 200 | 200 | 200 | 200 | 200 |
| Promotion (%) | | -4 | -8 | -4 | -2 | | |
| Promotion (absolute) | | -8 | -16 | -8 | -4 | | |

**Table 26 – Promotion Planning Example 3**

Although the example above referred to a promotion carried out on the product level, it is possible to plan promotions at any level of the planning hierarchy (e.g. for a product group or an entire brand). Promotional plans that are based on an aggregated set of data are distributed to product level automatically.

When releasing the unconstrained DP plan to SNP, only one key figure can be selected and its values are then transferred to SNP. When using Promotional Planning, it is necessary to write a macro that adds the corrected forecast to the promotional values and stores it subsequently in a new key figure. Do not overwrite either the corrected forecast, nor the promotional planning key figures! When releasing the DP plan to SNP, use this new key figure instead of the corrected forecast.

#### 3.3.10.1 Promotion Evaluation

The task of promotion evaluation is to provide the planner with feedback regarding the monetary aspect of the promotion. Promotion evaluation is an optional activity that needs to be activated per promotion if required. It uses two profiles, the revenue factor and promotion cost profile. In the revenue factor profile, the achievable turnover per sold unit is defined. The promotion cost profile contains the cost of the promotion per period. The overall promotion profitability is calculated according to the following formula:

Promotion Profitability for month x = Revenue Factor * Planned Quantity - Period Cost for month x

The promotion evaluation functionality in its current form is thus very basic, as it does not cater for quantity depended cost and other important factors. The profiles allow storing the required data in special time series or as key figures in the InfoCube.

### 3.3.11 Forecast Data Flow

Within any InfoCube, a minimum amount of Key Figures is required in order to carry out the Demand Planning (Forecasting) function. These Key Figures together with their logical interdependencies are explained in the following chapter. The Key Figure for Promotion Planning is obviously only required if this function is utilized. Their relation is graphically illustrated in the data flow diagram underneath.

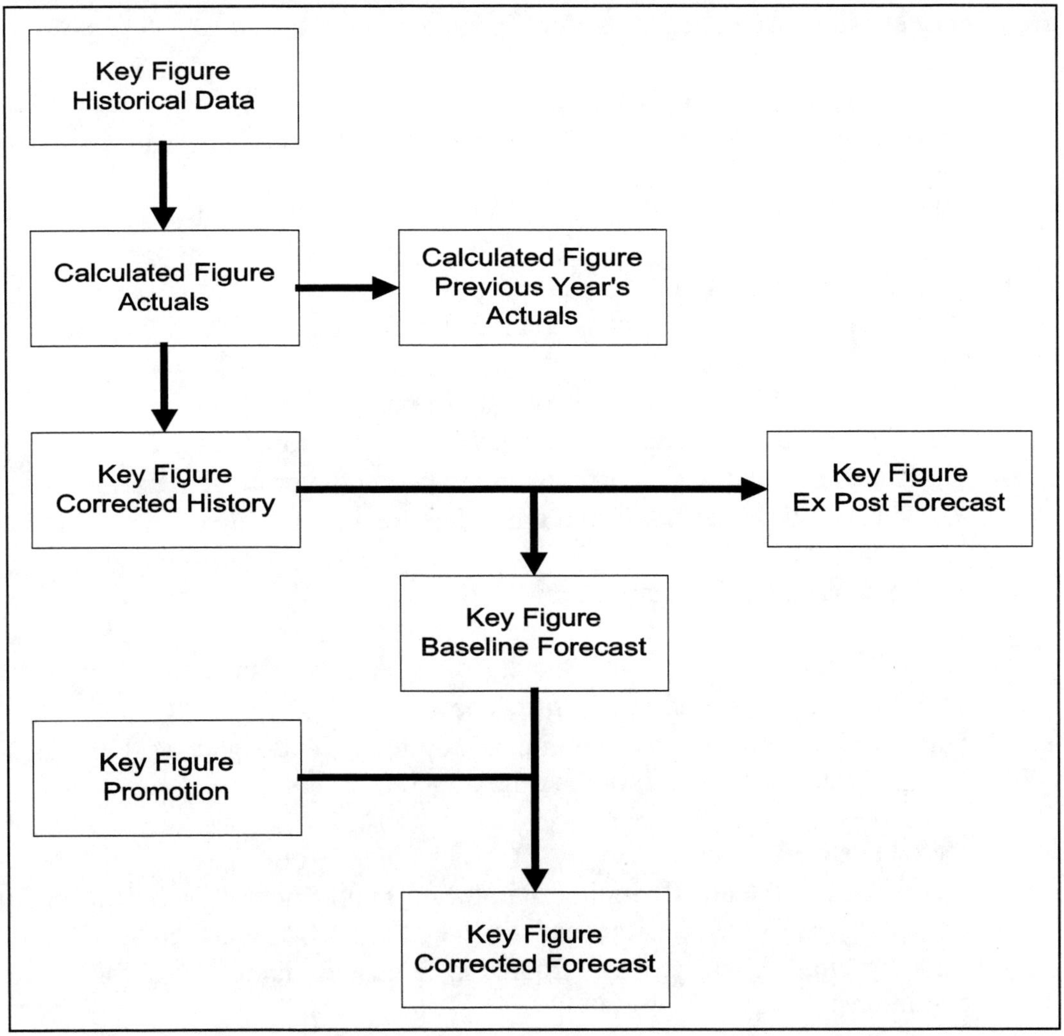


**Graphic 29 – Forecast Data Flow**

All key Figures can be made visible in the Interactive Planning Screen main view with names as defined when designing the Planning Book. The "Original History," which is not a Key Figure, can be put on the main view as well.

1. Historical Data, also called Historical Input
   - Defined in Univariate Forecast Profile together with the planning version as the "Historical Input Key Figure".
   - Defined in MLR Forecast Profile together with the planning version as the "Historical Input Key Figure".
   - Displayed in Interactive Planning.

2. Original History, also called Actuals
   The Original History key figure is a calculated figure and not a key figure that is stored in the InfoCube.
   - This figure differs from the Historical Data only in the following case:
     - Only one product chosen when performing the forecast
     - Phase In or Phase Out profile maintained in the product master
     - Material Forecast flag set in univariate forecast profile or in interactive planning
     - Univariate forecast carried out

     If all these conditions are met, the system calculates an adjusted history called "Original History" or "Actuals" which can be displayed.
   - This figure is not stored in the InfoCube.
   - Displayed in Interactive Planning as "Actuals" and again as "Previous Year Actuals" with a 12 months time offset.

3. Corrected History
   - Defined in InfoCube Planning Parameter in segment "Technical Field Assignments: Corrected Forecast" as "Key Figure Corrected History"
   - The Original History key figure is adjusted under the following conditions:
     - Outlier Correction flag set in univariate profile or used in Interactive Planning
     - Corrected History flag set in univariate profile or used in Interactive Planning
     - Average Number of Days entry field maintained in univariate profile or used in Interactive Planning

     If any of these conditions are met, the system calculates an adjusted history called "Corrected History" which can be displayed.

- Can be edited in Interactive Planning
- Visible in the Interactive Promotion Planning screen with the Key Figure name

4. Original Forecast, also called Baseline Forecast
   - Defined in Master Forecast Profile in the field "Key Figure"
     Only the Key Figure is defined here, but not the planning version. The planning version used to read data depends on the data selection and the planning version used to store data depends on the used Univariate or MLR profile.
   - The Original Forecast will be adjusted in the following case:
     - Only one product chosen when performing the forecast
     - Phase In or Phase Out profile maintained in the product master
     - Material Forecast flag set in univariate profile or used in Interactive Planning
     - Univariate forecast carried out

     If <u>all</u> these conditions are met, the system recalculates the forecast figures before displaying them.
   - Defined in InfoCube Planning Parameter in segment "Technical Field Assignments: Corrected Forecast" as "Key Figure"
   - Defined in InfoCube Planning Parameter in segment "Technical Field Assignments: Promotion Planning" as "Key Figure"
   - Displayed in Interactive Planning
   - Visible in Interactive Promotion Planning screen with the Key Figure name

5. Corrected Forecast
   - Defined in InfoCube Planning Parameter in segment "Technical Field Assignments: Corrected Forecast" as "Key Figure Corrected Forecast"
   - The Original Forecast key figure is adjusted under the following conditions:
     - Average Number of Days entry field maintained in univariate profile or used in Interactive Planning

     If <u>any</u> of these conditions are met, the system calculates an adjusted history called "Corrected History" which can be displayed.

- Can be edited in Interactive Planning
- Displayed in Interactive Planning
- Visible in the Interactive Promotion Planning screen with the Key Figure name

6. Ex Post Forecast
   - Defined in InfoCube Planning Parameter in segment "Technical Field Assignments: Corrected Forecast" as "Key Figure for Ex Post Forecast"
   - Displayed in Interactive Planning

7. Promotion
   - Defined in InfoCube Planning Parameter in segment "Technical Field Assignments: Promotion Planning" as "Absolute Key Figure promotion"
   - Always stored in absolute figures
   - Displayed in Interactive Planning

### 3.3.12 Output of Demand Planning

The result of the Demand Planning exercise is a realistic prediction of future demand per product, time period and location (either manufacturing sites with own stocks or distribution centers). This plan is not optimized in terms of technical feasibility or profitability; it just predicts the anticipated quantities that can be sold. It therefore represents maximum quantities, rather than achievable throughput of the supply chain network. Constraint based optimization is the domain of Supply Network Planning which is the next step in the process.

Demand plans can be stored in various versions, and APO allows passing multiple planning versions to SNP. This is helpful for example to investigate the feasibility of altered supply chains and/or for checking up capacity constraints before the final forecast figures are released. The relation between SNP and DP planning versions is a one to multi relation where a specific DP version can be copied several times to different SNP planning versions. This allocation is done using option "Model/Planning Version" in Master Data Maintenance of SNP.

The release can take place as an on-line task for individual products or in batch mode. In order to carry out the release in batch mode, a Release Profile needs to be created. The batch release is a type of Mass Processing. For further information regarding Mass Processing, refer to the appropriate chapter. While releasing the unconstrained DP plan to SNP, it is necessary to define the locations to which the demands must be allocated. This applies to both, the interactive and batch release. The allocation of an appropriate location is the task of Location Management.

Should you run the APO system as a stand-alone system, ensure that the assignment of the Business System Group to the Logical System is correct (path Tools > APO Administration > Settings > System Group > Assign Logical System). All five definitions for R/3 flag, Release, Master, Update, and ATP Update Mode should be left blank.

The unconstrained DP plan can not only be released to SNP but also to an R/3 system where the DP plan is used to create R/3 Independent Requirements. For further information on releasing the DP plan to SNP or R/3, please refer to the SNP section of this book.

When releasing the unconstrained DP plan to SNP, only one key figure can be selected and its values are then transferred to SNP. When using Promotional Planning, it is necessary to write a macro that adds the corrected forecast to the promotional values and stores it subsequently in a new key figure. Do not overwrite either the corrected forecast, nor the promotional planning key figures! When releasing the DP plan to SNP, use this new key figure instead of the corrected forecast.

#### 3.3.12.1 Forecast Changes

Forecasts obviously need to be changed as and when required. This is done using the Interactive Planning screen or in batch mode. A change could entail deleting a quantity completely for a period. To do so, overwrite the old quantity with a Zero.

After the revised forecast was saved, a new release of the demand forecast to SNP needs to be carried out. With the new release, the old forecast values in SNP will be replaced with the new ones. In this case, do not select "Create new Orders" or the newly released forecast values will be added to the already existing ones in SNP, instead of replacing them. In a separate step, a new SNP planning run (Heuristics, Optimizer, or CTM) needs to be carried out to adapt the SNP plan to the changed set of forecast data (independent requirements).

#### 3.3.12.2 Location Management

DP allows planning at any level of a freely definable hierarchy. This hierarchy usually starts on a high level such as company, region or even worldwide and is consolidated or broken down level-by-level using aggregation and distribution factors. Commonly, the lowest level from a business feasibility point of view is the forecast per product and customer. As said before, it is totally up to the individual business which levels are planned. See also the chapter "Planning Approach." In order to pass over these demands to SNP where they will be transformed to SNP forecasts or demand objects (they used to be called Independent Requirements in R/3) it is necessary to allocate each demand to exactly one location of the type "Plant" or "Distribution Center". The reason for this is that SNP plans procurement and transport orders for locations of these types only. A forecasted demand, which is basically the same as an "Independent Requirement" in R/3, can only exist at such location types.
APO offers two different ways to accomplish the distribution of demand (Location Split) over the locations.

- Location defined as Characteristic Value
  In this case a characteristic that represents the plants and/or distribution centers exists. While forecasting is carried out, the key figure for this characteristic is populated with the demand per product and location. During release to SNP, these key figures are transferred to SNP.
- Location not defined as Characteristic Value or not used
  Should no key figure for a characteristics value per location exist or should the existing one not be used, the location split is carried out according to pre-

defined ratios. The location-split definition can be per product or product range and can be time phased.



### 3.3.13 Mass Processing

Mass Processing is used to create forecasts in batch and to release the unconstrained DP plan to SNP. Carrying out these tasks in batch mode is releasing the planner's time and utilizing the system resources during off peak hours where these jobs do not negatively affect the responsiveness of the system.

- Forecasting
  Up to now we were dealing with interactive forecasting. This method, where the planner interacts with the APO system and carries out the planning is obviously not adequate to process larger amounts of data. In order to do so, the system offers the creation of forecasts without user intervention. In a typical business scenario, a forecast batch job is carried out monthly and provides the base from which onwards the planner works in an interactive mode. The planner can concentrate on products that are of strategic importance and/or require check up and further refinement. The alert monitor provides valuable input for this follow up task. Categorized messages guide the planner through this task, pointing out products where an exception occurred. Mass Processing can be carried out at any level of aggregation for a given planning book and planning version. Macros can also be run during mass processing.
- Release to SNP
  Mass processing is also used to release the DP plan. In order to start this batch job a release profile has to be created. The release of the DP plan to SNP is usually done with the same frequency as the creation of forecasts. In most cases this happens on a monthly basis.
- Release to R/3
  It is required to release the forecast to R/3 in situations where only the DP functionality of APO is used. Within R/3 the forecast values are used to create independent requirements.

### 3.3.14 Supported Requirements Strategies

APO supports as standard three different Requirements Strategies. It is possible to add other strategies if required. Consumption of the forecast is depending on the requirements strategy.

- Strategy 10 Make to Stock Production
  Using the Make to Stock strategy, production is carried out irrespective of the incoming sales orders and solely based on the demand plan. For planning purposes, sales orders are ignored. This is the requirements strategy typically used in mass production.
  - Incoming sales orders do not consume the forecast.
- Strategy 20 Planning with Final Assembly
  Production is planned according to the specified demand plan as well as sales orders when using this Make to Stock requirements strategy. Usually the demand plan is the driver for the longer term planning and a prioritized mix of demand plan and sales orders are used for the operational planning.
  - Incoming sales orders consume the forecast.
- Strategy 30 Planning without Final Assembly
  This Make to Order strategy is applied in situations where semi-finished products are manufactured in a make to stock environment, and the final assembly only takes part after a sales order was received. With the creation of the sales order, the production of the finished product is kicked off. Components for the finished products are taken from stock as they had been produced independently before. This requirements strategy is used for example in the PC industry where all components are bought or manufactured beforehand. With the sales order, the final assembly according to the customer's specification is carried out.
  - Incoming sales orders consume the forecast of the finished product.
- Strategy 40 Make to Order Production
  Using the Make to Order strategy, production is carried out only based on incoming sales orders. Dependent requirements are thus created only at time of sales order receipt.
  - Incoming sales orders consume the forecast.

Forecasts are consumed with every incoming sales order for requirements strategies 20 and 30 in such a way that the planned demand closest to the sales order on the time axis is consumed first. With backward consumption the closest planned demand in the past is used first, with forward consumption the closest planned demand is used in the future. As another option, backward/forward consumption is possible. The three options are illustrated in the following graph. On the top is the backward consumption mode, followed by the forward and backward/forward consumption mode.

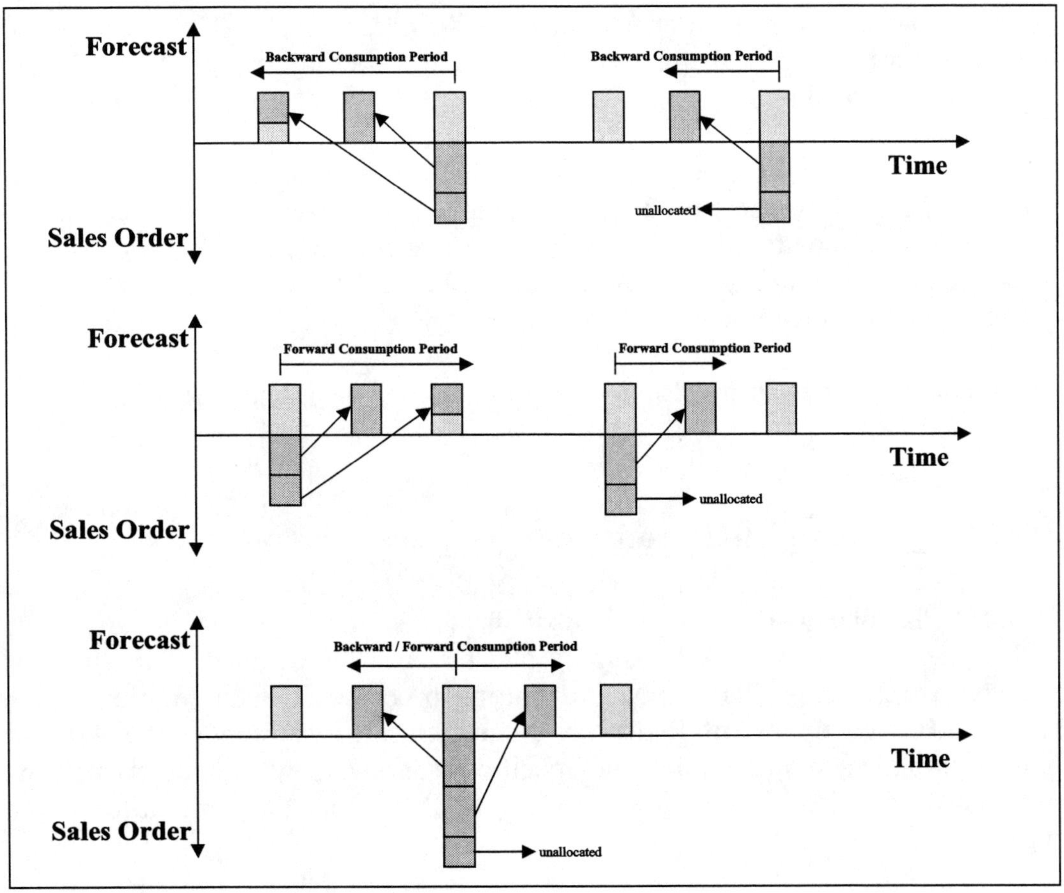


**Graphic 30 – Forecast Consumption**

Please note that the consumed forecast is the forecast defined in SNP and not the one defined in DP! This has two consequences to think about. Firstly when creating a sales order outside of the period for which SNP has forecast values, no forecast consumption can take place. Secondly when copying DP forecasts to SNP for periods where already forecasts existed, there is a potential to lose information about forecasts already consumed. The latter problem could be overcome by copying the forecast that might already be reduced back to DP. In DP a comparison of original and retransmitted forecasts from SNP would reveal this. In a third step the DP forecast would have to be adjusted by these figures before being copied to SNP.

With APO the same product can be allocated to different requirements strategies. This is required if the same product for example is sold in a Make to Order and in a Make to Stock environment. In this case the two requirement types would have to be planned separately. This can be accomplished by defining a characteristic "Strategy" in the InfoCube.

Requirements Strategies are also dealt with in the SNP section.

### 3.3.15 Supported Production Types

Demand Planning works independent of the Production Types as it only deals with demands, but not with the supply that matches the demand. SNP supports with release 2.0 only Discrete Manufacturing processes. As an addition to the release 2.0, the support of Repetitive Manufacturing was announced. Process Orders are also supported, but a specific Process Flow Scheduler will be introduced at a later stage. Refer to the SNP section for more information regarding Production Types.

## 3.4 The DP Data Environment

APO DP is tightly integrated with the SAP new data warehouse called Business Information Warehouse (BW), which is also a New Dimension Product (NDP). All historical data to be used by APO as well as forecast data generated by APO is being stored in BW.

Information in BW is stored in what is called an InfoCube. This n-dimensional info cube stores all transaction data from R/3 or another On-line Transaction Processing (OLTP) system required for APO. Additionally, some other data required by APO is stored in BW as well. This could be, to name two examples a global forecast (e.g. car sales for a country) as well as predictions of competitors' sales. The InfoCube needs to be set up in the lowest denominator approach. If any of the APO (and in this instance BW) users require sales data per product, customer and week, then all data has to be stored on this level. APO is using this InfoCube, and it is up to those who set up APO initially to determine the level of aggregation required.

The advantage of the InfoCube setup is that various planners can plan on their individual aggregation levels without a need for duplicating data. Planning can be on a high level such as sales per brand name, month and country (which is ideal for strategic planning) or per product, week and customer to monitor and plan customer efficiency.

Various planning versions using the same historical data allow a "What If Analysis" on exactly the required level of detail. As all planning versions use the same historical data, there is no problem with data consistency. Historical data is stored in the planning version Zero.

Data required for performing Demand Planning and saving forecasts is stored in several places, which can be grouped into the areas as depicted below.

- InfoCube
    - Historical Data
    - Forecast Data
- Profiles
    - Forecasting
    - Alert

- Life Cycle
- Patterns
  - Seasonal
  - Life Cycle
  - Promotional

On the following pages we shall go through the concepts of the InfoCube and how the data stored in the InfoCube interacts with the various profiles and patterns.

### 3.4.1 InfoCube

The InfoCube is the construct used to store all historical as well as forecast data. It does not store any parameters, profiles or the promotion catalog. Promotion plans are stored in tables and update the forecast data in the InfoCube. InfoCubes are also used in the SAP Business Information Warehouse (BW), and APO is fully integrated not only with R/3 but also with BW. Key Performance Indicators (KPI) are defined in BW and calculated using data in BW. They are visible within APO just like one's own data. The Key Performance Indicators were defined in collaboration with the Supply Chain Council and are based on Best Practices.
In order to achieve seamless integration APO uses the On Line Analytical Processor (OLAP). OLAP is the tool, which allows the APO user to:

- create and maintain InfoCubes, which are used to read historical data and to write forecasts,
- set up communication rules between the OLTP system and the BW portion of APO, and
- to write data directly to the InfoCube from sources such as a spreadsheet.

In essence the InfoCube contains all historical transaction data required to perform the forecast. This data needs to be updated regularly in a time interval depending on the planning cycle. A monthly update run is absolutely sufficient when forecasting is carried out on a monthly basis. The InfoCube furthermore contains the forecast that was created using APO.
In order to use APO forecasting functionality; it is not required to have a BW system; every APO system comes with its own small BW subset. It is not possible

to create any InfoCube based reports within APO. If this or the usage of key performance indicators is a business requirement, it is necessary to get a full BW system. APO uses BW technology for its data storage but does neither share the data as such nor does it need a dedicated hardware to do so.
Set up and maintenance of the InfoCube is carried out using the Administrator Workbench. See the appropriate chapter for more information.

**Logistics Information System (LIS) and Business Information Warehouse (BW)**

When trying to understand the tasks of the Business Information Warehouse (BW), one might get the idea that the Logistics Information System (LIS), which is part of R/3, could provide the same type of data and functionality to APO. This is a correct assumption, and in principle there should be no problem doing so. The matter is that SAP has decided to use BW technology and not LIS. For this reason any discussion of advantages and disadvantages is rather academic and will bear no fruit.
BW appears to be the long-term strategic product, which will replace similar functions and data currently stored in the LIS. At the moment LIS cannot provide any data to APO, as there are no standard interfaces or similar functionality available. APO on the other hand could be fed with LIS data via the detour of extracting LIS data to a spreadsheet and then consequently being uploaded into APO.

#### 3.4.1.1 Logical Structure

An InfoCube contains data that is required to perform a forecast and to compare forecasts with actual data. Based on this definition, it is required from the InfoCube to provide time-based historical demand data and to store the forecast in a way that it is possible to compare the two sets of data as well as various forecasts with each other. The minimum level of detail for quantity-based demand information is "What & When ", and additionally "How Much". This is the fundamental concept of any demand information system irrespective of the technical implementation. The "What & When" in the InfoCube is called

Characteristics, and the "How Much" is the Key Figure. A graphical way of showing this situation is by means of a table as done below. The point where the "What" row crosses the "When" column is the "How Much" cell.

| | | **Dimension Time / Characteristic** | | |
|---|---|---|---|---|
| | | **Month 1/99** | **Month 2/99** | **Month 3/99** |
| Dimension | Pr. # 1 | 10 | 20 | 15 |
| Product with | Pr. # 2 | 30 | 35 | 40 |
| Characteristic | Pr. # 3 | 20 | 20 | 25 |

**Table 27 – Basic InfoCube Example**

We have in our example the dimension "Product" with the characteristic "Product Number" which is defined per row. The dimension "Time" with its characteristic "Month" can be found per column. It is totally immaterial which characteristic is put into the row and which into the column. We could have also put all characteristics into the columns or rows. Why do we need dimensions and characteristics, as they seem to have a one-to-one relation? The answer is that we do not really need them here in our basic example, but in reality an InfoCube will contain much more information. Characteristics will then be grouped logically into Dimensions. Let's go further and assume we want to know how much demand we had, not only per product, but also per product group. We shall now break down the dimension "Product" into its two characteristics "Product Number" and "Product Group". The result is as follows:

| | | **Dimension Time / Characteristic** | | |
|---|---|---|---|---|
| | | **Month 1/99** | **Month 2/99** | **Month 3/99** |
| Dimension | Gr. A, Pr. # 1 | 10 | 20 | 15 |
| Product with | Gr. A, Pr. # 2 | 30 | 35 | 40 |
| Characteristics | Gr. A, Pr. # 3 | 20 | 20 | 25 |

**Table 28 – Extended InfoCube Example**

Please note that aggregated quantities per month and product group, the so-called Key figures, can be calculated and that for the total of the subordinate products there is no need to store data. Every time an update on our small table above is carried out, we require the information product group, product, month, and quantity. Care is required nevertheless if a product moves from one product group to another. This is an imminent problem to any information system, and there are several approaches for such a case. The SAP Business Information Warehouse (BW) allows setting up a hierarchy of Characteristics. This is not a required function for APO. We shall therefore not further elaborate on this possibility. Within Demand Planning, data is automatically aggregated and distributed according to the Proportional Factors or Pro Rata. See the chapter "Aggregation & Distribution" for more information. We still have not defined what the relation is between dimensions and characteristics. Any characteristic must be allocated to one and exactly one dimension of an InfoCube. A dimension can have several characteristics attached to it. There is no rule which characteristic has to be put together with which other characteristic into a dimension. Also no rule exists how many dimensions are needed. Four characteristics could be in four different dimensions or put all together into the same dimension. It would have no impact on the planning process or on the level of detail of planning. We shall go through an example in the chapter "Characteristic Value Combination".

Would it make sense to define a new characteristic "Year" within the dimension "Time" if we need the demand figures per year? Certainly not as there is a mathematical relation between month and year. Twelve months make one year. As this is a constant relation, we do not need to have two characteristics within the dimension "Time." The use of a macro to calculate yearly demand would be more appropriate in this case. Just be careful when working with the time expressions Week and Month, as there is no fixed relation between them. Week 5 in the year 2000 as an example is part of the months January and February. To cope with this problem, it is required to define the two characteristics Week and Month. This is done for example when working with the APO reference InfoCube. The APO reference InfoCube called DP_REFER contains some basic settings that can be used when creating one's own InfoCube.

Up to now our model has two dimensions, Product and Time which were shown in a two dimensional table. We shall now add a third dimension, which we call "Customer" and allocate the Characteristic "Customer Number" to it. Our more sophisticated model has now three dimensions, which is graphically represented by the cube shown below. Ever wondered where the name InfoCube comes from?

It is obvious that this principle also works with more than 3 dimensions and 4 characteristics. The limitations of the BW InfoCube are a maximum of 16 dimensions and 256 characteristics. There is no additional constraint on the maximum number of characteristics per dimension (not necessarily exactly 16 characteristics per dimension).

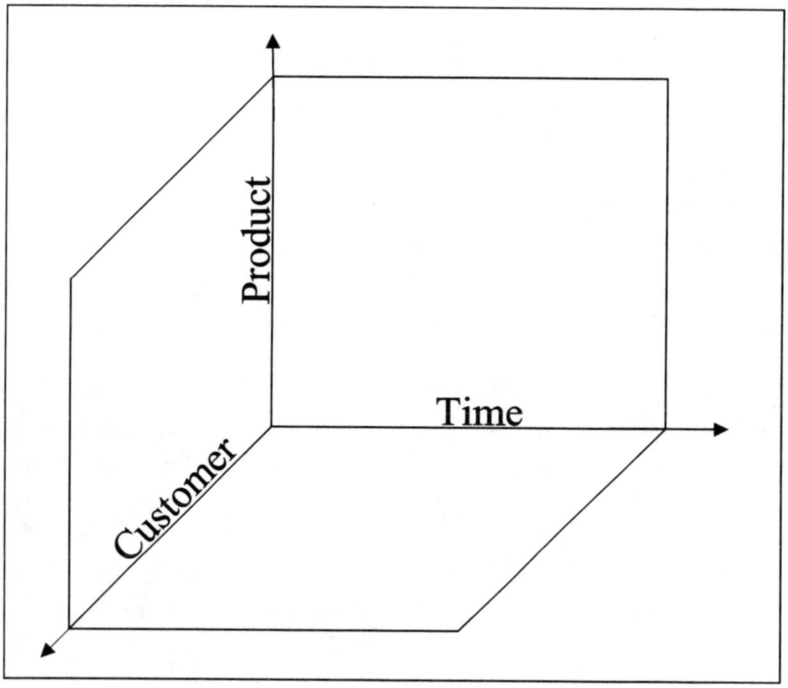


**Graphic 31 – DP InfoCube**

Everything said above applies to the storage of historical data as well as to the storage of planning (forecasting) data. There are actually only two differences.

1. Historical data in the InfoCube is stored only once in Planning Version Zero. The OLTP system or other data sources update it.
2. Forecasting data is stored potentially more than once to represent multiple scenarios in multiple Planning Versions.
   APO updates it.

Version Management deals with the management of the various forecast versions. Planning versions can be created and deleted and data stored in a planning version can be copied to another one. Several planning versions can also used when populating the data environment required for Supply Network Planning. Please refer to the chapter "Version Management".

APO comes with a large amount of predefined Info Objects. The generic term Info Objects describes Characteristics (which are grouped in Dimensions), Key Figures, Unit Characteristics, and Time Characteristics. Please refer also to the chapter "Info Objects".

Planning in DP is carried out by means of defining the Key Figure values. Before this can be done, it is necessary to activate a certain combination of characteristics. They are also referred to as "Characteristic Value Combinations".

We have concentrated up to now on the definitions required for storing historical data. In our example we always assumed one key figure, which was the sales quantity. In practice one would most probably add other key figures such as turnover or average price. More key figures will be added to enable the storage of forecasts. Used key figures should not have any mathematical relation as this would result in data redundancy. But, as shown in the example below, there is no rule without exception.

| | | Dimension Time / Characteristic Month 1/99 | | |
|---|---|---|---|---|
| | | Key Figure 1 Sold Quantity | Key Figure 2 Average Price | Key Figure 3 Turnover |
| Dimension | Pr. # 1 | 10 | 1.00 | 10.00 |
| Product with | Pr. # 2 | 30 | 1.10 | 33.00 |
| Characteristic | Pr. # 3 | 20 | 1.20 | 24.00 |

**Table 29 – Multi Key Figure InfoCube Example**

In this example the Turnover key figure could have been easily calculated by multiplying the key figure Sold Quantity with the key figure Average Price. The reason why this was not done is that the planner wants to see, on an aggregated level, the average price per product group as a key figure. Note that this average must not be weighted. In this example based on the aggregation rule "Average" the result on the product group level is 1.10 and not 1.12, which would be the weighted average. To get the weighted average per product group, it is useful to deploy the Macro technique and calculate the figure where appropriate.

When should data redundancy be tolerated?

- To enable non weighted average values on a higher level.
  This was shown above.
- To improve the responsiveness of the system.
  It is often faster to read more (redundant) data than to calculate it whenever required.
- To allow planning in multiple key figures.
  If it is practice to plan on a high level in a monetary unit, which then needs to be transferred into a quantity, it is required to store the factor "price per unit". Once the turnover figures have been planned, one or several macros can translate these turnover figures with the help of the price per unit to a quantity-based forecast.

What is explained above is a very basic setup that obviously would not be sufficient in a real-world planning environment. In a typical live system multiple key figures can be found. They are:

| | |
|---|---|
| • Sales in Units (History) | as in the OLTP system |
| • Sales Revenue | as in the OLTP system |
| • Average Price | as in the OLTP system |
| • Corrected History | corrected by APO |
| • Sales Plan 1 (Statistical Forecast) | e.g. initial plan as a result of a trend model |
| • Sales Plan 2 (Corrected Forecast) | manual correction applied |
| • Sales Plan 3 (Consensus Based Forecast) | result of sales plan alignment |
| • Sales Plan 4 (Composite Forecast) | combination of the Sales Plan 2 and 3 |
| • Promotion Planning | adding of promotions |
| • Final Sales Plan | plan that will be copied to SNP |
| • SNP Plan | constrained plan coming from SNP |
| • Historic Sales Plan | shows the last sales plan that was made |

Obviously not all these key figures are required. The final determination of key figures to be used depends on the exact business requirements. It is good practice to define some placeholders (or dummies) when setting up a new InfoCube, as it is a very difficult task to integrate new key figures into an existing database. In order to do this, the content of the entire InfoCube would have to be deleted and somehow repopulated from an external data source.

APO allows copying the constrained SNP plan back to DP. This enables the comparison of the DP with the SNP plan, which reveals forecasts that cannot be met by the supply network. It is necessary to allocate a Category to a DP key figure in order to release the SNP plan to DP. When the release takes place, the system matches such demands in SNP with key figures in DP that have the same category. For more information regarding the definition and setup of categories refer to the chapter "Profiles" in the SNP section.

An InfoCube has exactly one quantity unit of measure (UoM) that is used for the storage of quantity related planning data. It is advisable to define this unit of measure in thousands of pieces or any other neutral unit. The use of units like pallets or boxes is rather risky as pallet or box sizes might change over time and are not the same for all products. In some cases planning in weight or volume units is the better option. The selection of the planning unit of measure is a fundamental task. Once defined and loaded with data, the InfoCube cannot be changed anymore.

Key figures are displayed in the base unit of measure as defined in the InfoCube. Any other unit of measure can be used as a display unit provided it is defined in the product master. Units of measure based on the International System of Units (SI) can be converted without explicit definition in the product master. The SI system is based on seven different basic units from which all other measurements are derived (e.g. 1000g = 1 kg). It also links non-metric units like inches and pounds to the base units. A unified unit of measure for all products is required to facilitate the aggregation and distribution of key figures through all levels of the planning hierarchy.

Should the product ranges be too diverse to have the same base unit of measure in planning, a so-called planning unit needs to be introduced. This dimension free planning unit of measure will have to be transferred into a product specific unit of measure when the DP plan is released to SNP. The dimensionless planning unit of measure as well as the product specific unit of measure need to be defined in the product master.

A special situation exists where the relation between units and weight or volume is not constant. This is known as "variable or catch weight", which is a function within the R/3 industry solution Oil. In order to follow a consistent planning approach, it is advisable to use only one unit of measure within APO that can be used by DP, SNP, and PP/DS.

For the DP environment, one might want to work with multiples of the defined unit of measure (e.g. pieces in SNP and PP/DS and thousands of pieces in DP).

### 3.4.1.2 Technical Structure

Technically the InfoCube is a collection of two different types of tables, the Fact Tables and the Dimension Tables. They are joined together in a "Star Schema".

Dimension Tables are made up of a key, a dimension number, and the characteristics within the dimension. As there is a maximum of 16 dimensions, no more than 16 dimension tables can exist. Dimension tables do not contain any key figures. The graphic further down shows the dimension tables for the example used in the previous chapter. The used key in this example is fictitious.

The Fact Table is made up of an access key and all the relevant key figures. The access key represents a unique combination of characteristics. The combination of each of the up to 16 dimension tables forms the Fact Table access key. A graphic of a fact table based on our previous example is shown below.

| Fact Table | | | |
|---|---|---|---|
| Key | Sold Quantity | Average Price | Turnover |

**Graphic 32 – InfoCube Fact Table**

| Dimension Product | | |
|---|---|---|
| Key | Product Number | Product Group |
| 123 | 1 | A |
| 124 | 2 | A |
| 125 | 3 | A |

| Dimension Time | |
|---|---|
| Key | Month |
| 223 | 1/99 |
| 224 | 2/99 |
| 225 | 3/99 |

| Dimension Customer | |
|---|---|
| Key | Customer Number |
| 323 | X |

**Graphic 33 – InfoCube Dimension Table**

Dimension and Fact Tables are joined together in a "Star Schema". The up to 16 points of the star represents the dimension tables, and in the middle of the star, you can find the fact table. This can be seen in the graphic below.

| Dimension Product | | |
|---|---|---|
| Key | Product Number | Product Group |
| 123 | 1 | A |
| 124 | 2 | A |
| 125 | 3 | A |

| Fact Table | | | |
|---|---|---|---|
| Key | Sold Quantity | Average Price | Turnover |
| 123-223-323 | 10 | 1.00 | 10.00 |
| 124-223-323 | 30 | 1.10 | 33.00 |
| 125-223-323 | 20 | 1.20 | 24.00 |

| Dimension Time | |
|---|---|
| Key | Month |
| 223 | 1/99 |
| 224 | 2/99 |
| 225 | 3/99 |

| Dimension Customer | |
|---|---|
| Key | Customer Number |
| 323 | X |

**Graphic 34 – InfoCube Star Schema**

### 3.4.1.3 Setup and Maintenance

Setup and maintenance of the InfoCube is done primarily using the Administrator Workbench. This is a powerful highly graphical and intuitive easy to learn application. Strictly speaking, it is not really an APO application. Its origin is the Business Information Warehouse where it is used for exactly the same purpose. The normal APO user will never use the Administrator Workbench, as its task is solely the creation and the structural maintenance of the InfoCube as the main repository for data required in DP. The following chapter will give a brief overview of the Administrator Workbench functionality required for APO. For those interested in more details I suggest to get BW specific literature.

The Administrator Workbench is primarily used to maintain the following elements.

- Info Objects
  Characteristics, Key Figures, Unit-, and Time Characteristics are the four object types, which make the group of Info Objects. Info Objects can be grouped in Object Catalogs for easy retrieval and logical grouping. APO comes standard with a large number of predefined Info Objects and often one of them can be used without further maintenance.
- Info Areas
  An Info Area is used to group various Info Cubes. This is with practical relevance for APO if Vendor Managed Inventory (VMI) functionality is deployed. For each VMI customer, a separate InfoCube has to be defined. It is also useful when using Product Allocations in Global ATP, as each Product Allocation Group requires its own InfoCube.
- Info Cubes
  The InfoCube is the heart of Demand Planning. All historical data as well as all forecast data is stored in an InfoCube. It is arranged in Dimensions, which in turn have one or multiple Characteristics and Key Figures. The Administrator Workbench is used to define all these relations. Multiple Info Cubes can share the same Info Objects.
- Info Sources
  Every InfoCube must be linked to an Info Source in order to be populated with data. Info Sources define Transfer Structures, Transfer Rules, and

Communication Structures. The Source System is one of many Application Components.

- Source Systems
  The Source System describes in combination with the Info Package the layout of the data provided by the data originating system (R/3, CSV type spread sheet, etc.). A Source System is linked to an Info Source, which provides finally the InfoCube with data.

As said above, it is not really necessary to fully understand the technicalities of the InfoCube setup and its surrounding environment. The setup is a once off activity and should be done by a BW specialist. Some additional information required for each InfoCube has to be defined in the separate transaction "Configure InfoCube Parameters".

### 3.4.2 Info Objects

APO comes with a large amount of predefined Info Objects. The generic term Info Objects describes Characteristics (which are grouped in Dimensions), Key Figures, Unit Characteristics, and Time Characteristics. All these info objects can be used instead of creating new ones when setting up the APO InfoCube. Info Objects can be grouped in Info Object Catalogues. Some of the Info Objects are mandatory to define a meaningful InfoCube or are required for logical reasons. When creating a new InfoCube it is recommended to use the SAP delivered InfoCube "DP_REFER" as a template.

Once the InfoCube is populated, new Info Objects can only be added or existing ones deleted after the InfoCube is being set to "inactive." This will delete all data stored in the InfoCube!

The list below shows some of the predefined Info Objects and their respective usage. Note the following explanations:

| Dimension | | Characteristic | |
|---|---|---|---|
| Description | Technical Name | Description | Object Name |
| Version | "InfoCube"IC1 | Version | APODPVRSI |
| Time | "InfoCube"ICT | Calendar Day | 0CALDAY |
| | | Calendar Year/Week | 0CALWEEK |
| | | Calendar Year/Month | 0CALMONTH |
| | | Calendar Year | 0CALYEAR |
| Unit | "InfoCube"ICU | Unit Key | 0UNIT |
| Data Packet | "InfoCube"ICP | Change Run ID | 0CHNGID |
| | | Record Type | 0RECORDTP |
| | | Request ID | 0REQUID |

**Table 30 – Info Objects**

1. The technical dimension name is made up of the InfoCube name followed by ICT, ICU, or ICP for mandatory dimensions and then IC1 through to IC13 for all others including the Version Dimension.
2. The Dimension Time must have at least one characteristic. Some of the predefined time dimensions are shown in the list; others that are used when using Fiscal Year Variants are also available.
3. When viewing the technical structure of an InfoCube, the Unit dimension (if used) is not displayed.
4. The Data Packet Dimension stores system-related data. It does not need to be set up.
5. In order to perform aggregation and distribution, it is required to define proportional factors. DP_REFER contains a proportional factor named APODPDANT. If it is required to aggregate and distribute key figures according to more than one proportional factor, then one needs to set up multiple Proportional Factors.

## 3.4.3 Profiles

DP is using several profiles that are linked to an InfoCube. The main one is the Master Forecast Profile, and an InfoCube can have more than one of it. The user can pre-select the Master Forecast Profile or select at run time which one to use. This is handy, as not all products that have to be forecasted will necessarily require exactly the same forecast parameters. The profiles used for forecasting and their main parameters are dealt with in the following chapters.

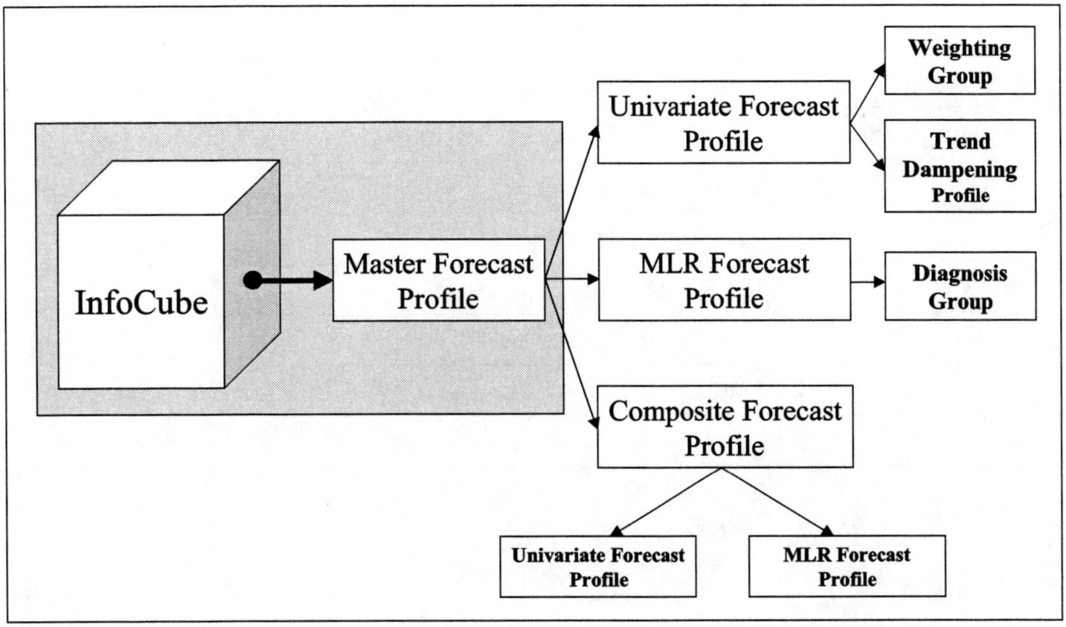


**Graphic 35 – DP Profiles**

The Master Forecast Profile is InfoCube dependent; this means a specific Master Forecast Profile can only be used in conjunction with a specific InfoCube. In opposition to this, the Univariate, MLR, and Composite Profiles are InfoCube independent. Therefore, when dealing with several InfoCubes, the same Univariate, MLR, and Composite Profiles can be used. The Composite Profile itself refers to one or multiple MLR and/or Composite Profiles. This cascading of profiles allows a flexible "mix and match" of profiles and avoids unnecessary data maintenance. In some cases there are links to profiles and other profile-like entries. The diagram above shows the profiles with their relationships.

There are a few other profiles used in Demand Planning. The following table lists them and points to the chapter where more information can be obtained.

| Profile | Chapter |
|---|---|
| Planning Book | Planning Book |
| Time Bucket | Time Buckets |
| Trend Dampening | Time Series Based Forecasting |
| Weighting Group | Time Series Based Forecasting |
| Diagnosis Group | Causal Forecasting |
| Phase In | Life Cycle Management |
| Phase Out | Life Cycle Management |
| Like Modeling | Life Cycle Management |
| Release | Output of Demand Planning |
| Alert | Alert Monitor |

**Table 31 – DP Profile Overview**

#### 3.4.3.1 Master Forecast Profile

This profile defines the start and end date of the forecast or the number of periods to be forecasted. It also defines the start and end date of the historical data to be used or the number of periods for which historical data will be used. With the help of these parameters, the forecast is carried out either for a fixed period or starting from the period following the current one for a certain amount of periods. The

Master Forecast Profile also points to exactly one Multiple Linear Regression Profile, one Univariate Profile, and one Composite Forecast Profile. Multiple Master Forecast Profiles can be defined per InfoCube. The Master Forecast Profile to be used is defined in the selection ID. The following list contains the parameters that can be defined.

- Key Figure
  Define the key figure into which the forecast result (not the corrected forecast) has to be written.
- Period
  Specify the period used for forecasting.
- Material Forecast
  Set this flag if you want to use the Phase-In, Phase-Out, or Like Modeling feature. All required product parameters for this functionality are stored in the respective product master. It will only be applied if this parameter is set.
- Alert Profile
  Link an alert profile to the forecast master profile.
- Forecast Horizon
  The horizon can be specified in two ways, fixed with a *from* and a *to* date, or alternatively floating depending on the system date. For the second option, simply specify the number of periods to be forecasted, and do not specify a date. In this case the forecast horizon starts by default after the current period as per system date and lasts for the number of periods as specified here. This is the normal setting in a live environment. Alternatively specify a *from* and *to* date explicitly. The system will automatically add the number of periods reflected by these dates. This feature is useful for development and testing purposes where no live data is available. Assuming you have loaded the InfoCube with some historical data it is possible to run all forecasts with a fixed start date.
- History Horizon
  The history horizon is specified the same way as the forecast horizon. It is also possible to use fixed or floating dates.
- Model Selection
  The model selection links a Univariate, MLR, and Composite Profile to the Master Forecast Profile.

DP

### 3.4.3.2 Univariate Profile

Here you find all parameters required for running a time-based forecast. Foremost, a default-forecast strategy is defined (e.g. seasonal model) with all its relevant factors like Alpha, Beta, Gamma, and Sigma Factor. It also defines the average number of workdays per planning period. Refer to the chapter "Workday Correction" for more information. The last section of the Univariate Profile flags the errors the system has to calculate in order to evaluate the forecast (e.g. MAD, MSE). A default button for this profile populates the majority of fields with default values according to best practices. The following list contains parameters that can be defined.

- Historical Input
  - Version & Key Figure
    Define the DP version and key figure where the univariate forecast has to be written. You can write the forecast into a version different to that where the historical data is stored.

- Model Parameters
  These parameters are used as a default every time a forecast is started the first time. In Interactive Planning, the planner can change them on the Model and Parameter tab for subsequent forecasts.
  - Forecast Strategy
    This is the forecast strategy used. Select one of the Univariate strategies <u>or</u> the MLR strategy!
  - Periods per Season
    The default number of periods per season used for seasonal and trend seasonal models.
  - Alpha, Beta, Gamma, and Sigma Factor
    As and where required, the factors defined here are used by the respective models. Refer to the explanation of the strategies for further information.
  - Weighting Group
    This profile like entry is used for a Moving Average model.
  - Trend Dampening Profile

The Trend Dampening Profile is an optional parameter for the trend and seasonal trend models.

- Diagnosis Group
  The diagnosis group is used to define upper and lower limits of control parameters that are calculated when performing the univariate forecast. Should a result fall out of any of the defined values, an alert can be generated. In order to receive an alert it is required to create a macro and activate it in the planning book.

- Control Parameters
  The control parameters apply to all forecast strategies. They are explained in detail with the various forecast strategies.
  - Without Zero Consumption
    Ignore periods without any consumption so that these periods do not influence the forecast.
  - Outlier Correction
    Correct Outliers based on the Sigma Factor and the Mean Absolute Deviation (MAD).
  - Use Corrected History
    After calculating the corrected history, it is not used automatically for the forecast. This is only done if this flag is set.
  - Adjust Corrected History
    Set this flag if you want the corrected history to be calculated (adjusted). This flag must be set in order to make the above flag meaningful.
  - Average Number of Days
    Defining a value in this field activates the Workday Correction feature. If left blank, no Workday Correction takes place.

- Forecast Errors
  APO can calculate various forecast error figures. Define here which one should be calculated. As each calculation requires processing time, only such should be activated that are used by the planner. In Interactive Planning, the planner can also activate them if required. The errors that can be calculated during a univariate forecasting run are:
  - MAD Mean Absolute Deviation

- ♦ Error Total Total Error
- ♦ MPE Mean Percentage Deviation
- ♦ MAPE Mean Absolute Percentage Error
- ♦ MSE Mean Square Error
- ♦ RMSE Square Root of the Mean Square Error

For these error measurements, upper limits can be defined in a diagnosis group. Exceeding the defined values in the diagnosis group can lead to the creation of an alert (see above under "Model Parameters"). Forecast Errors are dealt with in detail in the chapter "Forecast Accuracy Analysis".

### 3.4.3.3 Multiple Linear Regression Profile

The main parameters defined here are the Diagnosis Group that defines various MLR parameters and the used independent variables. The alert monitor can be used to automatically inform the planner should any of the parameter values be out of the acceptable range. The following list contains parameters that can be defined.

- Diagnosis Group
  The diagnosis group is used to define some upper and lower limits of control parameters that are calculated when performing an MLR-based forecast. Should a result fall out of any of the defined values, an alert can be generated.

- Historical Input
  - ♦ Version & Key Figure
    Define the DP version and key figure where the univariate forecast has to be written. You can write the forecast into a version different to that where the historical data is stored.

- MLR Variable
  - ♦ Independent Variables
    Specify here a key figure of the InfoCube as an independent variable. Press the "Key Figure" button to link a key figure to the profile. Using one

key figure or time series only makes the Multi Linear Regression a Single Linear Regression. It is also possible to specify a time series either instead or additionally to a key figure. Press the "Time Series" button to link a key figure to the profile. Before a time series can be used, it must be created using the "Time Series" button. The Time Series pop up window allows specifying the time series ID and description as well as the number of periods for which data will be entered. In the next step, the values per period have to be defined (press "Edit Time Series" button) and define values as required.

- Version
  Specify the planning version of the key figure. This field only applies if the independent variable is a key figure.
- Transformation
  Should an independent key figure of a certain period influence the dependent variable (the forecast) with a time lag, then specify the number of periods of this time lag here. The time lag can be a positive or negative figure. This field only applies if the independent variable is a key figure.
- Start Date
  The start date can be specified only if a time series is used to describe an independent variable. By specifying a start date, the system can relate the first value of the time series to a period.

#### 3.4.3.4 Composite Forecast Profile

The Multiple Linear Regression Profile(s) together with the Univariate Profile(s) to be used for the creation of the composite forecast are defined here. In this profile, you can also specify time independent weighting factors or a time dependent weighting group. The Composite Forecast will return a result even if one of the input forecasts does not provide a result.

Let me give an example. We have specified a univariate and an MLR profile in the composite profile, each with a weight of 50%. The univariate forecast returns a result of 1000 pieces in a certain period. The MLR forecast is out of the tolerance as defined in the diagnosis group and does not return a figure for the same period. The overall result for this period is therefore 1000 plus Zero pieces divided by two, which makes 500 pieces.

### 3.4.3.5 Release Profile

The Release Profile is used when the unconstrained DP plan is released to SNP and when the constrained SNP plan is released (given back) to DP. This profile is only used for the batch background release and not for the on-line release. The following definitions can be made:

- Basic Settings
  - InfoCube
    Define the InfoCube used for the release.
  - Key Figure
    Specify here the key figure that carries the information that needs to be released to SNP to create the independent requirements. This is usually the corrected forecast key figure.
  - SNP Version
    Specify the SNP planning version into which the DP key figure will be released.

- Extras
  - Time Buckets Profile
    Specify the time bucket that is used to create the independent requirements in SNP. This time bucket must be in daily buckets.
  - Category
    The ATP category is used for the transfer of the SNP plan back to DP. Any SNP key figure that is characterized by this ATP category is used during the release to DP. This setting is only required if the transfer profile is to be used for transferring the SNP plan to DP.
  - Flag: Create New Orders
    With this flag set the system will create new SNP independent requirements for all forecast elements found in DP irrespective of

probably already defined SNP independent requirements. Set this option to improve system performance but only when transferring data the first time for the given period; otherwise a duplication of orders is likely to occur! Never set this flag when transferring an updated demand plan to SNP.

#### 3.4.3.6 Transfer Profile

The Transfer Profile is used when the unconstrained DP plan is given back to an R/3 system where independent requirements are created based on the transferred APO values. The "Basic Settings" are identical to those of the Release Profile (see above). Additionally, the following definitions can be made:

- R/3
  - Requirement Type
    Specify the material requirement type in R/3 used when transferring the DP plan to R/3.
  - Version
    Specify the R/3 demand version number. R/3 can have several versions of independent requirements.
  - Flag: Active
    Activate this flag if the R/3 demand version used is the active one.

### 3.4.4 Patterns

Patterns are actually a hybrid between master and transactional data. They are time-based information based on the planner's input or on system calculations. APO stores three types of patterns. They are the Seasonal, the Life Cycle, and the Promotional Patterns. These values cannot be found in the InfoCube, they are stored in conventional tables.
Similar to a pattern, Time Series Variables used in connection with MLR forecasts are stored outside the InfoCube.

## 3.4.5 Master Data Environment

In order to populate the InfoCube no master data at all needs to be set up. This is not a surprise as the InfoCube is a tool developed to store data in a data warehouse environment. As long as the data loaded into an InfoCube conforms to the Info Object settings in terms of length and type, no problems will occur. Even Demand Planning functions can be carried out without any master data.

As we have seen, Demand Planning does not require a lot of master data to be set up. The main task is the creation and population of the InfoCube. In addition to this, profiles and patterns, which are also types of master data, need to be set up carefully before demand planning can be carried out.

### 3.4.5.1 Location

Locations can be manufacturing plants, distribution centers, suppliers, or vendors. In general a location is any place where products either come from, go to or where they are stored. Although most probably defined as a characteristic in the InfoCube, no location master data needs to be set up in order to populate it. Forecasting could be carried out without any reference to a location. In this case it is required to define the distribution of the forecast over the various locations when releasing the forecast to SNP. See also the chapter "Location Management". When selecting a location during the forecasting process using the search facility, the location description is displayed if a corresponding location master record was defined. But even if this is not the case, a location can be selected using the search facility and be used in forecasting. Location master records must be defined before releasing the unconstrained DP plan to SNP!

### 3.4.5.2 Product

The term 'product' relates to any type of material from component to finished product. It is not necessarily a tangible unit. Although products must be loaded into the InfoCube in order to perform the forecasting, no product master data needs to be set up for the initial step of loading the InfoCube. Any product and/or location can be loaded into the InfoCube irrespective of whether master records exist or not. When selecting a product during the forecasting process using the search facility, the product description is displayed if a corresponding product master record was defined. But even if this is not the case, a product can be selected and used in forecasting. Nevertheless, a product master must be defined in order to use Life Cycle Management or Promotional Planning functions in forecasting. For more details refer to the chapter "Life Cycle Management".

Product master records must be defined before releasing the unconstrained DP plan to SNP! The product master must have the same unit of measure as the InfoCube unit of measure, either as the base of unit of measure or as an alternate unit of measure.

### 3.4.5.3 Characteristic Value Combination

There is no Characteristics master record that can be updated by the planner. Characteristics, which are together with the Key Figures one of the four types of Info Objects, are defined in the InfoCube as part of the initial set up.

Characteristic Value Combinations are needed to carry out planning of demand for a certain combination of characteristics. Characteristic Value Combinations are also referred to as Planning Objects. There are two ways of creating Characteristic Value Combinations:

- Mass Generation based on historical data
  In this mode, APO creates characteristic value combinations for all combinations of characteristics that can be found within a certain period. The period under observation can be specified. This means that planning can be

carried out on the same level as sales were reported in the period under observation. Note that the planning can be carried out on the same level of detail; it does not have to be carried out on the same level. When planning on higher levels, APO applies distribution rules to spread the forecasted figures over the subordinate elements. Combinations of characteristics are created in an InfoCube whenever a demand occurred. It is required to specify the planning version to be used as a basis for the calculation of Characteristic Value Combinations.

- Individual Generation
  It is possible to additionally define any specific characteristic value combination for such combinations of characteristics where no demand was reported in the period under observation. This can be done in two ways, with or without graphical support. This is required for example for any new products where no history exists.

For practical reasons, the mass generation of characteristic value combinations should be carried out first. In a second step, all those combinations missing will be defined one by one.

The creation of characteristic value combinations is planning version independent. Once the characteristic value combinations are created, they are stored in the InfoCube using a version called "APOMASTER".

**Example:**
Cumulated sales figures for the month July 99 are shown below. We have the two products needles and pins, two customers Brown and Smith, and we deliver from our two locations Denver and Atlanta. The first table contains all possible permutations with the exception of one.

| Product | Customer | Location | Sales Quantity |
|---|---|---|---|
| Needles | Brown | Denver | 200 |
| Needles | Brown | Atlanta | 400 |
| Needles | Smith | Denver | 100 |
| Needles | Smith | Atlanta | 300 |
| Pins | Brown | Denver | 300 |
| Pins | Brown | Atlanta | 200 |
| Pins | Smith | Denver | 500 |

**Table 32 – InfoCube Example 1**

There are no sales of the product Pins to customer Brown from our location Atlanta. This is depicted in the table below.

| Product | Customer | Location | Sales Quantity |
|---|---|---|---|
| Pins | Smith | Atlanta | 0 |

**Table 33 – InfoCube Example 2**

Running Mass Generation based on historical data in July 99 creates seven different characteristic value combinations. The only non-existing characteristic value combination is "Pins – Smith – Atlanta" as no demand occurred for this combination in July 99. We now also want to plan our product pins to customer Smith from our location Atlanta. For this reason we manually create this combination.

# 3.5 The DP Transactions

In the following chapters we will have a look at the main DP transactions, which is foremost the Supply Chain Cockpit, the DP Interactive Planning screen, and the Promotional Planning screen.

## 3.5.1 Supply Chain Cockpit

The graphical presentation of data has come a long way since the first release of an R/3 system, and APO uses a very appealing environment for most of the daily planning tasks to be performed. It is called "Supply Chain Cockpit," and indeed out of this cockpit, the majority of tasks can be performed.
The Supply Chain Cockpit guides the user through all tasks such as

- Demand Planning,
- Supply Network Planning,
- Production Planning & Detailed Scheduling, and

The DP specific main tasks, forecasting and promotion planning, are not performed directly out of the Supply Chain Cockpit. In order to perform forecasting, the user has to jump from the Supply Chain Cockpit into the DP Interactive Planning Screen. This can be done via the Supply Chain Cockpit menu structure or using one of the Control Panel buttons (see also the chapter "Control Panel"). Unfortunately, there is no way to get from the Supply Chain Cockpit directly into the Interactive Promotion Planning Screen. The user is forced to either leave the Supply Chain Cockpit or to open a new session. Starting from the Supply Chain Cockpit or the DP Interactive Planning Screen, the user can also access the Alert Monitor. The Alert Monitor is a central tool and provides the user with information regarding any problem in the supply chain irrespective of a specific source. The upcoming alerts are grouped according to the APO area (e.g. alerts for Demand Planning) and can further be filtered so that in a multi-user environment only the responsible planner receives specific messages.
The DP Interactive Planning Screen can also be called up directly from the APO tree structure. The access via the Supply Chain Cockpit does not provide any advantages compared to the direct access. It is merely a matter of convenience to

jump from the Supply Chain Cockpit to the Interactive Planning Screen directly and is only required if the same planner has both responsibilities or if the SNP planner needs to have a quick look at the DP situation.
The functional details of the Supply Chain Cockpit are dealt with in detail in the SNP section, as the Supply Chain Cockpit is primarily an SNP tool. There we shall also go through the Supply Chain Engineer, which is a graphical tool used to define the whole supply chain network with all locations and its dependencies as well as the Alert Monitor.
For more information regarding the Supply Chain Cockpit, refer to the SNP section where the Supply Chain Cockpit appearance is dealt with in more detail.

#### 3.5.1.1 Control Panel

The Control Panel in the Supply Chain Cockpit is a collection of buttons that can be activated user specific and appear at the bottom of the Supply Chain Cockpit screen. They can be displayed either enlarged or in small size to not take away too much of the valuable screen space. Irrespective of the size, the buttons have the same functionality. Amongst the buttons is one named "DP" which allows accessing the DP Interactive Planning screen and the DP Alert Monitor.

#### 3.5.1.2 Alert Monitor

The Alert Monitor can be accessed from the DP Interactive Planning Screen, from the Supply Chain Cockpit, or directly from the APO tree structure. The Alert Monitor, when activated from out of the Supply Chain Cockpit or the DP Interactive Planning screen, provides the user with structured information regarding all detected alerts.

In this chapter we shall only deal with the DP related tasks. For the other views, refer to the appropriate sections. DP is the only area within SNP where the user can define own alerts; all other areas have only predefined rules. A user profile determines which user receives which alerts. This ensures that a planner is not cluttered up with messages that belong to another planner. This is achieved by allocating an alert profile to a user. In order to see alerts the following activities must have been carried out:

- Link of Alert Profile to Master Forecast Profile
  Allocation and definition of the alert profile is done in the transaction for master forecast profile maintenance. This link must be done for all used master forecast profiles in use. To maintain an alert profile within the forecast profile maintenance program select "Go to – Alert Profile". Use the same alert profile name as in the Supply Chain Cockpit. The use of the alert profile can be restricted (see the SNP section).
- Definition and Activation of Macros
  Define macros as and when required. For further information regarding the creation of macros refer to the chapter "Advanced Macros".
- Link of Planner User ID to an Alert Profile
  This can be done in the Settings transactions for the Supply Chain Cockpit.

For more detailed information regarding the setup of the Alert Monitor refer to the chapter "Alert Monitor" in the SNP section.

### 3.5.2 DP Interactive Planning Screen

For those knowing the R/3 forecasting environment (and screens) only, I can promise a real positive surprise when starting to work with the DP Interactive Planning Screen for the first time. The DP Interactive Planning Screen offers various tools for viewing and updating data such as historical demand and forecasts. Furthermore a wide variety of default planning book settings defined by the planner can be accessed. The Interactive Planning Screen appears with a number of views, which the planner selects to perform interactive planning. The views and their appearance are defined per planning book in the planning book profile. The main view is user-defined, and needs to be customized. This is explained in the "Planning Book" chapter.

- Planning View
  The Planning View appears like a two dimensional spreadsheet. Working with it is as easy as working with any other spreadsheet. Its name, which appears on the tab, can be defined per planning book.

The columns represent time buckets (weeks or months) as defined in the Time Bucket Profile that is linked to the Planning Book. Linked to the Planning View and defined in the planning book information screen are two time bucket profiles, one dealing with the display of historical data, the other one with the forecast data. For further information regarding the definition of Time Bucket Profile, please refer to the appropriate chapter.

The rows of the Planning View represent the key figures or other data required in order to perform the forecasting task. Only Key Figures that are defined in the InfoCube that is linked to the selected planning book can be used. Besides these key figures, rows with other types of information can be defined. Useful data to be displayed in these rows are:

- Original History
- This Year's Actual Sales
- Previous Year's Actual Sales
- Corrected History
- Original Forecast
- Corrected Forecast
- Promotion

Entire rows or parts of a row can be totaled. For each row attributes are defined. They include parameters like "Display only" versus "Update allowed" or "Info Cube Text" versus "Planner Defined Text". The Aggregation and Distribution type of a key figure can be defined only if this has not been done in the InfoCube parameters already. For more information regarding the Aggregation and Distribution of data, refer to the appropriate chapter.

The data of the entire spreadsheet of the planning view can be downloaded to Microsoft Excel for further processing. It is also possible to upload data from Microsoft Excel into the DP planning view.

A number of screen tabs representing "Standard Views" are provided by SAP. These standard views offer forecast data in spreadsheet and graphical form as well as system messages and forecast evaluation figures (calculated errors). Graphical display is depending on the planner's preference and can be in various formats. Graphically presented forecast figures can be clicked on and dragged to new levels. This also updates the table behind the graph. The historical data used for each of the forecasting models can be seen on the Planning View. The Standard Views are as follows:

- Forecasting View
  This view displays either the forecast result based on a Time Series model such as the Constant or the Seasonal Model, or a Multiple Linear Regression (MLR) model, or a Composite model.
- Causal View
  Here, only the result of a Multiple Linear Regression (MLR) model is displayed.
- Composite Forecast View
  The combination of a Time Series Based and a Causal forecast can be seen here.

Note that the different views represent different forecast results based on the same data. The data on which the forecasts are based can be seen on the Planning View. Results in one planning view can be kept while a new forecast is carried out in another view.

Quantity key figures are displayed in the base unit of measure as defined in the InfoCube and currency key figures are displayed in the base currency as defined in the InfoCube. Any other quantity related unit of measure could be used as a display unit provided it is defined in the product master. Units of measure based on the SI system can be converted without explicit definition in the product master. SI system units relate volumes, weights or any other scientific measurement to each other (e.g. 1000g = 1 kg).

In addition to these Planning and Standard Views as described above the Interactive Planning Screen also offers a data selection area in the form of a tree structure. The planner uses this area for selecting objects such as products and locations for which he or she wants to perform the forecast. Selection criteria can be named and stored. Later these selections can be called up again. Also see the chapter "Selection Variants".

Working with the Interactive Planning Screen is further simplified by the use of Context Sensitive Menus. The eight available Context Sensitive Menus are grouped into those that work on "Grids" and those that work on "Charts". Grids (or spreadsheets) and charts can be found on several views depending on the definition in the planning book. Graphics can be switched off to improve the system responsiveness.

Context Sensitive Menus for grids can be activated for

- One or multiple rows,
- One or multiple columns,
- One or multiple cells, and
- The entire grid.

Context Sensitive Menus for charts can be activated for the

- X axis,
- Y axis,
- A row's graphical element in the chart, and
- The entire chart.

Depending on the element the cursor is positioned on, a context sensitive menu pops up when pressing the right mouse button.

APO uses macros to distribute and aggregate data from one planning level to the next. Macros are defined calculation procedures to manipulate data shown in the Interactive Planning Screen. The aggregation and distribution macros are predefined and therefore only need to be applied rather than developed and applied. For further information regarding macros see the chapter "Advanced Macros".

### 3.5.2.1 Graphical Display

Any key figure of the InfoCube as well as any calculated row that is visible in the planning book can be displayed graphically. The display of the data and the selection process of possible data to be displayed depend on the selected planning view (tab).

The Main Planning View of the planning book is fully customizable in terms of which key figures of the InfoCube are shown or not. Any shown key figure can be flagged "Graphics Display" in the planning book design transaction and is subsequently made part of the graphics display. The selection of key figures to be displayed in the planning book design is a pre-selection, and the user can further restrict (not enlarge) this selection.

The Forecast View contains various SAP predefined key figures. Neither the selection of key figures can be influenced nor whether they are displayed in graphical form or not. The user can only restrict (not enlarge) the graphical presentation of the predefined key figures.

The Causal View contains various SAP predefined key figures and all influencing factors of the MLR profile. All these figures are displayed in the graphic. The user can only restrict (not enlarge) the graphical presentation of the predefined key figures and MLR influencing factors.

The Composite View contains the forecast results of all components as specified in the composite profile. In addition to this the new composite forecast and the corresponding ex-post forecast are displayed. The user can only restrict (not enlarge) the graphical presentation of the displayed values.

Following elements of the graphic can be formatted (per user) according to user specifications.

| | |
|---|---|
| General Settings | Activate context sensitive menu anywhere in graphic |
| Plot Area | Double click on plot area (not grid area) |
| Gridlines | Double click on grid area |
| Y – Axis | Double click on Y– Axis |
| X – Axis | Double click on X– Axis |

A multitude of settings can be done for these graphical elements, one of them being the suppression of individual lines that are not required. Some of the settings are valid for all views (tabs), others only for the selected view. All graphical settings done in the DP Interactive Demand Planning screen can be saved user specific by selecting the "Save Graphic Settings" button in the menu bar.

### 3.5.2.2 Selection Management

It is required to define the data environment (e.g. products and customers) before any planning can be carried out. A selection consists of the planning objects (products, plants, etc.) and the definition of a planning version. The combination of these objects is also referred to as Characteristics Value Combination. The planner can use Selection ID's to filter any data of the InfoCube for planning purposes. Based on the tree structure, the planner selects one or multiple elements of a planning object together with the planning version. This selection can be saved using a selection ID. By calling up this selection ID later again, the planner can immediately work in his or her planning environment without prior time-consuming data selection.

Selection ID's are linked to a specific planning version within the InfoCube. Furthermore selection ID's can be linked to a specific master forecast profile in the case where more than one forecast profile exists. After selecting a Characteristics Value Combination, with or without a Selection ID, the data is locked and no other planner can access this object combination.

Selections are built up in the DP Interactive Planning screen and are InfoCube dependent. Any planner with the appropriate authorization can perform this step. In a second step that is carried out in the "Maintain Selection Assignments" transaction, the selection ID's can be allocated to one or several users. Selection Management provides the following benefits:

- The creation of user specific selection ID's facilitates an easy data selection as the individual user does not have to build up his or her data environment again and again when opening a planning book.
- Several users can share the same selection ID's. This ensures that the data selection is consistent.
- Users can be limited to only use selection ID's. This is helpful for inexperienced or casual DP users (see Collaborative Planning).
- The selection ID pop-up window shows only user specific and relevant selection ID's, which supports a "cleaner" user-interface.

Selection ID's can be deleted in the separate transaction "Delete Selections", which is also used to delete selection ID's from areas other than DP (e.g. SNP).

### 3.5.2.3 Notes Management

In APO Demand Planning it is possible to capture notes alongside with any historical or forecast values. The free-text-notes are edited using the SAP editor. Different notes can be captured per planning version, characteristics value combination and time period. Thus the note is linked to the lowest level information of the InfoCube. Additionally notes can be kept at any level of aggregation. Let me give an example. The planner makes a note of the forecast value of a certain product and locks the forecast value. Later, the product group, to which this product belongs, is planned separately. The planner now adds a new note to the product group and can at the same time quickly drill down to the note of the single product.

Maintenance of notes is started by activating the context sensitive menu on the cell (of the forecast or any other value) for which the note should be created or updated and selecting "Display Note". The note contains administrative information that shows amongst other information--the language and up to three titles as well as the date, time and user ID when created and last updated.

### 3.5.2.4 Version Management

APO can accommodate a huge amount of different planning versions with version Zero being the active one. This version by default carries all actual data. Before a new planning version can be used, it has to be created. This can be done directly out of the Interactive Planning Screen or in a separate transaction. Single key figures or the whole set of key figures can be copied from one planning version to another. Non-required planning versions should be deleted to support a good housekeeping. After the forecasting job has been carried out, one or multiple planning versions can be released to Supply Network Planning for further processing. The purpose for releasing more than one planning version to SNP could be to compare various demand plans and compare their feasibility and cost structure within SNP.

Planning versions can help to follow up on forecasted demand and how it changes over the time from the first forecast up to the moment where actual data exists. In this scenario the final forecasts for several periods are kept in saved versions that are not accessed for editing. The following table shows a spreadsheet that enables the planner to compare the change of forecast values over time and to finally compare it with the actual demand. It is based on a twelve month horizon with monthly planning intervals.

| Month | 00 | 01 | 02 | 03 | .. | 11 | 12 |
|---|---|---|---|---|---|---|---|
| 00 | Actual | Plan +01 | Plan +02 | Plan +03 | | Plan +11 | Plan +12 |
| 01 | Plan +12 | Actual | Plan +01 | Plan +02 | | Plan +10 | Plan +11 |
| 02 | Plan +11 | Plan +12 | Actual | Plan +01 | | Plan +09 | Plan +09 |
| 03 | Plan +10 | Plan +11 | Plan +12 | Actual | | Plan +08 | Plan +08 |
| .. | | | | | | | |
| 11 | Plan +02 | Plan +03 | Plan +04 | Plan +05 | | Actual | Plan +01 |
| 12 | Plan +01 | Plan +02 | Plan +03 | Plan +04 | | Plan +12 | Actual |
| 13 | Actual | Plan +01 | Plan +02 | Plan +03 | | Plan +11 | Plan +12 |
| 14 | Plan +12 | Actual | Plan +01 | Plan +02 | | Plan +10 | Plan +11 |

**Table 34 – Reporting Example**

Each row shows for a specific month the actual sales and the forecast for the following 12 months. All 13 data values there are taken from the current month's forecast. In the first month (00), the actual demand is in cell 00/00 and the planned (forecasted) demand can be found in the consequent cells of this row. The forecasted demand shown in this row is based on the forecast carried out in this month (00). The second row shows the actual demand of the month in cell 01/01 and the planned (forecasted) demand for the following months can be found in the consequent cells of this row and the very first cell of this row. This principle is carried forward for all rows.

Each column shows how the forecasted demand changes over time from one forecast run to the next. Every 12 months the actual demand shows up.

This spreadsheet can have as many rows as required. The number of data columns for a 12 months rolling forecast is 13. Note that each row requires data from a saved planning version. In order to generate such a report, it is necessary to have a full BW system installed since APO on its own does not allow reporting on data stored in the InfoCube.

### 3.5.3 Interactive Promotion Planning Screen

Promotion Planning is carried out in a special Interactive Promotion Planning program and not from within the Interactive Planning screen that is used to perform the forecasting task. The user interface is very similar to that of the Interactive Planning screen, and the usage of the screen corresponds as well. Unlike the Interactive Planning screen, the Interactive Promotional Planning screen cannot be customized at all. Column and Row layout is predefined and Key Figures are shown using the technical Key Figure name as defined in the InfoCube. Some Promotion Planning specific rows are added and again their names cannot be changed according to user requirements. To overcome this deficiency, it is possible to specify a "reference planning book" when accessing the Interactive Promotion Planning transaction. If a planning book is specified initially, the key figure names are taken over from it and displayed instead of their technical names. Data is shown in tabular form as well as in a graph, and it is possible to update data in both the table and the graph. On a second tab, all promotions for a product can be displayed.

Promotions are classified according to Application Type (Coupon Action, Price, Advertising, or TV Advertising) and Promotion Type (Quantitative Promotion or Qualitative Promotion). This classification allows for group promotions and selection according to their classification.

Promotions are defined in absolute figures or as relative figures in proportion to the baseline forecast. In order to view a baseline forecast, Promotion Planning should be performed after the initial forecast has been carried out. The result of the promotion plan updates the corrected forecast key figure and is thus immediately visible in the Interactive Planning screen. For this to happen, it is nevertheless a prerequisite to activate the promotion.
Access to the Promotion Planning screen is only via the tree structure and not from the DP Interactive Planning Screen. In a release later than 2.0 (patch 04), direct access from the DP Interactive Planning Screen will be possible.

The key figure that needs to be specified on the initial screen is that of the baseline forecast as defined in the InfoCube parameters. See also the chapter "Forecast Data Flow".

# 3.6 Authorization Management

New with release 2.0 was the introduction of Authorization Management. Authorization objects allow the execution of specific functions in APO. Some of them are module dependent; other general ones are used throughout APO. The DP specific authorization objects are listed in the following table. The General authorization objects follow in the table after that.

| Area | Authorization Object | Object Name / Object Description |
|---|---|---|
| DP | | |
| | C_APO_DPVR | Demand Planning Version |
| | | This authorization is used to give access to specific demand planning versions. |
| | C_APO_PLBK | Planning Book |
| | | Permits access to specific planning books in the DP interactive planning screen. |
| | C_APO_SELE | Data Selection |
| | | In order to use predefined data selection screens, this authorization is needed. |
| | C_APO_ADV | Advanced Macro Maintenance |
| | | Allows the maintenance of advanced macros. |
| | C_APO_MAC | Advanced Macro Usage |
| | | This authorization is needed to run advanced macros in the DP interactive planning screen. |

**Table 35 – DP Authorization Objects**

For demand planning, a special user exit exists that allows custom specific definition of authorization objects to introduce further restrictions and controls.

| Area | Authorization Object | Object Name / Object Description |
|---|---|---|
| General | | |
| | C_APO_FUNC | Demand Planning and Supply Network Planning |
| | | Allows selective user access control to various transactions within Demand Planning and Supply Network Planning |
| | C_APO_LOC | Master Data Maintenance, Location |
| | | Permits location master data maintenance on display, change, create and delete level. Requires access-authorization to the supply chain engineer. |
| | C_APO_PROD | Master Data Maintenance, Product |
| | | Permits product master data maintenance on display, change, create and delete level. Requires access-authorization to the supply chain engineer. |
| | C_APO_RES | Master Data Maintenance, Resource |
| | | Permits resource master data maintenance on display, change, create and delete level. Requires access-authorization to the supply chain engineer. |
| | C_APO_PPM | Master Data Maintenance, Production Process Model |
| | | Permits production process model master data maintenance on display, change, create and delete level. Requires access-authorization to the supply chain engineer. |
| | C_APO_PLAN | Production Model Plan |
| | | Permits production process model master data maintenance on display, change, create and delete level for the plan. |
| | C_APO_TLAN | Master Data Maintenance, Transportation Lane |
| | | Permits transportation lane maintenance within the supply chain engineer on display, change, create and delete level. Requires access-authorization to the supply chain engineer. |

**Table 36 – General Authorization Objects**

# 3.7 DP Guides

In the following chapters practical "How to do" guides are provided for some key tasks in DP. They obviously require access to an APO system. The demo InfoCube DP_REFER, if not already existing, should be created before continuing. To do so follow these three easy steps:

1. From the APO menu structure call transaction SE38.
2. Specify the program name /SAPAPO/RMDP_BW_INITIALIZE.
3. Select "Execute".

That is all; you should have now the InfoCube DP_REFER in your system.

## 3.7.1 Setting up the InfoCube

The creation of an InfoCube is easier than what one might think. The procedure below assumes that the InfoCube DP_REFER exists already (please see above). Note that clicking the right mouse button activates the context sensitive menu. This is true at least for right-handed people who have not reassigned the mouse buttons.

**1. Create Info Area (InfoCube tab)**

- Activate the context sensitive menu on folder InfoCubes and select Create Info Area.
- Specify name and description for the Info Area.

**2. Create Info Objects**

- Select the Edit Info Objects button (Shift F5) in the button bar.
- Name new required Info Objects, select their type and press the New button.

- For Key Figures enter the type and the data type of the key figure (check system delivered Info Objects to get some ideas). Define settings as required. For Characteristics enter the data type and the length of the characteristics. Activate and Save.

**3. Create Info Object Catalog**

- Select the Edit Info Objects button (Shift F5) in the button bar.
- Select the Info Objects Catalog button (Ctrl F6) in the button bar.
- Specify the name of the new catalog and select Edit.
- Enter a name and a description for the catalog of the characteristics.
- Using the Transfer Fields icon, copy the desired characteristics (for example newly created ones in the previous step) from the template to the structure. Once all Info Objects are added to the Info Object Catalog select Activate and Exit.
- Repeat the previous 4 steps for all Key Figures accordingly.

**4. Create InfoCube (InfoCubes tab)**

- Activate the context sensitive menu on <u>Your Info Area</u> and select Create InfoCube.
  Enter a name and a description for the InfoCube. Select DP_REFER as the reference InfoCube and select Enter.
- Select the Characteristics tab.
- All Info Objects of DP_REFER appear. Ensure that APODPVRSI is included in the structure. Select the characteristics from your Info Object catalog by clicking on the Info Object catalog icon in the upper right corner and double clicking on the name of your Info Object catalog (created in step 3).
- Copy the characteristics from the template to the structure using the Transfer Fields button in the middle of the screen. You must include APODPVRSI in the structure if not there already.
- Click on the Dimensions tab.

- Define at least two dimensions; one for the version (should be there already if you used DP_REFER) and one or more for the other characteristics. You do not need to create dimensions for time characteristics or units; these are created automatically.
- Click on the Assign tab.
- Select the characteristic you want to assign, click on the check box of characteristic and place the cursor on the dimension to which you wish to assign it and click on the Assign button and select Continue (F5).
- Click on the Time Characteristics tab.
- Copy at least one of the Time Characteristics from the template to the structure.
- Click on the Key figure tab.
- Copy the key figures from the template to the structure using the Transfer Fields button (triangle pointing to the left). You must include APODPDANT in the structure. You can also select the key figures from your Info Object catalog by clicking on the Info Object catalog icon in the upper right corner and double clicking on the name of your Info Object catalog (created in step 3).
- Choose Activate and Exit.
- Leave the Administrator Workbench.

**5. Configure InfoCube**

From the APO main menu select Supply Chain Planning > Demand Planning > Environment > Current Settings > Configure InfoCube Parameters.

- Specify Your InfoCube.
- Define the General Planning Parameters Base Unit of Measure, Currency, and Factory Calendar.
- Configure all Key Figure Planning Parameters. Refer to the chapter "Forecast Data Flow".
- Define the Characteristics Planning Parameters Product (the characteristic where the product number is), Location Split (select No Location Split and specify the characteristic where the location number is), and the Time Period of the used Time Characteristic.

- Define the method of aggregation or distribution for key figures as required.
- Save and exit.

You now have a fully functional InfoCube. The next steps deal with loading data into this InfoCube. Note that this task cannot be done anymore once a data load took place! Even deleting the data will not solve this restriction.

## 3.7.2 Creating Source Data

In most cases the link to R/3 will not be available as of day one, and it is required to load some test data using an Excel spreadsheet. When creating the spreadsheet, ensure that you create the columns in exactly the same sequence, as you will later define in the step "Loading the InfoCube." No headers must be used in the spreadsheet. Select the entire spreadsheet and define the cells as "Text" as otherwise all leading Zeroes will be truncated. Specify for the version type "0000000000" and for the proportional factor "1". Date fields must be in the following format (with leading zeroes):

- Month mmyyyy
- Week wwyyyy
- Day yyyymmdd
- Period ppppyyyy

Save the file in comma delimited (.csv) format. Should you use Key Figures in your InfoCube, which you do not want to populate with data, put them at the end of the communication structure. In this case they do not need to be put in the spreadsheet at all.

## 3.7.3 Loading the InfoCube

After the InfoCube structure has been defined and we have a data source, it is the next logical step to populate the InfoCube with this data. All paths are defined assuming you start in the APO main menu. Most of the work will be done in the Administrator Workbench.

Start the Administrator Workbench (Supply Chain Planning > Demand Planning > Environment > Current Settings > Administrator Workbench). The Administrator Workbench can also be found in the IMG. We shall now go through a number of steps that are all carried out from within the Administrator Workbench. To do so we have to joggle between various tabs.

1. **Create Source System (Source Systems tab)**
   - Activate the context sensitive menu on the Folder Source Systems and select Create Source System.
   - Select File System, Manual Meta Data, Data using File Interface and select Enter.
   - Enter a name and a description for the Source System and select Enter.

2. **Create Application Component (Info Sources tab)**
   - Activate the context sensitive menu on the Folder Info Sources and select Create Application Component.
   - Enter a name and a long description for the Application Component and select Enter.

3. **Create Info Source (Info Sources tab)**
   - Activate the context sensitive menu on Your Application Component and select Create Info Source.
   - Select Transaction Data and then Enter.
   - Enter a name and a long description for the Info Source and select Enter.

4. **Assign Source System to Info Source (Info Sources tab)**
   - Activate the context sensitive menu on Your Info Source and select Assign Source System.
   - Enter the name of Your Source System and select Enter.
   - Enter all Info Objects of the InfoCube (Characteristics, Time Characteristics, and Key Figures) into the column Info Object. The Info Objects must be entered in exactly the same sequence as they appear in the

data columns of the Excel spreadsheet you created earlier. Input data only into this one column called Info Object; the other fields are populated automatically.

- Activate the check box Delta Update. Select Save and Cancel.

5. **Maintain Communication Structure (Info Sources tab)**
   - Activate the context sensitive menu on Your Info Source and select Maintain Communication Structure. Confirm any possibly upcoming information messages.
   - Transfer all Info Objects from the template to the Communication Structure. To do so click either selectively on the Transfer Info Object button (triangle pointing to the left) or the Transfer all Info Objects button (2 triangles pointing to the left), then Activate.

6. **Maintain Transfer Rules (Info Sources tab)**
   - Activate the context sensitive menu on Your Source System and select Maintain Transfer Rules, then Activate.

7. **Create Update Rules (InfoCubes tab)**
   - Activate the context sensitive menu on Your InfoCube and select Create Update Rules.
   - Enter the name of your new Info Source and select Enter.
   - Note that the status must be green for all key figures; if this is not the case something must have gone wrong in one of the previous steps. Do not continue without rectifying the problem, as the data load will not be successful.
   - Select Activate, Save and Exit.

8. **Create Info Package and Load Data (Info Sources tab)**
   - Activate the context sensitive menu on Your Source System and select Create Info Package.
   - Enter a description and select Enter. The following parameters have to be defined:
     - External Data tab:
       - Load external data from: Client Workstation

  - Control File: No
  - File Type: CSV File
  - Data Separator: switch the Hex setting off and use the character comma (,).
  - Escape Sign: switch the Hex setting off and use the character inverted comma (").
  - File Name: define the path of the spreadsheet file on your local PC.
- External Data Parameters tab:
- Thousand Separator: use the character colon (:).
- Character for Decimal Point: use the character point (.).
- Select Save.
- Choose the Schedule tab and execute Start.

If everything worked well, you should now have data in your InfoCube! To verify this, call up the transaction "LISTCUBE" from the APO menu structure. Select B for InfoCube type and define your InfoCube. The transaction behaves pretty much like SE16 in R/3. Define your selection (most probably all key figures and choose Enter. The content of the InfoCube should appear. Assuming this was successful, we can continue. Go to the next and final step.

If you want to reload data into the InfoCube, delete all existing data in the InfoCube first and then proceed as follows.

- Activate the context sensitive menu on <u>Your Info Package</u> and select Info Package Scheduler.
- Change any of the definitions as required.
- Choose the Schedule tab and execute Start.

Repeat the following step as well.

**9. Maintain the Characteristic Value Combinations**

- From the APO tree structure follow the path Demand Planning > Master Data > Maintain Characteristics.
- Specify your InfoCube.
- Select Generate Characteristic Combination. Define Source Version Zero, define a time interval and execute. You can safely define a time interval greater than the one used in your InfoCube.

Have a look again at your InfoCube data as described in step 8. There should be some new lines in it representing the newly created Characteristic Value Combinations. They are stored with version "APOMASTER".



## 3.7.4 Defining the Planning Book

The following chapter deals with the creation of a planning book. I shall explain the basic steps required. It obviously depends on the key figures in the InfoCube what has to be defined in the planning book. To get a basic setup I suggest following the instructions exactly in the sequence as described. Following Prerequisites must be fulfilled:

- 2 Time Bucket Profiles (one for the historical data and one for the forecast) are defined.
- The InfoCube is created (not necessarily loaded) and the Planning Parameters have been defined.
- All required Forecast Profiles are defined.

Go to the Planning Book Design Utility (APO main menu > Supply Chain Planning > Demand Planning > Environment > Current Settings > Define Planning Book).

1. **Create Planning Book Header**
   - Select Planning Book > Create. Specify a name and choose Enter. You can refer to an existing Planning Book in the Copy from section. Note that the referred Planning Book must be for the same InfoCube as the new Planning Book. In this case the Row Structure and/or the Advanced Macros can be copied into the new Planning Book.
   - On the upcoming screen define the following:
     - InfoCube the Planning Book refers to
     - Type of planning book (Standard or Internet)
     - Planning View Name (any)
     - Planning View Text (any, this text will appear on the Interactive Planning Screen as a tab name)

- Select the Forecasting Views (Forecasting Methods) which should be available to the planner in the Planning Book
- If you want the creator to be the only one who can change the Planning Book select the "only be creator" button.
- Specify a fixed start date for the forecast horizon if you do not want the forecast horizon to be the period following the current one depending on the system date.
- Select the Time Bucket profiles for the Forecast and the Historical Data.
- Use the "Buckets Profile" button if no time buckets are defined yet. This will bring you into the Time Bucket Profile Maintenance.
- Choose Enter. Changes to the majority of these settings can be done by selecting Go to > Planning Book Info from the main screen. You should have now a pretty empty planning book in front of you.

2. **Define Planning Book**

To view all unallocated key figures, press the "Key Figures" button. This opens another area on the screen that provides this information.

- To insert the historical and forecast data key figures:
  1. Click on the first row and activate the context sensitive menu, select "Assign Structure". Select the key figure representing the historical data.
  2. Activate the context sensitive menu on the newly created row and select "Row Attributes". Define a user-defined text if required.
  3. Select the row created in step 1 and activate the context sensitive menu. Select "Special Functions – Insert Previous Year's Actuals". Repeat step 2 for the newly created row.
  4. Select the row created in step 1 again, and then activate the context sensitive menu. Select "Special Functions – Insert Actuals". Repeat step 2 for the newly created row.
  5. Select the last row, activate the context sensitive menu and select the "Attach Row" function.
  6. Select the row created in step 5, and then activate the context sensitive menu, select "Assign Structure". Select the key figure representing the Forecast data. Repeat step 2 for the newly created row.

7. Select the row representing the Forecast data and activate the context sensitive menu. Select "Special Functions – Corrected History". Repeat step 2 for the newly created row.
8. Select the row representing the Forecast data again and activate the context sensitive menu. Select "Special Functions – Corrected Forecast". Repeat step 2 for the newly created row.

- To insert the promotion data key figure:

9. Select the row representing the Forecast data once more and activate the context sensitive menu. Select "Special Functions – Absolute Promotion". Repeat step 2 for the newly created row.

- To insert the ex-post forecast data key figure:

10. Select the row representing the Forecast data once more and activate the context sensitive menu. Select "Special Functions – Ex-Post Forecast". Repeat step 2 for the newly created row.

- To insert any other key figures:

11. Select the row after which you would like to insert a new key figure, activate the context sensitive menu and select the "Attach Row" function.
12. Click on the row created in step 11, and activate the context sensitive menu and select "Assign Structure". Select a key figure as needed. Repeat step 2 for the newly created row.
13. Repeat the last two steps as required.

Note that there are more elegant ways to define the planning book. The path shown ensures that nothing is forgotten and also gives the beginner a chance to understand what he or she is doing. Start and experiment after the first planning book works.

Instead of using the "Assign Structure" option of the context sensitive menu, you can also drag any key figure displayed in the "Unallocated Key Figures" area onto a tree structure element representing an empty row. Use this option only after you defined the key figure that represents the historical data.

Should the key figures (rows) not appear in the sequence as required, simply select a row in the table section on the right while pressing the <Shift> key. Drag the row to the new place as required and drop it there.

## 3.7.5 Creating Advanced Macros

The definition of macros is a task one needs to get used to. We shall go here through the creation of two macros. The first macro is very basic and adds two lines to give the result in the third. The second macro is used to trigger an alert. Macros are created in a special transaction called the "Macro Builder". Go to the Macro Builder by selecting "APO main menu > Supply Chain Planning > Demand Planning > Environment > Current Settings > Macro Builder". Select a planning book as well as a view, and press Enter. Often, there is more than one way to achieve a certain task. I shall guide you to the one I found to be the easiest. Should you make any mistakes and want to change an element, simply activate the context sensitive menu on it and select "Attributes". Selecting "Delete" will delete the element and put into the clipboard.

<u>Create Macro 1:</u>

The first macro will pick up the corrected forecast (row 4) of each period and multiply it by the anticipated sales price (row 10) to give the anticipated turnover for the forecast, which will be stored in row 11.

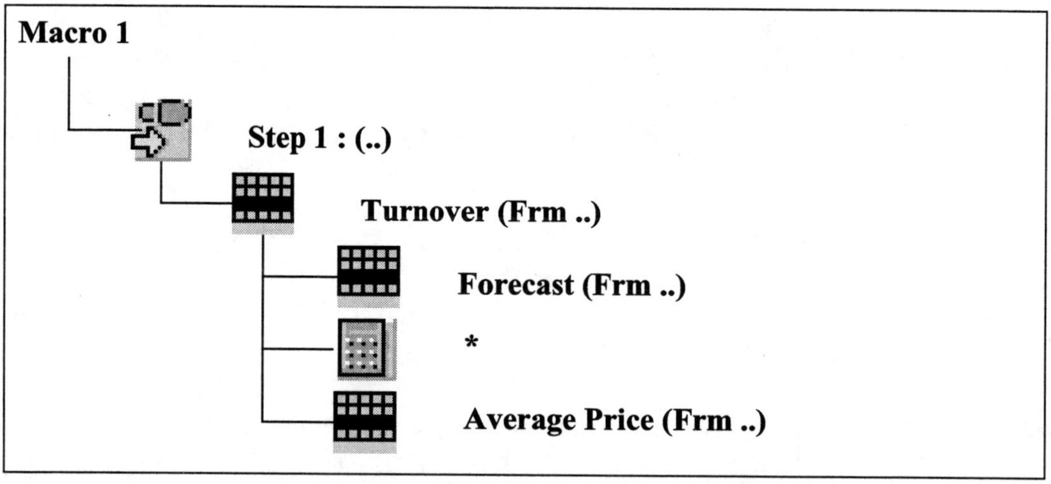

## Graphic 36 – Structure Macro 1

1. Drag and drop the Macro icon from the Elements section onto the Macros icon in the Macro section. Define the name of the macro (Test Macro 1) on the upcoming screen and leave the other two options unselected. Then press Enter.

   The status color of the macro is red.
2. Drag and drop the Step icon from the Elements section onto the newly created macro (Test Macro 1) icon in the Macro section. Define the name of the macro step (Step 1) on the upcoming screen and leave the other options unchanged. The system suggests processing the macro in accordance with the time bucket profiles of the InfoCube. Then press Enter.

   The status color of the macro remains red.
3. Drag and drop the Row icon from the Elements section onto the newly created macro step (Step 1) icon in the Macro section. Select the row that will be used in this macro step (Row 11) on the upcoming screen and leave the other options unchanged. Then press Enter.

   The status color of the macro remains red.
4. Drag and drop the Row icon from the Elements section onto the newly created icon (Turnover) in the Macro section. Choose "Create in next level" on the pop-up window. Select the row that will be used in this macro step (Row 4) on the upcoming screen and leave the other options unchanged. Then press Enter.

   The status color of the macro remains red.
5. Drag and drop the Operator/Function icon from the Elements section onto the newly created icon (Corrected Forecast) in the Macro section. Choose "Append" on the pop-up window. Select the operator that will be used to be "multiplication" (the "*" symbol). Then press Enter.

   The status color of the macro remains red.
6. Drag and drop the Row icon from the Elements section onto the newly created icon (the calculator with an * sign) in the Macro section. Choose "Create in next level" on the pop-up window. Select the row that will be used in this macro step (Row 10) on the upcoming screen and leave the other options unchanged. Then press Enter.

   The status color of the macro remains red.

7. This step is not mandatory and can be skipped. Select the Macro 1 icon in the macro section and press the Check button on top of this section. A pop-up window displays the message "Error-free check executed". Press Enter.
   The status color of the macro changes to yellow.
8. Select the Macro 1 icon in the macro section and press the Activate button on top of this section. A pop-up window displays the message "Generation completed: Macros saved". Press Enter.
   The status color of the macro changes to green.
9. Drag and drop the Macro 1 icon from the Elements section onto the Default icon in the Events section. The default tree structure is opened automatically and the new macro is inserted. Then press Enter.
   The status color of the macro remains green.

<u>Create Macro 2:</u>

The second macro will pick up the corrected forecast (row 4) of each period and check the forecast value. An alert will be generated if this value is greater than 10,000. The following graphic depicts the structure of macro 2.

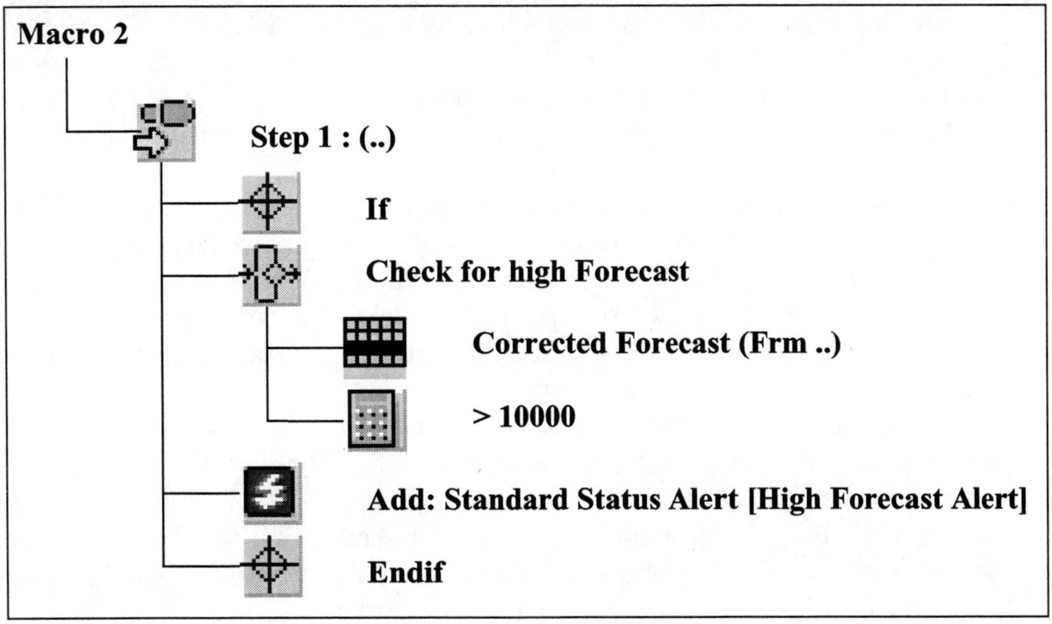


**Graphic 37 – Structure Macro 2**

1. Drag and drop the Macro icon from the Elements section onto the Macros icon in the Macro section. Define the name of the macro (Test Macro 2) on the upcoming screen, and leave the other two options unselected. Then press Enter.

   The status color of the macro is red.
2. Drag and drop the Step icon from the Elements section onto the newly created macro (Test Macro 2) icon in the Macro section. Define the name of the macro step (Step 1) on the upcoming screen, and leave the other options unchanged. The system suggests processing the macro in accordance with the time bucket profiles of the InfoCube. Then press Enter.

   The status color of the macro remains red.
3. Drag and drop the Control Statement icon from the Elements section onto the newly created macro step (Step 1) icon in the Macro section. Choose "Create in next level" on the pop-up window. Select the "If" statement on the upcoming screen. Then press Enter.

The status color of the macro remains red.

4. Drag and drop the Condition icon from the Elements section onto the newly created icon (If) in the Macro section. Choose “Create in next level” on the pop-up window. Define the name of the condition (Check for high Forecast) on the upcoming screen. Then press Enter.

   The status color of the macro remains red.
5. Drag and drop the Row icon from the Elements section onto the newly created icon (condition “Check for high Forecast) in the Macro section. Choose “Create in next level” on the pop-up window. Select the row that will be used in this macro step (Row 04) on the upcoming screen, and leave the other options unchanged. Then press Enter.

   The status color of the macro remains red.
6. Drag and drop the Operator/Function icon from the Elements section onto the newly created icon (Corrected Forecast) in the Macro section. Choose “Append” on the pop-up window. Select the operator that will be used to be “greater than” (the “>” symbol) and specify the value “10000”. Leave a blank between the operator and the value. Then press Enter.

   The status color of the macro remains red.
7. Drag and drop the Alert/Status icon from the Elements section onto the newly created icon (condition “Check for high Forecast) in the Macro section. Choose “Append” on the pop-up window. Select the alert text “High Forecast Value” on the upcoming screen, and leave the other options unchanged. Then press Enter.

   The status color of the macro remains red.
8. Drag and drop the Control Statement icon from the Elements section onto the newly icon (condition “Check for high Forecast) in the Macro section. Choose “Append” on the pop-up window. Choose “Create in next level” on the pop-up window. Select the “Endif” statement on the upcoming screen. Then press Enter.

   The status color of the macro remains red.
9. This step is not mandatory and can be skipped. Select the Macro 2 icon in the macro section, and press the Check button on top of this section. A pop-up window displays the message “Error-free check executed”. Press Enter.

   The status color of the macro changes to yellow.

10. Select the Macro 2 icon in the macro section, and press the Activate button on top of this section. A pop-up window displays the message "Generation completed: Macros saved". Press Enter.

    The status color of the macro changes to green.

11. Drag and drop the Macro 1 icon from the Elements section onto the Default icon in the Events section. The default tree structure is opened automatically and the new macro is inserted. Then press Enter.

    The status color of the macro remains green.

# 4 Supply Network Planning

## 4.1 Introduction

SNP is the logical follow up of DP. The start of Supply Network Planning is the release of a so-called unconstrained forecast, which was generated using Demand Planning functionality. It is good practice to release (copy) only such demand into Supply Network Planning that lies within the next 2 to 3 months of the forecast. This reduced horizon is then used for further planning and optimization. Output of this activity is planned orders for procurement (required goods purchases), production, and planned transport orders (intra company movements). After the planning and optimization has been carried out, it is necessary to go one level further down and schedule planned orders for production in the case of in-house production. Deployment and Transport Load Build are the last activities after the production has been carried out.

SNP plans the areas of Manufacturing, Purchasing, Distribution, and Transportation based on previously defined Independent Requirements, Dependant Requirements, Sales Orders, and other upcoming requirements. It not only considers transportation and production cost when deriving a plan, but also optimizes the usage of production and transportation facilities. The SNP Optimizer selects the production location taking into account the production cost as well as the transportation cost between locations. The Deployment Optimizer, another optimizing program within APO, optimizes specifically the usage of transportation resources. In order to use the optimizing functionality, it is essential to know production and transportation cost as exact as possible. This also applies where several production and or transportation modes are possible. SNP optimizes according to "penalties" that have to be set up precisely. These penalties work like a point system with the worst scenario being allocated the highest penalty. Doing so allows freedom from absolute production and transportation cost, using instead a relative scale.

SNP's power rises and falls with the exact knowledge of cost structures and their reproduction using penalties. The problem is which company knows the exact production costs and, even more often a problem, the exact transportation costs? Planning and optimizing according to both is currently not the norm but leads potentially to enormous cost savings.

## 4.2 Overview

The three main elements of SNP are:

- Planning and Optimization
- Deployment
- Transport Load Builder

The output of Planning and Optimization is a medium term production, purchasing and distribution plan. These plans are available to the planner for further refinement and alert processing. This is an important step specifically after a heuristic planning run as this method provides a plan that is not necessarily feasible. Deployment can be run in a heuristic approach and in an optimization mode. Transport Load Builder ensures economical transport loads, but is not a route optimizer.



SNP requires a substantial amount of master data to be set up. The main elements are the Product Master, Production Process Model, Location Master, Resource Master, Transportation Lanes, and Quota Arrangements. The use of various Profiles simplifies the day-to-day maintenance of master data. The Supply Chain Model is finally created using the Supply Chain Engineer, a graphical tool that simplifies this task tremendously.

APO has a function which allows information feedback from Supply Network Planning to Demand Planning. The idea is to give the demand planner (forecaster) confirmed data back to judge the operational feasibility of the demand plan created earlier. The forecast figures can then be seen as a constraint based demand.

In the case of in house production, planned orders for production are available to Production Planning and Detailed Scheduling for further processing. SNP orders need to be specifically released to PP/DS. During this process, amongst other activities, the production type PPM is exploded. Any orders that have at least one activity within the specified Production Horizon are dealt with by PPDS and cannot be changed anymore by SNP. The APO Production Horizon can be compared with the R/3 Fixing Period.

### 4.2.1 The SNP Planning Steps

The process flow of Supply Network Planning functionality is different depending on the procurement type of the product. For all externally procured (purchased) products or internally procured products sourced from an alternative Manufacturing Plant or Distribution Center, the following three step sequence applies:

1. Planning and Optimization
2. Deployment
3. Transport Load Builder

Internally procured, that means at this specific location manufactured products go through a five-step process at the manufacturing location:

1. Planning and Optimization
2. Release Supply Network Plan to PP/DS
3. Perform Finite Scheduling in PP/DS
4. Deployment
5. Transport Load Builder

Step 3 above can be further broken down into its sub-activities. Please refer to the detailed description about PP/DS to obtain more information. Note that a product that is sourced from an alternate location triggers another planning process in this originating location. The activities in this alternate location are again dependent on the procurement type of the product in this location. Ultimately, this leads to a multilevel planning effort up to the moment where the product in a location is either manufactured or bought from a vendor.

# 4.3 The SNP Methodology

## 4.3.1 SNP Demand Calculation

What is the demand at a certain point in time? Well, it depends on how you have customized the system. APO offers a highly flexible approach for calculating the demand. It comes standard with a whole lot of settings. It is advisable to first try to fully understand them and in a second step change them to cater for the exact business requirements.

All stock, receipt (supply), and issue (demand) elements are allocated to SNP categories. The SNP categories are also referred to as the ATP categories as they are also used to setup the ATP logic. Each ATP category is matched to an R/3 MRP element, but keep in mind that the used identifiers are totally different. In the case of demand calculation, obviously only those elements referring to demand are of interest. The definition of the ATP categories cannot be changed.
ATP categories are allocated to Category Groups whereby any ATP Category can be allocated to several Category Groups. APO comes with a whole set of defined Category Groups, which work but need to be adapted to suit individual business requirements.
The last allocation step is to link the Category Groups to the SNP Key Figures. The SNP Key Figures must not be mixed up with the DP Key Figures, although they deal with a similar topic.
To make the definition of demand a bit more flexible, but also a bit more difficult, APO offers the possibility to link exactly three different Category Groups to each of the five SNP Key Figures. The use of three Category Groups allows defining the demand differently with respect to the Short, Medium, and Long Term Plan. The split into three time segments (not more, not less) is fixed, but, if not required, the same Category Group could be linked to all three time segments. This does not apply to the Forecast Key Figure as the Category Group linked to this Key Figure is composed only of exactly one SNP Category.

Within SNP the following five Demand Key Figures are defined.

- Sales Order Demand
  Allocated to this key figure should be a category group, which in turn contains all such categories that deal with Sales Orders and related documents. A related document could be, for example, a Customer Enquiry or a Scheduling Agreement. Objects belonging to these categories and category groups originate in an OLTP system such as R/3.
- Dependant Demand
  APO creates as a result of a planning run or when orders are created interactively Dependant Demand if required (that means if the planned product has a PPM or BOM structure). All such Dependant Demands can be found in this key figure. Dependant Demands can also originate from the OLTP system. They are grouped together in Category Groups, which again are linked to the key figure.
- Planned Distribution Demand
  During an SNP planning run, the Planned Distribution Demand is calculated. Planned distribution demand represents all planned stock movements between locations in APO. All objects making up planned distribution demand are allocated to certain categories and then grouped in category groups. These category groups are then linked to this key figure.
- Confirmed Distribution Demand
  Confirmed distribution demand is the output of Deployment activity. Demand objects are either converted planned distribution demands or newly created planned distribution demands. These demands are allocated to categories as well, which in turn are allocated to Category Groups and finally to this key figure.
- TLB Confirmed Distribution Demand
  The TLB run finally provides the planning of the imminent shipment. The TLB confirmed distribution demands are also allocated to categories, which in turn are allocated to Category Groups and finally to this key figure.
- Forecast
  The forecast originates in DP and is represented by a single category that is allocated to a single category group and finally to this key figure. Depending on the requirements strategy and the consumption mode, this figure is reduced by incoming sales orders.

Note that although APO predefines the Key Figure names, it is up to the implementing team to allocate ATP Groups and ATP Categories appropriately to these Key Figures. The Transport Load Builder (TLB) uses separate definitions for Demand and Supply. Please refer to the chapter "Transport Load Builder".

What are the benefits of this rather complex setup?
The flexible allocation of demand elements to make up the total demand at a given time allows setting up APO precisely and according to the business needs. Depending on customer order behavior, production capabilities, and distribution network lead times, the Supply Chain model can be optimized to ensure low stock levels and in time delivery. Below is a graphic showing a typical time behavior in the sales environment.



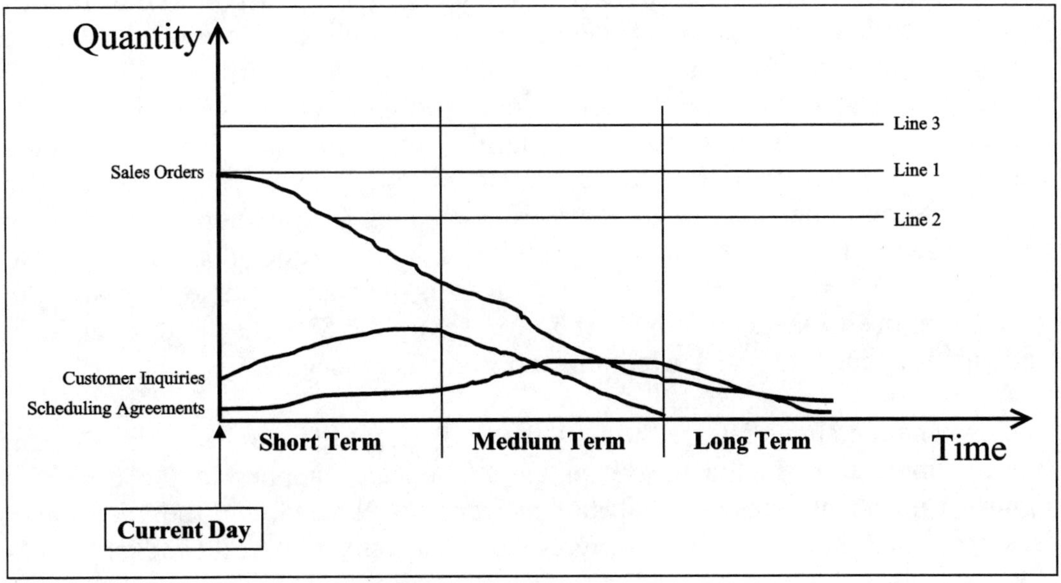


**Graphic 38 – Demand Time Dependency**

The graph is based on a constant model with forecast being consumed by the incoming sales orders. Sales orders are increasing to their maximum on the current day. Customer inquiries start in the medium term segment, rise and thin out again as some of them are converted to sales orders. Some remain and should be deleted if they run into the past. Scheduling agreements are long standing contracts and start in the long-term segment. They first increase and will then fall again as every scheduling agreement call-off reduces this figure (a call-off turns into a sales order). The forecast remains steady as long as no sales orders are received and reduces with incoming sales orders. Shown in the graph is the total of sales orders and forecast, which remains constant. Line 1 above assumes that sales orders are received in exactly the amount predicted in the forecast, line 2 shows an underestimated forecast, and line 3 an overestimated forecast. The above graph is a simplified example as there are several other parameters that might influence the characteristics of the curves.



The strength of the flexible APO setup is that, depending on the time segment, SNP planning can consider different demand categories or not. While running SNP, the system will cater for demand for scheduling agreements, customer inquiries, quotations, and sales orders only in the long term as all the four elements are part of the total demand in our (assumed) model. Medium term, the demand is made up of sales orders, scheduling agreements, and quotations only as we allow our customers to have a late call off and quotation to sales order change, but no late customer inquiry to sales order change. In the short term, we only accept sales orders in our models as a late call off or quotation to sales order change are also not accepted anymore. This is just an example, and it really depends on the business environment how to set up the SNP Key Figures and how to divide the time into Short, Medium, and Long Term segments.

The explanation above referred to how the SNP Key Figure Sales Order Demand is setup in relation to the time segments. The same applies to the SNP Key Figures Dependant Demand, Distribution Demand Planned, and the Distribution Demand Fixed. For the SNP Key Figure Forecast, only one ATP Category exists. Therefore exactly the same Category Group is allocated towards the three time segments, or, if three Category Groups are defined exactly the same ATP Category will be allocated to all Category Groups.

A further refinement when calculating the demand is the split of time according to the Forecast Horizon. Within the Forecast Horizon (that is starting from the present for the number of the days defined here), Total Demand is calculated according to the following formula:

| | |
|---|---|
| Total Demand = | |
| | Sales Order Demand |
| + | Dependant Demand |
| + | Planned Distribution Demand |
| + | Confirmed Distribution Demand |
| + | TLB Confirmed Distribution Demand |

After the end of the Forecast Horizon, Total Demand is calculated according to the following formula:

| | |
|---|---|
| Total Demand = | |
| | Maximum of (Sales Order Demand) and (Forecast) |
| + | Dependant Demand |
| + | Planned Distribution Demand |
| + | Confirmed Distribution Demand |
| + | TLB Confirmed Distribution Demand |

This allows coping easier with situations where the forecast was over or understating the actual demand. Within the Forecast Horizon (which is actually the time where the system does not bother what the forecast is) demand is calculated irrespective of the forecast. After the end of this Forecast Horizon, APO compares the SNP Key Figure Sales Order Demand with the SNP Key Figure Forecast and uses the greater of the two before adding the other SNP Demand Key Figures. Again the question when the Forecast Horizon should be set depends on the individual business. The Forecast Horizon should cover the period where the sum of demands as defined in the SNP Key Figure "Sales Order Demand" is more or less stable. It must also be long enough to allow for increased or reduced procurement and/or distribution in the case where the forecast was not correct.

The following graphic shows an example of how the SNP demand key figures relate to each other.

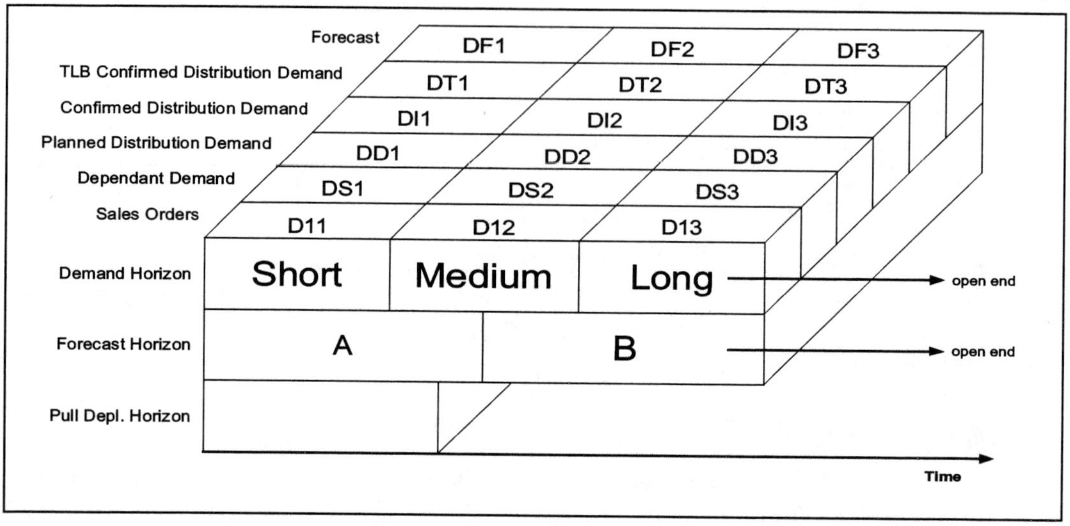


**Graphic 39 – SNP Demand Key Figures Setup**

Underneath is an example of the setup of the SNP Demand Key Figures. Please refer to the chapter ATP Categories for a list of ATP categories, which are linked to the SNP Key Figures, listed here. Also see the SNP Interactive Planning screen chapter where these definitions are used as well. The category group for forecast (DFCST) is also split up into three groups although the same category (FA) is allocated to it always.

| Key Figure | Key Figure Name | Time Segment | Cat. Group | Cat 1 | Cat 2 | Cat 3 | Cat 4 | Cat 5 |
|---|---|---|---|---|---|---|---|---|
| DMDP1 | Sales Order Demand | Short | D11 | BM | | | | |
| | | Medium | D12 | BL | BM | BN | | |
| | | Long | D13 | BK | BL | BM | BN | |
| DMDSE | Dependant Demand | Short | DS1 | AY | EL | | | |
| | | Medium | DS2 | AY | EL | | | |
| | | Long | DS3 | AY | EL | | | |
| DMDD1 | Distribution Demand planned | Short | DD1 | | | | | |
| | | Medium | DD2 | BH | EB | ED | | |
| | | Long | DD3 | BH | EB | ED | | |
| DMDDF | Distribution Demand confirmed | Short | DI1 | | | | | |
| | | Medium | DI2 | EG | EH | | | |
| | | Long | DI3 | EG | EH | | | |
| DMDDT | Distribution Demand TLB confirmed | Short | DT1 | BI | EJ | EK | | |
| | | Medium | DT2 | BI | EJ | EK | | |
| | | Long | DT3 | BI | EJ | EK | | |
| DFCST | Forecast | Short | DF1 | FA | | | | |
| | | Medium | DF2 | FA | | | | |
| | | Long | DF3 | FA | | | | |

**Table 37 – SNP Demand Key Figures**

The table underneath gives an example of a demand time stream. For illustration purposes the SNP Key Figure "Sales Order Demand" is further broken down into its Categories.

SNP

| Horizon | | Short | | | Medium | | | Long | | |
|---|---|---|---|---|---|---|---|---|---|---|
| | | Day | | | | | | | | |
| | | 1 | 2 | 3 | 4 | 5 | 6 | 7 | 8 | 9 |
| SNP Key Figure | Category | | | | | | | | | |
| Sales Order Demand | Total | 100 | 100 | 90 | 80 | 70 | 60 | 135 | 90 | 30 |
| | - Inquiry | | 50 | | 40 | | 10 | 5 | 10 | 0 |
| | - Quotation | 200 | | 20 | 5 | 5 | 10 | 15 | 5 | 5 |
| | - Order | 100 | 100 | 90 | 70 | 40 | 40 | 90 | 60 | 25 |
| | - Schedule | | 100 | | 5 | 25 | 10 | 25 | 15 | 0 |
| Distr. Demand (planned) | | | | 20 | 15 | 15 | 10 | 10 | 5 | 5 |
| Distr. Demand (firmed) | | | 30 | | 15 | 10 | 5 | 0 | 0 | 0 |
| Distr. Demand (TLB firmed) | | 50 | 45 | 40 | 0 | 0 | 0 | 0 | 0 | 0 |
| Dependant Demand | | 10 | 20 | 15 | 10 | 5 | 5 | 5 | 0 | 0 |
| Forecast Demand | | 100 | 100 | 110 | 130 | 160 | 160 | 110 | 140 | 175 |
| Total Demand | | 160 | 165 | 145 | 120 | 100 | 180 | 150 | 145 | 180 |
| | | Forecast Horizon | | | | | | | | |

**Table 38 – SNP Demand Calculation Example**

The gray shaded areas in the upper section of the table indicate which Categories are used to calculate the SNP Key Figure "Sales Order Demand". In the lower section of the table, the gray shaded areas indicate which SNP Demand Key Figures are used to make up the Total Demand.

## 4.3.2 SNP Supply Calculation

Like the Demand definition, the Supply definition is also highly customizable but not to the same degree. As said before, all stock, receipt (supply), and issue (demand) elements are allocated to SNP Categories. For further explanation of ATP Categories as they are also called refer to the chapter "SNP Demand Calculation".

For SNP Supply Calculation purposes, the Category Groups are linked to the SNP Supply Key Figures. There are also three time-different Category Groups per SNP Supply Key Figure. The use of three Category Groups allows defining the supply differently with respect to the Short, Medium, and Long Term Plan. The split into three (not more, not less) time segments is fixed, but if not required the same Category Group could be linked to all three time segments.



Within SNP the following seven Supply Key Figures are defined.

- Planned Production Supply
  Planned production orders are created by the SNP run or interactively by the SNP planner.
- Joint Production
  Joint Production products are also referred to as by products. While manufacturing the main product, the by-product is manufactured at the same time. For APO purposes it is of no interest whether the by-product is manufactured purposely or not. Under the SNP key figure you find only the by-product, not the main product, which can be found under the SNP key figure Planned Production Supply.
- Firmed Production Supply
  Allocated to this key figure should be category groups that contain all such categories that deal with production orders, which are firmed. Objects belonging to these categories and category groups represent orders dealt with by PP/DS. They are already in a finite planning status.
- Planned Distribution Receipt Supply
  In this key figure, planned orders generated by the SNP run should be seen.
- Confirmed Distribution Receipt Supply

In this key figure, planned orders generated by the Deployment run should be seen.

- TLB Confirmed Distribution Receipt Supply
  In this key figure, planned orders generated by the TLB run should be seen.
- In Transit Supply
  In this key figure, all products that have left the sending location but have not yet arrived in the receiving location should be seen.

Note that although APO predefines the Key Figure names, it is up to the implementing team to allocate ATP Groups and ATP Categories appropriately to these Key Figures. The Transport Load Builder (TLB) uses separate definitions for Supply. Please refer to the chapter "Transport Load Builder".



The Total Supply is calculated according to the following formula:

| | |
|---|---|
| Total Supply = | |
| | Firmed Production Supply |
| + | Joint Production |
| + | Planned Production Supply |
| + | Planned Distribution Receipt Supply |
| + | Confirmed Distribution Receipt Supply |
| + | TLB Confirmed Distribution Receipt Supply |
| + | In Transit Supply |

The following graphic shows an example of how the SNP supply key figures relate to each other.

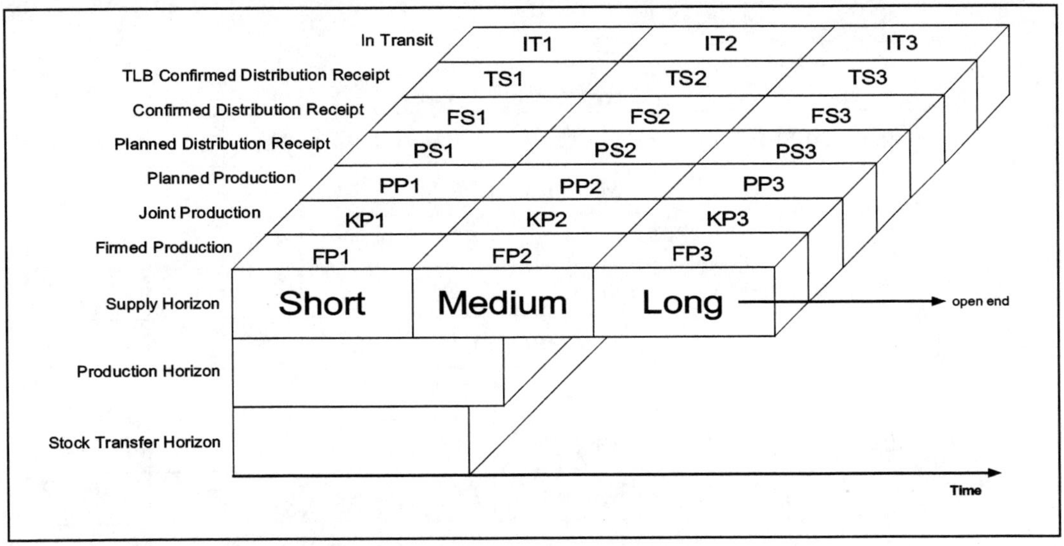


**Graphic 40 – SNP Supply Key Figures Setup**

Underneath is an example of the setup of the SNP Supply Key Figures. Please refer to the chapter ATP Categories for a list of ATP categories, which are linked to the SNP Key Figures listed here. Also see the SNP Interactive Planning screen chapter where these definitions are used as well.

| Key Figure | Key Figure Name | Time Segment | Cat. Group | Cat 1 | Cat 2 | Cat 3 | Cat 4 | Cat 5 |
|---|---|---|---|---|---|---|---|---|
| FPROD | Production firmed | Short | FP1 | AC | AD | | | |
| | | Medium | FP2 | AC | AD | AJ | | |
| | | Long | FP3 | AC | AD | AI | AJ | |
| KPROD | Joint Production | Short | KP1 | | | | | |
| | | Medium | KP2 | EM | | | | |
| | | Long | KP3 | EM | | | | |
| PPROD | Production planned | Short | PP1 | | | | | |
| | | Medium | PP2 | EE | | | | |
| | | Long | PP3 | EE | | | | |
| PSHIP | Distribution Receipt planned | Short | PS1 | | | | | |
| | | Medium | PS2 | | | | | |
| | | Long | PS3 | AG | EA | | | |
| FSHIP | Distribution Receipt confirmed | Short | FS1 | | | | | |
| | | Medium | FS2 | EF | | | | |
| | | Long | FS3 | EF | | | | |
| TSHIP | Distribution Receipt TLB confirmed | Short | TS1 | BF | EI | | | |
| | | Medium | TS2 | BF | EI | | | |
| | | Long | TS3 | BF | EI | | | |
| ITRAN | In Transit | Short | IT1 | EI | | | | |
| | | Medium | IT2 | EI | | | | |
| | | Long | IT3 | EI | | | | |

**Table 39 – SNP Supply Key Figures**

The table underneath gives an example of a supply time stream. For illustration purposes the SNP Key Figure “Firmed Production Supply” is further broken down into its Categories.

| Horizon | | Short | | | Medium | | | Long | | |
|---|---|---|---|---|---|---|---|---|---|---|
| | | Day | | | | | | | | |
| SNP Key Figure | Category | 1 | 2 | 3 | 4 | 5 | 6 | 7 | 8 | 9 |
| Production (firmed) | Total | 150 | 200 | 100 | 50 | 50 | 0 | 100 | 100 | 0 |
| | Pr/O – released | 150 | 150 | 50 | | 30 | | 10 | | |
| | Pr/O – created | | 50 | 50 | 50 | | | 50 | | |
| | Pl/O – firmed | | | 80 | | 20 | | 40 | 50 | |
| | Pl/O – not firmed | | 100 | | 50 | 20 | | | 50 | |
| Joint Production | | | 10 | 70 | 20 | 10 | | | 10 | |
| Production (planned) | | | 20 | 50 | 80 | 90 | 120 | 100 | 140 | 100 |
| Distribution Receipts (planned) | | | 30 | | 20 | | 10 | 50 | 0 | 100 |
| Distribution Receipts (confirmed) | | 10 | | 40 | 50 | 50 | 100 | | | |
| Distribution Receipts (TLB confirmed) | | 0 | 10 | 20 | | | | | | |
| In Transit | | 100 | 90 | 100 | 50 | 0 | 0 | 0 | 0 | 0 |
| Total Supply | | 250 | 300 | 220 | 250 | 200 | 220 | 250 | 250 | 200 |
| | | Production Horizon | | | | | | | | |
| | | Stock Transfer Horizon | | | | | | | | |

**Table 40 – SNP Supply Calculation Example**

The gray shaded areas in the upper section of the table indicate which Categories are used to calculate the SNP Key Figure "Firmed Production". In the lower section of the table, the gray shaded areas indicate which SNP Supply Key Figures are used to make up the Total Supply.

## 4.3.3 ATP Categories

Underneath is a list of ATP categories as defined in APO. Some of these categories are used within SNP to calculate the Demand and Supply situation. This was explained in the previous chapters.

| ATP Category | Short Text | Description |
|---|---|---|
| AA | PrcOrd (C) | Process order (created) |
| AB | PrcOrd (R) | Process order (released) |
| AC | PrdOrd (C) | Production order (created) |
| AD | PrdOrd (R) | Production order (released) |
| AE | NtwOrd (C) | Network order (created) |
| AF | NtwOrd (R) | Network order (released) |
| AG | PurRqs | Purchase requisition |
| AH | PO memo | Purchase order memo |
| AI | PlOrd. | Planned order (not firmed, unconfirmed) |
| AJ | PlOrd. (F) | Planned order (firmed, unconfirmed) |
| AK | PlOrd.(NC) | Planned order (not firmed, confirmed) |
| AL | PlOrd.(CF) | Planned order (confirmed, firmed) |
| AM | MatRes | Material Reservation cannot be withdrawn, location-relevant |
| AN | MatRes (W) | Material Reservation can be withdrawn, location-relevant |
| AO | MatRes (N) | Material Reservation cannot be withdrawn, not location-relev. |
| AP | MatRes(WN) | Material Reservation can be withdrawn, not location-relevant |
| AQ | MatRes | Material Reservation cannot be withdrawn, location-relevant |
| AR | MatRes (W) | Material Reservation can be withdrawn, location-relevant |
| AS | MatRes (N) | Material Reservation cannot be withdrawn, not location-relev. |
| AT | MatRes(WN) | Material Reservation can be withdrawn, not location-relevant |
| AU | OrdRes | Order reservation cannot be withdrawn |
| AV | OrdRes (W) | Order reservation can be withdrawn |

SNP

| ATP Category | Short Text | Description |
|---|---|---|
| AW | OrdRes | Order reservation cannot be withdrawn |
| AX | OrdRes (W) | Order reservation can be withdrawn |
| AY | DepReq | Dependent requirements |
| AZ | DepReq | Dependent requirements |
| BA | SubReq | Subcontractor requirements |
| BB | SubReq | Subcontractor requirements |
| BC | StTRes | Stock transfer reservation |
| BD | StTRes | Stock transfer reservation |
| BE | SchLne | Line in a scheduling agreement |
| BF | PchOrd | Order item schedule line |
| BG | Returns | Purchase order returns item |
| BH | PrqRel | Stock transport requisition |
| BI | ConRel | Stock transport order |
| BJ | SagRel | Scheduling agreement release |
| BK | Inquiry | Customer inquiry |
| BL | Quotation | Customer quotation |
| BM | SalesOrder | Sales order |
| BN | SchAgr | SD scheduling agreement |
| BO | SA-ESA | Scheduling agreement w/external services |
| BP | Contr. | Contract |
| BQ | FreeDelvry | Delivery w/o charge |
| BR | Deliv. | Delivery |
| BS | CusReq | Customer requirements |
| BT | ReturnsDel | Returns delivery |
| BU | QM lot | Inspection lot |
| CA | Stock/tsfr | Stock in transfer (location to location) |
| CB | SafetyStck | Safety stock |
| CC | Stock | Valuated, unrestricted-use stock |
| CD | ConsiStock | Valuated, unrestricted-use consignment stock |
| CE | SubconStck | Valuated, unrestricted-use subcontracting stock |
| CF | InspctnStk | Stock in quality inspection |
| CG | InspConStk | Consignment stock in quality inspection |
| CH | InspSubStk | Subcontracting stock in quality Inspection |
| CI | BlockedStk | Blocked stock |
| CJ | BlckConStk | Blocked consignment stock |

| ATP Category | Short Text | Description |
|---|---|---|
| CK | RstrUseStk | Restricted-use stock |
| CL | RsUseCnStk | Restricted-use consignment stock |
| CM | RsUseSbStk | Restricted-use subcontracting stock |
| CN | TsStkSb | Stock in transfer (storage location to storage location) |
| DD | Stock | Stock |
| EA | SNP: Preq | SNP: Purchase requisition |
| EB | SNP:Rel.PR | SNP: Release for stock transfer requisition |
| EC | VMI-SO | VMI sales order |
| ED | SNP:VMI-SO | SNP: VMI sales order |
| EE | SNP:PL-ORD | SNP: Planned order |
| EF | DEP: Preq | Deployment: Purchase requisition |
| EG | DEP: Preq | Deployment: Release for purchase requisition |
| EH | DEP:VMI-SO | Deployment: VMI sales order |
| EI | TLB: Preq | TLB: Purchase requisition |
| EJ | TLB:Rel.PR | TLB: Release for purchase requisition |
| EK | TLB:VMI-SO | TLB: VMI sales order |
| EL | SNP:DepDmd | SNP: Dependent demand |
| EM | SNP:PL-JP | SNP: Receipt from joint production |
| FA | FC-DEM | Planned independent requirements |

**Table 41 – ATP Categories**



## 4.3.4 Scrap Calculation

APO offers two ways to calculate scrap values. In a top down approach for each product, an assembly scrap value can be defined in the product master. The "Assembly Scrap" is a product dependent parameter. This scrap value applies if the product is the one to be assembled which means it is on the top level of the PPM (or BOM). If the assembly scrap value is maintained, all components required are supplied to the production process in a higher number according to the assembly scrap value. This applies independent of the used PPM.
This option should be used in an environment where, only at the end of the process, the usability of the product can be tested after all components have

already been utilized in the manufacturing process of the product. An example would be the manufacturing of PC motherboards.

A second possibility is a bottom-up approach where scrap value can be defined that applies to the product if it is a component in a PPM (or BOM). The "Component Scrap" is defined in the PPM and is a process dependent parameter. Only the single component will be supplied in a higher number to the production process and only if this is defined in the used PPM. Component Scrap can be defined time dependant.
This option should be used in an environment where, during the production process, components are likely to have different scrap percentages and/or where interim process checks can reveal non-usable products. Examples are multi-step assembly lines with interim quality tests.

Care must be taken if both scrap percentages are used, as the system will calculate scrap values in the top down and bottom up approach.

Example 1: Assembly Scrap

| | |
|---|---|
| Assembly Scrap Value | 20% |
| Required Quantity | 1000 pieces |
| Planned Process Quantity | 1000 pieces/80% = 1250 pieces |

⇒ All components will be supplied with a 25% surplus.

Example 2: Component Scrap

| | |
|---|---|
| Component Scrap Value | 20% |
| Required Quantity | 1000 pieces |
| Planned Process Quantity | 1000 pieces/80% = 1250 pieces |

⇒ The single component will be supplied with a 25% surplus.

## 4.3.5 Version Management

The SNP version is linked to exactly one DP version. This allocation is done in Master Data Maintenance of SNP (option "Version"). An SNP planning version is linked to exactly one model, but each model can be used in conjunction with several planning versions. The active SNP version is "000," the active SNP model is "000" as well. Transactional data is version dependent and as default only the active version "000" contains the transactional data. When copying an SNP version to another as an option, transactional data can be copied across as well.
With the current 2.0 release, only one planning version can be set to be active. In a later release, various planning versions can be flagged as "active". This means that transactional data from an OLTP system will be available to more than one planning version. It will then be possible to define, for example, two supply chain models with their own planning versions, one for each country.
Master data is not copied across planning versions, as it is either model dependent (transportation lanes) or made available for a planning version (e.g. products). Nevertheless, Master Data can be made version specific. This can be done in the respective master data maintenance programs. Note that version-specific master data is not updated when the non-version specific master record is updated. Planning version-specific master data can be deleted using the Version Management function. Note that this function only allows deleting of <u>all</u> version-specific master data.
In DP the various planning versions are used to distinguish the various product forecasts. These different forecast versions are then brought across to SNP into several SNP planning versions where the forecast's feasibility is determined using the same SNP model (paths 0 and 1). In order to carry out a What-If analysis alternative, (different) SNP models could be used to test the feasibility of a certain DP forecast (path 2). Various combinations of these base principles can be set up.

The following example gives an overview of a possible scenario.

- Path 0 is the "active" path (gray shaded)
- Path 1 is used for an alternate forecast based on the current supply network.
- Path 2 is used to test an alternate supply network based on the current forecast.

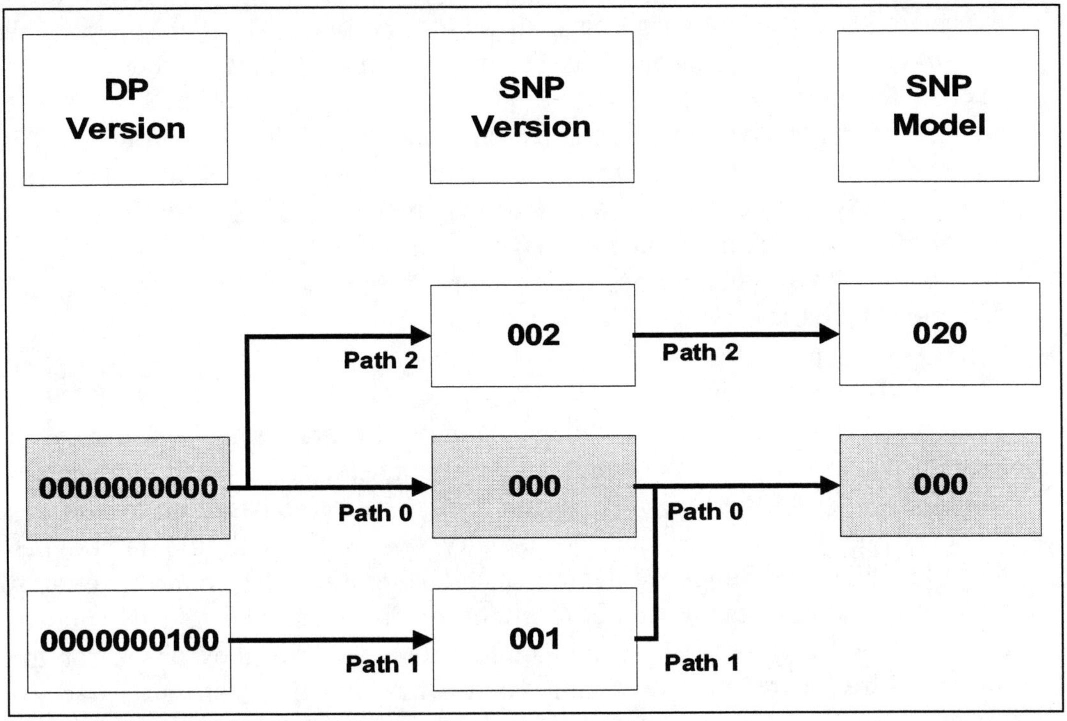


**Graphic 41 – DP & SNP Planning Version**



## 4.3.6 Planning and Optimization

Planning and Optimization can be carried out using three different methods. They vary in terms of the level of optimization on the one side and practicability on the other. They are:

- SNP Heuristics
  This method can be compared to an MPS run in R/3 where products are planned according to the requirements date. During the run backward and forward, scheduling is carried out, but resource capacity constraints are not taken into account. Because the heuristic method does not take any such constraints into account, it is usually the case that the result leads to capacity

overloads. It is the planner's task to adjust the heuristic plan separate per location to achieve a feasible plan. For more information see further down for the chapter Interactive Planning.
Demand is accumulated per period (or time bucket as it is called in APO). The length of the time buckets is freely definable from day to week to month. This method does not consider available capacity (it is infinite) or component availability. Static or dynamic pegging of supply orders back to the originating demand is not possible as Supply Network Planning combines all demands of a certain period into one bucket.

- SNP Optimization
  The SNP Optimizer employs the programming techniques "Linear Programming" and Multiple Integer Linear Programming". All relevant factors such as capacity constraints and available stocks are taken into account simultaneously during the program run. Optimization is based on lowest cost whereby the system uses various penalty costs. The solution is the best feasible plan based on lowest overall cost. The optimum takes into account all defined constraints and costs. It is important to understand that the penalty costs attached to products for non- or late delivery are a key driver for this process. Great care must be taken when setting up the cost data. Static or dynamic pegging of supply orders back to the originating demand is not possible as Supply Network Planning combines all demands of a certain period into one bucket. Optimization is carried out across all locations to derive an overall optimum.
- Capable-To-Match
  Capable-To-Match (CTM) is a planning algorithm, which considers constraints and priorities in the search for a solution. The found solution is feasible but not necessarily optimal as it will stop searching after a feasible solution has been found. Unlike the other procedures in SNP, it uses individual demands, which allows pegging from the supply order through to the originating demand. CTM creates supply orders at one or multiple locations based on available capacities and set priorities. It will return a "Not Capable To Match" message if it cannot find a solution.
  CTM is a tool capable of delivering a result based on the more-detailed Single or Multiple Activity Resource and not only on the simplified Bucket Resource. This is an option, but if used the short-term feasibility of the derived plan is guaranteed. The aforementioned other planning runs are used

to create global plans based on some simplifying assumptions. Both cannot be going down to the operational level as CTM does. Running CTM provides the planner with a quick check to determine any free capacity that could be used for a demand in question. CTM can use the same PPM as Production Planning & Detailed Scheduling and not only the simplified one as the other procedures do.

I dedicated a lot of space to the CTM planning algorithm, as it is a really different way of matching demand and supply. Unfortunately, this functionality is not dealt with adequately, and a lot of questions remain unanswered when going through APO documents or the Help functions.

Each of these methods has got its distinct advantages and disadvantages, which will be explained in the next chapters. It is purely a business decision which method to use, and this decision can be made on a day-by-day basis. Products are not flagged for a certain method; it purely depends on which program is started when performing the planning run. Obviously each of the methods requires some specific master data that need to be maintained.



#### 4.3.6.1 SNP Heuristics

SNP Heuristics is based on the unconstrained plan that was released from Demand Planning. This plan can be released to one or multiple SNP versions thus allowing What-If scenarios. The Heuristics run creates planned orders for production, external procurement and transportation. The decision between these three options is based on settings in the product master and the transportation lane. The product master procurement type on the GR/GI tab determines whether a product is produced at the own location (procurement type "E") or whether it has to be externally procured (procurement type "F"). With the procurement type "X," a check is carried out to determine the appropriate way of procurement. If a quota arrangement exists, external procurement is triggered; otherwise internal procurement is used. External procurement includes procurement at a vendor and transportation from an alternate location. SNP does not require special procurement types, as it is the case in R/3. An existing transportation lane with a valid quota indicates that procurement from the alternate location is permitted (see the chapter Quota Arrangement). The Heuristics is a netting procedure, comparing demand at a location against stock, fixed procurement, and in-transit quantities. Fixed procurement orders include fixed planned orders for production and planned orders for procurement that cannot be changed anymore. Any product, finished or component, that is part of the SNP model is planned.

#### 4.3.6.1.1 Quota Arrangement



Quota Arrangements are used to define the percentages that are shipped from or to one location to the other. They determine the possible sources of supply for planned orders for transportation (from an owned location), as well as for external procurement (from a supplier). Quota Arrangements always refer to a certain product; they are not a global location parameter. In case of planned orders for transportation they replace the "Special Procurement Types" known form R/3, and in case of planned orders for external procurement, they serve as a "Source List" for the product. Quota Arrangements exist on top of the transportation lane, which means they can only be created if a transportation lane exists. Inbound quota arrangements determine how the requirement is split over various possible sourcing locations. Outbound quota arrangements determine how available quantities are distributed. Quota Arrangements are defined in the Supply Chain Engineer.

The technique of supplying products from several locations simultaneously is also referred to as "Multi-Sourcing." SNP offers a Multi-Sourcing per demand technique where every demand is distributed over the sourcing locations according to the quota arrangement. This is unlike the time- dependent quota arrangement where any given demand is supplied from one location only, and the quota arrangement is maintained over time by changing the supplying location.

For a step-by-step instruction to create quota arrangements refer to the chapter "Maintenance of Quota Arrangements".

#### 4.3.6.1.2 Source Determination

With APO, products can have different procurement types that determine whether a product is manufactured in-house, transferred from one location to another on demand, or procured externally. When running the SNP Optimizer or CTM, the system decides dependent on cost parameters (SNP Optimizer) or the category of the supply (CTM) from where a product is sourced. The Heuristics run does not perform any valuation of possible procurement options and needs a set of rules regarding where to obtain a product. This is done using the "Procurement Type," which can be found in the product master GR/GI tab. The options in this field similar than those in R/3 and comprise:

- F — External Procurement
  In case of a product requirement, a purchase requisition is created.
- E — In-house Production
  Creating planned production orders fulfills any requirements.
- X or " " — External Procurement or In-house Production
  With this option, the system firstly tries to create purchase requisitions, and only if this is not possible, planned production orders will be created.
- P — External Procurement Planning
  Products with this procurement type are not planned by APO and will be skipped entirely during the planning run.

Note that there is no "Special Procurement Type" as in R/3. This is not required as the pure existence of a transportation lane defines the possibility to source a product from a location. When creating purchase requisitions in the Heuristics run, the system will first check for quota arrangements. If quota arrangements are maintained, the purchase requisitions will be created according to the quota. More than one purchase requisition can be created for one demand if multiple quotas are maintained. Quota arrangements can only be maintained "on top" of transportation lanes, or in other words, a transportation lane between the product demanding location and the possible source location must exist. A location can represent another (own) location or an external supplier. Purchase requisitions for own locations will finally lead to a planned transport order during deployment, others will become planned orders for purchasing. Should no quota arrangement exist, a purchase requisition without reference to a location is created. This logic is depicted in the following graphic. In this example a demand exists in a distribution center for a product with the procurement type "F" for external procurement.

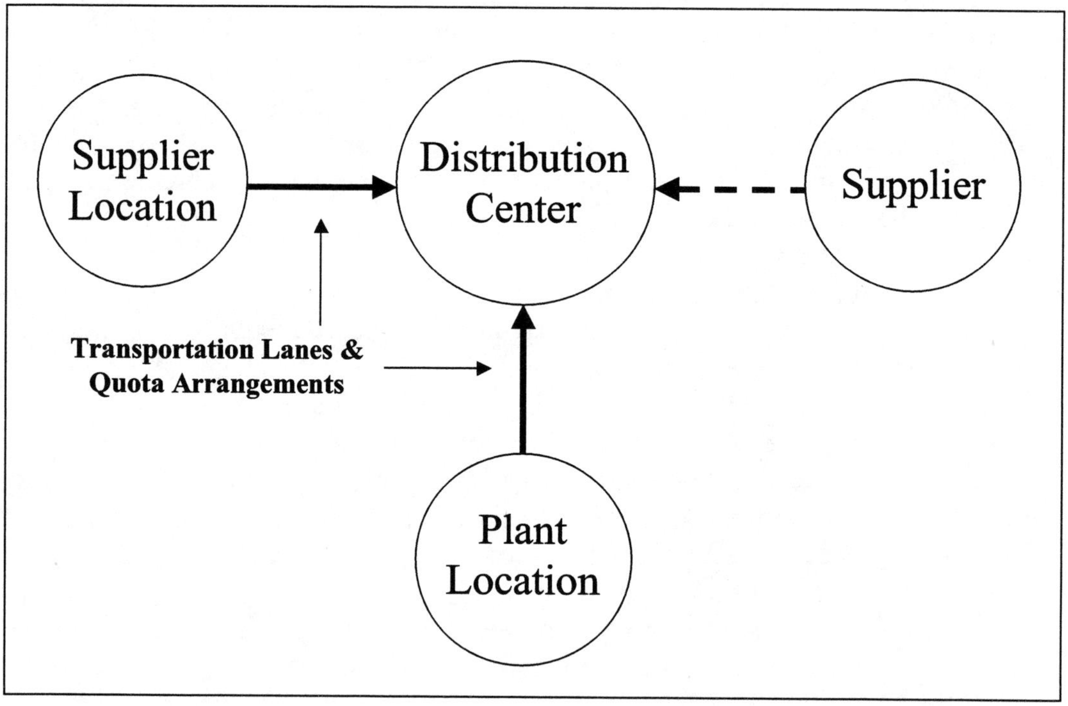


**Graphic 42 – Source Determination**

In all three cases the SNP Heuristics run creates "SNP Purchase Requisitions" in the distribution center location. Additionally, in the plant and supplier location demand elements are created. Quota arrangements can be used for the plant and supplier location only. A supplier that is not defined as a location in APO cannot be allocated a quota.

#### 4.3.6.1.3 Heuristics Planning Run

Following planning modes are available.

- Location
  The Location mode, which is a single-level, single-location approach, works like the Network mode but is restricted to only one or multiple locations. The location run can be performed for more than one location at a time.
- Network
  Only finished products (no components) are planned in this single-level, multi-location approach. Although this is a single-level planning, a PPM explosion is carried out, and such components that are at the same time finished products are planned further. This mode is used when using the <SNP Heuristic> button in the SNP Interactive Planning screen.
- Multi Level
  This is a multi-level, multi-location planning run that plans the entire supply chain for the selected product. It includes the explosion of the PPM's to derive the components' requirements. On-line, which means in the SNP Interactive Planning screen, only one product can be planned at a time. This restriction does not apply to the batch background planning.

The order according to which the planning of products takes place depends on the order of the products in the selection screen. The location sequence for the multi-location planning modes is system determined.

The Heuristics does not consider available capacity (it is infinite) nor is component availability checked. This entails that the planner performs a mandatory capacity leveling after the Heuristics run (see the chapter Capacity Leveling). The output of the Heuristics planning run is planned orders for production, transportation, and/or external procurement.

#### 4.3.6.1.4 Capacity Leveling

The Heuristics uses PPM's of usage type "S" and Bucket Resources. Capacity is loaded into the bucket period without considering sequence constraints. Buckets are loaded as required, as the Heuristics assumes indefinite capacities. This is the same principle as for example with the R/3 MPS run. After the completion of the Heuristics run, the planner must level the capacity to make the plan feasible. In case of a capacity overload situation, an alert is generated to warn the planner. No further support is provided from the Heuristics run for capacity leveling purposes.

A capacity check tool that can be found in the SNP Interactive Planning screen, gives the planner a first overview of the impact the Heuristics run had on the resource capacity. This will immediately show the level of feasibility of the Heuristics plan.



A priority-based capacity leveling program shifts capacity loads to achieve a feasible plan. While performing capacity leveling, only the selected resource is taken into consideration. This means that while leveling one resource, another resource's load might become a problem due to a newly created overload situation. Shifting is carried out as follows:

- Backward
  With this capacity-leveling variant, which should be used to satisfy high priority demand, the system tries to overcome capacity violations by shifting it to an earlier date. This obviously does not constitute a due date violation.
- Forward
  Low priority demand can be shifted further into the future thus causing a due date violation.
- Backward/Forward
  This is a combination of the two variants as described above.

The definition of priorities is based on one of the following options:

- Decreasing (Increasing) Order Quantity
  Level such demand orders first, that have the highest (lowest) order quantity.
- Decreasing (Increasing) Target days Supply
  Level such demand orders first, that have the highest (lowest) target days' supply.
- Decreasing (Increasing) Product Priority
  Level such demand orders first, that have the highest (lowest) product priority.

If no priority rule is defined, the sequence is by random. For additional information on capacity leveling refer to the chapter "SNP Interactive Planning Screen".

### 4.3.6.2 SNP Optimization

The SNP Optimizer is one of the real key benefits available in APO. Whereby R/3 offers with its latest release lots of functionality similar and sometime identical to APO, nothing like the Optimizer can be found there. It is most probably the SNP Optimizer as the hub of an advanced Supply Chain Management, which will make companies adding APO to their existing R/3 installation. This does not mean that there are no good features within SNP; but none of them is as outstanding as the SNP Optimizer and to a certain degree the Deployment Optimizer, which will be discussed later.

The Optimizer is a network-orientated production, transportation, and purchasing planner. It is optimizing the network activities based on user-defined control and penalty costs aiming for the overall lowest cost. Due date and safety stock violations are taken into account via penalty costs associated with these elements. Product source determination is not static according to the master data setup but also follows the lowest cost principle. Dynamic multi-sourcing provides the ability to procure products internally and externally at the same time and dependent on overall lowest cost. In the current release, 2.0, no optimization (selection) of transportation lanes is carried out. The Optimizer uses quota arrangements that can be defined per product (see above). As an option the quota arrangements can be re-calculated (optimized) and the result be used to update the stored quota arrangements.

The Optimizer supports various methods, which are dealt with in the next chapter. The SNP Optimizer and Cost profiles, as well as various other parameters stored in the master data objects, influence the result of the optimization run.

#### 4.3.6.2.1 Optimization Parameters

The optimization run aims to find the solution with the lowest overall cost. This general task is influenced by various objectives that are all expressed in cost. Optimization is a reiterative process where the variables are changed to achieve the objective while considering the constraints. This is depicted in the graphic below. The interdependence of the cost parameters is dealt with in detail in the chapter "Optimization Cost Parameters" further down.



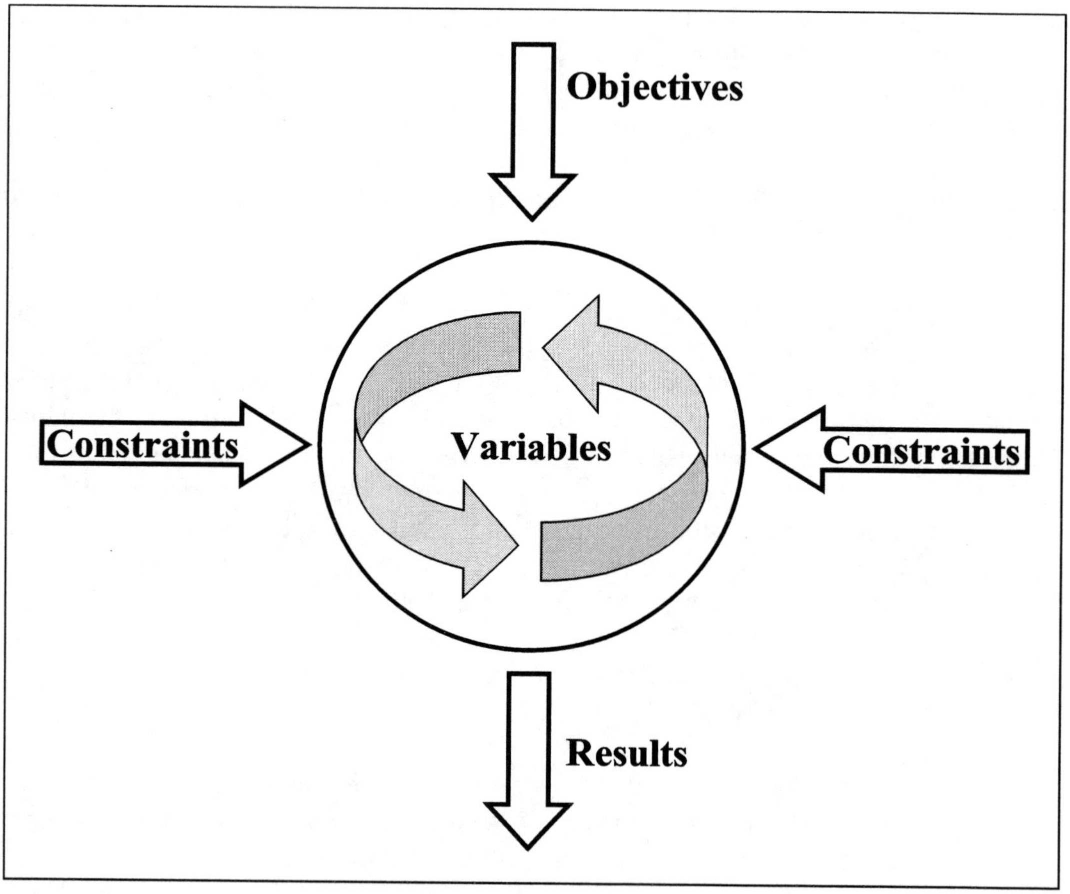


**Graphic 43 – SNP Optimizer Process**

Optimization can only be carried out according to exactly one objective. In the case of the SNP Optimizer, the objective is to minimize the overall cost. This general objective of the optimizer consists of various sub-objectives. The numerical relation of these sub-objectives is defined in the SNP Cost and Optimizer profiles. This is possible as they are all based on one common denominator, which is cost. The sub-objectives are listed below.

- Procurement Cost
  The cost of production (internal procurement) includes the component cost as well as the cost of using a resource. Various PPM's can point to different resources with different cost settings. Alternatively, the buying of the required product (external procurement) needs to be compared as an alternative.
- Transportation Cost
  The transportation cost together with the cost of the product at the alternate location can be compared with the production cost as well as the cost to purchase a product.
- Storage Cost
  The storage cost represents the cost incurred by storing products at a location and is dependent on the product's volume or weight.
- Penalty for Increasing Capacity
  One of the variables for the optimizer is to increase the capacity if shortages occur. Increasing of a capacity is usually only possible with additional costs over and above the normal per unit cost. This cost is expressed separately for production, transportation, storage, and handling capacities.
- Penalty for Late or Non- Demand Satisfaction
  An opportunity cost called Penalty for Late Demand Satisfaction ensures that the Optimizer does not delay deliveries to customers or into stock too much. Penalties are defined separately for non- and late delivery to customers and non- and late delivery into stock.
  The Penalty for Late Demand Satisfaction can be used to optimize on Profit. The higher the anticipated product profit is, the higher the penalty should be set up. If this is the case, the optimizer tries to first and utmost ensure that demands for those products with high penalty (profit) are satisfied first.

The found solution is based on constraints. All but two of these constraints are hard constraints that cannot be ignored. The following constraints are used.

- Production Capacity
  Production Capacity is limited. Two capacity variants are used. One represents the normal capacity, a second one the increased capacity. The usage of the increased capacity will be penalized according to the cost defined in the Penalty for Increasing Capacity parameter. This is a hard constraint as the capacity can only be increased to its maximum.
- Transportation Capacity
  The same as said above applies.
- Handling Capacity
  The same as said above applies.
- Safety Stock
  The decision to keep safety stock is strategic and should be adhered to by the Optimizer as far as possible. This constraint is used to ensure specified safety stock levels are maintained. This is one of the two soft constraints, as the required safety stock level can be violated.
- Demand Due Date
  The second soft constraint is the Demand Due Date. Worst case scenario is that the demand can only be fulfilled later than requested. There is (in theory) no limit to the lateness.

In order to find a solution, the optimizer not only can change the time sequence of events, it can also change some variables so that a solution can be found. The optimizer can use the following decision variables.

- Sourcing
  The product source can be changed between production, transportation, and external procurement.
- Production Lot Size
  The production lot sizes can be changed to achieve the cost optimum.
- Transportation Lot Size
  The transportation lot sizes can be changed to achieve the cost optimum.
- Capacity Increase
  Capacities can be increased within limits to accommodate higher demand than the standard capacity can cope with.

### 4.3.6.2.2 Optimization Methods

APO offers two different methods for the Optimization run. Optimization is a balancing act between trying to achieve the best solution on one side and managing the load (both system and data maintenance) on the other side. Depending on the chosen method, the SNP optimizer program is written using Linear Programming (LP) techniques or Mixed Integer Linear Programming (MILP). The two different methods are as follows:

- Continuous Optimization

  Simplex Based Algorithms using Linear Programming

  The Primal and Dual Simplex Algorithm Method belong to this group that takes all available data into consideration. SAP uses the ILOG library functions called CPLEX. This includes a specific simplex method variation, called the "Interior Point Method". The Interior Point Method can be used as an option. The optimizer detects product flow problems within the network and solves them with special algorithms. The variables used in the Optimizer model are continuous. Continuous variables are such that have no specific possible values but only a valid range. Let me give an example. The quantity that can be moved using a specific transportation lane shall be anything from (obviously) Zero to one thousand tons. We have a continuous variable as it can continuously change from the minimum to the maximum.
- Discrete Optimization

  Branch and Bound Methods using Mixed Integer Linear Programming

  The Discrete Optimization Method is also based on all available data. The main difference form a data point of view is that the used variables are made discrete. Branch and Bound methods covering all possible combinations usually have very long run times. It is therefore important that the optimizer eliminates all non-successful branches as early as possible. This is achieved by applying specialized filtering techniques. Discrete variables have predefined possible values and cannot just be set to any value. If we pick up the example from above, on the transportation lane we can now move goods in multiples of one hundred tons. We now have 11 possible values for the variable (Zero, 100, 200,….. 1,000 tons). Discrete Optimization allows the definition of restrictions to break the complexity of the problem into smaller pieces and thus improving the runtime.
  - Time Decomposition

The optimum solution is always based on a certain time frame. If the start and/or end date of the optimizer run is changed, the result changes as well. The longer the time span, the more data has to be considered, and the longer the run will take. Time Decomposition offers the possibility to break down the time span into smaller time buckets. The solution for each time bucket takes much less time than the solution for the entire time span. If, for example, a time span of four weeks is subdivided into four one-week buckets, the time to find the optimal solution for each of the one week buckets is much less than a fourth of what it would take without Time Decomposition. With this method the buckets are optimized sequentially. The result is not an overall optimum but various sub-optimums.

- Product Decomposition
  The Product Decomposition method groups products and then finds an optimum solution for one group of products after the other. The number of product groups can be defined in the SNP Optimizer profile. The higher the number of product groups, the more the result will deviate from the overall optimum.
- Priority Decomposition
  With Priority Decomposition the optimizer works sequentially through the solution finding process by grouping problems of the same priority. Priority for customer demand is set to 1, for forecast demand to 2. The safety stock priority can be set to 1, 2, or 6. The highest priority problem is solved first, followed by the next highest and so on.

A note on the side to those who love to check whether a program is working properly and returning the correct result. A very basic data setup in a test environment has most probably already a few thousand if not a million possible scenarios. To follow them up manually is absolutely impossible. In a typical live environment, the amount of data and resulting possibilities is enormous. What is left for the user is to trust that the programming was done correctly.

#### 4.3.6.2.3 Optimization Cost Parameters

The SNP Cost and Optimizer profiles contain various factors that are used when the total cost for an SNP plan is calculated. The cost of the various objects is specified in the master data of these objects. The cost structure elements that are used by the Optimizer when applying capacity variant 1 (normal capacity) and 2 (increased capacity) can be seen in the following table.

| Cost Element | | Capacity Variant 1 | Capacity Variant 2 |
|---|---|---|---|
| Resource | Production | | X |
| | Transport | (X) * | X |
| | Transport Product Specific | X | |
| | Storage | (X) * | X |
| | Storage Product Specific | X | |
| | Handling | | X |
| PPM Header | | X | X |
| Product Priority | Late Delivery | X | X |
| | Non Delivery | X | X |
| Safety Stock | | X | X |

**Table 42 – Cost Elements**

- The product independent transport and storage costs are only used as long as no product specific transport and/or storage is defined.

The cost parameters are the driving force behind the result of the Optimizer. When implementing APO, it is necessary to carefully plan the cost parameters and run a lot of test runs with different sets of parameters to understand their impact on the result.

#### 4.3.6.2.4 Optimization Planning Run

The SNP optimizer can be started from the Interactive Planning screen. In this case the SNP planning version and the time frame defined on the initial screen are used as input parameters for the Optimizer run. When starting the Optimizer, the Optimizer and Cost profile have to be specified. The used master data is as defined in the SNP model that is attached to the SNP version. Depending on the planning method, all or only a subset of the products is used in planning. The SNP Optimizer can also be carried out as a background job.

The output of the SNP optimizer run is planned orders for production, transportation, and/or purchasing. The orders are created in liveCache and are accessible for further processing. Alerts are created as and when required. They can be seen in the Supply Chain Cockpit and the Interactive Planning screen.



### 4.3.6.3 Capable-To-Match

Capable-To-Match (CTM) allows an efficient match of demand and supply specifically in situations with supply shortages. It can be used to create mid-term production and distribution plans just as the Heuristics or the Optimizer. The difference compared to the other two SNP planning tools is that it can use also the more detailed Single/Multi Activity Resources. Therefore it can consider sequencing constraints in the resource and thereby delivering a short-term feasible plan. Furthermore demands can be pegged with supplies. CTM uses Constraint Based Propagation techniques, which is a combination of traditional program logic and artificial intelligence. CTM uses the ILOG library for fast constraint propagation.
Three different planning methods are available. These methods allow selection according to the "pegging" status of a certain product in demand. Pegged orders are orders where a specific demand object is linked to production orders and/or other supply objects (e.g. stock or planned order for procurement). SAP talks of an "Order Net" where these objects can be linked (pegged) or not.

- A pegged demand is a demand where a link exists between the demand (e.g. a sales order) and a supply element (e.g. the production order to satisfy the sales order demand). Pegging works in both ways, which means that it is also possible to trace from a supply through to the demand. Pegging can be "Fixed" or "Dynamic." Typically sales orders in a make to order environment have a fixed pegging relation to a production order. The planner can fix a dynamic pegging link. Any pegging relation that is not fixed (yet) is dynamic.
- Unpegged demands are all of those where no relation exists between demand and supply. In other words, we have a requirement, but no source has been defined yet to satisfy this demand.
- An order that also exists in an OLTP system (e.g. R/3) is seen as a "fixed order" by definition. This ensures that the APO CTM run will not change anything during the planning run that is already dealt with in the OLTP system. The fixing of an order must not be confused with its pegging relation that can be fixed or dynamic.

Pegging techniques are further explained in the PP/DS section. CTM is a network-oriented planning tool that considers the planning situation along the entire supply chain in all locations. It checks stocks as well as procurement and transportation constraints. However it does not work out an optimal, but a feasible solution.



#### 4.3.6.3.1 CTM Planning Methods

In order to understand the different CTM planning methods, we have to discuss what a fixed planned order is. A planned order is set to "fixed" by the planner when it should not be changed (re-planned) anymore. In R/3 this was called "firming" of an order. In addition to this manual fixing procedure, all planned orders that were transmitted to an OLTP system are fixed automatically in APO. This is done to avoid further processing of an order in APO while the OLTP system probably changes it. Caution should be exercised as to not mix up fixed (or firmed) planned orders with such that have a fixed pegging relation! The three CTM planning methods are as follows.

1. Plan only unpegged orders

This is used typically if a new demand arises which has not been catered for before. The result will be that the system shows when and where it is possible to squeeze in a planned order to satisfy the new demand. It also checks all component requirements.

- ➢ Existing planned orders, which have a fixed or dynamic pegging relation, including fixed orders are not considered.
- ➢ The result is the first best supply fit for the new demand.

2. Plan all except orders with fixed pegging relations
   In this case all planned orders with no fixed pegging link will be re-planned. This option is helpful to re-plan all planned orders with no fixed pegging relation due to an assumed inefficient production plan or because circumstances have changed since the last optimization run (e.g. an unexpected breakdown of a resource). Existing orders are re-planned, but will not be deleted (the pegging link remains the same). In a case where new demands have arisen since the last planning run, this method will optimize both, existing orders with no fixed pegging relation, and those that have to be created additionally. Existing orders are re-planned, but not deleted. New planned orders might be created.
   - ➢ Existing planned orders, which have fixed pegging relations and all fixed orders are not considered.
   - ➢ The result is the first best supply fit for all demand except those where fixed pegging relations or fixed orders already existed.
3. Re-plan all orders
   With this method all planned orders with fixed or dynamic pegging link are deleted together with their respective pegging relation. This enables a from-scratch planning for all those orders, which do not have a fixed or dynamic pegging relation.
   - ➢ Existing planned orders that also exist in an OLTP system are not considered.
   - ➢ The result is the first best supply fit for all demand except those where fixed planned orders existed already.

The following table provides an overview of the CTM planning methods and the conditions under which an order is planned or re-planned by the respective method. Only if all conditions in a row for a given product are true, CTM will consider the planned order.

| | Pegging Relation | | | Order Situation | |
|---|---|---|---|---|---|
| CTM Planning Method | Not Pegged | Dynamic | Fixed | Fixed | Active in OLTP |
| 1 | Yes | n/a | n/a | n/a | n/a |
| 2 | Yes | Yes | No | No | No |
| 3 | Yes | Yes | Yes | Yes / No | No |

**Table 43 – CTM Planning Methods**



### 4.3.6.3.2 CTM Planning Approach

CTM matches prioritized demand with categorized supply. What does this mean? Each demand element (e.g. sales order or forecast demand) is allocated a priority. The most important demand element receives the highest priority, the second most important the second highest priority and so on. As CTM is a method that tries to satisfy important demand first, the prioritization must be carried out carefully. This prioritization does not have to be carried out manually. It is rules-based. The prioritization can be based on the following parameters.

- Customer — A customer that is defined in APO as a location can have a priority setting in the location master. This means that CTM can only prioritize customers that are defined in the Supply Chain Engineer.
- Product — Each product can have a priority defined in the product master SNP2 tab.
- Order Type — The order type reflected by the ATP category can be given a priority.
- Due Date — No setting is required as CTM works on an oldest first (first come – first served) principle.

Each demand element is prioritized according to the four definitions above. The prioritization definition is carried out on the Demand tab of the CTM Overview screen. It is not required to define rules for all these priorities. In fact none of them need to be defined. In this case the only, and obvious, priority is the date.

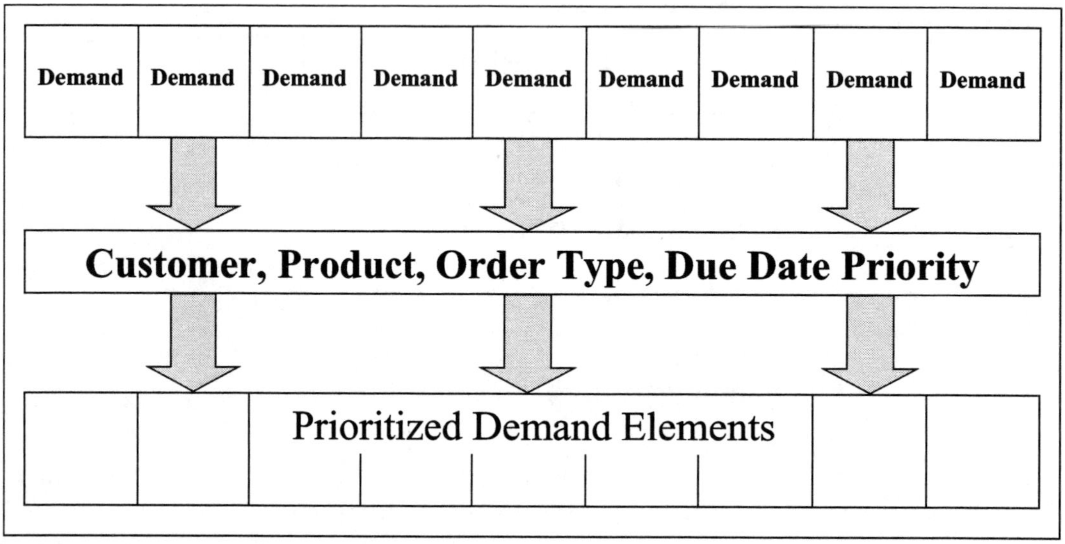




**Graphic 44 – Demand Prioritization**

In addition to the prioritized demand, CTM requires that all supply elements be categorized. The term supply element refers to stock (inventory) and to planned orders for external procurement. Planned orders for internal procurement cannot be made a supply element.

The first step in supply categorization is the definition of the supply categories. Up to 6 categories can be used in a single CTM planning profile. Each supply category will be allocated to the search strategy and be given upper and lower limits for which they will be valid.

<u>Example:</u>

Step 1: We create the supply categories "Supply Category 1" through "Supply Category 6". Supply Category 6 will be the one with the highest limits indicating the "worst" overstock situation. Supply Category 5 will be the one with next highest limits and so on.

Step 2: Now all the 6 supply categories are allocated to the search strategy "SS01". We want this strategy to search first for supply elements of supply category 6, then for such in supply category 5 and so on. If no supply elements are found in the supply categories 6 through 3, we want CTM to check for production possibilities and if that fails the search must continue in supply category 2 and then 1. The search strategy will look like this:

| Sequence | Supply Category Number | Supply Category Name |
|---|---|---|
| 1 | 6 | Supply Category 6 |
| 2 | 5 | Supply Category 5 |
| 3 | 4 | Supply Category 4 |
| 4 | 3 | Supply Category 3 |
| 5 | ** | **** Production **** |
| 6 | 2 | Supply Category 2 |
| 7 | 1 | Supply Category 1 |

**Table 44 – Search Strategy SS01**



In sequence 5 we have the supply category "**" which defines production. It is automatically included in the table, and we only have to stipulate its sequence number.

Step 3: We now need to define upper and lower limits for each of the supply categories per product and location. This is referred to as defining the Supply Limits. Our Supply Limit ID is "001" and we give it the name "Supply Limit 001". Supply Limits also have a validity period, let's say from 01.01.99 through to 31.12.99. As we have 6 different supply categories, we will define 5 supply limits. Supply limits are cascaded. This means that Limit Number 1 in the supply limit table is the upper limit for supply category 1 and as well the lower limit for supply category 2. Limit Number 5 is the upper limit for supply category 5 and the lower one for supply category 6. Supply category 6 does not have an upper limit. The Supply Limit table for product X1 at location LA looks as follows:

| Product | Location | Dates | | Limits | | | | |
|---|---|---|---|---|---|---|---|---|
| | | Start | End | 1 | 2 | 3 | 4 | 5 |
| X1 | LA | 01.01. 1999 | 31.12. 1999 | 100 | 200 | 300 | 400 | 500 |

**Table 45 – Supply Limits 001 (1)**

We could also add other products and/or locations to this table as well as different validity dates for the same location product. This task might become extremely laborious when dealing with a few hundred products at various locations and with changing supply limits. We will later see how default values can be used that are defined independent of products. The table above stipulates that any supply element of product X1 at location LA that exceeds a quantity of 500 belongs to supply category 6, any between 400 and 500 belongs to category 5 and so on. Should we have a demand for product X1, CTM will check for the search strategy and react accordingly. Three scenarios are of interest. The Demand is assumed to be 50 on 01.11.99.

1. Total Supply Element Quantity = 350
   The quantity 350 points to supply category 4.
   The search strategy SS01 determines that supply elements in groups 6 through 3 must be used before production is invoked. This results in a match of the demand with an existing supply element.
2. Total Supply Element Quantity = 150
   The quantity 150 points to supply category 2.
   The search strategy SS01 determines that only supply elements in groups 6 through 3 must be used before production is invoked. As there is not sufficient supply, CTM will check whether enough

capacity and components are available to raise a planned order for production for product X1.

2a. This procedure results in a match of the demand with a planned order if capacities and components are available,

or

2b. the search for supply elements will be continued if not enough capacity and/or components are available. In this case, as we have 150 on hand, the demand will be matched with an existing supply element (in supply category 2).

3. Total Supply Element Quantity = 10
The quantity 10 points to supply category 1.
This scenario is an extension of 2a or 2b. If we follow the 2a logic, there is no difference. In the case of 2b, where not sufficient capacity and/or components are available, the demand cannot be matched.

This is a basic example that could be refined much further incorporating safety stock options, CTM constraints, and so on. One major drawback up to now was that we have to define the supply limits per location product. CTM also offers the usage of default values. These default values can be defined from the supply limit screen. After the supply limits per location product are captured, a time stream needs to be generated (button "Generate Periods Ctrl+F8"). Define in the upcoming screen for which location products you want to generate the time stream (button "Change"), the period dates for the time stream, and up to 5 default limits. Leave the "Overwrite Existing Periods" flag cleared and the "Continuous" flag on. Then generate the periods.



Example:

| Product | Location | Dates | | Limits | | | | |
|---|---|---|---|---|---|---|---|---|
| | | Start | End | 1 | 2 | 3 | 4 | 5 |
| X1 | LA | 01.01. 1999 | 31.12. 1999 | 100 | 200 | 300 | 400 | 500 |
| * | * | 01.04. 1999 | 31.10. 1999 | 10 | 20 | 30 | 40 | 50 |

**Table 46 – Supply Limits 001 (2)**

The periods are generated for the period from 01.04.1999 through to 31.10.1999. The 5 default values are 10, 20, 30, 40, and 50. Our supply limit table from above does not change its appearance on the screen, but we can assume that it logically looks like this. The asterisk is a placeholder for any location product that was defined in the selection when generating the periods but does not have its own supply limit values. Further note that the default values have their own distinct validity period.

During the supply categorization step, each supply element is linked to a supply category. Supply elements as well as supply categories have quantities that do not necessarily match. In such a case the supply elements can either be split across several supply categories or be linked to the lowest level supply category. The "Split Supply" flag on the Supply tab drives this.



Example:

| **Supply Element** | **Quantity** | | **Supply Category** |
|---|---|---|---|
| | **Single** | **Cumulated** | |
| 1 | 60 | 60 | 1 |
| 2 | 60 | 120 | |
| 3 | 60 | 180 | 2 |
| 4 | 60 | 240 | |
| 5 | 60 | 300 | 3 |
| 6 | 60 | 360 | 4 |
| 7 | 60 | 420 | |
| 8 | 60 | 480 | 5 |
| 9 | 60 | 540 | |
| 10 | 60 | 600 | 6 |
| 11 | 60 | 660 | |
| 12 | 60 | 720 | |

**Table 47 – Supply Element Allocation without Split**

On a specific day we have 15 supply elements (e.g. planned orders for procurement) with a quantity of 60 each. The supply limits are as defined in the previous example above. If the "Split Supply" flag is not set the following allocation will be carried out:

Splitting of a supply element so that it can belong to more than one supply category has no impact on the underlying planned order; it merely means that the same supply element is member of more than more supply category. If the "Split Supply" flag is set the following allocation will be carried out:

| Supply Element | Quantity | | Supply Category |
|---|---|---|---|
| | Single | Cumulated | |
| 1 | 60 | 60 | 1 |
| 2 | 40 | 100 | |
| | 20 | 120 | 2 |
| 3 | 60 | 180 | |
| 4 | 20 | 200 | |
| | 40 | 240 | 3 |
| 5 | 60 | 300 | |
| 6 | 60 | 360 | 4 |
| 7 | 40 | 400 | |
| | 20 | 420 | 5 |
| 8 | 60 | 480 | |
| 9 | 20 | 500 | |
| | 40 | 540 | 6 |
| 10 | 60 | 600 | |
| 11 | 60 | 660 | |
| 12 | 60 | 720 | |

**Table 48 – Supply Element Allocation with Split**

Splitting of the supply elements has an even bigger impact if rather big supply elements exist. If we assume for example that we had, instead of 12 discrete supply elements with a quantity of 60, each only one big supply element with a quantity of 720, then the whole supply element would have been allocated to supply category 1.

The following graphic provides an overview of the Supply Categorization procedure.

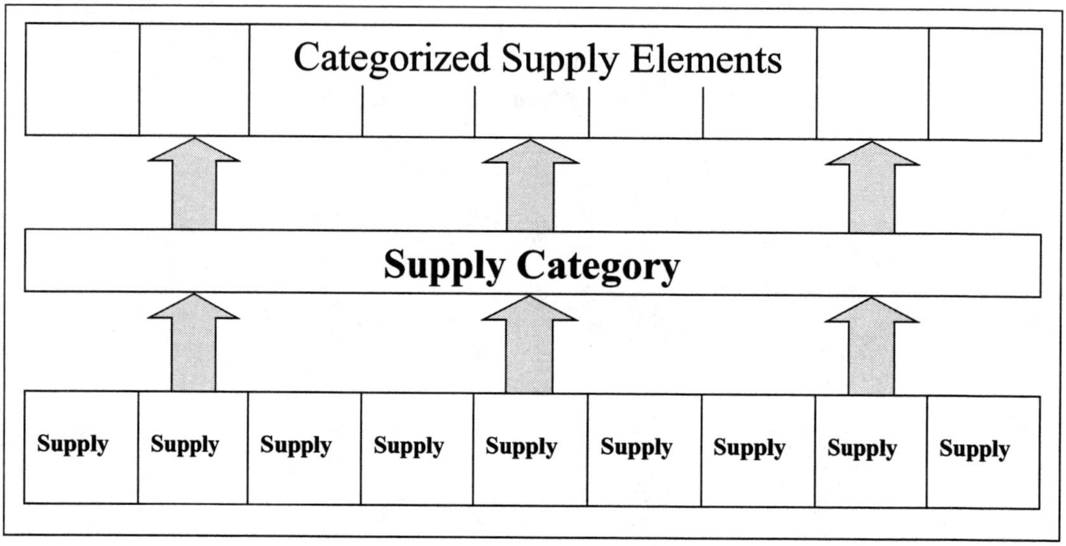


**Graphic 45 – Supply Categorization**

In a first step demand prioritization and supply categorization is carried out, then CTM searches sequentially according to the search strategy through all supply categories and exploits the production and transportation capabilities. The search is hierarchical and independent of the location of a product. In the above example, CTM first searches for supply elements of supply category 6 in all locations as defined in the SNP model or in the CTM work area if a CTM work area is defined (search before production). Only if this search is not successful, the supply elements of supply category 5 are checked, and again this happens across all locations as defined. This search is continued through supply categories 4 and then 3 before an attempt is made to check for production. Should production not be feasible, the search continues through supply categories 2 and 1 (search after production). Should this also be unsuccessful, the demand cannot be matched.

While checking the transportation and production capabilities during the search, CTM checks for the first feasible solution in terms of transportation and production capacity as well as component availability. If a feasible solution was found, the search stops and the demand is matched.

Therefore CTM provides <u>a feasible</u> and <u>not an optimum</u> solution.

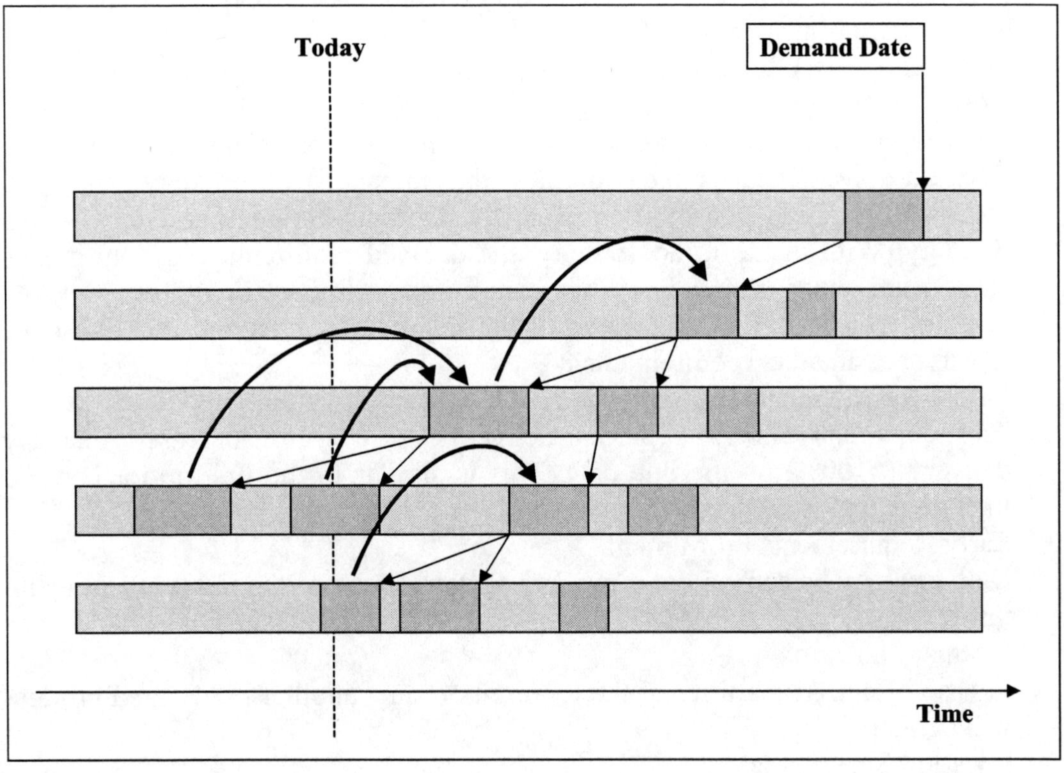


**Graphic 46 – CTM Search Tree**

The diagram above depicts such a search. Starting from the requested demand date, CTM checks all levels. It backs up to the next higher level and "closes" this branch if a constraint violation is encountered. The curved lines upwards indicate such a back up. After CTM finds a solution, it stops the search. For this reason it does not check another feasible solution. The non-adjoined blocks show this situation.

#### 4.3.6.3.3 Rules Based CTM

CTM allows influencing the demand-supply matching process by using customer specific constraints. This allows a high degree of control as various factors can be used to influence how the matching of demand and supply is carried out. Following constraints can be defined:

1. Delayed (partial) Requirements Fulfillment
   With this option, also referred to as "Partial Shipment," the delivery can be delayed either entirely or partially by a definable maximum number of days. The Late Demand Strategy defines the impact of the delay on other requirements. Two possibilities exist, the Domino Strategy and the Airline Strategy. With the Domino strategy, the delayed requirement will influence (delay) all other demands. When using the airline strategy, the delayed demand will be shifted to the end of the requirements list and thus not have any impact on other requirements.
2. Partial Requirements Fulfillment
   This constraint allows a partial delivery (<100%) or increased quantity delivery (>100%) on the due date. This is similar to the first option, but no time deviation is allowed.
3. Early Requirements Fulfillment
   Delivery may be carried out a number of days ahead of the requirement using this option.
4. Product Substitution
   In case of non-availability of the required product another predefined product will be delivered.
5. Location Substitution
   Can the required product not be delivered from the requested location another location will be used for shipment.

The following graphic illustrates options 1 through 3.

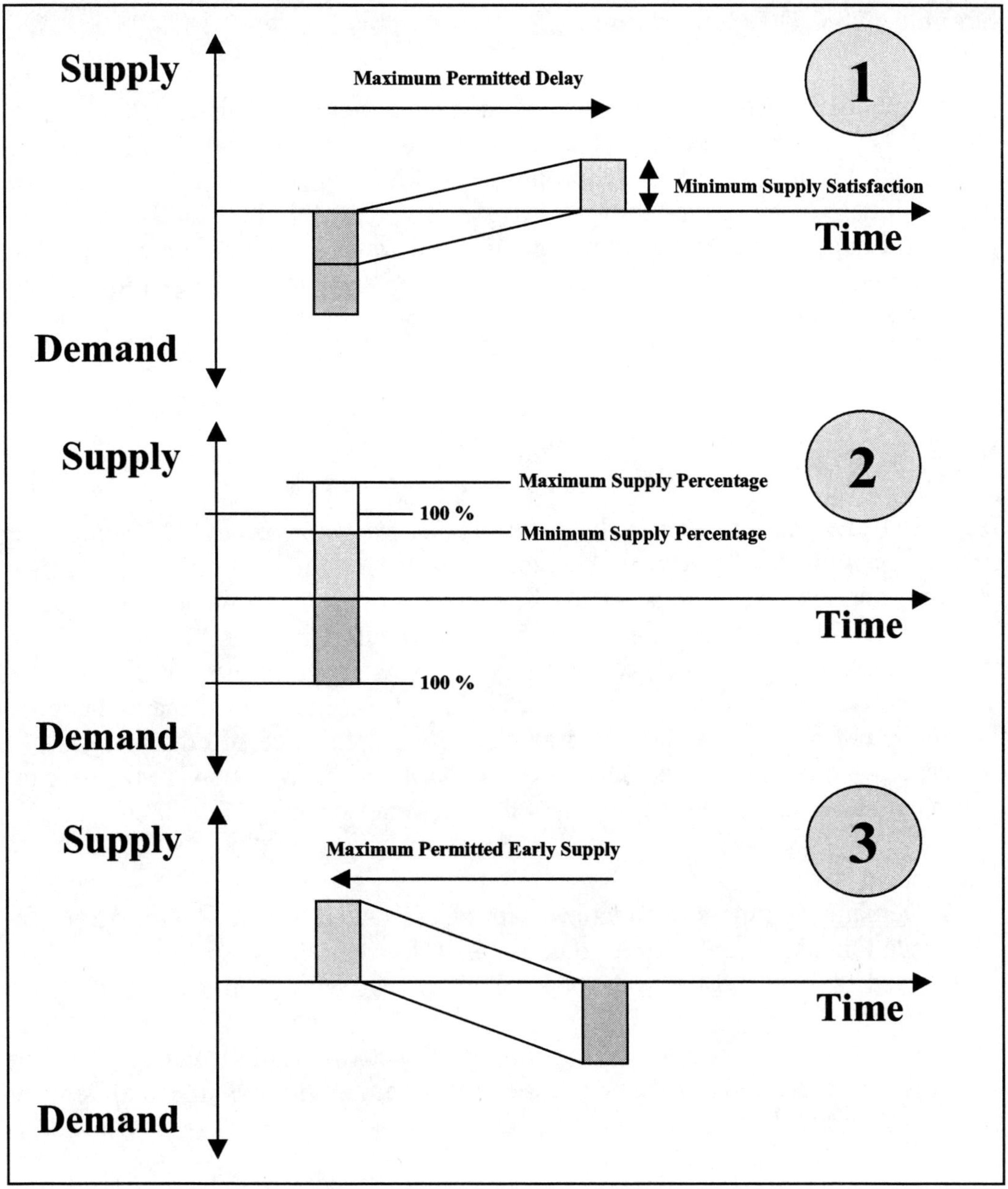

1
Supply
Demand
Maximum Permitted Delay
Minimum Supply Satisfaction
Time
2
Supply
Demand
Maximum Supply Percentage
100 %
Minimum Supply Percentage
Time
100 %
3
Supply
Demand
Maximum Permitted Early Supply
Time


SNP

**Graphic 47 – CTM Constraints**

Constraints defined on customer level use ATP principles. This entails that Rule Based CTM works only after at least some of the ATP customizing has been carried out. For the constraints 1 through to 3 default values can be defined in the CTM Global Customizing Settings Profile. They are applied in the case of a supply shortage where no customer specific constraint settings are maintained. In this chapter we will not go through all requirements and settings required for activation of Rules Based CTM.



#### 4.3.6.3.4 CTM Overview Screen

The CTM Overview screen is the maintenance program for the CTM planning profile. Besides this function it has some other functionality built in, which is really worth looking at. These accessories are really good, and it stands to reason that the same level of user support will be implemented in other APO areas. Some of the functionality is accessed directly on a tab, other via the Edit menu. Alternatively, a dedicated button exists. These options include the maintenance of the four CTM profiles as described above, the maintenance of other profile like entries, and additionally the functions as described below. The CTM Overview screen can be accessed via the SNP and PP/DS menu structure.

- Demand Tab
  A Demand Simulation function can be activated on this tab. After this simulation has been carried out, a "List Demand" button appears. When selected, a list is displayed showing all demands with the CTM assigned priority.
  This function might not work properly if activated immediately after the profile was created. In such a case, it is required to exit the maintenance session and go back into it.

- Supply Tab

A Supply Simulation function can be activated on this tab. After this simulation has been carried out, a "List Supply" button appears. When selected, a list is displayed showing all supplies with the CTM assigned category.
This function might not work properly if activated immediately after the profile was created. In such a case, it is required to exit the maintenance session and go back into it.

- Edit Menu
  The function "Check Your Data" is my favorite. It can also be started using a menu button, which looks like a scale. After it has been activated, master data required for the CTM run is checked for completeness and logical coherence. On the upcoming screen, the test can be limited as required. At the end of the check, an interactive list is displayed. It is grouped according to the master data used in CTM. The elements are as follows.
  - Location Products
  - PPM's
  - Resources
  - Shipments (means Transportation Lanes)

  Location information, which is also used by CTM, is unfortunately not included in this check. Any area where problems were encountered is yellow-shaded. Simply drill down to the master data object involved to finally see the data which the system questions.



#### 4.3.6.3.5 CTM Planning Run

CTM is a method that requires that all demands are prioritized and all supplies be categorized. The priority of a demand is not an attribute of the demand element (e.g. the sales order), nor is the category of a supply element an attribute of it. The categorization and prioritization is carried out dynamically and based on the respective CTM profile setting every time a CTM planning run is started. For this reason, the CTM run is carried out in a multi step procedure.
Step 1: Demand Prioritization

Starting the "Simulation" function in the CTM Overview screen tab "Demand" can simulate this step. Doing so provides an overview of how CTM will prioritize demands.

Step 2: Supply Categorization
Starting the "Simulation" function in the CTM Overview screen tab "Supply" can simulate this step. Doing so provides an overview of how CTM will categorize supplies.

Step 3: Build CTM Application Model
In this step all other CTM rules as specified in the CTM profiles are linked to the model. Rules as specified in Rules Based CTM are attached to the model. This is the preparation of the "CTM engine" start.

Step 4: Match Demand and Supply
The matching takes place on a dedicated CTM engine server or on the APO server. In either case the destination (RFC Destination) has to be defined in customizing.

Step 5: Delete, create, and update orders in liveCache
The result of the CTM run is finally used to update the liveCache.



The Optimizer creates reports that are accessible from the SNP menu under the Reporting option. The reports provide the resulting overall costs as well as its components. It is very helpful top evaluate the results when performing a what-if analysis.

- The Optimizer Log Data report provides statistics about the optimization run.
- The Backlog Report provides information about products with requirements in the past.

Should no report be available, check the table /SAPAPO/SNPOPT. In order to store reports, the field "LGNUM" should have a value of greater than Zero.

### 4.3.7 Comparison

APO offers three different planning methods, which immediately poses the question why one needs more than one and which one is the best. Before this question can be answered we should have a look at the factors considered by the three planning methods. This is done in the table underneath.

| | Heuristics | Optimizer | CTM |
|---|---|---|---|
| Lot Sizing | X | X | X |
| Calendar | X | X | X |
| Safety Stock | X | X | X |
| Lead Times | X | X | X |
| Scrap Parameters | X | X | X |
| Component Availability | X | X | X |
| Transportation Lanes | X | X | X |
| Quota Arrangement | Uses | Updates | |
| Production Capacity | | X | X |
| Transportation Capacity | | X | |
| Handling Capacity | | X | |
| Storage Capacity | | X | |
| Costs | | X | |
| Alternate Resource | | X | |
| Alternate PPM | | X | |
| PPM Time Dependent Parameters | | X | X |
| Product Priority | | X | X |
| Location Priority | | | X |
| Demand (Customer) Priority | | | X |
| Supply Category | | | X |
| Constraints | | | X |
| Pegging Network | | | X |

**Table 49 – SNP Planning Strategies**

Basic requirements are obviously met by all three planning methods. The main difference between the Heuristics and the Optimizer is that the Heuristics does not consider any capacities or costs. Costs are not considered by CTM either, but therefore it has a whole set of priority rules other than cost. The next table provides an overview of the results offered by the three planning methods.

| | **Heuristics** | **Optimizer** | **CTM** |
| --- | --- | --- | --- |
| Multi Location | X | X | X |
| Feasible Infinite Plan | | X | X |
| Optimized Plan | | X | |
| Feasible Finite Plan | | | X |
| Pegging | | | X |

**Table 50 – SNP Planning Run Results**



We see that all three methods are multi-location capable, but only the Optimizer can provide a cost optimized plan. Both, the Optimizer and CTM create feasible plans but based on different goals. The Optimizer plan is cost-optimized; the CTM plan is just feasible but not optimized. An advantage of CTM is that it also offers finite scheduled orders thus ensuring that the derived plan is feasible down to the operational (PP/DS) level. As a "by-product," CTM creates a pegging network as it can use time-continuous resources.

The Optimizer should be used in an environment where there is space to optimize. In situations governed by product shortages and/or late deliveries, CTM might be the better solution. This is specifically true when there is a business requirement to match demand and supply customer specific with different sets of rules. One must also not underestimate the amount of work that has to be put into the maintenance of cost (penalty) parameters for the Optimizer and into the supply categorization and demand prioritization for CTM. Where is the place for the Heuristics? The Heuristics can be used if neither of the constraints described above are valid for the business or in situations where the mid-term plan is not too difficult to maintain manually. I doubt that the typical APO user falls under this category. There is nevertheless a very good application for the Heuristics. In situations where either the Optimizer or CTM is used as the standard method, it makes sense to run the Heuristics for "checking" purposes. The benefit of using, for example, the Optimizer is that it detects bottlenecks automatically and creates plans that avoid an over-usage of certain resources. This usually comes at a price but is transparent to the planner. The Heuristics just loads resources as needed and will therefore point immediately to resources that are bottlenecks. This is a helpful exercise as it is good business practice to investigate why certain bottlenecks exist and what can be done to solve the problem in the future. The minimum the planner can do, then, is ensure his or her attention on these identified bottleneck resources identified by the Heuristics.

Last but not least, a word about the runtime. It comes without surprise that the Heuristics is the fastest. The Optimizer requires the most processing power with CTM being in-between.



### 4.3.8 Deployment

The aim of the Deployment run is to generate a Transport Plan, which identifies all required movements between plants, distribution centers, customers (including VMI) and suppliers. Deployment compares existing demand based on the Supply Network Plan with available stocks at the various locations. The deployment activity takes place directly after planning and optimization has taken place (in a pure trading environment) or alternatively after finite scheduling in PP/DS and production has been finished (in a production environment). The SNP Heuristics, the SNP Optimizer, and CTM create planned transport orders. So does the Deployment run and the Transport Load Builder. The difference is the planned orders ATP category and thus allocation to an SNP Key Figure. The following table gives an example.

| SNP Supply Key Figure | ATP Category | ATP Category Name | Generated by |
|---|---|---|---|
| Distribution Receipt planned | EA | SNP Purchase Requisition | SNP Heuristics, Optimizer, or CTM |
| Distribution Receipt confirmed | EF | Deployment Purchase Requisition | Deployment Heuristics or Optimizer |
| Distribution Receipt TLB confirmed | EI | TLB Purchase Requisition | TLB |

**Table 51 – Planned Orders Flow**



Deployment works with the "Available to Deploy (ATD)" quantity. The calculation methodology is explained in the chapter "ATD Calculation." The aim of the deployment run is to generate single product transport (shipment) recommendations. The deployment works within the user- definable pull and push deployment horizons. The pull deployment horizon is defined in the SNP Demand Profile, the Push Horizon in the SNP Supply Horizon. One the following three situations applies to any product/location combination:

- Demand > ATD
  In a situation where the demand is greater than the available supply, APO applies so called "Fair Share Rules." As the name depicts, a fair share rule is a set of rules and conditions with the aim to distribute products with insufficient stocks to all sources of demand in a fair way. Fair share distribution logic is defined per product in the product master record. It is possible to use a deployment profile to which a product is linked. See the master data chapter for more information about using profiles. The following Fair Share Rules are available:
  - Rule A
    Distribute source ATD supply proportionally to all locations according to demand.
  - Rule B
    Distribute source ATD supply in such ways that target stock levels are increased by approximately the same percentage in all locations.

  - Rule C
    Distribute source ATD supply proportionally to all locations according to priority of demand at target location.
- Demand < ATD
  Whenever ATD stocks exceed the demand, APO can apply so called "Push Rules". These rules, which again are defined in the product master, stipulate how excess stock at the source location is distributed to the target locations. In this scenario the stock is pushed to the target location earlier than the defined requirement. This is done amongst other reasons to release warehouse capacity at the source location. The options APO offers will only bring forward the distribution of products, which are in demand in a target location. The idea is that it is not of any harm to bring forward the distribution of products, as they will be required in either case some time later (Early Push, not Additional Push). The push logic does not violate any "Target Days' Supply" at the receiving location. Following Push Rules exist:
  - Rule P
    Distribute source stock for demand within push horizon. This rule is used when applying the "Push/Pull" option to the product.
  - Rule X
    Distribute source stock for all known demand. This rule is used when applying the "Pull" option in the product master or (irrespective of the settings in the product master) when the Deployment Optimizer is used.
- Demand = ATD
  By default the Pull Distribution as described above applies. No push or pull takes place as the ATD quantity matches the demand and no excess stock exists.

The following options can be set per product:

- Pull Distribution
  Stock is pulled from the target location as required. Distribution occurs according to the due date specified at the locations. Stock exceeding ATD remains at the source location. Fair share rules might be applied.
  The target location receives anything required in the Pull Horizon on a required date if stocks permit.
- Pull/Push Distribution

All demand within the Pull Horizon is met through deployment immediately, without regard to the requirement dates specified by the target location. Excess stock might be pushed to the receiving location for demands within the push horizon.
The target location receives anything required in the Pull Horizon immediately plus potentially more stock.

- Push Distribution
  All requirements defined in the system are met through deployment immediately.
  The target location receives stock early and irrespective of stipulated demand date.

The Pull and Push Deployment Horizons stipulate the number of days which the Deployment run considers when calculating the total deployment demand at the supplying location. Any demands outside these horizons are not considered (exception is Push Distribution).
The deployment run can also fulfill customer orders according to the priority defined in the R/3 sales order. This option, if chosen, has first priority before any push, pull, or fair share allocations take place.



#### 4.3.8.1 ATD Calculation

The ATD quantity that is used in Deployment and TLB is not necessarily the available or physical stock that can be found at the respective location. The calculation rule for the ATD quantity can be defined individually per location in the location master record. There are two fields in the location master record, ATD Receipts and ATD Issues, that determine which supply and demand elements are taken into consideration when calculating the ATD quantity. Allocated to these two fields are ATP Category Groups that in turn are made up of various ATP Categories. Should no specific ATD rules be linked to the location, the system will take all supply and demand categories into consideration. When running Deployment or TLB the system performs the following 4-step calculation to derive the ATD quantity for a certain period:

1. Calculate Demand according to the SNP Demand Profile

2. Calculate preliminary available stock by adding up the stock on hand and the Receipts according to ATP Category used in the ATD Receipts field.
3. Calculate ATD Quantity by subtracting backlog quantity and Issues according to ATP Category used in the ATD Issues field.
4. Compare ATD quantity calculated with Demand

#### 4.3.8.2 Heuristic Deployment



Heuristic Deployment compares demand arising at all requesting locations with available stock at the source location. It neither takes any resource constraints into consideration, nor does it optimize the usage of transport enablers. Therefore the result is a plan of what should and can be dispatched, but it is ignoring economical (optimizing) considerations or any other "real world" constraints. Neither freight consolidation nor mode and carrier selection is supported with the current release. The requirement date of a demand can be seen as a hard constraint that is not changeable by the Deployment run. The stock available to deploy is calculated according to the "Available to Deploy" (ATD) settings at the source location (see chapter ATD Calculation). In case of product shortage Fair Share rules might be used. Push rules might be applied in situations where an overstock situation is detected. Refer to the explanations above in the chapter "Deployment'.

During the Heuristic Deployment, the SNP created recommended transport orders are re-processed. The Deployment run is performed per sourcing location or for several locations as well as for single or multiple products. Various settings influence the Deployment run. The main ones are:

- Deployment Horizon Define the deployment horizon in days
- Do not change Order Setting this flag ensures that SNP created orders will not be changed by the Deployment run.
- Reduce Order Set this flag if SNP created recommended transport orders should be reduced by the deployed amount as in the newly created recommended transport order.
- Delete Order If this flag is set all SNP created recommended transport orders will be deleted after the Deployment run irrespective of whether any open quantity remains

or not. This option should only be set in conjunction with the "Reduce Order" flag and if no open quantities are likely to remain.

- Deploy to Order — In R/3 customer (sales) orders can be prioritized. Set this flag if the Deployment run must consider these priority settings.

The output of the Heuristic Deployment run that can be assessed and changed in the SNP Interactive Planning screen are again recommended transport orders per product. To obtain further information on editing recommended transport orders refer to the chapter "SNP Interactive Planning Screen."



### 4.3.8.3 Optimized Deployment

Optimized Deployment is a network-focused approach that strives to achieve cost optimized distribution of products. It uses transportation and non-delivery cost as the cost input parameters. The optimum is defined as the lowest cost result while using the storage capacity in receiving locations as constraints. In case of product shortages, the fair share rule A is utilized while the push rule P is used in the case of oversupply. Planning is carried out per product or for all products and always for the entire distribution network. The Deployment Optimizer takes into account the costs (penalties) and the priority defined per product and the transportation capacities. As it is the case with the Heuristic Deployment run, the Optimized Deployment run assesses the SNP created recommended transport orders and reprocesses them.

The output of the Optimized Deployment run that can be assessed and changed in the SNP Interactive Planning screen are again recommended transport orders per product. The results although usually not required can be edited using the SNP Interactive Planning screen. To obtain further information on editing recommended transport orders, refer to the chapter "SNP Interactive Planning Screen".

### 4.3.8.4 Comparison

Comparing the two Deployment modes, heuristic and optimized, might at first appear to be a bit unfair. Why should anyone use a heuristic mode if there is an optimizer? The optimizer is a sophisticated tool that should be used in complex distribution network environments where a multitude of transport modes and routes coupled with various product-sourcing points is present. Optimization requires choices, and that is where the heuristic deployment run has its justification. Remember that before the Optimizer can provide valuable results a high number of cost (penalty) definitions as well as capacity definitions have to be carried out. As with any optimizing software, the quality of the result is extremely dependent on accurate data. A balance must be found between theoretically possible and feasible solutions. APO will not solve any problem as long as the data input is not clean. A phased approach is also an option worth thinking about. In phase 1 the heuristic approach is used to give the user handling experience and confidence in his or her and the system's capabilities. Later in phase 2 the Optimizer is implemented. Following are examples where the usage of the Optimizer is not required.

- Single point-to-point transportation lane per product
  In situations where only one sourcing location exists, the Optimizer cannot provide any new insight.
- Optimization not required
  A Company using for example UPS or FedEx for the distribution has no impact on finite routing. The cost is also fixed for any specific route. This is similar to the point above.
- Transportation cost irrelevant
  If the transportation cost is too low compared to the overall product cost, the Optimizer will deliver correct results but the results might not be worth the effort put in.

Both the heuristic deployment and the optimizer have their benefits. It really depends on the business requirements, which of the two modes is more suited.

## 4.3.9 Transport Load Builder

The building of transport loads is a two-step process.

1. In the first step, the Transport Load Builder picks up the single product transport order recommendations generated in the deployment run, and combines them to multi-product Transport Orders. Transport order quantities are multiples of the rounding value defined in the lot size profile. TLB considers minimum and maximum capacities of transportation enablers (e.g. trucks). Transport limitations are defined in the Transport Load Builder profile, which is linked to the transportation lane. TLB can be described best as the finite scheduling step in Transportation Management. The result of the transport load builder run is depending on the type of receiving location. It creates
   - Transport Orders for plant to plant movements, or
   - Sales Orders for VMI customers.

   For further information regarding VMI customers see the appropriate chapter. TLB allows the definition of multiple transportation modes per lane and the assignment of priorities (0 to 10 with 0 being the highest priority) per mode. No optimization of the transport mode takes place. The suggested transport mode is always the one with highest priority; others are shown as alternatives. It is not possible to define additional constraints with the current release. Additional constraints could be transport conditions (e.g. temperature) or mixing restrictions (e.g. no chemicals together with food). Any unresolved requirements are displayed in a list. Multi-product transport orders can also be built manually or changed after the TLB run takes place.
2. After step one has been completed, a second task, called "Build Consolidated Loads" needs to be performed. In this manual step, various TLB generated transport orders are combined into loads, which represent a physical load. Each load consists therefore of one or multiple transport orders and those in turn of one or multiple transport order items.

To obtain more information regarding the calculation of the Available-to-Deploy (ATD) quantity used by the Transport Load Builder, see the chapter "Deployment".

## 4.3.10 Output of Supply Network Planning

The result of the Supply Network Planning exercise is a constraint-based realistic tactical plan for production (and distribution). The plan is not automatically feasible as it might be based on bucket resources (see above comparison of methods). The operational aspect of distribution is handled within Supply Network Planning by using Deployment and Transport Load Builder functionality. In the case of production, the Supply Network Plan is handed over to Production Planning & Detailed Scheduling where finite scheduling of the production takes place. There is no need to specifically transfer the plan to Production Planning & Detailed Scheduling. Once saved, the plan is available for finite scheduling if the planned orders fall within a specified period (production horizon). SNP planned orders need to be converted to PP/DS planned orders (see below).



## 4.3.11 Release Management

Within the SNP Release Management two options are available, the release of the unconstrained DP plan from DP to SNP, and the release of the constrained SNP plan to DP. The first option is also available within the DP environment and is explained in detail in the chapter "Output of Demand Planning", which can be found in the DP section.

### 4.3.11.1 Release DP Plan to SNP

Demand that has been established in DP needs to be released to an SNP planning version. Once the demand is in the planning version, SNP and PP/DS will use it simultaneously. The conversion of SNP orders to PP/DS orders (see the PP/DS section) only converts SNP created planned orders for production and for transportation as well as the purchase requisitions. Other demand elements, such as sales orders or other requirements, are transferred to the APO system into an

SNP planning version from the OLTP system directly. SNP and PP/DS do not change these demands. SNP and PP/DS can create dependent demands during the planned order creation.

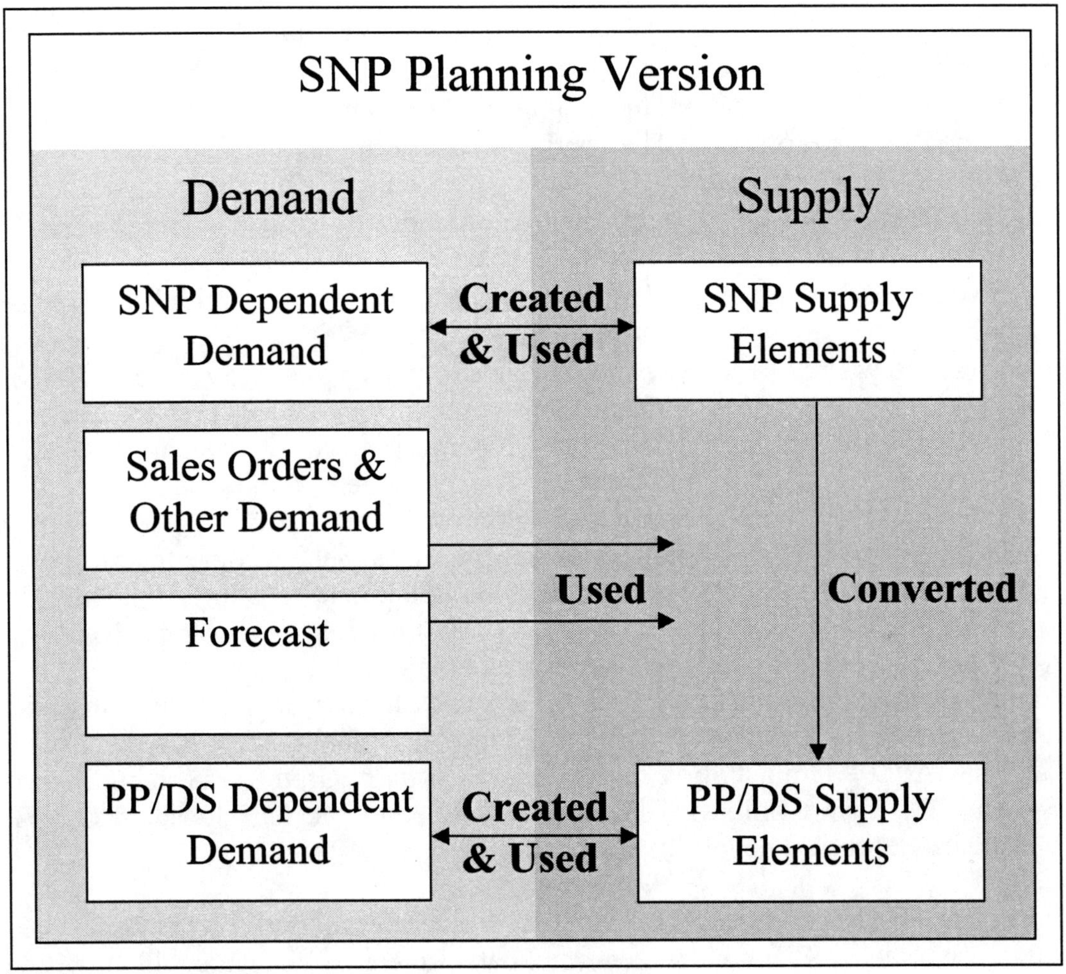


**Graphic 48 – Demand and Supply Elements**

In Supply Network Planning, an SNP planning version is linked to exactly one SNP model, but each SNP model can have several planning versions linked to it.

The SNP version is linked to exactly one DP version. This allocation is done in Master Data Maintenance of SNP; the path is “Supply Network Planning – Master Data – Model/Planning Version”. When releasing a DP plan the following parameters can be specified:

| | |
|---|---|
| • Product | Mandatory for interactive (online) release only |
| • Location | Optional |
| • InfoCube | This defines the data source |
| • Time Buckets Profile | The profile used determines the time roster of the SNP planning horizon (daily buckets) |
| • Date Range | Mandatory definition of start and end of SNP planning horizon |
| • SNP Planning Version | Mandatory as a DP version can be used to populate various SNP versions. |
| • Create New Orders | With this flag set, the system will create new SNP independent requirements for all forecast elements found in DP irrespective of probably already defined SNP independent requirements. Set this option to improve system performance but only when transferring data the first time for the given period; otherwise a duplication of orders is likely to occur! Never set this flag when transferring an updated demand plan to SNP. |



Should you run the APO system as a stand-alone system, ensure that the assignment of the Business System Group to the Logical System is correct (path Tools > APO Administration > Settings > System Group > Assign Logical System). All five definitions (the R/3 flag, Release, Master, Update, and ATP Update Mode) should be left blank.

Forecasts obviously need to be changed as and when required. This is done using the DP Interactive Planning screen or in batch mode. A change could entail the complete deletion of a quantity for a period. To do so, overwrite the old quantity with a Zero. After the revised forecast was saved, a new release of the demand forecast to SNP needs to be carried out. With the new release, the old forecast values in SNP will be replaced with the new ones. In a separate step a new SNP planning run (Heuristics, Optimizer, or CTM) needs to be carried out to adapt the

SNP plan to the changed set of forecast data (independent requirements). In this case the "Create New Orders" flag must not be set!

When creating new (supply) orders automatically during the release of the DP plan, a problem might arise for products that are procured via transfer from another location. Let me give an example. Product A in the distribution center X is procured via stock transfer from another location, the distribution center Y. In case of a requirement, the system will then automatically create a planned order for transportation if there is no sufficient stock in location X. This far everything works well. If now the procurement type in location Y points back to location X as the possible source, another planned order for transportation will be created. We have then closed the loop, and the same procedure starts again. This is an endless loop, and you will have to abandon this process sometime if it is not stopped (without result) by the system. The same problem exists when SNP orders are converted to PP/DS orders and the product is flagged for "Automatic Planning" in the product master PP/DS tab.



#### 4.3.11.2 Release SNP Plan to DP

The Supply Network Plan can also be copied (back) to the area of Demand Planning. It is stored in the Info Cube in a planning version. This feedback allows comparison of the two plans, the unconstrained Demand Plan and the constrained Supply Network Plan and, with that, the possibility of extended reporting as well as improvement of the Demand Plan. This activity is carried out either by the Supply Network Planner (push principle), or the Demand Planner (pull principle).
In order to transfer data from SNP to DP, the system uses a setting that can be found in the customizing of SNP Key Figures. For each SNP Key Figure, a Category can be defined. The Category defined in SNP is compared with the Category defined in DP (define the DP Category by using the transaction "Define Parameters for InfoCubes" in Current Settings of DP). Any DP Key Figure that matches an SNP Key Figure via this field Category will be populated with data during the transfer.
In order to use this function, it is required to define a DP key figure specifically for the SNP data. Various SNP versions could be used to feed the same InfoCube

using various DP versions. Another interesting aspect is to feed back two different SNP versions into DP using the same DP version but using two different DP key figures. By doing so one can easily compare the effect two different SNP versions have on the feasibility of the DP plan. When releasing an SNP plan, the following parameters can be specified:

| | |
|---|---|
| • SNP Planning Version | Defines from which SNP version data will be read. |
| • Product | Optional |
| • Location | Optional |
| • Date Range | Definition of start and end of SNP planning horizon |
| • InfoCube | This defines the data destination |
| • DP Planning Version | Defines into which DP version data will be written |

After all input data as described here is defined and the customizing settings have been done, the SNP to DP Key Figure assignment can be displayed on the initial release screen.



#### 4.3.11.3 Release DP Plan to R/3

The unconstrained DP plan can not only be released to SNP but also to an R/3 system where the DP plan is used to create R/3 Independent Requirements. The usage of this function makes good business sense if the DP module, but not the SNP module, of APO is used. This statement must be seen on a "per product" approach. Some products might be handled in SNP and their demand plan will be released to SNP, and others might be not handled in SNP, and in their case, the demand plan is given back to R/3. In addition to this scenario, there might be other requirements in an R/3 system for which the DP plan is needed. A possible application would be the creation of a budget that requires the forecasted sales quantities generated in APO.

## 4.3.12 Convert SNP Orders to PP/DS Orders

Planned orders for production, transportation, and purchase requisitions generated by SNP Heuristics, the SNP Optimizer or CTM need to be converted into PP/DS planned orders before they can be used within PP/DS. The same applies to all otherwise created SNP orders. During this process the orders are allocated a number that allows an easy synchronization with the OLTP system. During the conversion, planned orders for production are not changed with the exception of that the PP/DS PPM might have different quantity structures compared to the SNP PPM. SNP planned orders do not have to be converted into PP/DS planned orders in scenarios where SNP planning is carried out but no production planning or finite scheduling in PP/DS is required.



## 4.3.13 Specialized Customer and Vendor Relations

Within today's production and distribution environment, various industry specific special customer and vendor relationships can be found. A lot of business practices that are common [?] since years can often not or only partially be dealt with by the enterprise's application software. In the following chapters a few of these practices are explained together with their realization possibilities when using APO (and, where applicable R/3).

### 4.3.13.1 Vendor Managed Inventory

Vendor Managed Inventory (VMI) is a supplier customer relation where the vendor monitors the stocks at the customer and automatically replenishes theses stocks at the customer as and when they fall below previously agreed levels. Stocks sent to the customer are mostly sold with dispatch (sell-to VMI). The only difference to a normal sales order is that, in fact, the supplier decides when to sell (replenish). In some cases the actual sales transaction takes place at a later stage (ship-to VMI). For these constructs to work, it is necessary that the supplier maintains and monitors stocks on his own system. R/3 did not have any standard tools to do so. With APO this is now possible. A VMI customer is set up just the same way as any other location. It keeps track of the stock level at the VMI customer and can therefore easily be included in Demand Planning and Supply Network Planning.

VMI is becoming more and more standard in the Consumer Packaged Goods (CPG) industry sector. In addition to the logistical aspect described above, companies usually render into some type of risk sharing agreement where the vendor is obliged to take back stock from the customer if it cannot be sold in time. Furthermore, it is common practice to run areas within a shop as a type of a profit center where the vendor takes full responsibility for the profitability of the products sold. This might include pricing decision as well as the maintenance of the dedicated product area. Virtually the customer rents out a portion of the shop to the vendor.



APO supports VMI by allowing separate planning for such customers. Within DP an InfoCube per VMI customer can be created to allow individual forecasting. In SNP, a VMI customer is set up as a location with transportation lanes as required. DP integrates the VMI forecast, while SNP monitors the stocks at the VMI location. From a process point of view there is little difference between an internal company transfer (e.g. manufacturing plant to distribution center) and a VMI replenishment. Within SNP the TLB creates replenishment orders as and when required considering the customer stock level and other parameters (e.g. lot sizes).

#### 4.3.13.2 Consignment Stock

The term consignment stock describes stock owned by the supplier but already residing at the customer's warehouse. It can be used anytime at the customer's discretion and is payable only after consumption. Billing usually takes place periodically after confirmation of consumption or after a stock count. The risk of stock loss or damage is with the customer. Customer Consignment Stock is stock situated at the customer, Vendor Consignment Stock is stock made available by the vendor. Consignment stock functionality is fully supported by SAP R/3.

Consignment stock is very similar to Ship-To VMI (see above). The main difference between the two scenarios is that consignment stock is pulled by the customer, and VMI stock is pushed by the supplier.
A consignment customer can be defined in DP just like any other customer. In APO no special setup is required to model a consignment relation, whether it be for customer or for vendor consignment stock. This is so because the only difference between a consignment customer and a "normal" customer is the ownership of the stock.

#### 4.3.13.3 Direct Shipment

Direct Shipment, which is also referred to as Drop Shipment, refers to a situation where a customer sales order is received and the product is subsequently delivered directly from the vendor to the customer. The billing activity is performed by the company, which receives the sales order. The vendor merely delivers direct to the customer instead of to the warehouse. This must not be mixed up with a commission based business transaction where a sales order from a customer is directly forwarded to a vendor for further processing including delivery and billing. In this case a commission is paid based on the forwarded sales order.
APO can be modeled to support such a business construct. It is necessary to define both the customer and the vendor appropriately in SNP and to ensure that a transportation lane exist between them. Forecast consumption should be carried out at the own location and not at the vendor's location, as most probably no forecast exists for the vendor location.



#### 4.3.13.4 Subcontracting

A subcontractor is a company that manufactures an entire product or parts thereof for a customer in the customer's name. Often subcontractors are used to temporarily fill capacity gaps or to provide services for which the customer does not have the right specialized knowledge or machinery. The subcontractor is usually provided with all required components or semi-finished products and has to work strictly according to specified standards. Within SAP R/3 all required functions for subcontracting are existent. They include the creation of subcontracting orders with possible automated explosion of a BOM to specify all required components for the subcontracting order. Required components can be easily transferred to the subcontractor, and stocks at the subcontractor are monitored with a special stock type. Excess components can be kept at the subcontractor for later use or can be transferred back. R/3 has (at least with the current releases) two shortcomings, which are the absence of a transport order for the stock transfer to and from the subcontractor, and secondly there is no possibility to do capacity planning for and on behalf of the subcontractor. Often the latter is required, as lots of subcontractors are small to medium sized companies without sophisticated planning tools. This can be done now with APO. In APO the subcontractor can be defined as a location with resources as required.



In order to synchronize the planned transportation and planned production order, APO carries out the pegging of these two elements together at the same time in a 1 to 1 relation. At the same time R/3 uses these two planned orders to create a subcontracting order. The planned transportation order is for the finished product that has to be shipped back to the demanding location. It is not used for the provision of components required for the subcontracting process. The component requirements at the subcontractor can be dealt with using standard APO transport functionality. If subcontracting orders were captured in an R/3 system, APO creates a planned production order at the subcontractor's location as well as planned transport order. In both scenarios, the planned production order and the planned transportation order have the same order number in APO.

### 4.3.14 Mass Processing

Mass Processing is used to run the SNP Heuristics, SNP Optimizer, SNP Capable to Match, Deployment, and the Transport Load Builder in batch in predefined intervals and to release the unconstrained DP plan to SNP. Carrying out these tasks in batch mode is releasing the planner's time and utilizing the system resources during off peak hours where these jobs do not negatively affect the responsiveness of the system. All parameters defined for on-line processing are used the same way in mass processing. Alerts are generated in order to instantly focus on problem areas.

## 4.3.15 Supported Requirements Strategies

APO supports as standard four different Requirements Strategies. They correspond to the R/3 Production Strategies. It is possible to add other strategies if required. The four standard strategies are listed below.

- Strategy 10 Make to Stock Production
  Using the Make to Stock strategy, production is carried out irrespective on the incoming sales orders and solely based on the demand plan. For planning purposes, sales orders are ignored. This is the requirements strategy typically used in mass production.
  - Incoming sales orders do not consume the forecast.
- Strategy 20 Planning with Final Assembly
  Production is planned according to the specified demand plan as well as sales orders when using this Make to Stock requirements strategy. Usually the demand plan is the driver for the longer term planning and a prioritized mix of demand plan and sales orders are used for the operational planning.
  - Incoming sales orders consume the forecast.
- Strategy 30 Planning without Final Assembly
  This Make to Order strategy is applied in situations where semi-finished products are manufactured in a make to stock environment, and the final assembly only takes part after a sales order was received. With the creation of the sales order, the production of the finished product is kicked off. Components for the finished products are taken from stock as they had been produced independently before. This requirements strategy is used for example in the PC industry where all components are bought or manufactured beforehand. With the sales order, the final assembly according to the customer's specification is carried out.
  - Incoming sales orders consume the forecast of the finished product.
- Strategy 40 Make to Order Production

Using the Make to Order strategy production is carried out only based on incoming sales orders. Dependent requirements are thus created only at time of sales order receipt.

- Incoming sales orders consume the forecast.

With APO the same product can be allocated to two different requirements strategies. This is required if the same product for example is sold as a spare part (requirements strategy 10 or 20) and is used at the same time as a spare part. An example would be the motherboard of a PC. In this case the two requirements will have to be planned separately. The system creates separate planned production orders for requirements based on different strategies. Requirements Strategies are also dealt with in the DP section.

SNP

## 4.3.16 Supported Production Strategies

APO supports, as of release 2.0, only Discrete Manufacturing. As an addition to the release 2.0, the support of Repetitive Manufacturing was announced. Process Orders are supported with the current release, but a Process Industry specific Process Flow Scheduler will be available at a later stage. The main areas that will be affected by this new functionality are the resources and (obviously) the scheduler in PP/DS. The current scheduler (abbreviated DS-SFS) is optimized for a discrete manufacturing environment. The scheduler for repetitive manufacturing will be abbreviated RS, and the one used for the process industry orientated orders DS-PFS. A new resource type, the line resource, will be introduced for repetitive manufacturing. It will allow the definition of rates and product-specific rates for finite scheduling.

# 4.4 The SNP Data Environment

## 4.4.1 Profiles

Master Data setup used within Supply Network Planning is greatly simplified by the usage of so- called Profiles. While creating product master data, a profile can be linked to it, and any change performed on the profile is pulled through the master data automatically (link of profile to master data). Additionally information of a profile can be used as a reference source when creating master data without consequent automatic update (copy of profile to master data). The profile functionality is the same as the ones used in R/3 MRP (MRP and Forecast profiles). Some profiles are used as a general source of information and are not linked to any master data object. They serve the same purpose just as any other customizing entry. Furthermore there are profiles specifically used by the SNP Optimization run and some others for Capable-to-Match (CTM).



Below is an overview of SNP related profiles. Check the chapter "CTM Profiles" further down for specific CTM related profiles.

| Profile | Linked to | Usage |
|---|---|---|
| SNP Demand | Product Master | Time Dependant Calculation of Demand |
| SNP Supply | Product Master | Time Dependant Calculation of Supply |
| Demand | Product Master | Demand and Forecast Consumption Parameters |
| Requirements Strategies | Product Master Demand Tab<br>Demand Profile | Definition of Requirement Strategies |

| Profile | Linked to | Usage |
|---|---|---|
| Lot Size | Product Master | Production Lot Size Definition with single Rounding Value |
| SNP Lot Size (Edges) – Profile for Transportation Lanes | Transportation Lane | Transport Lot Size Definition with single Rounding Value |
| Rounding | Product Master Lot Size Tab<br>Lot Size Profile<br>Lot Size Profile for Transportation Lanes | Economical Multiple Step Rounding Calculation that supports several Rounding Values |
| Deployment | Product Master | Allocation of Fair Share and Push Rules |
| Transport Load Builder | Transportation Lane | Definition of Minimum and Maximum Load Parameters |
| SNP Global Category Settings | Global Profile with no link to specific master data | Allocation of ATP Categories to SNP applications |
| Time Buckets | Global Profile with no link to specific master data | Definition of Time Bucket used in SNP |
| SNP Optimizer | Global Profile with no link to specific master data | Used by the SNP Optimization Run |
| SNP Cost | Global Profile with no link to specific master data | Used by the SNP Optimization Run |

**Table 52 – SNP Profiles Usage**

The table underneath shows where the various profiles used within SNP can be maintained. It also contains “profile like” entities used in SNP. Check the chapter “CTM Profiles” further down for specific CTM related profiles.

| Profile | Product Master | SNP Current Settings | IMG Chapter |
|---|---|---|---|
| Lot Size | Yes,<br>Initial Screen | | |
| Demand | Yes,<br>Initial Screen | | |
| SNP Demand | Yes,<br>Initial Screen | Yes, but called “Demand” | Supply Chain Planning –Supply Network Planning - Profiles |
| SNP Supply | Yes,<br>Initial Screen | Yes, but called “Supply” | Supply Chain Planning –Supply Network Planning – Profiles |
| Deployment | Yes,<br>Initial Screen | Yes | Supply Chain Planning –Supply Network Planning – Profiles |
| Rounding | | Yes | Master Data – Product |
| Transport Load Builder | | Yes | Supply Chain Planning –Supply Network Planning – Profiles |
| SNP Lot Size (Edges) | | Yes | Supply Chain Planning –Supply Network Planning – Profiles |
| SNP Optimizer | | Yes | Supply Chain Planning –Supply Network Planning – Profile for the Optimizer |
| SNP Cost | | Yes | Supply Chain Planning –Supply Network Planning – Profile for the Optimizer |
| Requirements Strategy | | Yes | Master Data – Product |

| Profile | Product Master | SNP Current Settings | IMG Chapter |
|---|---|---|---|
| Global Category Settings | | Yes | Supply Chain Planning –Supply Network Planning – Category Groups |
| Time Buckets | | DP Current Settings only! | Supply Chain Planning - Demand Planning – Basic Settings |
| Phase In | Yes, SNP 1 View | | |
| Phase Out | Yes, SNP 1 View | | |
| Like Modeling | Yes, SNP 1 View | | |



**Table 53 – SNP Profiles Maintenance**

The following chapters deal with all available SNP profiles. The Life Cycle Management profiles are dealt with in the chapter "Life Cycle Management". Some parameters relating to SNP and PP/DS are grouped in a "Global Parameter". This global parameter is dealt with in the PP/DS section.

### 4.4.1.1 General SNP Profiles

#### 4.4.1.1.1 SNP Demand Profile

The SNP Demand Profile is one of two drivers that determine the calculation of demand at any specific point in time. The other driver for the demand calculation is the definition of Category Groups and their allocation to SNP Key Figures.

Please check the chapter "SNP Demand Calculation". Several parameters can be found in the Demand Profile. They are explained underneath.

- Demand Horizon 1
  This horizon defines the end of the Demand Short Term Planning Horizon, which is at the same time the beginning of the Demand Medium Term Planning Horizon. This figure in days specifies an interval starting on the present day.
- Demand Horizon 2
  This horizon defines the end of the Demand Medium Term Planning Horizon, which is at the same time the beginning of the Demand Long Term Planning Horizon. This figure in days specifies an interval starting on the first day of the Demand Medium Term Planning Horizon. After the end of the days specified here, the Demand Long-term Planning Horizon starts.

In a separate step category, groups are allocated to each of the three planning segments, Short, Medium, and Long Term Planning. Please refer to the chapter "SNP Demand Calculation". Note as well that the definition of the two Demand Horizons is independent of the definition of the Supply Horizons.

- Forecast Horizon
  The Forecast Horizon splits the future into two segments, and the figure defined in this parameter marks the end of the first time segment. It is defined in days and specifies an interval starting on the present day. It has an impact on how the total demand is calculated. Please refer to the chapter "SNP Demand Calculation".
- VMI Promotion Lead Time
  The VMI Promotion lead-time has a similar function as the Target Days Coverage field. Stipulate here the number of workdays for the calculation of the coverage required for all VMI promotion demand. The definition of the VMI promotion lead-time ensures that enough stock is available to cover promotions at a VMI customer. It is virtually a second safety stock.
- Pull Deployment Horizon
  The Pull Deployment Horizon stipulates the number of days, which the Deployment run considers when calculating the total deployment demand at the supplying location. Any demand outside this horizon is not considered.
- Period Split for Time Based Demand Distribution
  This setting determines how demand is distributed over time when performing the release of the unconstrained DP plan to SNP. The distribution of the

forecasted demand takes place by spreading it evenly over the periods. If for example the forecast was 1000 pieces per month, and the month has 20 working days (according to the respective factory location), the forecast in SNP would be 50 pieces per day. This is standard functionality that does not require any specific setting. The parameter here is specifically for situations where the forecast release takes place into a period that already started. Three options are available:

- Distribute the whole forecasted demand over the entire period even if part of the horizon is already in the past.
- Distribute a pro rata forecasted demand over the future period only. As a result the total demand distributed over the period is less than the DP forecasted demand.
- Distribute the whole forecasted demand over the remaining future period.



Example:
On September 1st, 1999 the forecast for the calendar week is released from DP. Part of the week is in the past already. The forecasted demand for this week is 900.

| Period Split Indicator | August 30 | August 31 | September 01 | September 02 | September 03 |
|---|---|---|---|---|---|
| Blank | 180 | 180 | 180 | 180 | 180 |
| 1 | | | 180 | 180 | 180 |
| 2 | | | 300 | 300 | 300 |

**Table 54 – Period Split Indicator Example**

#### 4.4.1.1.2 SNP Supply Profile

The SNP Supply Profile is used to determine the calculation of the available supply at any specific point in time. It works in conjunction with the definition of Category Groups and their allocation to SNP Key Figures. Please check the chapter “SNP Supply Calculation”. The Supply Network Planning Supply Profile parameters are explained underneath.

- Supply Horizon 1
  This horizon defines the end of the Supply Short Term Planning Horizon, which is at the same time the beginning of the Supply Medium Term Planning Horizon. This figure in days specifies an interval starting on the present day.
- Supply Horizon 2
  This horizon defines the end of the Supply Medium Term Planning Horizon, which is at the same time the beginning of the Supply Long Term Planning Horizon. This figure in days specifies an interval starting on the first day of the Supply Medium Term Planning Horizon. After the end of the days specified here, the Supply Long-Term Planning Horizon starts.

In a separate step category, groups are allocated to each of the three planning segments, Short, Medium, and Long Term Planning. Please refer to the chapter “SNP Supply Calculation”. Note as well that the definition of the two Supply Horizons is independent of the definition the Demand Horizons.

- Production Horizon
  This horizon defines the time within which SNP does not create any planned production orders. Planned production orders are created by SNP outside this period only, and then converted into PP/DS orders in a batch job. Within the Production Horizon, which is also referred to as the PP/DS Horizon, planned production orders are dealt with exclusively by PP/DS. For any unmatched (open) requirement that the SNP run finds within the production horizon, a planned order will be created just outside the production horizon. This is the same logic as it is used by the R/3 MPS run. This should only happen for products where “Automatic Planning” (see product master PP/DS view) is switched off.
  A global SNP and PP/DS parameter can be set defining the production horizon as well. This global value is used only in cases where the Production Horizon in the product master is not maintained (either as a direct input or via a profile).
- Stock Transfer Horizon
  The Stock Transfer Horizon defines the time within which SNP does not create any planned transportation orders. Planned transportation orders are created by SNP outside this period only. Only the Deployment run or TLB convert or create planned transportation orders within this period.

- Push Deployment Horizon
  In cases where an overstock situation was detected at the supplying location, the Deployment run tries to push products earlier than required to all those locations that require the products in question. It is important to understand that products will only be pushed earlier than required and only if demand exists in the receiving location (Early Push, not Additional Push). The Push Deployment Horizon stipulates the number of days, which the Deployment run considers when calculating the total deployment demand at the supplying location. Any demand outside this horizon is not considered. The Push Deployment Horizon is only used by the push rule "P". This push rule is used when applying the "Push/Pull" logic to a product.



#### 4.4.1.1.3 Demand Profile

This is not a typing mistake. APO really has an SNP Demand Profile (as discussed above) and a Demand Profile. The demand profile deals with several parameters grouped into four segments.

Segment 1: Requirements Strategy deals with the allocation of specific requirements (or production) strategy to the product and with the consumption of forecast (if applicable for the chosen production strategy).

1. Proposed Strategy
   The proposed (requirements) strategy defines the manufacturing strategy. Standard SAP delivered options are Make To Stock, Planning With Final Assembly, and Planning Without Final Assembly. For more information regarding the requirements strategies, see the chapter "Supported Requirements Strategies".
2. Consumption Mode
   Consumption of Forecast can be done backwards (consume forecast in period prior to consumption or earlier), forwards (consume forecast in period after consumption or later), or in forward / backward mode (combination of both). The parameter here defines which mode has to be used. Note that for the Requirements Strategy "Make To Stock" no forecast consumption takes place.

3. Backward Consumption Period
   In case of backward consumption of forecast, the number in this flag defines the number of working days allowed to go back. Should no forecast amount be available in this period, no forecast consumption will take place.
4. Forward Consumption Period
   In case of forward consumption of forecast the number in this flag defines the number of working days allowed to go forward. Should no forecast amount be available in this period, no forecast consumption will take place.
5. Assembly Planning
   As a rule the forecast of the product as specified in the sales order is consumed. With this flag set, the forecast of the product of the dependent requirement is consumed instead. A dependent requirement can be originated by a production order or by a transport order. The Assembly Planning flag should be switched on for the Requirements Strategy "Planning Without Final Assembly".



Segment 2: Dependant Demand deals with requirements created by the system when exploding a PPM.

6. Always Collective Requirements
   With this flag set, dependent requirements of various products are pooled together and only one requirement, which can cater for several demands, is created. In a situation where sufficient stock is available, the stock will be used before new orders are created. One product receipt caters for several demands. This applies irrespective of whether the higher level product is made in a make to order or in a make to stock environment. Lot sizing procedures can be applied and the cost recipient is the product.
7. Possible Customer Individual Requirements
   This option gives the same results if the higher level product is made in a make to stock environment. Should the higher level product be manufactured in a make to order scenario, the following applies. For each requirement an individual receipt element (planned order for production or external procurement) is created. Receipt is into individual sales order stock. The default lot size is exactly the required quantity. The cost carrier

is the demanding sales order. This flag must be set for example when using requirements strategy 30.

8. Collective Orders
   Component requirements are covered using collective orders in the case of Fixed Pegging. This is the equivalent to the R/3 Special Procurement Type 52.

Segment 3: Dynamic Pegging defines the permitted time span between demands and their corresponding supply elements. The settings here do not apply to Fixed Pegging relations.

9. Maximum Duration Backward Pegging
   The time entered here defines the maximum time allowed between a demand and the corresponding supply element that covers the demand. It defines the maximum time the demand may be ahead of the supply element. Should a supply element be linked with a demand element within this time span, no alert will be generated although the supply lies after the demand.
10. Maximum Duration Backward Pegging without Alert
    The time defined here works together with the above setting. It defines the maximum time the demand may be ahead of the supply without generating an alert. The time specified here should be less than the time specified above.
11. Maximum Duration Forward Pegging
    Defines the maximum time the supply element is allowed to be ahead of the demand. This ensures that supply elements that are far ahead of the demand are not used. By doing so the system ensures that demand and supply elements are close together.

For more information about Pegging, refer to the chapter "Pegging" in the PP/DS section.

Segment 4: Delivery Tolerances define the permitted over/under delivery percentages during the dynamic pegging process. Delivery in this context refers to the delivery of the supply element to the demand element. The demand element could also be for example another planned production order or a forecast requirement. The tolerance values can also be taken over from the sales order. In this case the default product values defined in the product master are ignored.

12. Under-delivery Tolerance
    Defines the percentage by which the supply element quantity may be short in comparison to the quantity requested by the demand element. Stipulate here the permitted maximum shortage percentage.
13. Over-delivery Tolerance
    This percentage is used calculate the quantity by which the supply element may exceed the quantity requested by the demand element. Stipulate here the permitted maximum oversupply percentage.
14. Flag Use Total Quantity
    Set this flag if a demand must consume always the entire quantity of a supply order.
15. Flag Use Total Stock
    Set this flag if a demand must consume always the entire quantity of a stock supply element.



#### 4.4.1.1.4 Requirements Strategy

Standard SAP delivered Requirements Strategies are Make To Stock, Planning With Final Assembly, and Planning Without Final Assembly. For more information regarding the requirements strategies, see the chapter "Supported Requirements Strategies". It is not advisable to change the delivered settings. If required, create new strategies. The parameters are grouped into two segments.
Segment 1: Planning Parameters

1. Category
   This setting defines the category (also known as the ATP category) that the system interprets as the base for procurement. Any element with the category specified here is seen as a requirement for which SNP has to create a procurement order.
2. Planning Segment
   The Planning Segment defines whether the product is manufactured in a make to order or make to stock environment.
3. Planning Version
   Defines the SNP version to be used.

Segment 2: Assignment

4. Assignment Mode
   The Assignment Mode determines whether and how sales orders consume the forecast.
5. Category Group
   A Category Group consists of various categories. The Category Group defined here stipulates all those documents with their corresponding categories that are used to consume the forecast. The Category Group is only defined if forecast consumption is to be carried out (see above setting). The Category Group used in the delivered system points to the category "BM", which is used for sales orders.



#### 4.4.1.1.5 Lot Size Profile

The Lot Size Profile, which is also sometimes referred to as the Production Lot Size Profile, is used to calculate the lot size used when creating planned orders. The following parameters, which are grouped into three segments, can be defined:
Segment 1: Calculation of Lot Size

- Lot Size Unit of Measure
  Planned orders will be created using this unit of measure. The unit of measure defined here needs to be maintained on product master level. Should it not be the product's base unit of measure, a conversion factor needs to be specified.
- Lot for Lot
  If this option is selected, the order quantity will be exactly the demand quantity. No rounding takes place.
- Fixed Lot Size (with Value)
  With this option the order quantity will be always exactly the same. Should the demand exceed this quantity multiple orders will be created.
- Maximum Lot Size Value
  A maximum lot size can be maintained to limit the quantity per order. It must be greater than the minimum lot size quantity. More than one order will be created if the demand exceeds the maximum lot size value
- Minimum Lot Size Value
  A minimum lot size can be maintained to ensure a minimum production order quantity. It must be less than the maximum lot size quantity.

- Rounding Value
  A rounding value is used to ensure that order quantities are in multiples of this number.
- Lot Size Always
  Lot size calculations always take place when manufacturing for an anonymous market (make to stock production). If this flag is set a lot size calculation is also carried out in a make to order environment.

Segment 2: Day's Supply

- Target Day's Supply
  Anticipated demand is calculated for the number of days specified in this parameter (see also "SNP Demand Calculation"). Consequently the production order quantity is adjusted in a way that the total of stock, anticipated receipts and the planned production order match the demand of the period as specified in this field. The Target Day's Supply is used by SNP but not by PP/DS.

Segment 3: (without name)

- Rounding Profile
  It is possible to branch into the Rounding Profile, should the rounding parameters offered in this profile not provide the required level of sophistication. The result of the calculation based on the Rounding Profile replaces all numerical settings in the Production Lot Size Profile.
- Assembly Scrap
  The Assembly Scrap defines the amount of scrap to be expected when the product using this profile is manufactured. Please refer to the chapter "Scrap Calculation".

Note that the lot sizing procedure is used even in the case of Make to Stock orders. In this case lots might be created with quantities greater than the actual sales order quantity.

#### 4.4.1.1.6 Lot Size Profile for Transportation Lanes

The Lot Size Profile for Transportation Lanes is used by the Transport Load Builder to ensure that suggested loads are within predefined parameters. The profile is linked to a transportation lane using the Supply Chain Engineer. The following parameters can be defined:

- Minimum Lot Size Value
  A minimum lot size can be maintained to ensure a minimum load. The suggested transport quantity will be at least the quantity specified here. It must be less than the maximum lot size quantity.
- Maximum Lot Size Value
  A maximum lot size can be maintained to limit the quantity per load. It must be greater than the minimum lot size quantity. More than one transport load will be created if the required transport quantity exceeds the maximum lot size value.
- Rounding Value
  A rounding value is used to ensure that transport order quantities are in multiples of this number.
- Rounding Profile
  It is possible to branch into the Rounding Profile, should the rounding parameters offered in this profile not provide the required level of sophistication. The result of the calculation based on the Rounding Profile replaces all numerical settings in this profile.



#### 4.4.1.1.7 Rounding Profile

The Rounding Profile is used to round up or down previously established demand. It can be linked to a product master in the Production Lot Size Profile and to a transportation lane in the Lot Size Profile for Transportation Lanes (see above). Each Rounding Profile has several levels. For each level a threshold value and a rounding value is defined. Let me explain how the final result is derived with the help of an example. To make it easier to understand, I have allocated to the different levels different package media.

Calculation:

Initial Step: Compare Original Demand with Threshold Value of level 1. If Original Demand is less than Threshold Value of level 1 then the Rounding Value equals the Original Demand (which means no rounding takes place). If the Original Demand is greater or equal than the Threshold Value of level 1 continue to step 1

Step 1: Divide Original Demand by Threshold Value of Level 3 and determine how many times the Rounding Value of Level 3 goes into the Original Demand Value. Do not consider the decimals now. We now have the number of pallets. Subtract the number of units on this pallet from the Original Demand, which gives us Demand 2.
Now compare Demand 2 with the Threshold Value of level 3. If Demand 2 is greater than the Threshold Value of level 2 then add 1 more pallets (round up) and we are finished. If not proceed to step 2.

Step 2: Divide Demand 2 by Threshold Value of Level 2 and determine how many times the Rounding Value of Level 3 goes into the Demand 2 Value. Do not consider the decimals now. We now have the number of cartons. Subtract the number of units in this carton from Demand 2, which gives us Demand 3.
Now compare Demand 3 with the Threshold Value of level 2. If Demand 3 is greater than the Threshold Value of level 2 then add 1 more cartons (round up) and we are finished. If not proceed to the next step.

Final Step: Divide Demand 3 by Threshold Value of Level 1 and determine how many times the Rounding Value of Level 1 goes into the Demand 3 Value. Round up to the next number. We now have the number of boxes.

Sounds maybe a bit complex, but it is not really. Each time the system has to round, it will go through the initial step and the final step. Additionally it will go through "n" calculation steps with "n" being the number of rounding levels minus 1.

| Level | Threshold Value | Rounding Value | Package Media |
|---|---|---|---|
| 1 | 6 | 10 | Box |
| 2 | 41 | 50 | Carton |
| 3 | 71 | 100 | Pallet |

**Table 55 – Rounding Profile Setup Example**

SNP

Here are some numerical examples for the model in the table above:

| Original Demand | Rounded Value |
|---|---|
| 8 | 10 |
| 43 | 50 |
| 83 | 100 |
| 134 | 150 |
| 161 | 170 |

**Table 56 – Rounding Profile Data Example**



#### 4.4.1.1.8 Deployment Profile

The Deployment Profile links a Fair Share Rule and a Push Distribution Rule to a product. Note that the Deployment Profile is only used by the Heuristic Deployment run and not by the Optimizing Deployment run. When using the Optimizing Deployment option, the distribution is based on the minimal penalty approach rather than on predefined rules.

1. Fair Share Rule
   This setting links one of the three fair share rules used in a pull distribution to a product or none if left blank. The Fair Share rules are explained in the chapter "Deployment".
2. Push Distribution
   Here, either push, pull or both methods are selected. The Push Distribution principles are explained in the chapter "Deployment".

#### 4.4.1.1.9 Transport Load Builder Profile

The Transport Load Builder Profile is used to provide the system with minimum and maximum parameters when creating transport loads. These parameters can be defined in volume, weight, and a third dimensionless unit. The TLB run checks all 3 limits simultaneously and ensures that none of them is violated.

1. Pull In Horizon
   The Pull In Horizon specifies the number of days in which TLB can check for additional requirements in cases where the minimum capacity is not reached. Should a load be too small then the system checks for additional requirements to enable a higher more economical load.
2. Volume Lower Limit
   Define the lower volume limit for the load in the unit of measure as defined in "Volume Unit of Measure."
3. Volume Capacity
   Define the upper volume limit for the load in the unit of measure as defined in "Volume Unit of Measure." Should the total requirements exceed the above limit multiple transport resources will be planned for.
4. Volume Unit of Measure
   This unit of measure is used for the two parameters above (e.g. $m^3$).
5. Weight Lower Limit
   Define the lower weight limit for the load in the unit of measure as defined in "Weight Unit of Measure."
6. Weight Capacity
   Define the upper weight limit for the load in the unit of measure as defined in "Weight Unit of Measure." Should the total requirements exceed the above limit multiple transport resources will be planned for.
7. Weight Unit of Measure
   This unit of measure is used for the two parameters above (e.g. kg).
8. Staging Area Lower Limit
   Define the lower unit limit for the load in the unit of measure as defined in "Staging Area Unit of Measure." The expression "Staging Area" refers to the area in a transport utility (e.g. truck) and describes the area where products can be loaded (staged).
9. Staging Area Capacity

Define the upper unit limit for the load in the unit of measure as defined in "Staging Area Unit of Measure." Should the total requirements exceed the above limit multiple transport resources will be planned for.

10. Staging Area Unit of Measure
This unit of measure is used for the two parameters above (e.g. pallets).

#### 4.4.1.1.10 Global Category Settings

The Global Category Settings define for the three SNP applications Heuristic (SH), Deployment (DH), and Transport Load Builder (TH) the ATP categories used for specific calculations. The profile is already defined in the delivered APO system and should not be changed.



#### 4.4.1.1.11 Time Buckets Profile

Within APO Time Buckets Profiles are used to define the period breakdown. When releasing the unconstrained DP plan into SNP, the number of days (buckets) defined in this profile determines the number of days for which requirements will be created into the future. Assuming you want to do planning in daily (and not weekly or monthly) buckets, the only thing that has to be carried out is to create a time bucket profile with daily buckets.

### 4.4.1.2 Optimizer Profiles

The SNP Optimizer Profile, in conjunction with the SNP Cost Profile, provides all parameters required for the SNP and Deployment Optimizer runs. For further information regarding the Optimizer run, please read the appropriate chapters.

#### 4.4.1.2.1 SNP Optimizer Profile

In the SNP Optimizer Profile the optimization method with the respective parameters can be set. Note that the selection of parameters used is dependent on the chosen optimization method. The following lists all parameters that can be set in the SNP Optimizer Profile

- Variant of Simplex Method
  Define the variant of the simplex method to be used. This setting is only used if the discretization method is not activated. There is no best setting for this field. The actual quality of the result as well as the runtime behavior depends on the data environment.
  - Dual  Dual Simplex Algorithm
  - Primal  Primal Simplex Algorithm
- IPM
  Use Inner Point Method. The Inner Point Method is an ILOG developed extension that can be used together with a Simplex method. This setting is only used if the discretization method is not activated.
- Time Decomposition
  Set this flag to enable Time Decomposition. Decreasing the time buckets (window size) supports a better runtime but also causes a worse optimization quality. When using this option, it is required to also define the "Initial Window Size for Time Decomposition" (see below). This works only in conjunction with the Simplex method.
- Product Decomposition
  When using Product Decomposition, the total planning problem is broken down into smaller groups of planned products. Decreasing the product partitions supports a better runtime but also causes a worse optimization quality. When using this option, it is required to also define the "Partition for Product Decomposition" (see below). Product Decomposition can be used with the simplex method and the discretization method.
- Initial Window Size for Time Decomposition
  The Window Size defines the number of time buckets that are combined in the Optimization run per time decomposition step. The time buckets in SNP are usually days and therefore the number of time buckets that can be defined for

SNP

Time Decomposition is the number of days combined in one optimization step. The Basic Solve considers all days together as one "big" bucket. The SAP recommended value range is from 2 to 5. Setting this value to 1 makes the quality of the result similar to this of the Basic Solve (Simplex) Solution. Greater values improve run time but lower the quality of the solution. This works only in conjunction with the Simplex method.

- Partition for Product Decomposition
  In this field define the percentage of products that should be considered in each optimization group. In a sequential approach, each group of products is then optimized separately. The SAP recommended value range for the partition is from 1 to 30%. Smaller values improve run time but lower the quality of the solution. Product Decomposition can be used with the simplex method and the discretization method.
- Hard Prioritization
  With Hard Prioritization switched on, the Optimizer strictly adheres to the demand prioritization settings. This works only in conjunction with the Simplex method.
- Safety Stock Priority
  When using Hard Prioritization (see above), the priority value for the safety stock priority can be changed from its default value 6 (lowest priority) to either 1, which is the same as customer demand, or 2, which is the same as forecast demand. The Safety Stock Priority Setting has no impact on the run time or the quality of the output. This works only in conjunction with the Simplex method.
- Discretization Method
  Select one of the two available discretization methods as required or set this field to "None". Discretization does not permit the selection of "Time Decomposition" or "Hard Prioritization".
  - None
    No discretization sets the optimizer into the simplex method, which is either primal or dual, as specified in the "Variant of Simplex Method" field.
  - Full Search
    A "full search" discretization optimization mode ensures that the provided result is the objective optimum based on all specified constraints. This is true as long as the run time was not limited.

SNP

  - Partial Search
    The "partial search" discretization optimization mode provides a reasonably good, but worse, result compared to the "full search" mode. Its benefit is an improved run time.
- Maximum Number of Iterations
  For discretization methods, the maximum number of iterations (also referred to as the search limitations) limits the number of attempts to find an improved solution. A greater the number of permitted iterations increases the likelihood to find the optimal solution.
- Maximum Runtime
  When using discretization methods, the maximum runtime in the format <mm,ss> can be preset.
- Rounding Limit for Transportation Variable
  The rounding limit (or rounding threshold) for transportation variables is used in conjunction with the "partial search" discretization method and is used to transform the continuous transportation lot size values into integer values. The value range is from 1 through to 99.
- Rounding Limit for Production Variable
  The rounding limit for production variable is used in conjunction with the "partial search" discretization method and is used to transform the continuous production lot size values into integer values. The value range is from 1 through to 99.
- Storage Product Allocation Quantity
  Set this flag if you want the Optimizer to consider available product dependent storage capacity that is defined in the product master GR/GI tab (field Material Storage Location Resource). The definition of a product dependent warehouse (storage) resource overrides a possibly defined product independent (location specific) resource. The Optimizer cannot increase product dependent storage capacities!
- Handling Resources
  Set this flag if you want the Optimizer to consider available product independent handling capacity. The handling resource is defined per location and is therefore product independent. No product dependent handling resources can be defined.
- Storage Capacity

Set this flag if you want the Optimizer to consider available product independent storage capacity that is defined in the location master. All products in a location that do not have a specific resource allocation in the product master (see above) share the available storage capacity.

- Transport Capacity
  Set this flag if you want the Optimizer to consider available product independent transportation capacity. The available transportation capacity is determined via the transportation's lane transport resource assignment.
- (Minimum and) Maximum Transport Lot Size
  The transport lot size is limited if this flag is set. If used with the simplex method then only the maximum is limited, if used with the discretization method both the minimum and maximum are limited.
- (Minimum and) Maximum PPM Lot Size
  The PPM lot size is limited if this flag is set. If used with the simplex method then only the maximum is limited, if used with the discretization method both the minimum and maximum are limited.
- Production Capacity
  Set this flag if you want the Optimizer to consider the available production resource capacities.
- Discretize Transport Resources
  With this flag set, transportation capacities are increased in incremental steps, as required for the discretization method optimization.
- Discretize Transport Lot Sizes
  With this flag set, transportation lot sizes are increased in incremental steps, as required for the discretization method optimization.
- Discretize PPM
  With this flag set, PPM lot sizes are increased in incremental steps, as required for the discretization method optimization.
- Discretize Production Capacity
  With this flag set, production capacities are increased in incremental steps, as required for the discretization method optimization.
- Rounding Profile for Production Times
  SNP planning is bucket-oriented in terms of available capacity and product availability. The standard assumption is that within a bucket it does not matter when exactly an operation has to take place, when the components are

required, and when the finished product can be expected. If the bucket is defined as a weekly bucket and based on the assumption stipulated above, we do not know exactly what is happening within this week. This approach, although sufficient for most SNP related planning, is too rough when it comes to optimizing.
The Rounding Profile for Production Times allows the definition of a rounding limit, which is used to determine whether the finished product availability is set to the beginning of the current or the following bucket. The following example illustrates this procedure.
Example:

The optimizer determines availability of the product to be on the 12th of January 2000. The bucket size is a week, and the question is now whether to set the availability to the 10th of January 2000 (beginning of the bucket) or to the 14th of January 2000 (end of bucket). The time period within the bucket is 5 days.

Case 1: Rounding Limit = 0.3
In this case the calculation of 0.3 * 5 days returns a value of 1.5 days. Our expected receipt is on day 3. As 3 is greater than 1.5, the receipt is scheduled to be at the end of the current bucket (which is the same as the beginning of the next bucket).

Case 2: Rounding Limit = 0.7
In this case the calculation of 0.7 * 5 days returns a value of 3.5 days. Our expected receipt is on day 3. As 3 is smaller than 3.5, the receipt is scheduled to be at the beginning of the current bucket.

- Rounding Profile for Transportation Times
  The Rounding Profile for Transportation Times follows the same logic as the Rounding Profile for Production Times (see above).

The following table provides an overview of the SNP optimizer profile settings (parameters) and their applicability to the SNP optimization methods. Dark gray shaded cells with an "X" indicate that the option can be used with the optimization method.

SNP

| Method / Parameter | Simplex | Discretization |
|---|---|---|
| Variant of Simplex Method | X | |
| IPM | X | |
| Time Decomposition | X | |
| Product Decomposition | X | X |
| Initial Window Size for Time Decomposition | X | |
| Partition for Product Decomposition | X | X |
| Hard Prioritization | X | |
| Safety Stock Priority | X | |
| Discretization Method | | X |
| Maximum Number of Iterations | | X |
| Maximum Runtime | | X |
| Rounding Limit for Transportation Variable | | X |
| Rounding Limit for Production Variable | | X |
| Storage Product Allocation Quantity | X | X |
| Handling Resources | X | X |
| Storage Capacity | X | X |
| Transport Capacity | X | X |
| Production Capacity | X | X |
| Minimum and Maximum Transport Lot Size | Only Max | X |
| Minimum and Maximum PPM Lot Size | Only Max | X |
| Discretize Transport Resources | | X |
| Discretize Transport Lot Sizes | | X |
| Discretize PPM | | X |
| Discretize Production Capacity | | X |
| Rounding Profile for Production Times | X | X |
| Rounding Profile for Transportation Times | X | X |

**Table 57 – Optimization Parameters**

#### 4.4.1.2.2 SNP Cost Profile

The SNP Cost Profile provides all cost (penalty) factors (multipliers) required for the SNP and Deployment Optimizer runs. The following lists all factors that can be defined in the SNP Cost Profile. For further information regarding the Optimizer runs refer to the appropriate chapters. Note that the resource capacity variant 1 is used as long as sufficient capacity is available. The capacity variant 2 is used only if the capacity defined in capacity variant 1 is not sufficient. Multipliers based on "increased capacity" are therefore only applied if capacity variant 1 does not provide sufficient capacity. Multipliers can be values between Zero and One, in which case the original value is lowered using the factor specified in the parameter.

- Cost Multiplier Production Process Model
  In each Production Process Model (PPM) you define a (output quantity dependent) penalty. The cost multiplier in this parameter picks up this cost and multiplies it accordingly. The PPM dependent variable penalty does not include the cost of components used in the planned order. This multiplier does not affect the variable cost for the usage of the resource either.
- Cost Multiplier Procurement
  Multiplies the procurement cost of the product as defined in the product master GR/GI tab. The procurement cost consists of quantity dependent and independent elements. The multiplier effects both.
- Cost Multiplier for Production Capacity Increase
  Multiplies the penalty for additional use of resource as defined in the resource capacity variant 2. It comes only into effect if the capacity defined in capacity variant 1 is not sufficient. There is no multiplier for capacity variant 1.
- Cost Multiplier for Transport Capacity
  Multiplies the penalty for use of a transportation resource. This multiplier uses the settings of the resource capacity variant 1.
- Cost Multiplier for Transport Capacity Increase
  Multiplies the penalty for additional use of transportation resource as defined in the resource header. This multiplier uses the settings of the resource capacity variant 2.
- Cost Multiplier for Storage Capacity

Multiplies the penalty for use of a storage resource. This multiplier uses the settings of the resource capacity variant 1.

- Cost Multiplier for Storage Capacity Increase
  Multiplies the penalty for additional use of storage resource as defined in the resource header. This multiplier uses the settings of the resource capacity variant 2.
- Penalty for insufficient Safety Stock
  Unlike all parameters explained above, this setting is an absolute value and no multiplier! Here you define the penalty applied to the SNP solution when a product falls below the minimum safety stock level. This value will be applied to all products that fall below the minimum safety stock level exactly the same way and irrespective of any other parameters. It is also quantity independent, which means that there is no difference whether the safety stock is Zero or just below the minimum level.
- Cost Multiplier for Handling Capacity Increase
  Multiplies the penalty for additional use of handling capacity as defined in the resource variant 2. It comes only into effect if the capacity defined in capacity variant 1 is not sufficient. There is no multiplier for capacity variant 1.
- Cost Multiplier for Delivery Delay
  The product master allows on the SNP1 view the definition of penalties for Late and Non-Delivery. These values are defined separately for Sales and Forecast requirements. In the case of forecast requirements the term "delivery" refers to the time where the stock is posted on hand. The delay penalty can be set to come only into effect after a certain (grace) period. With the Cost Multiplier for Delivery Delay parameter, these penalties can be multiplied as required. The penalty and this multiplier are per base unit of the product and day. It is applied to both, the penalty for sales order and forecast demand.
  The Penalty for Late (and Non) Delivery can be used to optimize on Profit. The higher the anticipated product profit is, the higher the individual product's penalty should be set up. If this is the case, the optimizer tries to first and utmost ensure that demands for those products with high penalty (profit) are satisfied first. This and the following cost multiplier can be used to balance this profit-orientated optimization with other goals.
- Cost Multiplier for Non Delivery

This parameter works the same as the one explained above. The only difference is that the Cost Multiplier for Non Delivery comes into effect in situations of non-delivery. The penalty and this multiplier are per base unit of the product and day. It is applied to both, the penalty for sales order and forecast demand.

The table below gives an overview of all cost multipliers that can be defined in the SNP Cost Profile. The penalty for falling below the safety stock level is not included, as it is an absolute cost value and not a multiplier.

In the column "Resource", the numbers 1 and 2 depict the resource capacity variant that is used by the multiplier.

| **Basis** | **Time** | **Quantity** | |
|---|---|---|---|
| **Master Data** | **Resource** | **Product** | **PPM** |
| **Cost Multiplier** | | | |
| Production Process Model | | | X |
| Procurement | | X | |
| Production Capacity Increase | 2 | | |
| Transport Capacity | 1 | | |
| Transport Capacity Increase | 2 | | |
| Storage Capacity | 1 | | |
| Storage Capacity Increase | 2 | | |
| Insufficient Safety Stock | n/a | n/a | n/a |
| Handling Capacity Increase | 2 | | |
| Delivery Delay | | X | |
| Non-Delivery | | X | |

**Table 58 – SNP Cost Profile Parameters**

#### 4.4.1.3 CTM Profiles

CTM is using its very specific own profiles, and there is virtually no interdependence between other SNP and PP/DS settings. Some global settings are required that define the interaction of CTM with the rest of SNP. The main CTM profile called "CTM Planning Profile" can only be maintained at one particular place that can be reached via the following path: "Supply Chain Planning – Supply Network Planning – Planning – Mass Processing – Capable-to-Match." The screen coming up is also referred to as the "CTM Overview screen" The CTM Overview screen displayed there is the driver for the whole CTM environment and from there, some of the required CTM profiles can be created and updated as well. The table below gives an overview of CTM related profiles and how they are linked to each other. Profile marked with an (*) in the column "IMG" can be maintained in the IMG chapter "Supply Chain Planning – Supply Network Planning – Capable to Match".

| CTM Profile | Linked to | Usage | IMG |
|---|---|---|---|
| CTM Global Customizing Settings | Global Profile with no link to specific master data | Global CTM settings that define the interaction of CTM with SNP and PP/DS | * |
| CTM Planning Profile | Global Profile with no link to specific master data | Main CTM profile that governs the CTM run | |
| CTM Time Stream | CTM Planning Profile Planning Data | Defines the Time Buckets | * |
| Supply Categories | CTM Planning Profile | Name definition of Supply Categories | * |
| Search Strategies | CTM Planning Profile | Link of Supply Categories to a Search Strategy | * |
| Priority of Order Categories | CTM Planning Profile | Definition of Demand Priorities | * |

| CTM Profile | Linked to | Usage | IMG |
|---|---|---|---|
| CTM Work Area | CTM Planning Profile | Defines the Work Area for the CTM Planning Run | |
| CTM Supply Limits | CTM Planning Profile | Defines per product individual supply limits and defaults | |
| CTM Constraints | CTM Planning Profile | Activation of CTM Constraints | |
| Time Zone | CTM Planning Profile | Options for the Time Display | |

**Table 59 – CTM Profiles**

SNP

In the following chapters, all CTM related profiles are explained. The CTM Planning Profile, which is maintained in the CTM Overview screen, is put at the end as it is referring to other individual CTM profiles.

#### 4.4.1.3.1 CTM Global Customizing Settings

The following CTM Global Customizing Settings can be made:

- Planning Method
  Select either SNP or PP/DS Planning.
- Generate Orders for
  Select either SNP or PP/DS. Planned orders created by the CTM run are either SNP or PP/DS planned orders. Choose SNP if you do not want CTM to impact PP/DS planned orders. In this case the CTM generated planned orders need to be released to PP/DS just like any other SNP planned orders (e.g. such planned orders created using the SNP Optimizer).
- PPM Selection
  Production Process Models have a usage indicator stipulating in which area they can be used. Although this indicator suggests that only SNP, PP/DS, or CTM can use PPM's, in actual fact CTM can use all three. This must also be

seen in connection with CTM's ability to use bucket or time continuous resources. The usage of resources is defined in the PPM. PPM's with the usage indicator "S" use bucket resources, such with usage indicator "P" use time continuous resources.

- Use Rules
  Enable the usage of CTM customer substitution rules.
- Default Values for Constraints
  Constraint definition in CTM is rules based. The above flag determines whether CTM customer substitution rules are used. The following parameters deal specifically with CTM constraints. Please refer to the chapter "Rules Based CTM" for detailed information.

1. Delayed Requirements Fulfillment
   - Flag Allowed Yes/No
   - Maximum Postponement
     Define the maximum number of days a demand may be postponed. If only postponement and no partial delivery is allowed, set the Minimum Portion for Partial Delivery to 100%.
   - Minimum Portion for Partial Delivery
     This is the minimum percentage required for a partial postponed delivery. The maximum postponement is defined in the Maximum Postponement parameter.
   - Strategy Demand Satisfaction
     Select the CTM strategy for late delivery (either "D" or "A") as required.
2. Early Requirements Fulfillment
   - Flag Allowed Yes/No
   - Maximum Period for Early Fulfillment
     Define the maximum number of days allowed for early delivery.
3. Partial Requirements Fulfillment
   - Flag Allowed Yes/No
   - Minimum
     This is the minimum percentage of a requirement that must be fulfilled. The remaining quantity remains unsatisfied for the order.
   - Maximum

Indicate whether more than the required quantity may be shipped. In other words, is the customer willing to accept oversupply and up to which limit. Indicate an allowed 5% oversupply with an entry of 105%.

#### 4.4.1.3.2 CTM Time Stream

The CTM time stream allows the definition of up to 4 different types of periods, days, weeks, months, and quarters. For each of the period types, the number of periods is specified. No gaps exist in this time stream. It can be specified with a fixed or relative start date. Once all settings have been done, the actual time stream is created. It can be viewed by pressing the "Display Planning Periods – Ctrl+F3" button. The following fields are part of the CTM Time Stream:

- Time Steam ID
- Start of Generation
    - Fixed Starting Date
      Select this radio button, and specify a fixed start date for the CTM planning run. This option is only suitable in cases where a certain CTM time stream is intended for single usage, as otherwise it has to be changed before every new run for a new period. This option is specifically helpful in a testing environment.
    - Relative Start
      Select this radio button to have a CTM run starting date relative to the system date. Planning starts on the current day or a number of days in the future as specified.
    - Time
      This field is populated automatically.
- Planning Period Definition
    - Period Type 1
      Select a period type for the period next to the start date of the planning run.
    - Number of Periods
      Specify the number of periods for the first period type.

- Period Type 2
  Optionally, select a period type for the period after the previously defined first period of the planning run.
- Number of Periods
  Optionally, specify the number of periods for the second period type.
- Period Type 3
  Optionally, select a period type for the period after the previously defined second period of the planning run.
- Number of Periods
  Optionally, specify the number of periods for the third period type.
- Period Type 4
  Optionally, select a period type for the period after the previously defined third period of the planning run.
- Number of Periods
  Optionally, specify the number of periods for the fourth period type.

- End Date
  The end date is generated automatically based on the entries made in the CTM Time Stream profile.



#### 4.4.1.3.3 Supply Categories

In this profile simply define Supply Categories consisting of an identifier and a name. These supply categories will be used in the next step where various supply categories are linked to a search strategy.

#### 4.4.1.3.4 Search Strategies

The Search Strategy is used to determine the demand prioritization and links the previously defined supply categories to a search strategy. One supply category named "**Production**" and with the identifier "**" is automatically put into all search strategies. The sequence can be defined as required, and the production

supply category can have any sequence number. While performing the CTM run, the system will search for supply according to this sequence and also check for production possibilities according to this search strategy. Note that a search strategy with the identifier "blank" exists. This search strategy contains one entry only with the supply category "Production".
If no supply categories besides "production" are defined in a search strategy, CTM will immediately check for production and not consider any other supplies. This is technically correct, but does not really make business sense.

#### 4.4.1.3.5 Priority of Order Categories

The supply categorization of demand elements is defined within this profile. Allocate in this profile a priority to every required ATP category. Logically it makes sense to only allocate priorities to ATP categories that describe a demand (e.g. sales orders) and not to those that describe supplies (e.g. purchase orders).
The ATP category of a demand has no influence on the CTM match of demand and supply if no priorities are defined in this profile. This might be a desired situation.



#### 4.4.1.3.6 CTM Work Area

The CTM Work Area maintenance program can be accessed via the Goto Menu. To create a new CTM work area, simply type in a name and press <Enter>. The right side of the screen then displays all products for all locations. Using the "Choose" button, which looks like a funnel, you can restrict this list to location products of a certain SNP model. Location products have to be selected individually as no blocking of lines exists. The triangle symbol to the left will then move the selected location products into the CTM work area. The double triangle moves all products across. Location products can be easily removed using the same technique.

#### 4.4.1.3.7 CTM Supply Limits

The CTM Supply Limits can be defined only after the Supply Categories have been set up and must be maintained before Supply Limits and/or Supply Splitting is defined on the Supply tab. Specify a Supply Limit ID and description. Specify then a product and/or a location to which you want to attach supply limits. The definition of a product and/or location in the selection section works like a default setting for the supply limits maintained in the supply limit profile. It is also possible to define the supply limits individually without any entry in the selection section. In the list below this section define all supply limits with start and end date as well as the limits 1 through to 5.
Supply limits need to be generated after they have been created. To do so, activate the “Generate Periods - Ctrl+F8” button.



#### 4.4.1.3.8 CTM Constraints

CTM Constraints are based on CTM rules, which are dealt with in the chapter “Rules Based CTM”. The CTM Constraints function in the CTM Overview Screen links the CTM rules to the CTM Planning Profile. Additionally it is required to activate (allow the usage of) the constraints in the CTM Global Customizing Settings profile.

#### 4.4.1.3.9 Time Zone

CTM is a network oriented planning tool that can at the same time deal with down-to-the-second scheduling. It is therefore important to consider the individual time zones of the locations that are part of the planning task. The Time Zone, which can be accessed via the Control Data Menu, determines which time is displayed. The following options are available:

| | |
|---|---|
| Time Zone of Location | Use the time zone valid for the respective location. |

| | |
|---|---|
| Local Time Zone of User | Display all times in the time zone of the user as defined in the user master record. |
| All Times are displayed in UTC | Use Universal Time Coordinated (UTC). Note that daylight savings time is not used when applying UTC |

#### 4.4.1.3.10 CTM Planning Profile

The CTM Planning Profile, which is maintained in the CTM Overview screen, is the heart of the CTM run. Here, various CTM profiles are linked together and complemented by other parameters. The screen appears with 6 tabs that are explained in this chapter. Start the maintenance of the CTM planning profile by defining a CTM Planning Profile name, and then follow through the tabs as indicated.



- Planning Data
  After creating a CTM Planning profile, the system switches to this tab automatically. Define in the Planning Area section the SNP version to be used and a CTM Work Area if desired. For more information regarding the usage of CTM work areas, read the appropriate chapter. In the Time Stream field, specify the CTM Time Stream to be used. If you press <Enter> at this moment, a warning is coming up if the active SNP version was selected. The Time Stream Definition section providing detailed information about the selected CTM Time Stream is displayed as well.
- Strategies
  The Strategies tab contains five sections.
  The first section called "Planning Mode" defines the planning mode used by CTM when selecting this profile. Refer to the chapter "CTM Planning Methods" for more information.
  In the second section, Planning Area, it is required to define whether the CTM run is carried out for the SNP model or for a CTM work area. In the latter case, it is necessary to define a CTM work area in the Planning Data tab (see above).
  The scheduling direction, forwards or backwards, is defined in the third section.

In the fourth section the Pegging Type, fixed or dynamic, is defined.
The Search Strategy is linked to the CTM Planning Profile in the fifth and last section. Select here any of the search strategies defined in the Search Strategies Profile (see the previous chapters). After selecting a search strategy and pressing the <Enter> key the details of the selected strategy is displayed. Note that a search strategy with the identifier "blank" exists. This search strategy contains one entry only with the supply category "Production."



- Demand
  Define the priority sequence by selecting one after the other of the Demand Prioritization criterions. The Demand Prioritization criterion selected first is priority one, the next one priority two and so on. Not all of the criterions need to be selected. The possible criterions are:

| | | |
|---|---|---|
| 01 | Order Type | If this option is selected, ensure that the "Priority of Order Categories Profile" was maintained. |
| 02 | Date | This refers to the date of the demand order |
| 04 | Product Priority | Prioritization is according to location product. |
| 05 | Location Priority | Prioritization is according to location. |

  After pressing the <Enter> key, the name of the selected Demand Prioritization is displayed. If none of the Demand Prioritization criterions was selected, the system prioritizes automatically by demand date only. For more information on Demand Prioritization, refer to the chapter "CTM Planning Overview". A Demand Simulation function can be activated on this tab. Please refer to the chapter "CTM Overview Screen".
- Supply
  With this option the individual or default supply limits are linked to the CTM Planning Profile. In order to carry out this step, the Supply Categories as well as the Supply Limits need to be defined. Select the "Use Supply Limits" button to activate the usage of supply limits. Activate the "Split Supply" button if required. In the lower section of the screen, select the "Other Allocation" button, and define the Supply Category that carries the lowest (upper and lower) limit. Repeat this step up to 6 times to define all supply categories. When selecting the "Safety Stock" button, CTM will create a planned order to replace the safety stock automatically if it has to use it to satisfy demand. In this table you should define all supply categories that are linked to the search strategy as stipulated on the Strategies tab. This should be done in the inverse sequence of that used in the search strategy. For more

information on Supply Categories, refer to the chapter "CTM Planning Overview".
A Supply Simulation function can be activated on this tab. Please refer to the chapter "CTM Overview Screen".

- Settings
  The Settings tab displays the status of the CTM run during the planning run.
- Planning Run
  After all parameters have been defined, the CTM Control Panel on the Planning Run tab should show the Planning Version, Model Name, optionally the CTM Work Area, and the Planning Period. Provided the assignment of the CTM optimization server has been carried out, you can now start the CTM planning run and obtain the CTM messages.

### 4.4.2 Master Data Environment

SNP and PP/DS require an extensive definition of master data. Data can be copied to APO, but after this it is possible to update information in R/3 or APO without appropriate synchronization. Data transfer between R/3 to APO is unidirectional to APO and asynchronous. Master data, in general, is model independent. Only the Transportation Lane and the Quota Arrangement are defined per model. Before master data can be used within a model, it has to be allocated (subscribed). In general, master data in APO is a subset of data stored in R/3, but it is at the same time enriched to cater for special functions not available in R/3. As said before, synchronization of APO with R/3 data still has to be fully developed. Stringent business rules have to be set up to avoid unsynchronized update of data in APO that is also defined in R/3. The minimum requirement here would be the possibility to define data that is resident in both systems to be a display only field in APO. As master data can only be transferred to APO, it cannot be the master system.

In order to use the master data objects Location, Product, Resource, and Production Process Model in SNP (and PP/DS), a 4-step process must be carried out:

1. Create master data object.
   In this step the master data object definition is carried out.
2. Add master data object to the SNP model in the master data maintenance transaction or in the Supply Chain Engineer.
   This step adds the master data object to the SNP model.
3. Optionally, add master data object to the work area in the in the Supply Chain Engineer.
   Now the master data object is made visible in the Supply Chain Engineer.
4. Add master data object in the Supply Chain Cockpit.
   Finally, the master data object is visible in the Supply Chain Cockpit and can be used in an SNP planning version.

An additional complication arises as some master data objects can be maintained version-specific. In this case the master data object definitions are different per planning version! This planning specific maintenance of master data objects is evoked automatically when maintenance is initiated from various planning screens (e.g. the SNP Interactive Planning screen).

The Supply Chain Engineer is dealt with in the chapter "The SNP Transactions."

#### 4.4.2.1 Supply Chain Model and Version

The supply chain model and planning version(s) are created in one transaction. This transaction provides an excellent overview of all supply chain models and their allocated planning versions. Models and planning versions can also be deleted or marked for deletion in this transaction. Furthermore, models and planning versions can be copied. When copying planning versions, version-specific master data is always copied across, and transactional data can be copied additionally. If transactional data is also copied, the new planning version will be totally independent of the active planning version.

In this transaction the SNP version is also linked to a DP version. It is only possible to release the DP plan to SNP after this link has been established.



#### 4.4.2.2 Location

Locations can be manufacturing plants, distribution centers, suppliers, or vendors. In general a location is anything where products either come from, go to or where they are stored. The location master record is rather small and therefore easy to maintain. All information that can be defined is situated on one screen, which is subdivided into five segments.

- Segment 1: Resources
  A handling resource can be defined per location. The Optimizer uses the handling resource if defined and activated in the SNP Optimizer profile. Furthermore a product independent storage (warehouse) resource can be defined per location. The Optimizer uses the product independent storage

(warehouse) resource if defined and activated in the SNP Optimizer profile. It is also possible to define a product specific storage warehouse resource.

- Segment 2: Calendar
  APO offers the possibility to define per location three different calendars. This allows a flexible definition of work hours depending on the task to be performed. The calendars defined here are not the factory calendars but the Time Streams.

| Calendar | Used by/for |
|---|---|
| Production | Components and Semi Finished Products |
| Storage | Goods Receipt, Transport Order, Finished Products |
| Shipping | Goods Issue |

- Segment 3: Deployment/ATD
  For Deployment and TLB purposes, ATP category groups (which in turn are made up of one or several ATP categories) can be linked to locations. This allows a user definable composition of used receipt and issue elements per location. The ATD (Available to Deploy) quantity with its elements "ATD Receipts" and "ATD Issues" can therefore be defined location specific. The system uses all supply/demand categories in the case where no entry is made in the ATD receipts/ATD issue fields. For further information see also the chapter "ATD Calculation".
- Segment 4: Control Parameters
  Locations have a user defined priority rating that is used for example when running CTM.
- Segment 5: Geographical Data
  For display purposes, in the Supply Chain Cockpit screen, it is necessary to define the longitude and latitude for each location. Additionally the time zone in which the location can be found is defined here. Geographical data can be entered when creating the location master. Alternatively, the geographical data is added automatically when allocating the location to an SNP model using the drag and drop functionality. In this case a popup screen appears allowing, confirming or fine-tuning the longitude and latitude of the location.

A location address can be maintained on the location master initial screen. Select the location and choose either create, change, or delete.

Locations are deleted in a two step process. Both of them are carried out from the "Initial Screen" of the transaction "Location Master Data Maintenance". Before

SNP

deleting a location, ensure that it is not used in other master data object like for example products.

Step 1: Set the deletion flag (under the menu option "Location").

Step 2: Delete the flagged locations by starting a batch job. This batch job that can be run either immediately or at a predefined time deletes the flagged locations only if no other dependent master data is attached to the location. This ensures that no unassigned products, resources or other master data objects are left behind without reference after the location was deleted.

While the location master record is deleted, its assignment(s) to supply chain model(s) ceases as well. There is no need to first detach a location from a supply chain model.



#### 4.4.2.3 Product

The term 'product' relates to any type of material from component to finished product. It is not necessarily a tangible unit. Product master data is defined globally and per location. Information is grouped logically and can be accessed easily by selecting the appropriate tab. The following explanation deals with all elements per tab. While accessing location-specific data it is possible to maintain global data at the same time. At any time the product number, the product description, and the base unit of measure are visible above the individual tabs.

Product memos can be added and maintained from any view, allowing the definition of any text. This is done using a basic text editor. Product memos can also be viewed and edited from various SNP and PP/DS transactions.

Another very useful new tool is the mass maintenance of products. On the selection screen, mass maintenance allows the definition of single discrete values of product (and/or location) numbers, the definition of a product (and/or location) number range, or the definition of multiple ranges. On the following screen, virtually all product master fields are displayed allowing the graphic selection of those that require the change. The last step is different for fields with restricted possible entries and for those that carry numerical values. For fields with possible entries, the new entry can be defined. Should the field be numerical, a new value can be defined or alternatively a calculation rule can be used. Available calculation rules are multiply, divide, add, or subtract. In this case the new value is derived from the old value. The same mass maintenance functionality is also available specifically for the penalties defined in the SNP1 tab.



| | Views | | Modules | | | | SNP |
|---|---|---|---|---|---|---|---|
| | Global | Local | DP | SNP | PP/DS | GATP | Version |
| Attributes | | | | | | | |
| Unit of Measure | | | | | | | |
| Classification | | | | | | | |
| Phase In / Phase Out | | | | | | | |
| SNP 1 | | | | | | | |
| ATP | | | | | | | |
| Administrative | | | | | | | |
| Demand | | | | | | | |
| Lot Size | | | | | | | |
| SNP 2 | | | | | | | |
| PP/DS | | | | | | | |
| GR/GI | | | | | | | |
| Extra | | | | | | | |

**Table 60 – Product Master Views**

The table above provides an overview of the product master views and the APO modules using it. The last column highlights all those product master views that contain information that can be defined SNP planning version specific. The product master needs to be assigned to any SNP model it is supposed to work with. This can be done in the Supply Chain Engineer or directly in the product master maintenance screen. Product master data can be made SNP version specific. This allows the independent maintenance of master data per SNP version.

Products are created on a global location independent level and additionally per location. Consequently, they can be deleted separately on location and global level. In order to delete a product on global level, no location dependent entry must exist anymore. In order to delete a product, it must also not be used in other master data object like for example PPM's. The deletion on global and/or location level is a two step process. Both of them are carried out from the "Initial Screen" of the transaction "Product Master Data Maintenance".

Step 1: Set the deletion flag (under the menu option "Product") for a product on global, location, or both levels. You can only delete the global level when all location dependent definitions are either also marked or already deleted.

Step 2: Delete the flagged products by starting a batch job. This batch job that can be run either immediately or at a predefined time, The idea is that this run deletes all flagged products only if no other dependent master data is attached to the them. This ensures that no unassigned PPM's or other master data objects are left behind without reference after the product was deleted.



While the product master record is deleted, its assignment(s) to supply chain model(s) ceases as well. There is no need to first detach a product from a supply chain model.

#### 4.4.2.3.1 Product Master Global Data

Global data is grouped into the following views represented each by a named tab.

#### 4.4.2.3.1.1 Attributes

The Attributes view is subdivided into three segments. None of theses segments refer to any predefined profile. The segment External Product Number displays the name of the External Product Number, which is composed of the Business System Group and the External Product Number (these are display only even in change mode).

In the second segment Weights and Measures/EAN, the weight and volume with their respective units of measure for the product are displayed. The weight and volume refer to the product in its base unit of measure. Additionally the EAN (bar code number) for the product is displayed.

The General Data segment consists of a field Product Group and the Stacking Factor. The Storage Position Factor determines whether a product can be stacked and if so how many levels are permitted. The Storage Position Factor is also referred to as the Stacking Factor. This information is used by TLB to determine the maximum stacking factor. The Product Group in this segment is the same format as on R/3 and not used by APO.

In an optional fourth segment up to 5 product attributes can be defined. This segment requires activation carried out in customizing. Please refer to the chapter "Product Attributes."



#### 4.4.2.3.1.2 Unit of Measures

The Unit of Measures tab displays as the minimum the base unit of measure. Additionally it shows all alternative units of measure that are possibly defined for the product. Each alternate unit of measure has a conversion factor that depicts the numeric relation to the base unit of measure. It is furthermore possible to allocate an individual EAN (bar code number) to each unit of measure.

#### 4.4.2.3.1.3 Classification

This tab is used to allocate a class to the product. Furthermore, it allows branching into the Rules Maintenance screen. Classification of products is required if Characteristics Dependent Planning is to be carried out.

#### 4.4.2.3.1.4 Phase In / Phase Out

The Phase In / Phase Out view is subdivided into three segments. Each of the three segments refer to specific profiles that can only be created and maintained out of the Product Master Maintenance program. Maintenance of the Phase-In and the Phase-Out Profiles are identical and allow defining the number of periods between the start and the end of the respective profile. The popup screen used to maintain these profiles allows the upper half to define how the demand increases or decreases over the time of the profile validity period. The lower half (which can be switched off) shows the captured data in graphical form (bars) thus enabling an easy control of the captured data. Per period any value between 0 and 100 (%) can be captured. Once these profiles are applied to the product, its demand can be corrected according to the percentages defined. It is up to the user to ensure that the start and end date specified for the product launch and the product discontinuation segments coincide with the number of periods defined in the respective profile. For further information and examples regarding the use of these profiles refer to the chapter “Life Cycle Management.” Note that this product view is used in Demand Planning. In order to deploy Lifecycle Management, it is therefore required to define a product master, although this is not mandatory for other DP functionality.

<u>Segment Product Launch</u>
Within this segment the start and the end of the product launch phase (Phase In) is defined as well as the name of the profile (time series) to be attached.

<u>Segment Phase Out Control</u>
Within this segment the start and the end of the product discontinuation phase (Phase Out) is defined as well as the name of the profile (time series) to be attached.

SNP

Segment Reference

As with the Phase In and Phase Out profiles, the creation and maintenance of the Like profile is done from within the Product Master Maintenance program. On the popup screen used to maintain the Like Profile, it is possible to stipulate one or multiple products whose historical data will be deployed when carrying out the demand planning for the product. If multiple products are referred to, it is necessary to choose either "Average" or "Sum". Average will take the average of all products in the profile, sum will take their total.

#### 4.4.2.3.1.5 SNP 1

The SNP1 view consists of one segment, which only deals with Penalty Cost. The settings here are used solely for the SNP Optimizer run. The first group of fields is used to define the penalty cost for customer requirements. The SNP Optimizer uses the Penalty for Non Delivery value to determine the opportunity cost associated with a non-delivery of a customer sales order. The second entry determines the penalty cost per day for late delivery to a customer. In the case of a late delivery to a customer the SNP Optimizer calculates this penalty per day for all days after the Maximum Delay, which is defined in the third field. Any delay less than the Maximum Delay does not lead to any penalty calculation. These penalties might get multiplied according to the settings in the SNP Cost Profile. The second group of fields in this view contains exactly the same fields as described above. The difference is that the second group deals not with customer requirements but with Forecast Requirements. For both groups a Delete button exists that deletes all three entries in one step if utilized. The definitions found in this screen are also referred to as "SNP Priority Classes".

The Penalty for Late and Non Delivery can be used to optimize on Profit. The higher the anticipated product profit is, the higher the product penalty should be. If this is the case, the optimizer tries to first and utmost ensure that demands for those products with high penalty (profit) are satisfied first.

#### 4.4.2.3.1.6 ATP

The ATP tab contains general as well as location-specific data. The tab symbol and the fields displayed change with the selection (general or location specific). The only two product fields on the global level deal with product allocations. The screen allows the input of the Product Allocation Procedure (field Product Allocation) and the Product Allocation Procedure Sequence (field Procedure Sequence). The location specific data fields are explained further down.

### 4.4.2.3.2 Product Master Location Data

Location specific data is grouped into the following views (tabs).

#### 4.4.2.3.2.1 Administrative

On this view the ID's of the planners responsible for the various planning tasks can be captured. If for example a specific SNP planner is defined in this view, and this planner is calling up an SNP planning job, he or she will only plan those products where the planner ID in the product master matches. This setting is not providing access control and must not be seen as an authorization check. It merely helps to pre-select products in a planning run. The four planners that can be specified here are the Production Planner (PP/DS), the Supply Network Planner (SNP), the Demand Planner (DP), and Transportation Planner (TP/VS).

#### 4.4.2.3.2.2 Demand

The Demand view can be maintained by simply specifying a Demand Profile. In this case all data previously specified in the profile is copied into the product master. From there data can either be edited as required or left without change. If data copied from a profile is edited in the product master, the link to the profile is broken and subsequent updates of the profile do not have any affect on the product master. Changes of the profile are carried through to the product master automatically only if the profile data was not changed in the product master. To break the link between the product master and the profile, simply delete the profile name in the product master. This will turn all profile-related fields from display only to editable. All fields on the Demand view can be found in the Demand Profile. For further information regarding the available fields on this view refer to the chapter "Demand Profile."

#### 4.4.2.3.2.3 Lot Size



Parts of Lot Size view can be maintained by simply specifying a Lot Size Profile. The majority of fields on this view can be found in the Lot Size Profile. For further information regarding the available fields in this profile refer to the chapter "Lot Size Profile". In addition to the fields in the Lot Size Profile, the following fields can be maintained:

| | |
|---|---|
| ♦ Safety Stock | Specify the target safety stock |
| ♦ Calculation of TSL | Specify the method for calculating the safety stock |
| ♦ Service Level | Specify the desired service level |

#### 4.4.2.3.2.4 SNP 2

The SNP2 view is subdivided into four segments. The first three segments are SNP Demand Profile, SNP Supply Profile, and Deployment Profile. Here again one can specify the corresponding profile to copy all data of the profiles into the product master. See also the explanations for the Demand view above. A fourth segment is called "Other Data." It contains the following four fields.

| | |
|---|---|
| ♦ Customer Material | The customer's product number can be put in here |
| ♦ VMI Purchasing Group | This field contains possibly a VMI specific purchasing group |

| | |
|---|---|
| ♦ Purchasing Group | Displays the Purchasing Group in the same format as R/3 |
| ♦ Priority | Used by CTM, the SNP and Deployment Optimizer to define the priority of the product |

#### 4.4.2.3.2.5 PP/DS

The PP/DS view is subdivided into three segments. None of theses segments refer to any predefined profiles.

Segment Automatic Planning for all Changes

In this segment the product's planning mode is set. The following options are available:

| | |
|---|---|
| ♦ Automatic Planning | PP/DS creates planned orders automatically for any upcoming product shortage. This is also true when PP/DS functionality is called from ATP (CTP functionality). The Automatic Planning feature is also referred to as "Incremental Finite Scheduling." |
| ♦ Manual Planning with Check | For upcoming requirements (including ATP (CTP) generated requirements), no planned orders are created. Nevertheless the system searches for a suitable supply element and if successful pegs the demand to the supply. The planner has to react manually only in the case of an unsuccessful search. |
| ♦ Manual Planning without Check | For upcoming requirements (including ATP (CTP) generated requirements) no planned orders are created. The planner has to always react manually and create planned orders as required. |

Segment Task List Explosion

Dependant requirements are created as a result of the BOM or PPM explosion. PP/DS offers two possibilities, to explode the APO resident PPM or the BOM, which resides on the connected R/3 system (if R/3 is the OLTP system). In customizing a global setting defines whether the PPM or BOM is used. In addition to this global setting, it is possible to define individually per product whether the PPM or BOM is to be used. Note that the BOM of the R/3 system can only be used within PP/DS. It is always required to create a PPM for SNP purposes, irrespective of the BOM/PPM explosion setting.

Segment Heuristic

The PP/DS Planning run uses, if not defined otherwise, a standard "built-in" planning algorithm. Define alternate other planning algorithms if required. SAP offers various alternative Heuristic-based algorithms (e.g. planning based on weekly lot sizes). If required specify such a algorithm in the field Function Module together with the Period Indicator and the Time Stream ID.



#### 4.4.2.3.2.6 GR/GI

The GR/GI view is subdivided into five segments. None of the GR/GI segments refer to any predefined profile.

In the Time segment the Planned Delivery Time, Goods Receipt and Goods Issue times are defined (in days). Various SNP programs use these time definitions when scheduling calculations are carried out.

The Stock segment displays the stock on hand at the location. This is obviously a display only field. It shows the overall stock in the location totaling all sub-locations (R/3 storage locations) and versions (R/3 batches).

The Procurement Type is the only field in the Procurement Type segment. It is used for example by SNP Heuristic to determine the valid mode of procurement. The SNP Optimizer decides on the procurement type depending on the cost situation. Please note that there is no "Special Procurement Type" as in R/3. This is not required as the pure existence of a transportation lane defines the possibility to source a product from a location. This makes even more sense when thinking about the SNP Optimizer. The decision to procure externally or internally is cost driven, as is the selection of the location from where to procure the product. Any location that has a transportation lane to the demanding location is considered.

The fourth segment, Resource, deals with the consumption of handling resources when the product has to be moved within the location. The figure is entered together with the appropriate unit of measure and refers to the base unit of

measure of the product. The same applies to the Storage Consumption. The third entry deals with the cost associated with storing the product. The warehouse (storage) resource used to store the product is the last field. The Optimizer uses the product dependent storage (warehouse) resource cost if defined in the product master and activated in the SNP Optimizer profile.
In the last, the fifth segment. a cost function can be defined. The cost function allows specifying fixed and variable procurement costs in lot size intervals. To create or update existing cost functions, specify the cost function name and select the Maintain button next to the field.

#### 4.4.2.3.2.7 Extra

The Extra tab is an optional tab that carries up to 5 product attributes on location level. This tab requires activation carried out in customizing. Please refer to the chapter "Product Attributes".

#### 4.4.2.3.2.8 ATP

The ATP tab contains general as well as location specific data. The tab symbol and the fields displayed change with the selection (general or location specific). The location specific data fields are:

| | |
|---|---|
| Location Dep. Procedure | This field allows the input of the Location Dependent Product Allocation Procedure. |
| Location Dep. Sequence | Here the Location Dependent Product Allocation Procedure Sequence is defined. |
| Check Mode | The check mode, which is called "Requirements Class" in R/3, is one of the parameters passed from R/3 to APO when an ATP request is to be carried out. Should this information be missing, then this fall back value is used. This is also helpful when linking a non-R/3 OLTP system to APO that might not have definitions similar to a check mode. |

| | |
|---|---|
| Check Horizon | The check horizon, which is called "Replenishment Lead Time" in R/3, determines the number of working days as specified in the factory calendar after which all requirements can be confirmed (if the ATP check rule uses this option). |
| ATP Group | The ATP group, which is called "Availability Check" in R/3, is one of the parameters used to determine how the availability check is carried out. The definition here is also a fall back value in situations where this information is not sent across from the OLTP system. |
| Checking Horizon Calendar | Factory calendar used in conjunction with the check horizon. |
| Display Unit of Measure | Defines the unit of measure used when displaying ATP results in APO. |

#### 4.4.2.3.3 Product Attributes

Up to 10 attributes can be defined per product, 5 each on global and location level. The activation of the global attributes adds 5 new fields to the Attributes tab. A completely new tab called "Extra" appears if attribute fields are defined (activated) on location level. The attributes are activated in the IMG (path APO > Master Data> Product > Freely Definable Names for Attributes). This option allows to activate this function and to allocate names that appear on the screen for all 10 attributes.

#### 4.4.2.4 Resource

An APO resource is characterized by having a capacity, which ultimately will have a load and might be planned for during the planning and optimization process. Resources are grouped in Resource Categories. Possible Resource Categories in APO are:

- Production Resources (work centers in R/3),
- Storage Resources (warehouses and storage types in R/3),
- Storage Handling Resources (e.g. fork lifts), and
- Transport Resources (e.g. trucks).

Transportation resources are the only category of resources that are not location specific. They are not planned for by PP/DS, but will be used in TP/VS planning tasks. Resource Categories cannot be changed once the resource has been created. The main function of a resource is that it has a capacity. These can be expressed in time (as it is the case for a work center, for example, 10 hours per workday for a production resource) or independent of time (e.g. 100 pallets in a Storage Resource). APO uses the acronyms "Bucket Resource" and "Time Continuous Resource" to define the type of resource. Time continuous resources are further broken down into Single and Multi Activity Resources. Bucket resources are used only in SNP, time-continuos resources are used in PP/DS and possibly for CTM based planning in SNP and PP/DS.

Since release 2.0 it is possible to also create Mixed Resources. A Mixed Resource is a combination of the two resource types, Bucket Resource and Time Continuous Resource. Mixed resources can be used for all resources with the category "Production". The other three resource categories are only used in SNP planning and do therefore not require the definition of time-continuous resources. With release 3.0 of APO, it is planned to introduce a new resource type, the tank resource. It will be a special type of storage resource catering for the special needs of storing products in tanks. Most types of resources are allocated to a specific location. The usage of Reference Resources simplifies the data maintenance in cases where multiple Resources with the same parameters need to be maintained individually. Work centers can be copied from R/3 to APO, where they are used to initially create resources.

The resource master needs to be assigned to any SNP model it is supposed to work with. This can be done in the Supply Chain Engineer or directly in the resource master maintenance screen. Resource master data can be made SNP version-specific. This allows the independent maintenance of master data per SNP version.

The following graph gives an overview of APO resource types and categories.

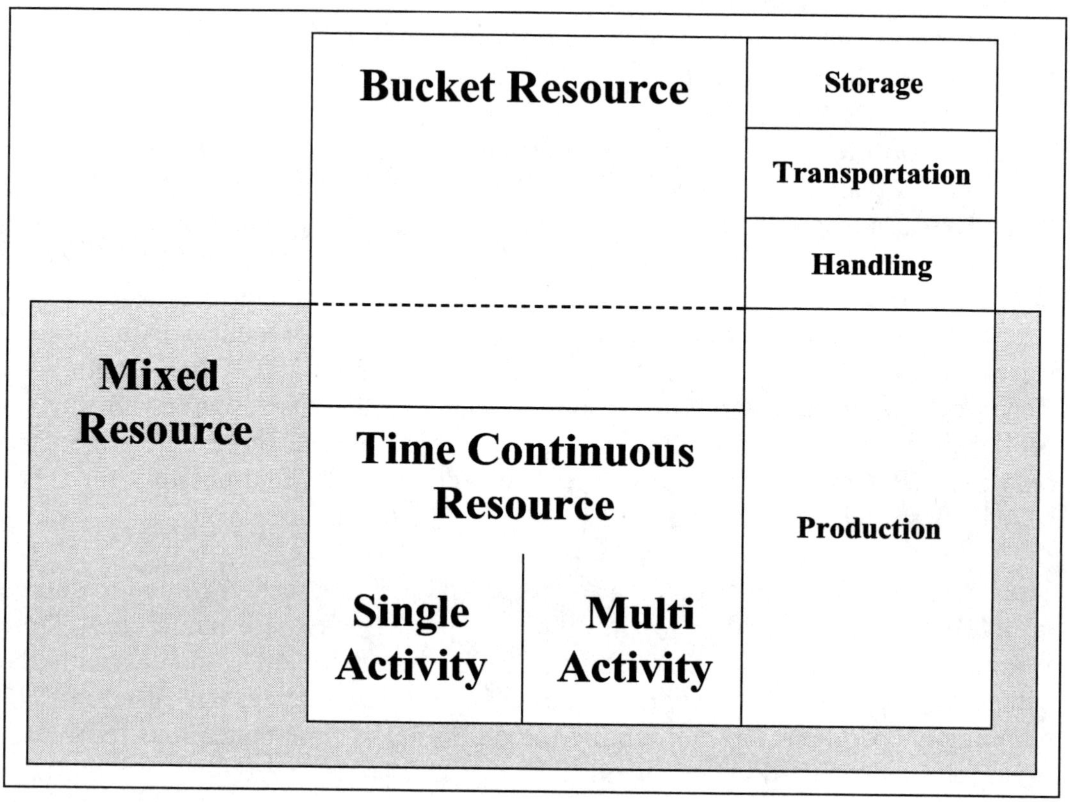


**Graphic 49 – Resource Overview**

A resource can be deleted from the header data screen after it has been selected. In order to delete a resource, it must not be used in any PPM or SNP model! Whenever an attempt is made to delete a resource the "Where Used List" is brought up automatically. If there is any entry, the deletion process cannot be carried out. To proceed in such a case, first change any PPM's that might use the resource and detach the resource then from any supply chain model. The deletion is then possible. No further warning is brought up and after the next <Save> the resource will be deleted.

The following chapter deals with the maintenance of bucket resources. They are used by all SNP applications except CTM, which can use both the bucket and the time-continuous resource. For information regarding time-continuous resources se the consecutive chapters. The maintenance of these two types of resources is different, although both have most fields in common.



#### 4.4.2.4.1 Bucket Resource

A Bucket Resource has a capacity that can be planned down to a daily level without considering sequencing constraints. It can have up to two different capacities (e.g. volume and weight for a truck). Finite scheduling is not possible for a Bucket Resource and thus Bucket Resources cannot be used by PP/DS. Both available capacities can be expressed as a quantity (e.g. 100 tons) or as a rate (e.g. 100 kg/day). The time aspect in the rate definition of a bucket resource is always "per day." It is also possible to define available hours per day as the capacity.
Capacity requirements coming from planned orders are loaded onto the resource considering only the available capacity within the time frame (day). This approach can possibly lead to a situation where several planned orders are loaded onto the resource although they all require starting at the same time. In this case finite scheduling, which will be carried out in PP/DS, detects a violation, and the production plan will have to be altered. The SNP Optimizer allows defining the time aspect of a bucket resource. Either one day or a multiple of days can be seen as one bucket in the Optimizer. Using multiple days improves the run time of the Optimizer but at the same time increases the likelihood of Finite Scheduling violations later on in the process.
Bucket Resources can be used by the SNP Heuristic run, the SNP Optimizer, and by CTM. The Transport Load Builder also uses them. The SNP Heuristic run only loads capacity requirements onto the resource, it does not carry out any capacity

feasibility checks. Please note that the SNP Optimizer only uses capacity variant 1 and capacity variant 2. In a first attempt the Optimizer uses the capacity variant with the lower capacity, and if not sufficient capacity is available, it will switch over to the other capacity variant. It does therefore not matter which of the two capacity variants provides the higher or the lower capacity.

The maintenance of the resource master is simplified by the use of "Definitions." The Definitions screen is accessible from within the Resource master data screen. For Bucket Resources only one Definition is used, which is the Quantities/Rates Definition. The maintenance of Definitions is dealt with in the chapter "Definitions."



The resource master maintenance screen provides on the upper half a table, which displays all selected resources (or which is empty for entry of new resources). On the lower half, 5 different tabs provide the same information in a different presentation. All data that can be found in the tabs, except that of the Short Texts and Characteristics tabs, is also displayed in the upper half of the screen. Information in the resource master is grouped using the following tabs (listed with the abbreviations used in the list underneath).

| | |
|---|---|
| General Data | GD |
| Planning Parameters | PP |
| Standard Capacity | SC |
| Short Texts | ST |
| Characteristics | CH |

Following is a list of all fields that can be maintained for Bucket Resources. Some of the Resource Data can be viewed in a table like layout only, while most of the details are displayed additionally on several tabs. Fields shown on the Characteristics tab need to be maintained in order to utilize the Block Planning functionality

| Field | Tab | Description |
|---|---|---|
| Resource | | Technical Name or Number of the Resource. |
| Short Description | | Name of Resource. |
| Resource Category | GD | Category of the resource. |
| Location | GD | Location in which the resource can be found or which is performing the planning task for it (e.g. for trucks). Displayed is location ID and name. |
| Time Zone | GD | Time zone of the location and thus resource; copied automatically from the location master. |
| Planner | GD | Planner responsible for the resource. |
| Factory Calendar | GD | Calendar that is used for this resource. |
| Active Variant | GD | Defines the active variant of capacity, which is only possible if capacity variants are maintained. The scheduler uses the active capacity variant. |
| Reference Resource (*) | GD | If no capacities are maintained for the resource, the system tries to use the capacity defined in the reference resource (if defined here). |
| Sort String | PP | This field is used in capacity planning to sort resources according to values other than the resource name. |
| Overload % | PP | The overload percentage is the maximum allowed overload for the resource. Any load above this value is seen as an overload. |
| Minimum Load % | PP | Defines a minimum load the resource should have below which it is identified as underutilized. |
| Finite Scheduling | PP | Defines that finite scheduling has to be carried out for this resource. This is obviously a contradiction, as bucket resources do not allow finite scheduling. This flag can be ignored for Bucket Resources. |
| Bottleneck Resource | PP | Defines the resource as a bottleneck. The SNP Optimizer can consider this flag. |

| Field | Tab | Description |
|---|---|---|
| Schedule on Grid | PP | If this flag is set, activities can only start at the beginning of the bucket period. |
| Cross Period Activity | PP | This field is also called "Activity Overlap Periods". It permits that an activity in this resource may start on one day and be continued on another. |
| Dimension | SC | Defines the dimension type (e.g. time) of the Standard Capacity defined on the standard capacity tab. This type must be the same as the one used for the Quantity/Rate definition. |
| < Capacity Button > | SC | The capacity button activates a pop up window that displays the valid bucket capacity. The definition of the valid capacity depends on various factors. Please refer to the chapter "Finding the Valid Capacity". |
| Number of Periods | SC | Number of periods that the defined capacities refer to if the capacities are time related. |
| Period Type | SC | Defines whether the capacity is time related (per day) or without relation to time. |
| Bucket Capacity | SC | This is the Standard Capacity of the Bucket Resource. |
| Unit of Bucket Capacity | SC | Defines the dimension of the Standard Capacity defined on the standard capacity tab. |
| Language | ST | Language for Short Description. Multiple descriptions in various languages can be maintained in parallel. |
| Short Description | ST | Name of Resource dependent on language defined above |

| Field | Tab | Description |
|---|---|---|
| Class Name | CH | This field allows the allocation of a class to the resource. Furthermore it allows branching into the Rules Maintenance screen. |
| < Detail Information Class > | CH | Displays detail information about the allocated class. |
| < Delete Classification > | CH | Deletes a class allocation |
| < Define Rules > | CH | Allows the definition of parameters used in Block Planning. |

**Table 61 – Bucket Resource Master Fields**



(*) The usage of a reference resource works the same way as the use of profiles in the product master. If a reference resource is specified during the creation of a resource, all fields of the reference resource are copied into the resource. As long as the name of the reference resource is not deleted in the resource any change in the reference resource is reflected in the resource.

Resource categories that can be maintained using the resource type "Bucket" include:

- Production
- Storage
- Handling
- Transportation

In the resource master maintenance screen, an individual tab can be found for the resource category "Transportation". Should a new resource be created via the transport tab, the resource category "Transportation" is applied automatically, and the resource will appear consequently under the transport tab only. When created via the bucket tab, the resource category has to be defined manually and the resource will appear consequently under the bucket tab. Other than that there are no differences.

#### 4.4.2.4.2 Time-Continuous Resource

Time Continuous Resources are broken down into the groups of Single Activity and Multi Activity Resources. These types of resources can be used for finite scheduling down to the second. Whenever a resource is loaded, which means a planned order requires capacity, the scheduling is carried out considering sequence constraints. This ensures that a resource can be used at any given point in time by:

- Exactly one planned order (Single Activity Resource),
- As many planned orders as activities exist in the resource or in other words exactly one planned order per capacity (Multi Activity Resource (option 1) with time based capacity defined only),
- As many planned orders as possible according to the unit-based capacity (Multi Activity Resource (option 2) with time and unit based capacity defined).

Operation split, that is the distribution of a production order operation over various resources, is not supported in release 2.0 (Multi Activity Resource (option 3) with time based capacity defined only). The resource type "Single Activity" or "Multi-Activity" can be used in conjunction with the resource category "Production." The following graphic provides an overview of the possible operation/activity allocation to resources.

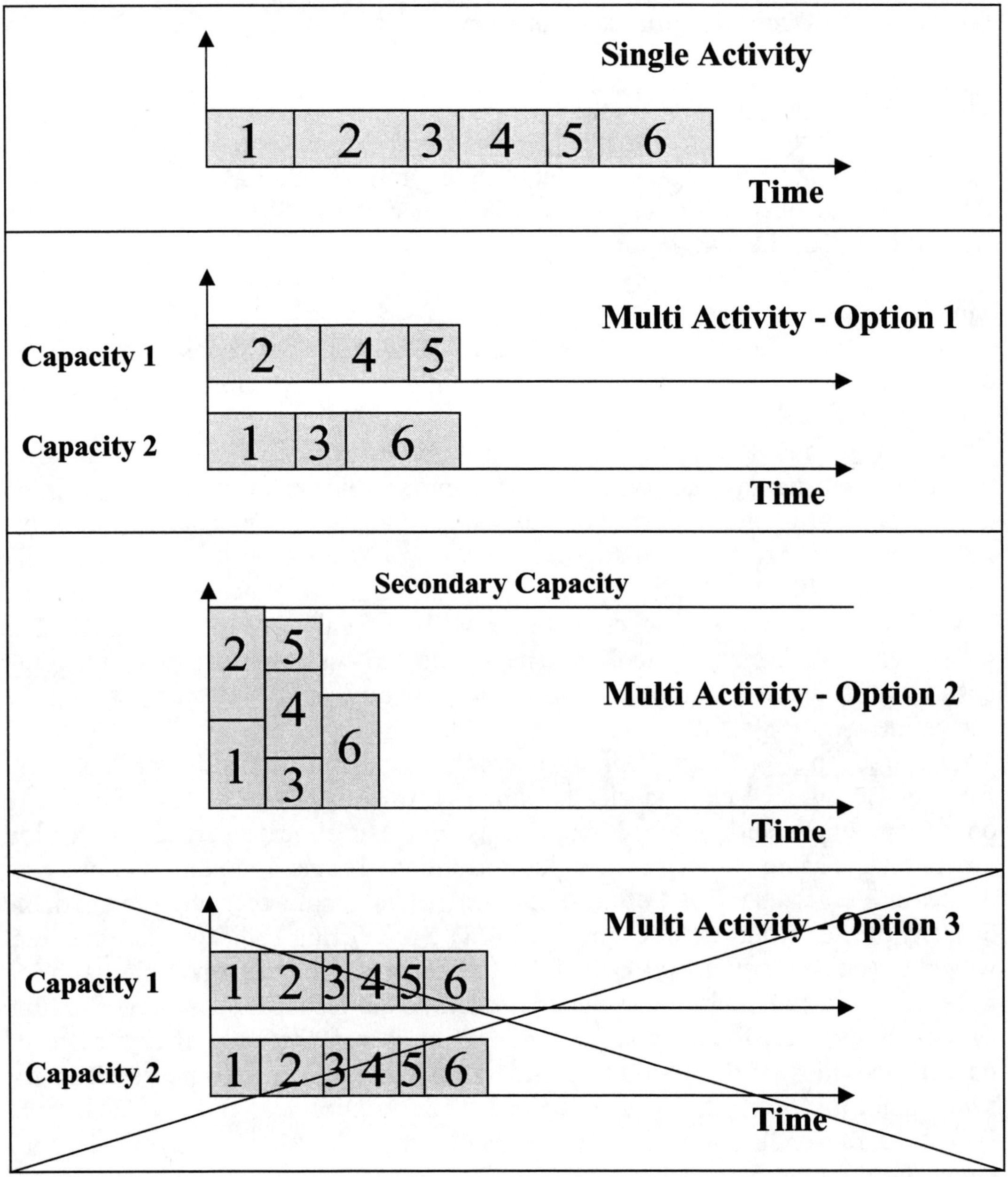
Single Activity
1 2 3 4 5 6
Time
Multi Activity - Option 1
Capacity 1
2 4 5
Capacity 2
1 3 6
Time
Secondary Capacity
2 5 4 1 3 6
Multi Activity - Option 2
Time
Multi Activity - Option 3
Capacity 1
1 2 3 4 5 6
Capacity 2
1 2 3 4 5 6
Time

**Graphic 50 – Time Continuous Resources**

Single Activity Resource
A Single Activity Resource is the same as an R/3 work center with one defined capacity. It has one capacity, which is expressed in time. Single Activity Resources can only be used by the CTM run and by PP/DS, not by the SNP Heuristics run or the SNP Optimizer.

Multi Activity Resource
A Multi Activity Resource is the equivalent of an R/3 work center with multiple capacities attached to it. Two options are available when defining the capacity of a Multi Activity Resource.
The first option is used in the case where a resource consists of several identical machines each having the same type and amount of capacity. With this option exactly one production order can be allocated to any of the machines within this resource at any given moment. An example would be a Drilling Work Center where three drills are available. Each of them can serve exactly one production order at a time and a production order will use only one of the drills. The parameter "Synchronized Start" can be applied to multi activity resources and ensures when applied that all activities at all capacities of the resource start at the same time.
The second option allows defining a second capacity restriction for the Multi Activity Resource. This capacity is expressed in relation to a unit of measure other than time. During scheduling the system can allocate several production orders for the same point of time as long as the total capacity (expressed in a unit of measure other than time) of all scheduled orders is not exceeding the available capacity of the resource. An example would be a Freezing Facility where the total weight based capacity is 100 kg and the total time capacity is 8 hours a day. The system can allocate multiple production orders to the resource at any point in time as long as the total freezing capacity of 100 kg is not exceeded. If it is required that all activities of the production orders allocated to the resource start at the same point in time, the "Synchronized Start" option can be set. The SNP Heuristics run or the SNP Optimizer cannot use Multi Activity Resources; they can be used by the CTM run and by PP/DS.

The difference in the maintenance of Single and Multi Activity Resources is only marginal, and is therefore dealt with together in this chapter.

The definition of available capacity is done either by setting up a Standard Capacity or by creating one or multiple capacity variants. The usage of standard capacity is a simple way of defining the available capacity for a resource. It does not allow to define precise shifts or shift sequences, nor does it allow to define breaks at predefined times. It is adequate for resources that are not a bottleneck and where finite scheduling can be carried out on the shop floor. Furthermore only one possible capacity, the standard capacity can be defined.
The use of capacity variants allows a precise down to the second definition of working and non-working time. This is achieved by means of precise shift and break times as well as efficiency rates per shift. Various capacity variants can be defined allowing the parallel definition of several scenarios. Any maintained capacity variant could be set to "Active." The scheduler that is accessed from the SNP Interactive Planning Screen uses the active capacity variant. Capacity variants have a validity period thus allowing easy maintenance of capacity related data. Should no capacity variant be defined (or valid), the system uses the standard capacity (see also the chapter "Finding the Valid Capacity"). For Standard Capacities only the start time, end time and break duration is maintained. They are available on all workdays according to the factory calendar.



The following two tables provide a complete overview of all fields that can be maintained for Single and Multi Activity Resources.

| Field | Tab | Description |
|---|---|---|
| Resource | | Technical Name or Number of the Resource. |
| Short Description | | Name of Resource. |
| Resource Category | GD | Category of the resource. |
| Location | GD | Location in which the resource can be found or which is performing the planning task for it (e.g. for trucks). Displayed is location ID and name. |
| Time Zone | GD | Time zone of the location and thus resource. |
| Planner | GD | Planner responsible for the resource. |

| Field | Tab | Description |
| --- | --- | --- |
| Factory Calendar | GD | Calendar that is used for this resource. |
| Active Variant | GD | Defines the active variant of capacity, which is only possible if capacity variants are maintained. The scheduler uses the active capacity variant. |
| Reference Resource (*) | GD | If no capacities are maintained for the resource, the system tries to use the capacity defined in the reference resource (if defined here). |
| Setup Matrix | PP | The setup matrix used for this resource (if any). See the PP/DS section for further information. |
| Sort String | PP | This field is used in capacity planning to sort resources according to values other than the resource name. |
| Maximum Overlap | PP | Defines the amount of time that two scheduled activities can overlap (planned order one not finished yet, but planned order two already starting). The higher this value the easier it is for the Optimizer to find a result. |
| Unit of Measure | PP | Unit of measure for the time defined above. |
| Finite Scheduling | PP | Defines that finite scheduling has to be carried out for this resource. |
| Bottleneck Resource | PP | Defines the resource as a bottleneck. The SNP Optimizer can consider this flag. |
| Dimension | SC | No dimension for a single activity resource can be defined. The field is shown but gray shaded. |
| < Capacity Button > | SC | The capacity button activates a pop up window that displays the valid single activity capacity. The definition of the valid capacity depends on various factors. Please refer to the chapter "Finding the Valid Capacity". |

| Field | Tab | Description |
|---|---|---|
| Start | SC | Start time of resource on workdays as defined in factory calendar. |
| End | SC | End time of resource on workdays as defined in factory calendar. |
| Break Duration | SC | Break duration of resource on workdays as defined in factory calendar. |
| Resource Utilization % | SC | Defines the effective time worked in the resource in form of a percentage of the total working time as defined above. |
| Productive Time in Hours | SC | This value is calculated by the system and shows the productive time in the resource taking into account start, end, and break times as well as the resource utilization. |
| Language | ST | Language for Short Description. Multiple descriptions in various languages can be maintained in parallel. |
| Short Description | ST | Name of Resource dependent on language defined above. |
| Class Name | CH | This field allows allocating a class to the resource. Furthermore it allows to branch into the Rules Maintenance screen. |
| < Detail Information Class > | CH | Displays detail information about the allocated class. |
| < Delete Classification > | CH | Deletes a class allocation. |
| < Define Rules > | CH | Allows the definition of parameters used in Block Planning. |

**Table 62 – Single Activity Resource Master Fields**

(*) The usage of a reference resource works the same way as the use of profiles in the product master. If a reference resource is specified during the creation of a resource, all fields of the reference resource are copied into the resource. As long as the name of the reference resource is not deleted in the resource, any change in the reference resource is reflected in the resource.

| Field | Tab | Description |
|---|---|---|
| Resource | | Technical Name or Number of the resource. |
| Short Description | | Name of Resource. |
| Resource Category | GD | Category of the resource. |
| Location | GD | Location in which the resource can be found or which is performing the planning task for it (e.g. for trucks). Displayed is location ID and name. |
| Time Zone | GD | Time zone of the location and thus resource. |
| Planner | GD | Planner responsible for the resource. |
| Factory Calendar | GD | Calendar that is used for this resource. |
| Active Variant | GD | Defines the active variant of capacity, which is only possible if capacity variants are maintained. The scheduler uses the active capacity variant. |
| Reference Resource (*) | GD | If no capacities are maintained for the resource, the system tries to use the capacity defined in the reference resource (if defined here). |
| Sort String | PP | This field is used in capacity planning to sort resources according to values other than the resource name. |
| Maximum Overlap | PP | Defines the amount of time that two scheduled activities can overlap (planned order one not finished yet, but planned order two already starting). The higher this value the easier it is for the Optimizer to find a result. |
| Unit of Measure | PP | Unit of measure for the time defined above. |

| Field | Tab | Description |
|---|---|---|
| Synchronized Start | PP | Flag that if set forces all operations that run in parallel to start at the same time. |
| Finite Scheduling | PP | Defines that finite scheduling has to be carried out for this resource. |
| Bottleneck Resource | PP | Defines the resource as a bottleneck. The SNP Optimizer can consider this flag. |
| Dimension | SC | Dimension describing the capacity of the resource. |
| < Capacity Button > | SC | The capacity button activates a pop up window that displays the valid multi activity capacity. The definition of the valid capacity depends on various factors. Please refer to the chapter "Finding the Valid Capacity". |
| Start | SC | Start time of resource on workdays as defined in factory calendar. |
| End | SC | End time of resource on workdays as defined in factory calendar. |
| Break Duration | SC | Break duration of resource on workdays as defined in factory calendar. |
| Resource Utilization % | SC | Defines the effective time worked in the resource in form of a percentage of the total working time as defined above. |
| Productive Time in Hours | SC | This value is calculated by the system and shows the productive time in the resource taking into account start, end, and break times as well as the resource utilization. |
| Capacity | SC | Secondary capacity of the resource. |
| Unit of Measure | SC | Dimension describing the secondary capacity of the resource. |

| Field | Tab | Description |
|---|---|---|
| Language | ST | Language for Short Description. Multiple descriptions in various languages can be maintained in parallel. |
| Short Description | ST | Name of Resource dependent on language defined above. |
| Class Name | CH | This field, which is the only one not on the grid allows to allocate a class to the resource. Furthermore it allows to branch into the Rules Maintenance screen. |
| < Detail Information Class > | CH | Displays detail information about the allocated class. |
| < Delete Classification > | CH | Deletes a class allocation. |
| < Define Rules > | CH | Allows the definition of parameters used in Block Planning. |

**Table 63 – Multi Activity Resource Master Fields**

(*) The usage of a reference resource works the same way as the use of profiles in the product master. If a reference resource is specified during the creation of a resource, all fields of the reference resource are copied into the resource. As long as the name of the reference resource is not deleted in the resource, any change in the reference resource is reflected in the resource.

The usage of a setup matrix only works with single activity resources. Setup status dependent automatic calculation of the required setup time is therefore not supported for Multi Activity Resources.

#### 4.4.2.4.3 Mixed Resource

The Mixed Resource, introduced to APO with release 2.0, is not another resource type but a combination of a bucket resource with either a single-activity or multi-activity resource. Consequently, there are two mixed resources, the single-mixed and the multi-mixed resource. The introduction of the mixed resources greatly simplifies the maintenance of resources as exactly the same resource master can be used for SNP, CTM, and PP/DS planning purposes. In general, the mixed resources contain all fields of the bucket resource and the single or multi-activity resource. This means that some of the information that can be found in the mixed resource master applies only to SNP planning, while other is valid only during PP/DS planning.

The table below gives a comprehensive overview of all fields used in all resource types. It does not include the resource type "Transportation," although a tab with this name can be found in the resource master. In reality, the transportation resource type is just a bucket resource. All fields of the bucket and transportation resource type are identical. With the new module, "Transportation Planning & Vehicle Scheduling" the transportation resource will be changed to also allow the definition of multiple dimensions (e.g. mass and volume capacity of a truck). Transportation Planning & Vehicle Scheduling is part of release 3.0.

A few fields that can be found in a bucket resource are not part of the corresponding mixed resource. These are the "Number of Periods" with the "Period Type" as well as the "Bucket Capacity" with the "Unit of Measure" thereof. There is also one field that can only be found in a mixed resource and not in the bucket resource. It is the "Loss Factor". Obviously they have got something to do with each other. When using a mixed resource, the bucket capacity is calculated using the net single-activity or multi-activity capacity and correcting it by the loss factor. For more information regarding the possible units of measure that can be used for defining the available capacity as well as the calculation of the bucket capacity, refer to the chapter "Finding the Valid Capacity."

| Resource Master Tab | Field Name | Bucket | Single | Single Mix | Multi | Multi Mix |
|---|---|---|---|---|---|---|
| None | Resource | X | X | X | X | X |
| | Short Description | X | X | X | X | X |
| GD | Resource Category | X | X | X | X | X |
| | Location | X | X | X | X | X |
| | Time Zone | X | X | X | X | X |
| | Planner | X | X | X | X | X |
| | Factory Calendar | X | X | X | X | X |
| | Active Variant | X | X | X | X | X |
| | Reference Resource | X | X | X | X | X |
| PP | Setup Matrix | | X | X | | |
| | Sort String | X | X | X | X | X |
| | Maximum Overlap | | X | X | X | X |
| | Unit of Measure | | X | X | X | X |
| | Overload % | X | | X | | X |
| | Minimum Load % | X | | X | | X |
| | Synchronized Start | | | | X | X |
| | Finite Scheduling | X | X | X | X | X |
| | Bottleneck Resource | X | X | X | X | X |
| | Schedule on Grid | X | | X | | X |
| | Cross Period Activity | X | | X | | X |
| SC | Dimension | X | | | X | |
| | < Capacity Button > | | X | X | X | X |

| Resource Master Tab | Field Name | Bucket | Single | Single Mix | Multi | Multi Mix |
|---|---|---|---|---|---|---|
| SC | < Bucket Capacity Button > | X | | X | | X |
| | Number of Periods | X | | | | |
| | Period Type | X | | | | |
| | Bucket Capacity | X | | | | |
| | Unit of Bucket Capacity | X | | | | |
| | Start | | X | X | X | X |
| | End | | X | X | X | X |
| | Break Duration | | X | X | X | X |
| | Loss Factor in % | | | X | | X |
| | Resource Utilization % | | X | X | X | X |
| | Productive Time in Hours | | X | X | X | X |
| | Capacity | | | | X | X |
| | Unit of Measure | | | | X | |
| ST | Language | X | X | X | X | X |
| | Short Description | X | X | X | X | X |
| CH | Class Name | X | X | X | X | X |
| | < Detail Information Class > | X | X | X | X | X |
| | < Delete Classification > | X | X | X | X | X |
| | < Define Rules > | X | X | X | X | X |

**Table 64 – Resource Master Fields Comparison**

#### 4.4.2.4.4 Standard Capacity

One standard capacity can be defined per resource. This is done on the Standard Capacity tab. There is no need to maintain any definitions in order to use standard capacities. Standard capacities are defined by specifying the numeric value together with a unit of measure (bucket resources) or a start and end time together with the break duration (time-continuos resources). For time-continuous resources a resource utilization factor can be defined that adjusts the net capacity. The standard capacity is only used if no capacity variants have been defined for the resource and made active. The Optimizer does not use the standard capacity, as it requires the capacity variants 1 and 2 to be maintained. In scheduling the standard capacity is used if no capacity variants are defined. The system does not enforce the maintenance of any capacity. Obviously, in such a case, the resource cannot be used at all. Also see the chapter "Finding the Valid Capacity."



#### 4.4.2.4.5 Capacity Variants

While using Capacity Variants, the maintenance of the resource master is greatly simplified by the use of "Definitions". The Definitions screen is accessible from within the Resource master data screen. Following Definitions exist:

- Shift Factors define the productivity; shift factors are linked to a shift.
- Breaks define break times; breaks are linked to a shift.
- Shifts define the shift start and end time; shifts are linked to a shift sequences.
- Shift Sequences define the sequence of individually defined shifts.
- Quantities/Rates define the output as a quantity without time relation or as a rate.

All definitions except the last are used for time-continuous resources. Bucket resources use only the Quantity/Rates definition. The following graphic depicts the relationship of these definitions. The maintenance of Definitions is dealt with in the chapter "Definitions".

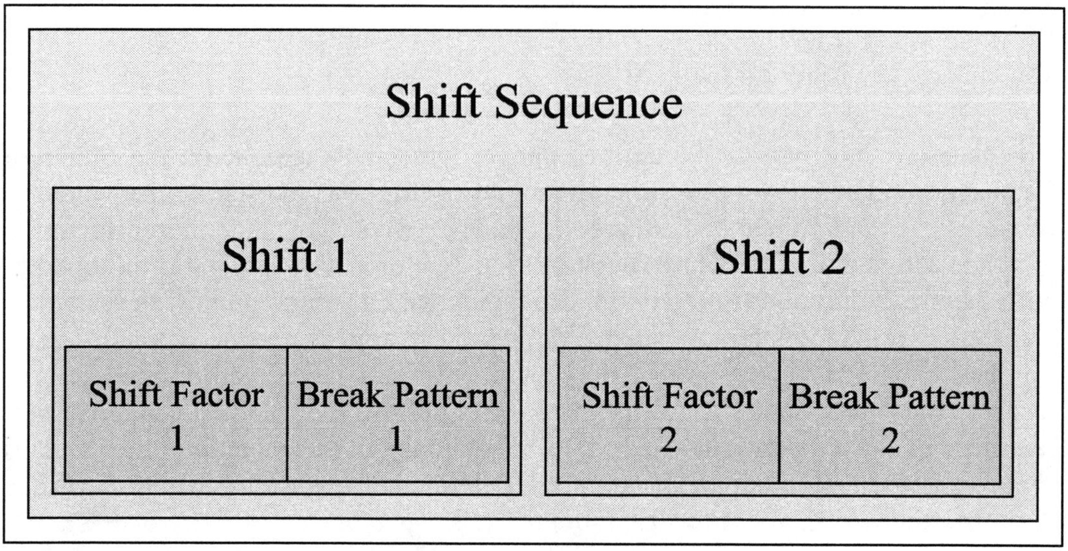


**Graphic 51 – Resource Definitions**



It is possible to link the same shift factor and break pattern definition to various shift definitions. The same shift definition can be linked to various shift sequences.

Capacity Variants for Bucket Resources

For bucket resources the capacity variant links the resource to a quantity/rate definition (see also the chapter "Definitions"). Various Quantity/Rates definitions can be linked to the same resource either for the same period or for different periods. Each capacity variant has a validity period. Additional Capacity Variant keys can only be defined when accessing the Resource master data maintenance from the PP/DS menu. To create a new capacity variant interval for a resource simply define the following:

- Capacity Variant  Numerical key of capacity variant
- Valid from  Validity start date
- Valid to  Validity end date

- Quantity/Rate Definition — Identifying number of the quantity/rate definition used for this capacity variant.
- Workdays — Determines whether the days in the quantity/rate definition are workdays according to the factory calendar of the resource, workdays, or non-workdays.

The Capacity Variants Overview screen displays a variant "0" if no capacity variant was maintained for the resource. Please note that the SNP Optimizer uses capacity variants 1 and 2 only. This is irrespective of whether they are marked as active or not. The capacity variant with the lower capacity is used as the "Default Capacity Version"; the one with the higher capacity is the "Additional Capacity Version."



Capacity Variants for Time-Continuous Resources

The capacity variant links the resource to a shift sequence. Shift sequences are defined using shifts, breaks, and shift factors (see chapter "Definitions"). Various capacity variants can be linked to the same resource, either for the same period or for different periods. Each capacity variant has a validity period. To create a new capacity variant interval simply define the following:

- Capacity Variant — Numerical key of capacity variant
- Valid from — Validity start date
- Valid to — Validity end date
- Shift Sequence — Name of shift the sequence used for this capacity variant.
- First Day — Day number within the shift sequence that represents the first day of the shift sequence. If for example the shift sequence is a weekly one with day one representing a Monday and the valid from date is a Wednesday this field must be set to 3.
- Workdays — Determines whether the days in the shift sequence are workdays according to the factory calendar of the resource, workdays, or non-workdays.

For resources without any defined capacity variants, a variant "0" can be seen on the overview screen. Periods with no capacity can be defined by simply keeping gaps between the valid to and valid from entries. It is also possible to specifically define shift definitions with Zero available capacity. This definition can, for example, be applied in periods where the resource is not usable due to a breakdown.

#### 4.4.2.4.6 Definitions

The Definitions Maintenance program is part of the Resource Maintenance program and can only be accessed from there. The following chapter explains all definitions with their respective fields and usage. Please note that all Definitions Maintenance screens show on the bottom half the fields Language, Name, and Short Description. This allows the naming of each Definition in various languages.



Shift Factor
The Shift Factor defines the efficiency during working time.

The efficiency is expressed as a percentage and called Resource Utilization. The shift factor is used together with the break time to calculate the available working time per shift. In case of Multi Activity Resources the number of capacities with unit of measure (if appropriate) are defined here as well. Shift Factors have a mandatory "Valid To" date and, as an option, a planner can be defined.

Break Patterns
Break Patterns define the non-working time.

They can be defined in two different ways. Option 1 is to specify a break start and end time, which automatically calculates the break duration. Use this option if a break has to occur at predefined times (e.g. the lunch break is at exactly 12.00). Option 2 allows defining the amount of time between the shift start and the start of the break. Additionally the break duration has to be defined. This option is used when it is required to ensure that a break occurs at least after a predefined amount of time (e.g. a break must start after four hours of work). It is advisable to use only one of the two options for a specific shift definition. Break Patterns have an option to define a planner.

<u>Shift Definition</u>
The Shift Definition stipulates the net available working time.

In the Shift Definition, the shift start and end time is specified together with the break pattern and shift factor. Note that no shift factors or break times are captured in the Shift Definition but the respective definitions are linked to the shift definition. The same break pattern and shift factor can be used several times thus reducing the amount of data capturing time tremendously. The output is the so-called Productive Time, which is calculated as follows:

| |
|---|
| Productive Time = (End of Shift – Start of Shift – Total Break Times) * Resource Utilization / 100 |

Shift Definitions have a mandatory "Valid To" date and as an option a planner can be defined.



<u>Shift Sequence</u>
The Shift Sequence defines the sequences of shifts within a given period.

Per day, up to 9 shifts can be defined. In a typical weekly shift sequence, one can find 7 entries, one per day, each with the respective shifts per day. It is important to also define the non-working days in such a definition. The shift sequence automatically restarts after the last day of the sequence. In the shift sequence one can define whether or not shifts are allowed to start or finish on non-working days. Shift Sequences have a mandatory "Valid To" date and as an option a planner can be defined. In an environment where exactly the same shifts occur daily (number and type of shifts), it is sufficient to define a shift sequence where one day is defined only. The definition is then valid for all working days.

The shift sequence as described above is used for Discrete Manufacturing and for Process Industry Orders. There are also shift sequences in the system that will be used in an upcoming release for Repetitive Manufacturing. These shift sequences allow the definition of product independent and dependent rates. Per rate definition, the number of time units and the output quantity per time unit can be stipulated. A new type of resource, the Line Resource will be introduced in conjunction with the material dependent rates.

Quantities/Rates

The Quantity/Rates Definition defines the bucket capacity.

It is the only definition used for Bucket Resources and is not used by Single/Multi Activity Resources. It contains the following fields:

- Quantity Rate — This is the name of the definition
- Valid to — Definitions only have a "valid to" date and thus are usable from the creation date onwards.
- Planner — The code for the planner responsible for the resource during the period.
- Number of Periods — Specify the number of periods (e.g. days) only if the definition is a rate (e.g. 100kg per day). Leave this field blank if the definition is a quantity.
- Period Type — The period indicator for the number of periods specified above. SNP only allows for days as a period type (or none).
- Bucket Capacity — Define the capacity in accordance with the two settings above. Note that the quantity/rate definition must have the same dimension as the capacity it will be linked to.
- Unit of Measure — Use a unit of measure in accordance with the period type for the quantity/rate definition.
- Costs — Specify the cost of using this quantity/rate. The definition of this cost (or penalty) is of utmost importance as the SNP Optimizer uses these cost figures to find the optimal solution.

The Quantities/Rates definition is used for SNP planning purposes. This planning procedure can be compared to Rough Cut Capacity Planning in R/3. In this planning step, it is adequate to plan not to the finest detail possible and ignore specific setup, tear down, and wait times, as long these activities do not constitute an abnormal high portion of the entire operation. Instead, it makes more sense to lower the available capacity of the bucket resource by a certain amount. The difference between this lowered available capacity defined in the Quantity/Rates definition and the real total capacity is then the "buffer." It will not be used by SNP, but can be used by PP/DS when finite scheduling is carried out if the time-continuous resource is adequately defined. When working with separate bucket and time-continuous resources, it is up to the planner to ensure that the master data is aligned appropriately. When using mixed resources, the relation between these two capacities is defined using the "Loss Factor." The loss factor percentage is the capacity portion that has to be taken off the time-continuous capacity when calculating the bucket capacity. The following graphic depicts this setup.

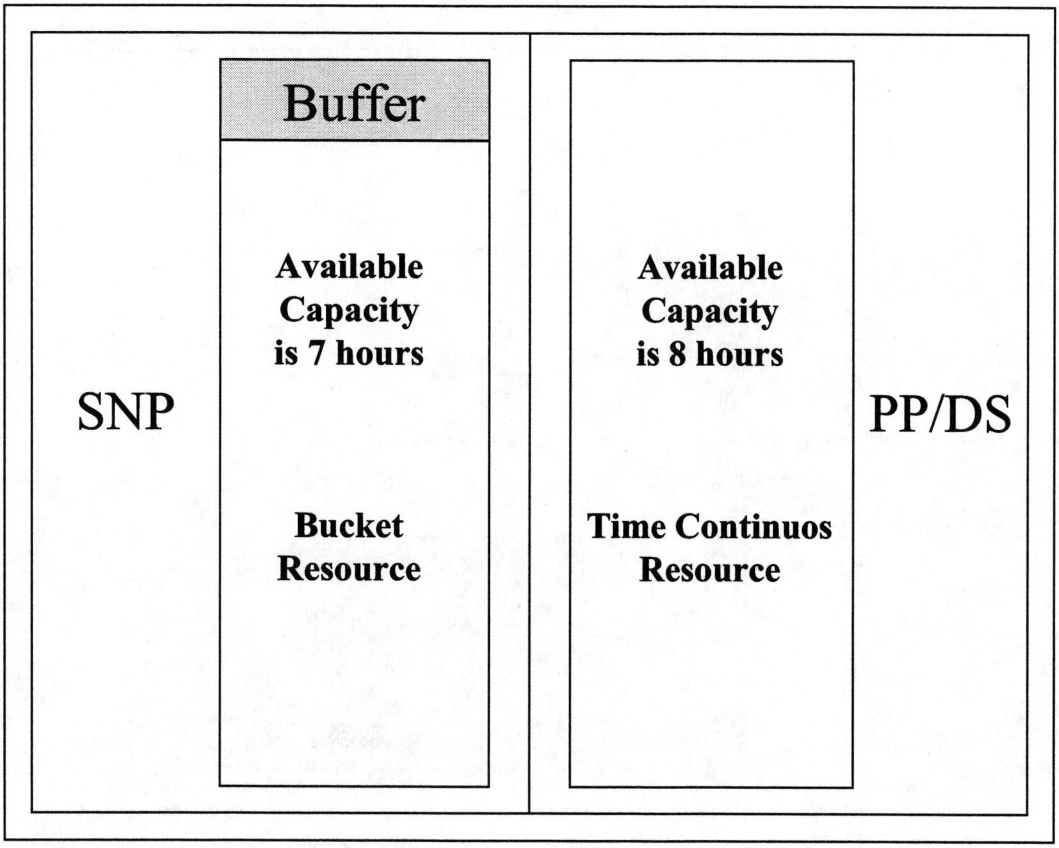


**Graphic 52 – Buffer Capacity**

The buffer in the above graphic is also referred to as the "Loss Factor". For more information see the chapter regarding mixed resources.

### 4.4.2.4.7 Finding the Valid Capacity

The search for the valid capacity is depending on the application area. It can be a rather complex task. The following diagram graphically illustrates the search procedure.

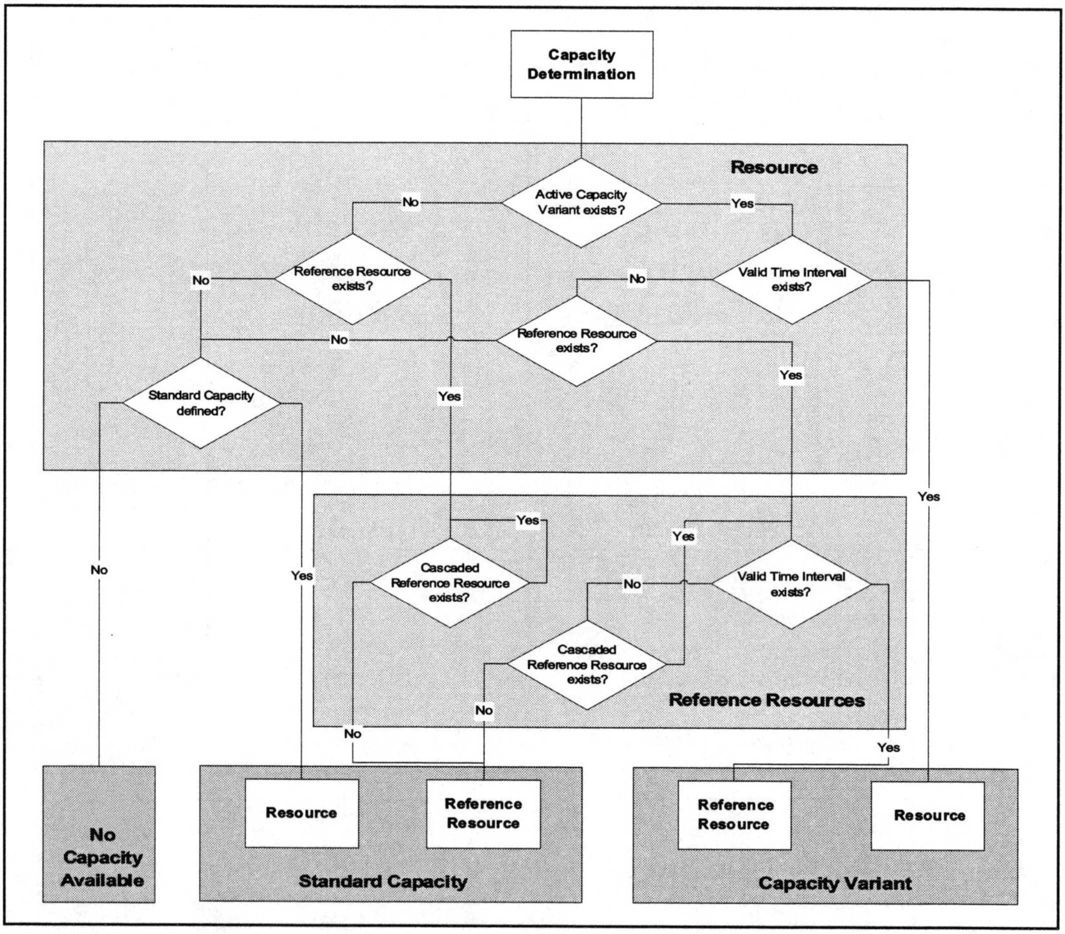


**Graphic 53 – Capacity Selection**

To facilitate an easier capacity maintenance, it is possible to link a resource to another resource (the reference resource) from which it will take over the capacity definitions under certain conditions. As can be seen in the graphic above, reference resources can also be cascaded. Whether this is advisable, is another question.

One or two capacity check buttons can be found on each of the standard capacity tabs of the resource master. When activated, the system finds the valid capacity according to the above graphic and displays the result in table form. The table can be saved locally for further processing using other PC programs. One capacity button can be found for bucket and time-continuous resources. For mixed resources two buttons are present, one for the bucket capacity, the other for the time-continuous capacity. Note that in order to use a capacity variant and not the standard capacity, the capacity variant must be defined for the resource and set as the active variant. Depending on the type of resources, different capacity types with individual dimensions can be defined. The capacity per working day is always the same for all days if the capacity data is taken from the standard capacity screen. When using capacity variants, the capacity can be different per day.



Bucket resources have a time or quantity-based dimension. When using a quantity-based dimension, it is possible to leave it without time relation (quantity), or to relate the quantity to the time (rate). Quantity definitions are used, for example, to describe the capacity of a truck or a warehouse. A time capacity is always expressed in a "per period" approach.

Single activity resources do not allow stipulating a dimension. The capacity is always expressed in time per working day. The productive time is calculated as follows:

| |
|---|
| Productive Time = (End Time – Start Time – Total Break Times) * Resource Utilization / 100 |

| |
|---|
| The available capacity equals the productive time. |

Single activity mixed resources provide the capacity figures for bucket and time-continuos calculations. Usually the capacity for a production bucket resource can be defined in a time unit or in other dimensions such as volume or mass for example. Single activity mixed resources take the productive time (see above), which could be derived from the standard capacity or active variant. This productive time is then reduced according to the loss factor to give the available capacity for the bucket capacity of the single activity mixed resource. As a consequence of this approach, it is only possible to define a time-related bucket capacity for a single activity mixed resource and no quantity or rate, as it is possible in a bucket resource. If the SNP planning must be carried out using a unit other than time, it is required to define the bucket resource and the time-continuos resource as separate entities. The bucket capacity is calculated as follows:



Bucket Capacity = Productive Time * (1 – Loss Factor / 100)

Multi activity resources are used in cases where the same type of activity is available in multiple units (e.g. three machines of the same type are one resource with the capacity counter set to 3). Another possibility is that the same machine can be used by multiple operations at the same time. In this case a total capacity in quantity is defined in the capacity counter and a unit of measure with a dimension other than time is specified. For case one, the calculation of available capacity is similar to this of single activity resources. The formula for the productive time is as follows:

Productive Time = (End Time – Start Time – Total Break Times) * Resource Utilization / 100

Total available capacity of the resource is the productive time multiplied by the capacity counter.

A further capacity restriction might be imposed on a Multi Activity Resource. This capacity referred as the secondary capacity is expressed in any unit of measure not equal to time.

Multi activity mixed resources provide the capacity figures for bucket and time-continuous calculations. In the case of the multi activity mixed resources it is not possible to define an alternate capacity (option 2, see above). A multi activity mixed resource takes the productive time (see above), which could be derived from the standard capacity or active variant. This productive time is then reduced according to the loss factor to give the available capacity for the bucket capacity of the multi activity mixed resource. As a consequence of this approach, it is only possible to define a time related bucket capacity for a multi activity mixed resource and no quantity or rate, as it is possible in a bucket resource. If the SNP planning must be carried out using a unit other than time, it is required to define the bucket resource and the time-continuos resource as separate entities. The productive time is calculated as follows:

| |
|---|
| Bucket Capacity = Productive Time * (1 – Loss Factor / 100) |

| |
|---|
| Total available capacity of the resource is the productive time multiplied by the capacity counter. |

The following table provides examples of possible capacity definitions for all types of resources and capacities.

| Resource Type | Capacity Type | Dimension | Definition | Resulting Capacity | Possible Capacity Variant |
|---|---|---|---|---|---|
| Bucket | | | | | |
| | Bucket | Time | 8 h / 1 day | 8 h / day | Time |
| | | Other | 1000 kg / 2 day | 500 kg / day | Rate |
| | | Other | 10 m3 | 10 m3 | Quantity |
| Single Activity | | | | | |
| | Time Continuos | <none> | Start Time = 08.00 | | |
| | | | End Time = 17.00 | | |
| | | | Break Duration = 01.00 | | |
| | | | Utilization = 90 % | 7.2 h / day | Shift Seq. |
| Single Activity Mixed | | | | | |
| | Time Continuos | <none> | Start Time = 08.00 | | |
| | | | End Time = 17.00 | | |
| | | | Break Duration = 01.00 | | |
| | | | Utilization = 90 % | 7.2 h / day | Shift Seq. |
| | Bucket | <none> | Productive Time = 7.2 h | | |
| | | | Loss Factor = 10 % | 6.48 h / day | Depends |
| Multi Activity | | | | | |
| | Time Continuos | <none> | Start Time = 08.00 | | |
| | | | End Time = 17.00 | | |
| | | | Break Duration = 01.00 | | |
| | | | Utilization = 90 % | | |
| | | | Capacity = 2 | 14.4 h / day | Shift Seq. |

| Resource Type | Capacity Type | Dimension | Definition | Resulting Capacity | Possible Capacity Variant |
|---|---|---|---|---|---|
| Multi Activity | | | | | |
| | Time Continuos | Other | Start Time = 08.00 | | |
| | | | End Time = 17.00 | | |
| | | | Break Duration = 01.00 | | |
| | | | Utilization = 90 % | | |
| | | | Capacity = 100 kg | 7.2 h / day & 100 kg (*) | Shift Seq. |
| Multi Activity Mixed | | | | | |
| | Time Continuos | <none> | Start Time = 08.00 | | |
| | | | End Time = 17.00 | | |
| | | | Break Duration = 01.00 | | |
| | | | Utilization = 90 % | | |
| | | | Capacity = 2 | 14.4 h / day | Shift Seq. |
| | Bucket | <none> | Productive Time = 7.2 h | | |
| | | | Loss Factor = 10 % | 14.4 h / day | |
| | | | Capacity = 2 | 12.96 h / day | Depends |

**Table 65 – Capacity Examples**

(*) The capacity of 100 kg must be seen as a further restriction of the multi activity resource. It operates for 7.2 hours per day and cope with a maximum of 100 kg at any time. The multi activity resource can handle in this case multiple operations as long as their total load does not exceed 100 kg.

SNP

### 4.4.2.5 Production Process Model (PPM)

#### 4.4.2.5.1 PPM Overview

The PPM is the most complex type of master data in APO. It represents a combination of a Bill of Material (BOM) and a Routing. This method is very similar to the Recipe known from R/3 PP-PI. The PPM provides all the information required for manufacturing a product. This includes required components and resources with the respective usage as well as the output product(s). It therefore is the key source of information for SNP and PP/DS when planning component requirements and/or resource consumption. The PPM has validity parameters for time and possible lot size. SNP and PP/DS are both using PPM's. The PPM used by the SNP Heuristics and the Optimizer is of type S (for SNP only) and contains less information than the PPM used by CTM, which is of type C (for CTM only) or by PP/DS, which is of type P (for PP/DS only). CTM can also use PPM's of type S or of type P. PPM's of type S can only work in conjunction with bucket resources and PPM's of type P work exclusively with time continuous resources. CTM can work with both as well as with PPM's of type "C."

Unlike in typical BOM's, we do not find a rigid relation of components used in the process, and finished products coming out of the process. Any product can be an Input if marked so, and any could be an Output. If two output products are defined, it is possible to create a PPM for either of the two or for both. In a situation where only one output product is used to create a PPM, it will be the only one that can be picked up by for example the SNP run for planning. The other output product is then a joint product (also called by-product or co-product) that cannot be planned on its own. There is no distinction between a by-product and a co-product as we can find it in R/3. The real difference in R/3 between the two definitions is a costing issue. APO does not deal with product costing and therefore does not need to distinguish.

On the top level and actually above the PPM, we find the Plan. The plan, which is not location specific, can be used to define several PPM's for several products.

Exactly one location specific PPM can exist in a plan per combination of location, validity period, and lot size range. The PPM can be named and given a description as required and does therefore not necessarily carry the name of an output product. The same plan can be used for one or multiple products depending on the number of output products defined in the plan. The following graphic shows an example where the two products "A" and "B" are output products of the same plan (they are joint products). The various PPM's within the plan are defined for different output products.

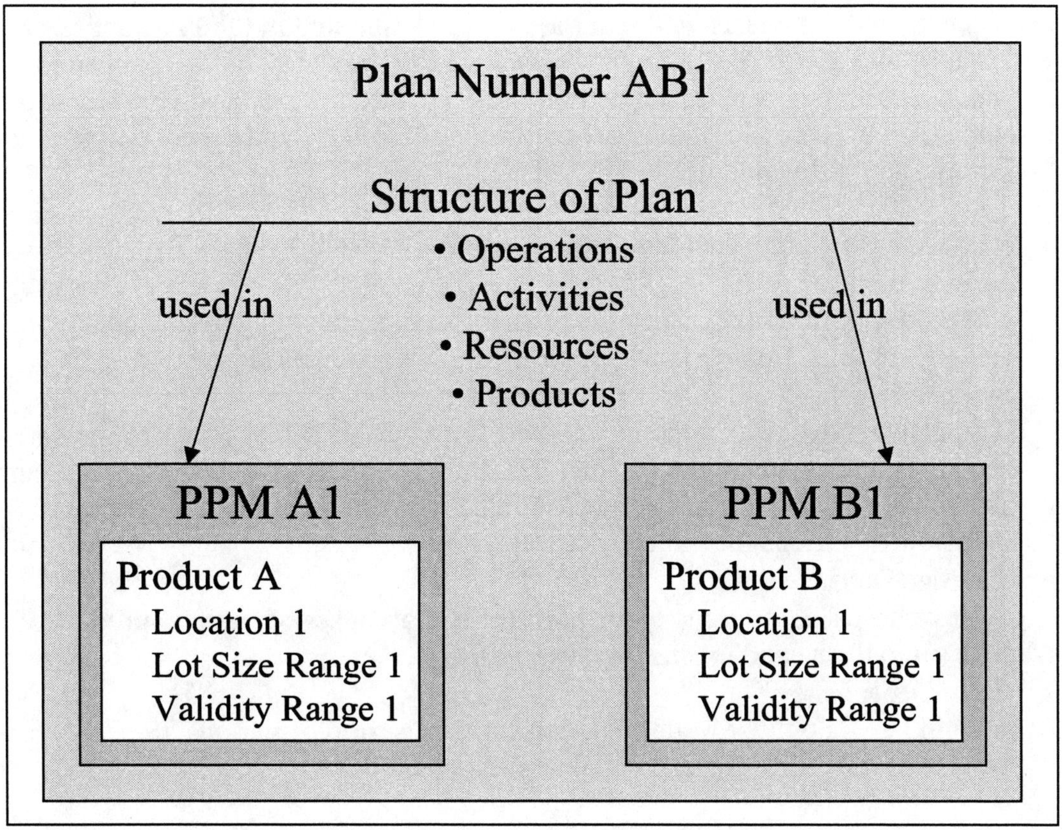


**Graphic 54 – PPM's and Plans**

It is required to create different plans if different PPM's are required for the same output product but for different locations, lot size ranges, or validity periods. Time dependent usage of input products (components) is modeled within the plan and does therefore not require the creation of different plans. The plan defines all specifics of a production process such as operations, activities, resources, and products/components. The PPM within a plan is a pointer that utilizes the structure of a plan and links it to an output product of exactly one location, lot size range, and validity periods. As the PPM is merely a pointer and not a structure like the plan it cannot be copied. A plan, on the other hand, can be copied as required. Note as well that the location stipulated in the PPM defines for which locations it can be used if there is a requirement. The location used in conjunction with the resource on activity level defines the physical location of the resource. In our example above, all planned orders for requirements of product "A" in location "1" would use the PPM "A1."



Why do we have plans? There are several reasons for using plans.

- Multi-Output
  Plans are helpful to describe a process-oriented production environment where not only multiple input but also multiple output products exist.
- Multi-Location
  The plan serves as a grouping method for all PPM's that relate to the same product in cases where the product is manufactured at several locations. Plans with all the PPM's that are defined within them can be easily copied and made available in various locations.
- Lot Size Dependency
  A plan is used to group several PPM's that describe output products in relation to their valid lot size ranges.
- Time Dependency
  Should PPM's only be valid for a certain time period or periods, then they can be grouped together elegantly in one plan.

On the plan header level following information can be captured.

- Plan usage (S, P, or C for SNP, PP/DS, or CTM only).
- The Cost Identifier, which is used by the SNP Optimizer.
- Plan descriptions in various languages.
- Products that can be produced with this plan.

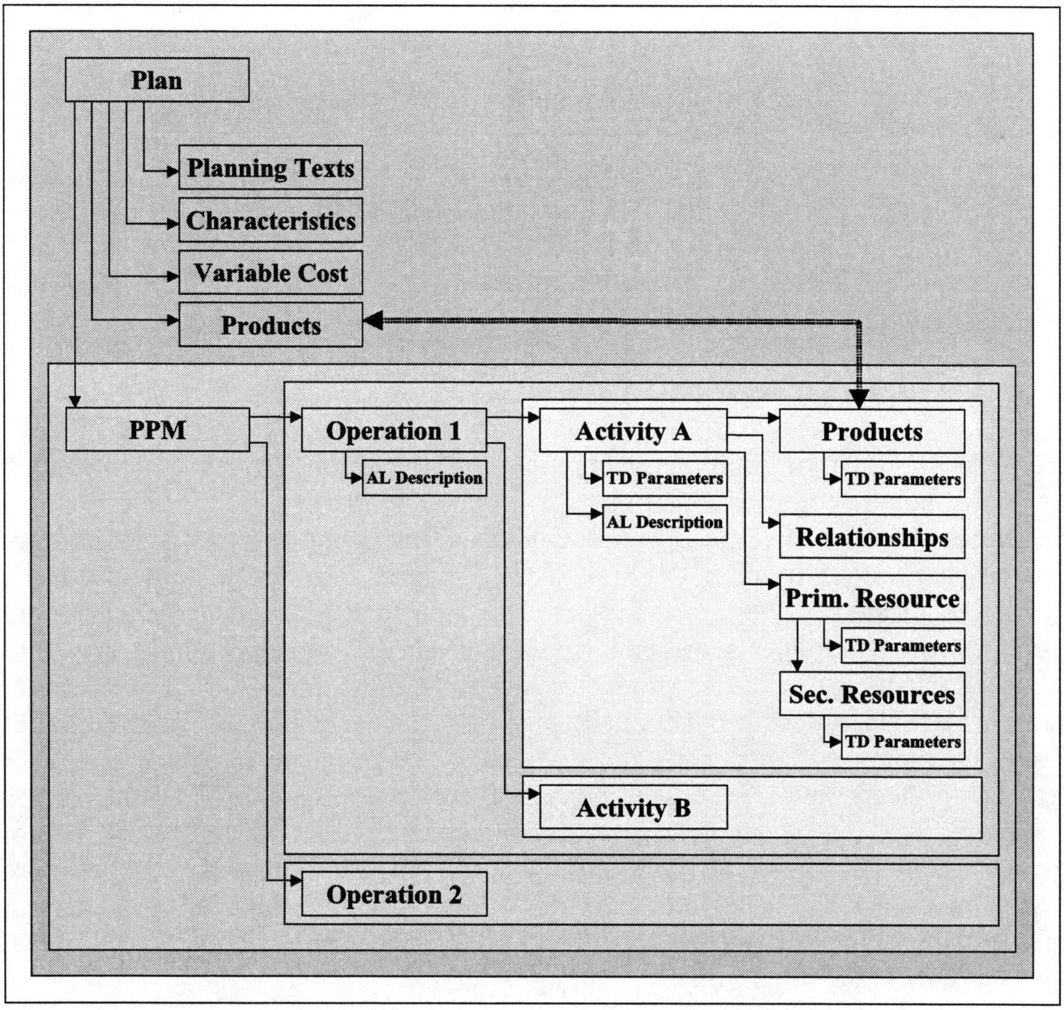


**Graphic 55 – PPM Structure**

The PPM is a highly structured set of master data. The difficulty is to set up the data consistently, as the data is not only related in a top down approach within a branch of the PPM but also cross branches. The structure of the PPM is as depicted in the above graphic. The abbreviation “TD” stands for Time Dependent, “AL” for Alternate Language.

One must keep in mind that the plan header information is information not for a specific PPM but for all PPM’s within the plan. Each plan contains potentially various sets of PPM’s. The PPM in the plan can be made usable for any and only for such an output product that is defined on activity level.

PPM’s can be deleted in a one step process. They should be deleted from any supply chain model beforehand.



**Operation and Activity**

A PPM has one or multiple operations. An operation groups activities that logically belong together. Each operation contains one or several activities. All activities within a specific operation must use the same primary resource. An activity has an activity type, which is Setup, Produce, Tear Down, or Wait (Queue Time). Allocated to these activities are the input and/or output products. Input products are components or semi finished products; output products are semi finished products or finished products. Any PPM must have at least one activity with a defined output product. SNP planning can be compared to Rough Cut Capacity Planning. For this reason it would not be adequate to plan within SNP for setup, tear down, and wait activities separately. For infinite scheduling purposes, it is sufficient to plan without these activities, as long they do not constitute an abnormal high portion of the entire operation. Instead, it makes more sense to lower the available capacity of the bucket resource by a certain percentage. This percentage is then the “buffer” that is not used by SNP, but can be used by PP/DS when finite scheduling is carried out.

The resources and their consumption are also defined on activity level. Duration and cost are specified per activity. One primary resource must be specified, and several secondary resources can be specified. The duration of an activity can be specified as a linear function of the output quantity or in a step function. The step function specifies the resource consumption per output quantity not in a linear way but in intervals (steps). Per step the duration of the step is defined and the resource consumption during this step. Step functions are useful in situations where the resource output is in multiples of the product's unit of measure. An example would be an extruder where per injection process 10 pieces are manufactured or a chemical process where the output quantity is a multiple of 100 kg. All steps have the same duration and consumption values. A Zero duration for the step depicts a liner function.

The identification number of operations and activities does not preempt a certain sequence. It is necessary to explicitly define the exact sequence of activities. This allows a totally flexible definition of any type of activity relation from simple line relations to highly complex networks. Any activity of any operation can be linked to any one or multiple activities irrespective of operations. This is done by means of building up relationships. The system displays predecessors and successors per activity, and it is sufficient to define the relation only once (either go to the predecessor activity and define the successor activity or vice versa). Relations between activities can be of type Start-Start, Finish-Start, Finish-Finish, or Start-Finish. It is possible to define for each such relation minimum and maximum deviations.



## PPM Network

As we have seen in the graphic above, a PPM that consists of one or several operations, each in turn has one to several activities. The number (or name) of the operation as well as the activity has no impact on this network at all. One can define that operation or activity 10 follows operation or activity 20 and so on. Each activity has to be brought in relation to other activities. For SNP PPM's these definitions are very basic. All relations are of the type "Finish-Start." For PP/DS PPM's more complex relations can be defined. They are dealt with in the PP/DS section.

## Modes

To add some more flexibility but also more complexity, the (SNP & PP/DS) PPM allows defining various Modes per activity. A mode represents a possible set of one primary and one or multiple secondary resource that are used in order to process an activity. Each mode represents an alternative that can be selected in order to carry out the activity. Note that secondary resources are used in APO to fulfill a requirement together with the primary resource. They complement each other. In opposition to this, resources defined in the various modes define various possible alternatives to fulfill the same capacity requirement. In bucket resource oriented PPM's, as used in SNP, there is usually only one activity per operation. For this reason, mode coupling is not a stringent requirement. For more information about mode coupling, which is a feature that can be found in PP/DS PPM's, refer to the PP/DS section. Scheduling is carried out according to exactly one resource (primary or secondary) as defined in the activity. The relation of various resource definitions is depicted in the graphic below.



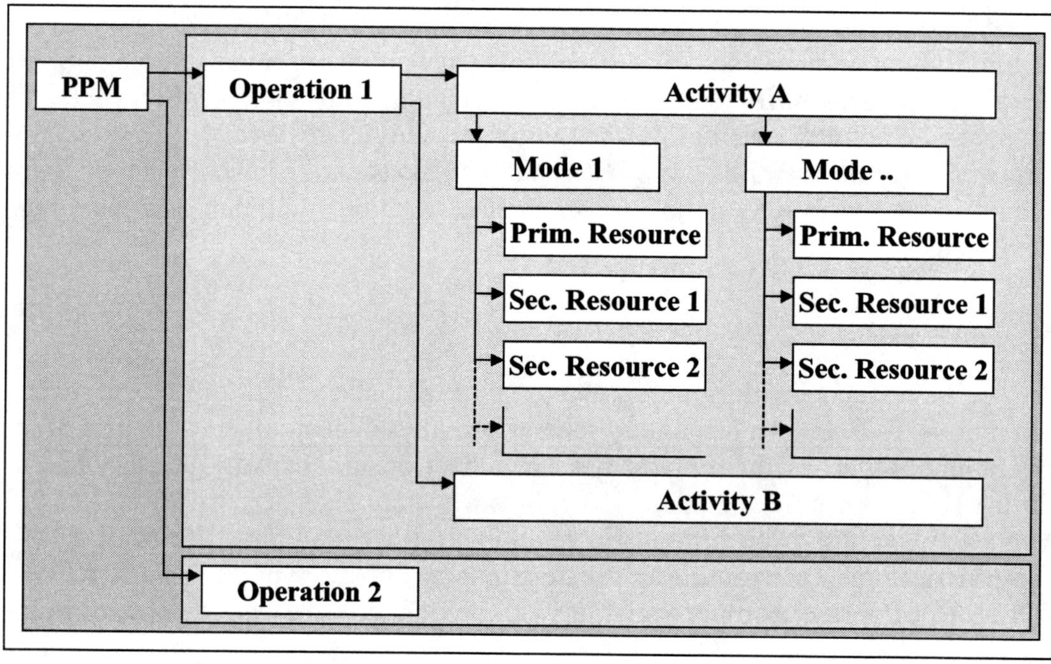


**Graphic 56 – PPM Modes**

Each activity has at least one mode. Duration and cost are specified per mode. The Heuristic run always uses the first defined mode.

## Time Dependent Parameters

Time Dependent Parameters allow the modeling of process parameters that change over time. In cases where time dependent parameters are maintained, the system will check to find a valid time interval. If the time dependent parameters do not apply to the time of the PPM explosion, the default value, if maintained, will be used. Time Dependent Parameters can be defined for the following processes.

- Scrap / Yield
  On activity level the scrap or the yield factor can be defined.
- Product Consumption and Penalty
  The consumption of products as well as the variable penalty for using the product can be defined on activity level. This also applies to output products. In this case the time dependent parameter defines the output quantity and associated penalty.
- Mode Fixed duration and Penalty
  Per mode the fixed duration parameter and the variable penalty for applying the mode can be defined.
- Resource Consumption and Penalty
  Per resource the consumption as well as the variable penalty for using the resource can be defined.

Any of the Time Dependent Parameters can be defined globally without specifying a specific SNP planning version or only for specific SNP planning versions.

## Resource Consumption Calculation

The time consumption per resource and mode in a PPM, which is defined in the "Secondary Resources Level" screen (see below) does not have to be specified in any relation to an output quantity on this screen. The time defined there must be seen in relation to the output product and quantity defined in the screen "Maintain Components."

In cases where no output product is defined for an operation, the time consumption specified in this particular operation has to be seen in conjunction with the output quantity of the following operation. This can be repeated through to the last operation that must have an output product. At the end, the PPM

describes the process of producing a product, and therefore at least one product in the last operation must be specified.
Care needs to be taken when scrap factors are applied in operations without output products. The calculation principles remain the same; it is just more difficult to understand the calculation and specify the time consumption data correctly.

## Consistency Check Tool

With all these possibilities when setting up a PPM, it is easily possible to forget something or to define inconsistent PPM's. For this reason APO offers a Check facility that verifies the logical consistency of the PPM. Only after this check has been carried out successfully, a PPM can be activated.

### 4.4.2.5.2 PPM Maintenance

In this chapter we will go through all fields required to set up a PPM for use in SNP. For more information regarding PPM's used for PP/DS, please refer to the PP/DS section. The structure of the PPM screens is depicted in the following graphic.

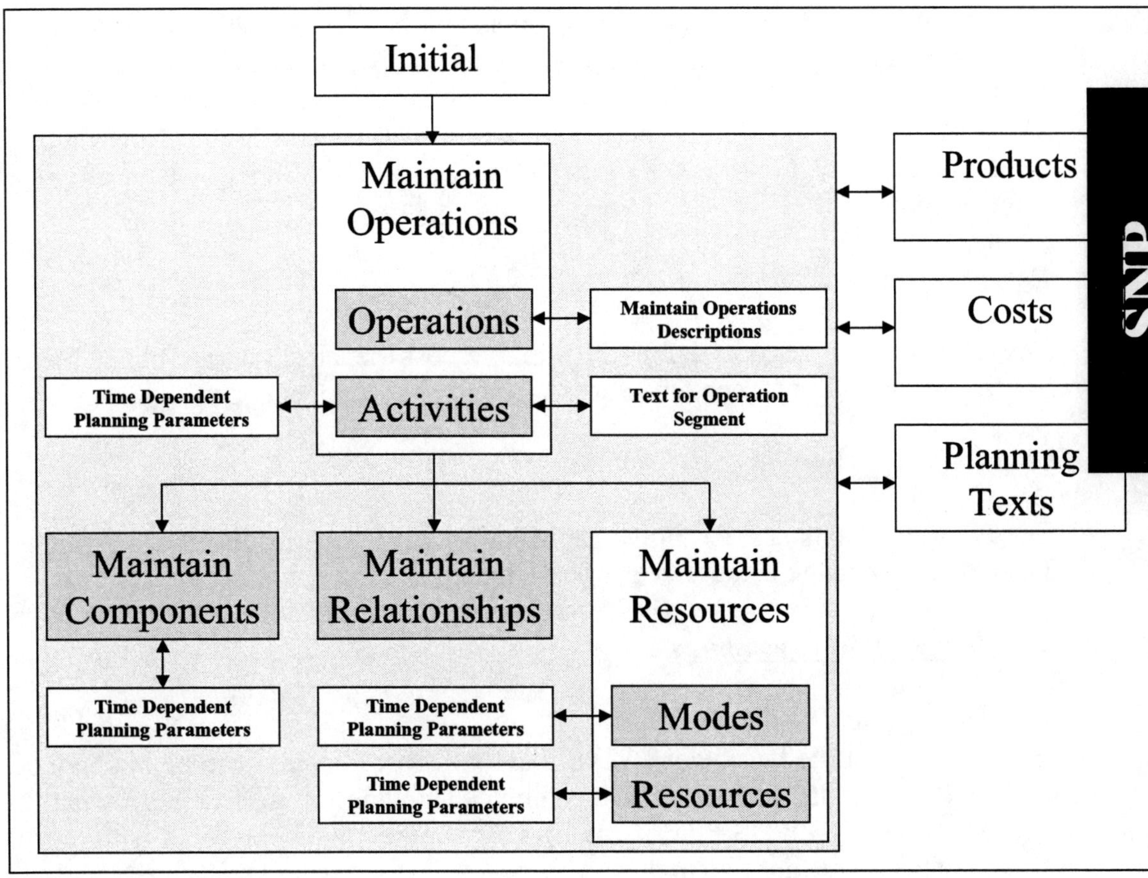


**Graphic 57 – PPM Screen Structure (SNP)**

**Initial Screen**

In order to create a PPM, a plan number and a plan usage has to be defined followed by its name on the next screen. This leads to the "Maintain Operations" screen.

**Products Screen**

The Products screen defines which products can be planned with the PPM. Only products that are defined as output products in the "Maintain Components" screen can be planned using the PPM. In this step you also assign the location for which the PPM is valid, the validity period as well as the lot size range. Note that the PPM name assigned on this screen is the one used in the Supply Chain Engineer and Cockpit.

**Costs Screen**

The Cost screen is used to define the variable cost (penalty) that is utilized by the SNP Optimizer. It must contain process as well as component cost.

**Planning Texts Screen**

The Planning Texts screen allows capturing of plan texts in different languages. The default language is the user's logon language.

**Screen Maintain Operations**

- Header Level
  On this level the two fields PP/DS plan and Cost Function can be maintained. The PP/DS plan field serves as a reference showing for an SNP PPM what the corresponding PP/DS PPM name is. This is purely a display field with (at the moment) no further function.
  The Cost Function field allows the definition of quantity dependent fixed and variable penalties, which are used by the Optimizer. Define in this field the Cost function to be used for this plan.

- <u>Operations Level</u>
  Following data can be maintained:
  - Operation — Name an operation as required. Multiple language descriptions can be captured by pressing the middle pushbutton next to the magnifying glass.
  - Description — Assign a name to the operation.

  Double click on the operations line or press the pushbutton with the magnifying glass to drill down one level to the activity. An operation can be deleted by selecting it and pressing the Delete Operation button. An operation can be deleted by selecting it and pressing the Delete Activity button.

- <u>Activity Level</u>
  Define the following data:
  - Activity Number — Specify any number as required.
  - Section — Give the activity a name in the field "Section." Pressing the pushbutton opposite the magnifying glass allows capturing multiple language descriptions.
  - Activity — Choose from Setup, Produce, Tear Down, and Wait (Queue) Time.
  - Activity Type — The activity description field is filled out automatically after pressing the <Enter> button.
  - Scrap (%) — Define a scrap percentage (if required). How scrap is calculated is dealt with in the chapter "Scrap Calculation."
  - Time Dependent — Time dependent parameters can be defined per activity by selecting the appropriate line and pressing the Time Dependent Planning Parameters button underneath the table.

  Double click on the activity line or press the pushbutton with the magnifying glass to get to the Maintain Components screen. An activity can be deleted by selecting it and pressing the Delete Activity button.

- <u>Sub-Screen Time Dependent Process Parameters: Activity</u>
  The upper section of this screen shows the standard scrap value used if none of the time dependent parameters apply. On this sub-screen, define the following data as required:
  - Valid Until — Define the valid until date. If there are periods in-between where the default scrap value as defined above should be used simply specify these periods here again and do not set the Scrap / Yield Indicator.
  - Scrap / Yield Indicator — Set this indicator so that the defined scrap value in this time dependent parameter is applied.
  - Scrap (%) — Define a scrap percentage. How scrap is calculated is dealt with in chapter “Scrap Calculation”.

  On the top of this screen is a “Scrap<->Yield” pushbutton. This is a toggle key, and pressing it will change the display from scrap to yield or yield to scrap. Press the “Version” pushbutton to enable definition of this time dependent parameter per SNP planning version.

**<u>Screen Maintain Components</u>**

This screen is a bit mixed up from a naming point of view. The screen name relates to components, the tab name to materials, the line to products, and the consumption is called material consumption. But it is all about products that can be input products (components) or output products (semi or finished). All input and output products are defined on this screen for SNP PPM’s.

Following fields can be maintained per activity on the Components screen:

- Product — Define the product number.
- Description — The description is a display only field.
- Valid from — The validity start date.
- Valid until — The validity end date.
- I/O — Specify whether the product is an input (I) or output (O) in this PPM.

- Consumption Mode — Select one of the consumption modes S, E, or C (for consumption being at the start, the end, or continuously).
- Material Consumption (v) — Define the variable consumption or output quantity of the product. This is measured in the product's base unit of measure.
- Base Unit — The base unit is a display only field.
- Time Dependent — Time dependent parameters can be defined per product by selecting the appropriate line and pressing the Time Dependent Planning Parameters button underneath the table.

A product allocation can be deleted by selecting it and pressing the Delete Component button.

- Sub-Screen Time Dependent Process Parameters: Component Alternative

  The upper section of this screen shows the standard fixed and variable product consumption values as well as the variable penalty used if none of the time dependent parameters apply. On this sub-screen, define the following data as required:

  - Valid Until — Define the valid until date. If there are periods in-between where the default consumption values as defined above should be used simply specify these periods here again, and do not set the Variable Parameter and/or Cost Indicator.
  - Variable Parameter — Set this indicator so that the defined material consumption value in this time-dependent parameter is applied.
  - Material Consumption — Define the variable material consumption in the base unit of measure.
  - Cost Indicator — Set this indicator so that the defined variable penalty value in this time dependent parameter is applied.
  - Penalty Variable — Define the variable penalty.

  Press the "Version" pushbutton to enable definition of this time dependent parameter per SNP planning version.

## Screen Maintain Relationships

The following fields can be maintained per activity on the Relationships screen:

- Operation — Select an operation.
- Activity Number — Select the activity within the operation as defined above.
- P/S — Select one of the two relation parameters V or N (for predecessor or successor). In an SNP PPM no time constraints and deviations can be defined.
- Activity Category — The activity category is a display only field showing the selected activity's category.
- Description — The description is a display only field showing the selected operations name.

Relationships need to be defined only in one direction. The system adds the counterpart automatically. Relationships can be deleted by selecting it and pressing the Delete Activity Relation button.

## Screen Maintain Resources

On the Resources Screen the primary resource can be maintained. Double click on the resource line or press the pushbutton with the magnifying glass to drill on level down to the secondary resources level.

- Primary Resource Level
  The following fields can be maintained per activity on the Primary Resources level:
  - Mode — Define a mode number.
  - Unit — Select the time unit for "Day" as SNP requires planning in daily buckets.
  - Duration Fix — Define the fixed duration as "1" for SNP.
  - Primary Resource — Select the primary resource for this activity.
  - Location — Specify the location of the resource used above.

- Pause not Allowed — Switch this flag on if activities must not be interrupted by breaks.
- Time Dependent — Time dependent parameters can be defined per product by selecting the appropriate line and pressing the Time Dependent Planning Parameters button underneath the table.

The maintenance of the primary resource needs to be continued on the screen with the secondary resources (see below). A mode definition with its primary resource allocation can be deleted by selecting it and pressing the Delete Mode button.

- Sub-Screen Time Dependent Process Parameters: Mode

  The upper section of this screen shows the standard fixed and variable resource consumption values as well as the variable penalty used if none of the time dependent parameters apply. On this sub-screen define the following data as required:

  - Valid Until — Define the valid until date. If there are periods in-between where the default consumption values as defined above should be used simply specify these periods here again and do not set the Variable Parameter and/or Cost Indicator.
  - Fixed Parameter — Set this indicator so that the defined material consumption value in this time dependent parameter is applied.
  - Duration Fix — Define the variable time resource consumption in the base unit of measure.
  - Duration Time Unit — Define the unit of measure used above for specifying the resource consumption.
  - Cost Indicator — Set this indicator so that the defined variable penalty value in this time dependent parameter is applied.
  - Penalty Variable — Define the variable penalty.

  Press the "Version" pushbutton to enable definition of this time dependent parameter per SNP planning version.

- Secondary Resources Level
  When switching to this screen, the primary resource is shown on the top line with some fields as display only. The fields below marked with an * need to be defined for primary resources as well. Following fields can be maintained per activity on the Secondary Resources level:
  - Resource — Define a secondary resource. The first line automatically shows the primary resource.
  - Location — Specify the location of the secondary resource. The first line automatically shows the location of the primary resource.
  - Multi Activity — The Multi Activity flag is a display only field and if switched on showing that the selected resource is a Multi-Activity resource. SNP can only work with Bucket resources.
  - * Unit — Define the unit of measure used when specifying the resource consumption (see below).
  - * Calendar — Mark exactly one resource per activity (primary or secondary) as a calendar resource. The marked resource with the defined resource consumption is used for scheduling purposes.
  - * Resource Consumption — Specify the resource consumption in the unit of measure as defined above.
  - Time Dependent — Time dependent parameters can be defined per product by selecting the appropriate line and pressing the Time Dependent Planning Parameters button underneath the table.

  A secondary resource allocation can be deleted by selecting it and pressing the Delete Resource button.

- Sub-Screen Time Dependent Process Parameters: Resource Consumption
  The upper section of this screen shows the standard fixed and variable resource consumption values used if none of the time dependent parameters apply. On this sub-screen define the following data as required:

- Valid Until — Define the valid until date. If there are periods in-between where the default consumption values as defined above should be used simply specify these periods here again and do not set the Variable Parameter Indicator.
- Variable Parameter — Set this indicator so that the defined resource consumption value in this time dependent parameter is applied.
- Resource Cons. (v) — Define the variable resource consumption in the unit of measure as defined below. For further explanation regarding the calculation of the resource consumption, refer to the chapter "Resource Consumption Calculation" further above.
- Unit of Measure — Define the unit of measure used when specifying the resource consumption.

Press the "Version" pushbutton to enable definition of this time dependent parameter per SNP planning version.



#### 4.4.2.6 Transportation Lane

Transportation Lanes represent the connection between two locations. They are direction dependent, which means that two transportation lanes have to be defined if goods movements take place in both directions. Several transportation modes can be allocated for the lane, if required on a per product level basis. Transportation lanes are master data objects that are model dependent. They can be created only in the Supply Chain Engineer. If the same transportation lane is required in two different models it has to be created twice. A transportation lane can have several validity periods and modes of transportation. At least one period and mode must be maintained. Per period and mode the following data can be maintained:

- Description — Name of the transportation lane.
- Transportation Planner — Responsible planner for the transportation lane.
- Transportation Calendar — Calendar used when scheduling activities on the transportation lane.

- Validity Period — Validity period of the transportation lane. Various validity periods can be maintained.
- Transportation Mode — Mode of transport (e.g. truck) of the transportation lane.
- All Products — This flag is set automatically. Note that the definition of individual products implies that these individual products have specific product-related parameters. It is nevertheless possible to move all products on the transportation lane. In order to move only specific products, deselect this flag and link the products in question to the transportation lane.
- Transportation Duration — Define the amount of days it takes to move goods from source to destination.
- Costs — The cost (penalty) associated with the usage of this mode and transportation lane. The Optimizer uses this value.
- Unit — Product unit of measure to which the costs and the TLB profile refer. Set this unit even if no TLB profile is used, as this is required by the SNP optimizer.
- Resource — Specify the name of the resource that is used. If no resource is stipulated here, the transportation lane has indefinite capacity. This should be done if for example the transport mode is an external carrier with "unlimited" capacity (e.g. UPS).
- Location of Resource — The system automatically adds the location to which the resource defined above belongs.
- TLB Profile — Link a TLB profile to the transportation lane to determine weight and volume capacity and their lower economical limits.

Various time periods can be defined repeating the above steps. The "Assign Transportation Method" button is used to add new transportation methods (modes) to an existing time period. To activate this function, the cursor must be positioned in a time period line. The upcoming screen allows to input data as described above. It is also possible to stipulate specific products that can be moved using this transportation lane and mode of transport. A list of all products assigned to a transportation lane can be viewed. To obtain this list, activate the context sensitive menu on the name of the transportation lane in the tree structure or on the line in the map. The system will display a list of all products specifically allocated to the transportation lane. Note that products must be created in the source and destination location! An option "Mass Maintenance" activated via the context sensitive menu on the transportation lane node allows the simultaneous generation and maintenance of various transportation lanes. Please refer to the SNP Guide "Maintenance of Transportation Lanes."



#### 4.4.2.7 Quota Arrangement

According to the APO terminology, quota arrangements are not master data. I cannot follow this definition and put the quota arrangement together with the other master data. Quota arrangements exist on top of the transportation lane, which means they can only be created if a transportation lane exists. Transportation lanes require that the locations they link are defined. Thus, the quota arrangement has the two prerequisites that the locations and transportation lanes are created prior to the creation of the quota arrangement. Inbound quota arrangements determine how the requirement is split over various possible sourcing locations. Outbound quota arrangements determine how available quantities are distributed. Quota Arrangements, like the transportation lanes can only be defined in the Supply Chain Engineer. Following parameters need to be maintained:

| | |
|---|---|
| • Quota Percentage | Numerical Value |
| • Inbound / Outbound | Flag |
| • Source / Target Location | Any Location in the SNP model |
| • Validity | Period in which Quota Arrangement is valid |
| • Lot Size Profile | Optional entry to determine Lot Sizing requirements |

#### 4.4.2.8 Cost Maintenance

Up to now, we have gone over various master data objects, and the majority had some fields that were dealing with some cost (or penalty) settings. All these cost settings must be maintained accurately if the optimizers are to produce a meaningful result. This can be a rather laborious task with lots of master data object accesses depending on the type of cost that has to be defined. The Cost Maintenance transaction greatly helps to reduce the amount of thinking regarding where which cost definition is stored exactly. It is the central cost-related maintenance program that updates the respective master data objects. It is sorted by cost type (e.g. production cost) rather than master data object (e.g. product master). This is a really sensitive approach and makes the cost definition task easier. As said above, this transaction does not maintain a new master data object. It merely updates already existing master data objects. It is for example required to define the capacity (supply) variants of a resource in order to maintain its cost with this transaction.

All data entered is for the supply chain model as specified on the initial screen. Note that the Cost Maintenance transaction can only be used on master data objects that are existing already and are maintained to the right level.

| Tab | Cost | Drill Down Step 1 | Drill Down Step 2 | Drill Down Step 3 | Cost Definition |
|---|---|---|---|---|---|
| Production | | | | | |
| | Production | | | | |
| | | PPM (SNP) | Production Resource (Bucket) | Supply Variant 1 | Resource Q/R Definition |
| | | | | Supply Variant 2 | Resource Q/R Definition |
| | | Production Resource (Bucket) | Supply Variant 1 | ➔➔➔ | Resource Q/R Definition |
| | | | Supply Variant 2 | ➔➔➔ | Resource Q/R Definition |
| | | Location | PPM (SNP) | ➔➔➔ | PPM Cost Function |
| | | | Production Resource (Bucket) | Supply Variant 1 | Resource Q/R Definition |
| | | | | Supply Variant 2 | Resource Q/R Definition |
| Transport | | | | | |
| | Transportation | | | | |
| | | Transportation Resource | Supply Variant 1 | ➔➔➔ | Resource Q/R Definition |
| | | | Supply Variant 2 | ➔➔➔ | Resource Q/R Definition |
| | | Transportation Lane | Transportation Mode 1 | ➔➔➔ | Product Independent Transport. Cost |
| | | | Transportation Mode n | ➔➔➔ | Product Independent Transport. Cost |
| | | | Transportation Mode 1 | Product | Product Dependent Transport. Cost |
| | | | Transportation Mode n | Product | Product Dependent Transport. Cost |

| Tab | Cost | Drill Down Step 1 | Drill Down Step 2 | Drill Down Step 3 | Cost Definition |
|---|---|---|---|---|---|
| Handling | | | | | |
| | Handling | | | | |
| | | Handling Resource | Supply Variant 1 | →→→ | Resource Q/R Definition |
| | | | Supply Variant 2 | →→→ | Resource Q/R Definition |
| | | Location | Handling Resource | Supply Variant 1 | Resource Q/R Definition |
| | | | | Supply Variant 2 | Resource Q/R Definition |
| Storage | | | | | |
| | Stock-Keeping | | | | |
| | | Storage Resource | Supply Variant 1 | →→→ | Resource Q/R Definition |
| | | | Supply Variant 2 | →→→ | Resource Q/R Definition |
| | | Location | Storage Resource | Supply Variant 1 | Resource Q/R Definition |
| | | | | Supply Variant 2 | Resource Q/R Definition |
| | | Product | Location | →→→ | Location Product Location Storage Cost |
| Others | | | | | |
| | Procurement | | | | |
| | | Product | Location | →→→ | Product Cost Function |
| | Delay / No Delivery | | | | |
| | | Product | →→→ | →→→ | Product Delay / No Delivery Cost |

**Table 66 – Cost Maintenance**

#### 4.4.2.9 Master Data Hierarchies

Hierarchies are used to show multi-level hierarchical relations of master data objects. The structure describes the possible relations of the master data objects. The master data objects are added later and make up the contents of the hierarchy. In APO, locations, products, location specific products, and resources can be added to structures. The creation of the hierarchy structure as well as the hierarchy is done in the APO IMG, the assignment of the master data objects is carried out in a separate step as part of master data maintenance. The same master data object can be made part of several hierarchies.

The APO master data hierarchies are used only in SNP.



### 4.4.3 Data in liveCache

The liveCache in APO contains the following data:

- Master Data
  These are the objects we discussed in the chapters above. The storage of the data takes place in conventional table structures and in liveCache. This is transparent to the user. Deletion of master data deletes the entries in liveCache at the same time.
- Order Network Data
  The Order Network Data is the information about all orders in APO. Orders can either originate in APO itself (e.g. newly created planned production orders) or be transmitted from an OLTP system (e.g. sales orders). Order data remain in liveCache as long as the order is "active." For testing purposes in a non-live environment a program (/SAPAPO/RLCDELETE) can be used to delete all or selected order data from the liveCache. This program must be used with extreme care as it can lead to data inconsistencies if applied wrongly!
- Time Series Data.

For each product the Time Series Data stipulates all demands and supplies. Global ATP for example uses this data to determine product availability. Time Series Data can be viewed from the main menu using following path: Global ATP > Tools > Product Availability Check > Display Time Series. An interesting aspect is that the time series is the only place where APO keeps information on sub-location level (R/3 storage location), version level (R/3 batch), and per account assignment.

## 4.5 The SNP Transactions

The main SNP transactions are the SNP Interactive Planning screen and the Supply Chain Cockpit.

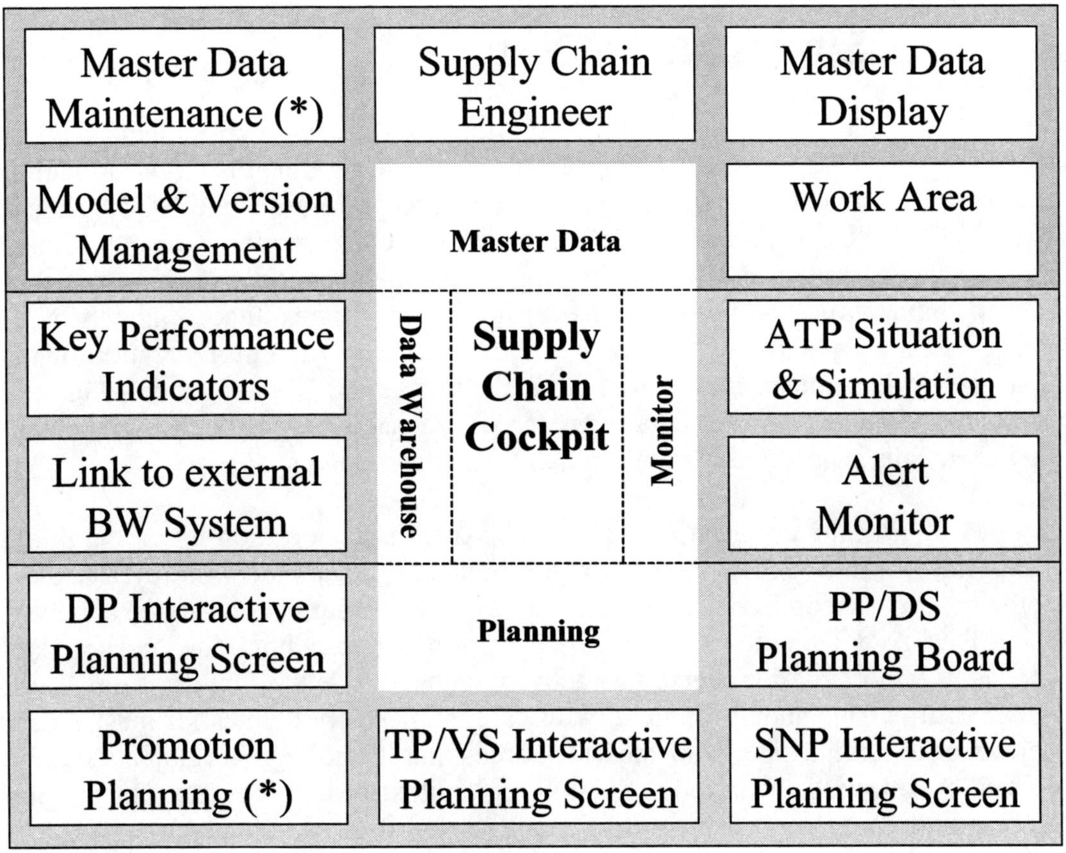


**Graphic 58 – The Hub Supply Chain Cockpit**

The Supply Chain Engineer is used to model the entire supply chain network that is visible in the Supply Chain Cockpit. It refers strongly to the data environment chapters and lays the foundations on which SNP planning is carried out. The Supply Chain Engineer is the APO central transaction (hub) starting from which the majority of the day-to-day tasks can be performed. The graphic above provides an overview of the functions that can be initiated from the Supply Chain Cockpit.

### 4.5.1 Supply Chain Engineer



The Supply Chain Engineer is a modeling tool used to link data objects such as locations, products, resources, and production process models to an SNP model. It is a common misconception that the SCE is used to model the SCC. This is wrong, as the SCE is the tool to define the supply chain model. It has an impact on the SCC, as in the SCC a certain supply planning version with its associated supply chain model is displayed. Nevertheless, the appearance of the SCC is defined separately and independently of the SCE. After the initial creation of the SNP master data objects it is required to make them available to a model. This can be done either in the master data maintenance transaction or in the Supply Chain Engineer. This is depicted in the graphic further down.

In order to allocate any master data object (except transportation lanes and quota arrangements) to a model, they must first be made part of the work area and by doing so they become visible in the Supply Chain Engineer. This is achieved using the "Add Objects to Work Area" option for the individual master data objects. It is possible to reverse this activity with the "Delete Objects from Work Area" option. This should be done with care, as it easily deletes all master data objects of a certain type from the work area. Single master data objects can be deleted by selecting them and activating the context sensitive menu. On the pop up screen select "Delete from Work Area". Master data can also be assigned to a supply chain model directly out of the respective master data maintenance transaction. The Supply Chain Engineer is the only place in the system where transportation lanes and quota arrangements can be created and maintained. This is due to the fact that they are model dependent master data whereby all other master data is model independent. Quota arrangements are a type of add-on for the location master. Once master data objects are visible in the Supply Chain

Engineer (they are part of the work area), they can be added to the model. This task is performed using the "Add to Model" option. The "Delete from Model" option reverses this allocation to a model.

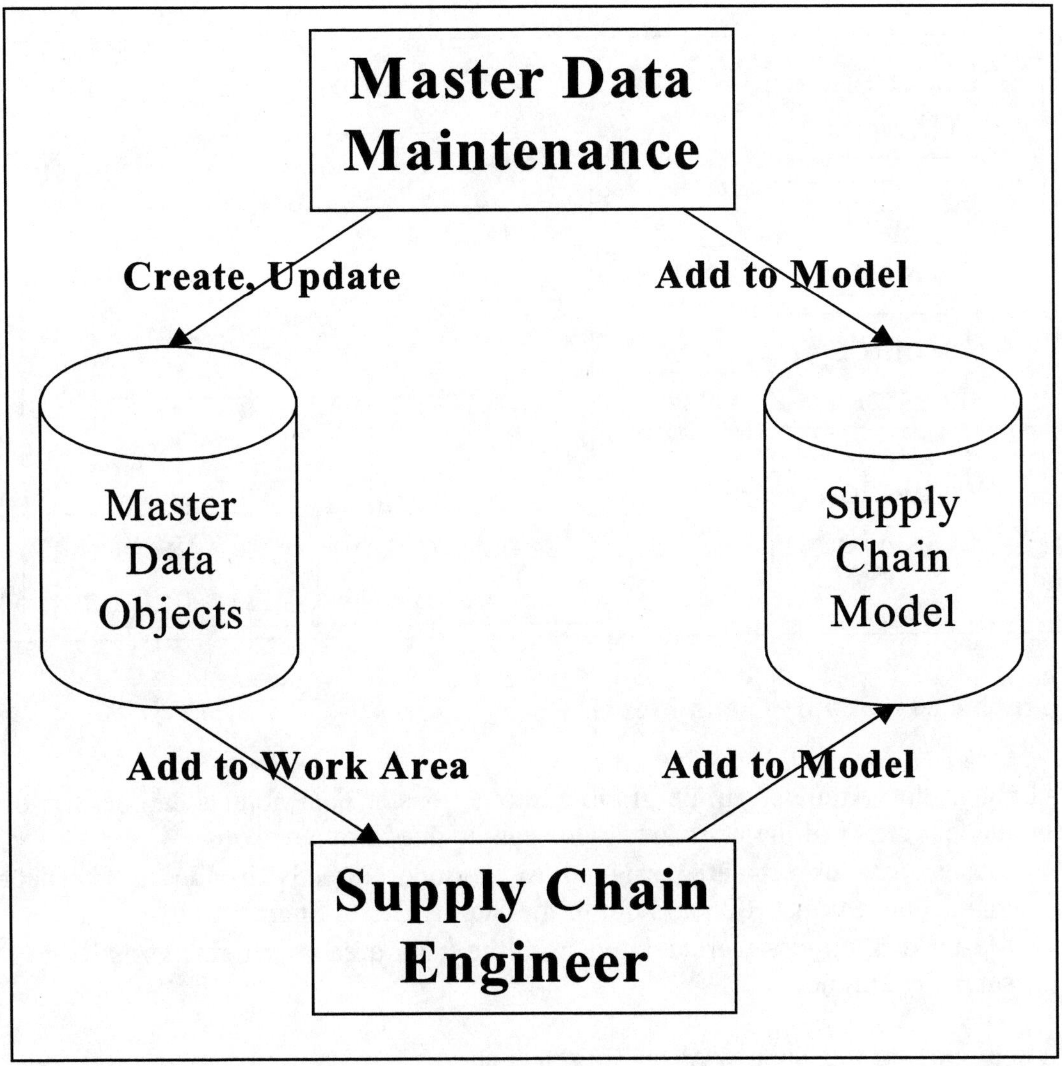


**Graphic 59 – Definition of the Supply Chain Model**

A Supply Chain Model can be seen as a collection of related master data. This is depicted in the graphic above.

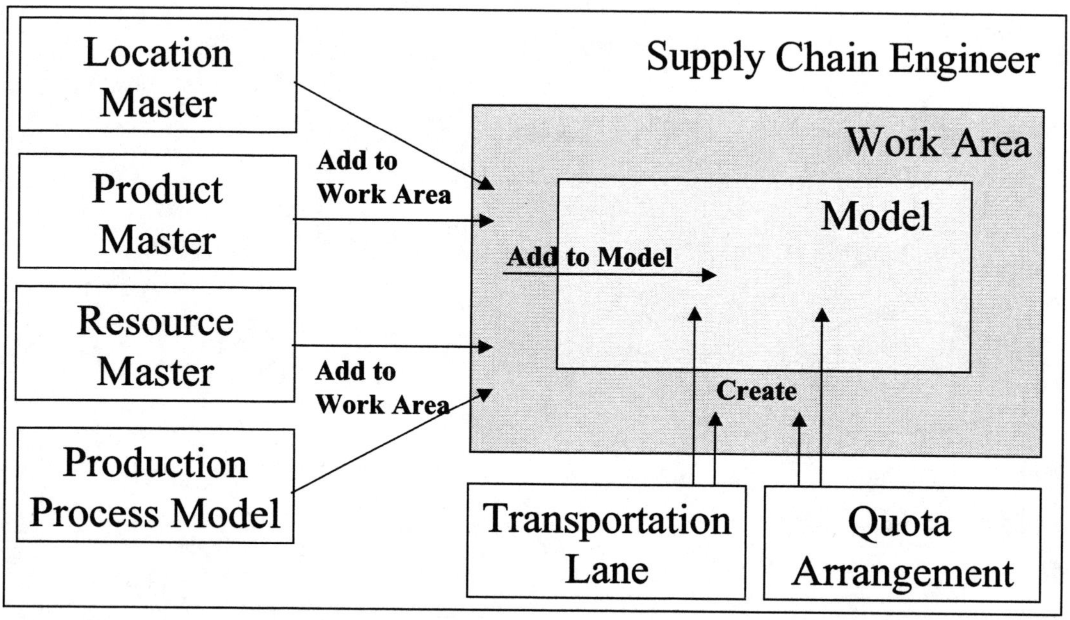


**Graphic 60 – Supply Chain Model**

Although not stipulated in the graphic above, master data objects can be part of the model but not of the work area. This can be due to two reasons:

- Master data objects are assigned to a model directly in the master data maintenance transaction and not in the Supply Chain Engineer.
- Master data objects were deleted from the work area after being assigned to a supply chain model.

When opening the Supply Chain Engineer the last used supply chain model and work area are prompted for use. The work area, which defines the master data objects that can be seen and used, is maintained in the Supply Chain Engineer. The work area defines the master data objects that are visible and available in the

Supply Chain Engineer session. If no work area name was stipulated the system will save the work area without a name. Master data objects according to the work area are available in the tree structure (left section of the screen) and in the case of locations also in the map (right section of the screen). Transportation lanes are not part of the definable work area as they are defined per model and automatically shown when opening the Supply Chain Engineer for a certain supply chain model. This means that all transportation lanes of a certain supply chain model are shown at any time.

Master data objects in the supply chain model do not have to be necessarily part of the work area and vice versa. The initial selection (based on the last saved work area) might get changed during a Supply Chain Engineer working session by adding new (or deleting redundant) data objects to (from) the tree structure or possibly the map display in case of locations.

Master Data objects can be added to the SNP model only in the Supply Chain Engineer. Adding data objects to the work area (which is shown in the tree structure) is the first step of making master data objects part of a supply chain model. In a second step the data objects can be made part of the model. Master data objects can be deleted from the work area and thus from the supply chain model only in the Supply Chain Engineer. Deleting data objects from the work area does not take them off the supply chain model. Data objects cannot be taken off the model without deleting them from the work area. If objects previously deleted from the work area are made part of the work area again they are automatically seen as part of the model again. That is obvious, as they were always part of the model and only not visible.

The deletion of master data objects in the model using the Supply Chain Engineer has no effect on the object in the Supply Chain Cockpit where it remains! Note that the Supply Chain Cockpit shows the combination of an SNP model and SNP Planning Version and changing the model does not change the model/version combination automatically.

The relation between SNP supply chain models, planning versions and their presentation in the Supply Chain Engineer and Cockpit will be discussed in the chapter "Supply Chain Cockpit."

### 4.5.1.1 User Profile

The user can define his or her individual working environment using the User Profile. In the user profile, various defaults can be set. Maintenance of the user profile is possible out of the SCE or directly from the menu structure. When maintaining the profile starting from the menu structure, more options are available. These additional options mainly deal with the graphical representation and are not part of the following table that lists possible settings for the SCE profile. The list also contains a cross-reference for all those settings that can be made in the SCC user profile.

| SCE | SCC | Field | Setting |
|---|---|---|---|
| General Tab | | | |
| X | X | Highlight Objects not in the Model | Select whether objects that are part of the selection but not part of the model should be highlighted in the tree structure. |
| X | X | Use Work Area as Filter for Display | Select whether locations that are part of the model but not of the work area should be displayed on the map. |
| Model Maintenance Tab | | | |
| X | | Assign Dependent Objects to Model | |
| X | | Include Dependent Location Products | |
| X | | Include Dependent Resources | |
| X | | Include Dependent PPM's | |
| X | | Maintain Geographical Coordinates | |

| SCE | SCC | Field | Setting |
|---|---|---|---|
| Query Tab | | | |
| X | X | Relative / Fixed Time Interval | Select either fixed or relative time interval to be used for queries. |
| X | X | Relative Time Interval | If you have selected to use relative time intervals, specify the time interval here. |
| X | X | Fixed Time Interval | If you have selected to use a fixed time, specify the start and end date and time here. |
| | X | Time Stream | Define a time steam for queries |
| X | X | Use Selection Dialog Box | Define which of the three views is to be used. |
| Transportation Tab | | | |
| X | | Transportation Method | Select one or multiple transportation methods that have should have allocated a common end of validity date when they are created. |
| X | | End of Validity for Transportation Method | Define the common end of validity date for <u>all</u> transportation methods selected above. |
| X | | Location Assignment Check of a Product | Select whether an error message must be created when assigning a product to a transportation lane that is <u>not</u> maintained in <u>both</u>, the source and the target location. |

**Table 67 – SCE User Profile**

On the initial screen, the last used supply chain model and work area is set as default when opening the Supply Chain Engineer.

## 4.5.2 Supply Chain Cockpit

The graphical presentation of data has come a long way since the first release of an R/3 system, and APO uses a very appealing environment for most of the daily tasks to be performed. It is called "Supply Chain Cockpit," and indeed out of this cockpit the majority of tasks can be performed.

The Supply Chain Cockpit guides the user through important tasks such as

- Demand Planning,
- Supply Network Planning,
- Production Planning & Detailed Scheduling, or
- Global ATP Checks.

In the following chapters I will explain the main elements of this Supply Chain Cockpit. We already went through the Supply Chain Engineer, which is the graphical tool used to define the whole supply chain network with all locations and its dependencies. Another module integrated into the Supply Chain Cockpit is the Alert Monitor, which provides the user with information regarding any problem in the supply chain irrespective of a specific source.

The SNP planning version that is displayed in the Supply Chain Cockpit is linked to exactly one supply chain model, but each model can work in conjunction with several planning versions. Using the Supply Chain Engineer, data objects are allocated to the supply chain model independent of an SNP planning version. The task of the Supply Chain Cockpit is twofold.

- Display information about the master data objects in the supply chain model dependent on the SNP planning version.
- 
- Display SNP planning version specific data such as alerts or key performance indicators.

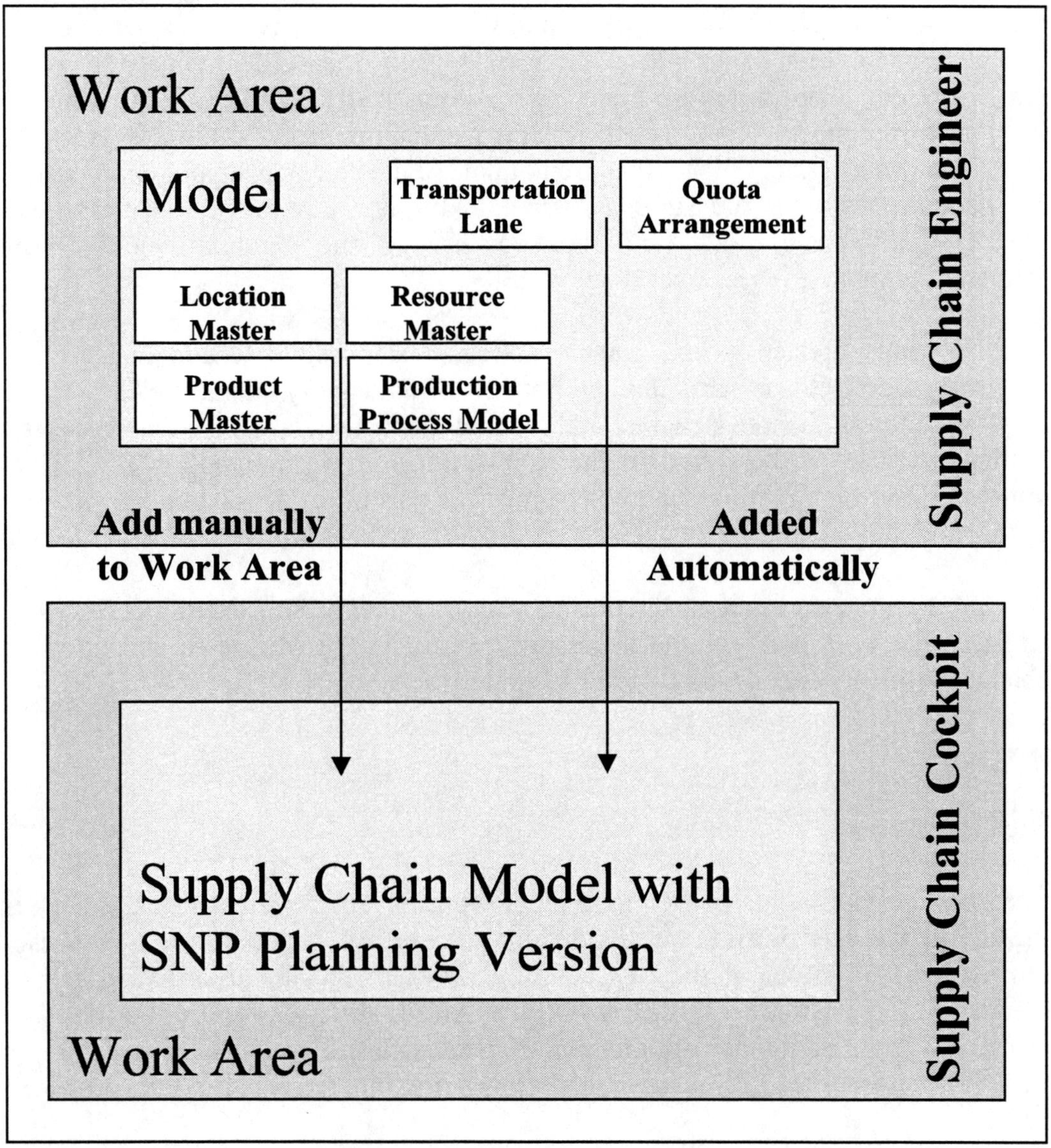


Graphic 61 – Supply Chain Planning Version

In order to retrieve information regarding a master data object of the selected supply chain model, it is necessary to add it to the SCC. Any master data objects except transportation lanes are made visible using the "Add Objects to Work Area" option. Transportation Lanes are automatically visible in all planning versions of the model. The "Delete Objects from Work Area" option reverses the allocation. Master data objects that are not part of the selected supply chain model can be made visible in the Supply Chain Cockpit, but they remain not being part of the supply chain model and thus not part of the planning version. The following graphic gives an overview.

Although not depicted in the graphic above, it is possible to add master data objects to the SCC work area that are not part of the supply chain model. What is displayed in both the tree structure and the map depends also on the Display Filter Settings, which can be found in the user settings. A further option (Highlight option) allows highlighting such objects that are part of the work area but not part of the model.



It is important to understand that during a session new master data objects can be added to the work area without necessarily changing the work area definition. A changed work area needs to be saved separately.

#### 4.5.2.1 User Profile

The user can define his or her individual working environment using the User Profile. In the user profile, various defaults can be set. Maintenance of the user profile is possible out of the SCC or directly from the menu structure. When maintaining the profile starting from the menu structure, more options are available. These additional options mainly deal with the graphical representation and are not part of the following table that lists possible settings for SCC profile.

| SCC | SCE | Field | Setting |
|---|---|---|---|
| General Tab | | | |
| X | X | Highlight Objects not in the Model | Select whether objects that are part of the selection but not part of the model should be highlighted in the tree structure. |
| X | X | Use Work Area as Filter for Display | Select whether locations that are part of the model but not of the work area should be displayed on the map. |
| Query Tab | | | |
| X | X | Relative / Fixed Time Interval | Select either fixed or relative time interval to be used for queries. |
| X | X | Relative Time Interval | If you have selected to use relative time intervals specify the time interval here. |
| X | X | Fixed Time Interval | If you have selected to use a fixed time specify the start and end date and time here. |
| | X | Time Stream | Define a time steam for queries |
| X | X | Use Selection Dialog Box | Define which of the three views is to be used. |
| X | | Entry Object Default | Define which of the four views is to be used. |
| X | | Query Object Pool | Define which of the three views is to be used. |
| Alert Monitor Tab | | | |
| X | | SNP Alert Profile | Define the SNP alert profile to be used. |
| X | | TLB Alert Profile | Define the TLB alert profile to be used. |
| X | | DP Alert Profile | Define the DP alert profile to be used. |
| X | | ATP Alert Profile | Define the ATP alert profile to be used. |
| X | | PP/DS Alert Profile | Define the PP/DS alert profile to be used. |
| X | | SNP Planning Profile | Select an SNP planning profile. |

| SCC | SCE | Field | Setting |
|---|---|---|---|
| Planning Tab | | | |
| X | | ATP | Allows specifying a default business event when checking the ATP situation. |
| X | | CTM | Allows specifying a default CTM profile for the CTM run. |
| X | | SNP | Allows specifying a default time buckets profile for the SNP run. |



**Table 68 – SCC User Profile**

The list also contains a cross-reference for all those settings that can be made in the SCE user profile. No alerts can be displayed if no alert monitor profile was selected in the alert monitor tab. It is also possible to branch to the alert monitor profile setup from the alert monitor view.

On the initial screen, the last used supply chain model, SNP planning version, and work area is set as default when opening the Supply Chain Cockpit The SNP planning version is linked to exactly one SNP supply chain model. As a consequence, the definition of the SNP planning version determines automatically the SNP supply chain model to be used.

#### 4.5.2.2 Tree Structure

The tree structure in the middle section of the left side of the Supply Chain Cockpit screen allows the selection of master data objects. Inside are five tabs representing the following data objects:

- Locations
  The locations tree structure is further broken down into plants, distribution centers, customers and vendors, activating the context sensitive menu on any of these objects in the sub-nodes allows displaying location and

product/location master data. Queries per location are activated in the same way. Note that queries within SNP are not user defined. They are predefined by APO and can only be used but not altered. Specific location specific Key Performance Indicators can be activated as well, but only if a separate BW system is installed. The same information as described here can be gained when activating the context sensitive menu on the object in the map.
Activating the context sensitive menu on any of the nodes (e.g. on the plant node) allows adding new data objects to the node.

- Products
  The product tree structure allows the display of product master data, product related queries, and key performance indicators. Products can also be added to the tree structure. Obviously this data cannot be obtained from out of the map.
- Resources
  The resources tree structure contains sub-nodes for production-, storage, handling, and transportation resources. As with locations for all data objects in the sub-node, different information can be obtained while on the node level new data objects can be added. This data can also not be obtained from out of the map.
- Production Process Models
  This tree structure's functionality is equivalent to that of the product.
- Transportation Lanes
  In the transportation lane tree structure, master data information per transportation lane can be obtained. Furthermore, queries can be started per data object. Note that it is not possible to add a transportation lane to the work area. It is made part of it automatically.

The tree and map section of the Supply Chain Cockpit screen can be narrowed (widened), which will give the other section more (less) space. For further information regarding Work Areas and subscribing of master data refer to the chapter "Supply Chain Engineer".

### 4.5.2.3 Network Display

The middle section of the right side of the Supply Chain Cockpit screen is dedicated to display the supply chain network in either geographical or logical mode. Various maps of all continents are available. The appearance of the maps can be adjusted or they can be totally switched off, which activates the logical view. In this case objects of the supply chain such as locations (plant, distribution center, customer, and vendor) as well as transportation lanes are displayed in network format without geographical reference. This option is useful if the supply chain is to be displayed in a format where the geographical location of the objects is of no interest or too complex and/or unclear. A zoom-in functionality allows zooming in on any portion of the display even if the map display function is switched off. To activate this function press the <Ctrl> key and simultaneously mark the zoom area using the mouse pointer. An overview screen can be activated that shows the position of the zoom area in relation to the overall map or network. The default map per user is defined in the User Specific Settings of the Supply Chain Cockpit. The tree and map section of the Supply Chain Cockpit screen can be narrowed (widened), which will give the other section more (less) space. Transportation lanes can have a validity period and the Supply Chain Cockpit allows displaying only those transportation lanes that are valid within a user specified time range.



### 4.5.2.4 Control Panel

The Control Panel in the Supply Chain Cockpit is a collection of buttons that can be activated user-specific and appear at the bottom of the Supply Chain Cockpit screen. They can be displayed either enlarged or in small size to not take away too much of the valuable screen space. Irrespective of the size, all buttons relating to APO areas have the same functionality. Each of these buttons has on the top the respective name and underneath a pictogram symbolizing the respective APO area. At the bottom is a small section that is activated (highlighted) if an alert in the respective area was detected. Depending on the alert priority, the error, warning, or information symbol can be seen. See also the "Alert Monitor" chapter. The following table summarizes the functionality that can be accessed for all control panel buttons that relate to APO areas. Please note that the sequence of buttons is user definable and not all (or any) buttons have to appear on the screen.

| Button | Call Functions |
|---|---|
| BW | Calculate Key Performance Indicators (KPI)<br>Business Information Warehouse |
| DP | DP Alert Monitor<br>DP Interactive Planning Screen |
| SNP | SNP Alert Monitor<br>SNP Network<br>SNP Product / Location<br>SNP Location / Resource<br>CTM |
| PP/DS | PP/DS Alert Monitor<br>Graphical Planning Table |
| Transport | Transport Alert Monitor<br>Transport Load Builder |
| ATP | ATP Alert Monitor<br>ATP Situation<br>ATP Simulation |

**Table 69 – Supply Chain Cockpit Buttons**

The BW call function is only possible if a separate BW installation exists. In addition to the APO module specific buttons, any master data object from the tree structure of the Supply Chain Cockpit can be dragged and dropped into the Control Panel section. This allows fast access to frequently used master data objects. The appearance of the button varies depending on the type of master data it represents.

## 4.5.3 Alert Monitor

The Alert Monitor can be accessed directly from the menu structure or from the SNP Interactive Planning screen and the Supply Chain Cockpit. Unlike the alerts in DP, alerts in all other areas such as SNP are predefined. They can be parameterized, but no new alerts can be added. The Alert Monitor, when activated from out of the Supply Chain Cockpit or the SNP Interactive Planning screen provides the user with structured information regarding all detected alerts. The screen is divided into three sections.

- Alert Type
  In this section on the upper left screen, an entry for each alert area (e.g. Demand Planning) can be found in the "View" tree structure. In the same section an entry for each alert type (e.g. MAPE Upper Limit Exceeded) is displayed in the "Alert View" tree structure. Double clicking on any entry in the tree structure activates the second screen section "Alert Object". In this section all objects that cause an alert are displayed.
- Alert Object
  This section on the bottom left of the screen displays in a tree structure all objects that cause an alert as described above. Double clicking on any entry in the tree structure activates the third screen section "Alert Details". In this section details of all objects that cause an alert are displayed.
- Alert Details
  Detailed information regarding any alert and the causing object are displayed in this section. The display layout depends on the alert type and alert object.

It is necessary to refresh the Alert Monitor to view the latest alerts while working in the Interactive Planning screen, the Supply Chain Cockpit, or the Alert Monitor itself. Alerts are not propagated upwards. Let me give an example. In a case where an alert exists for one of the input components of a planned order for production, the order as such does not have an alert.

In this chapter we shall deal with all alert views. Alerts in SNP are predefined similar to MPS or MRP exception messages in R/3. They are broken down into the areas of (core) SNP and TLB/Deployment. For DP, alerts can be custom defined by using macros or by using a diagnosis group. Please refer to the DP master forecast profile for further information regarding diagnosis groups. Furthermore, alerts can be defined for PP/DS and ATP.

In order to receive alerts, it is necessary to select all required alerts and save them in a profile. This profile is then linked in the Supply Chain Cockpit as a user specific setting to an SNP planning version. This link, as it is user specific, enables a selective display of alerts per user. Each alert is characterized by the following parameters:

- Activation Flag
  Only alerts that are flagged as active will be calculated and displayed. Select here all alerts that should be used in the profile.
- Description
  This is an SAP defined description of the alert. The field is "display only".
- Standard Priority
  The standard priority is SAP predefined. For alerts that allow the definition of threshold values, this standard priority is only used if no threshold values were maintained. This priority is used by default for all alerts where no threshold values can be defined. The field is "display only".
- Alert Check Rule
  This is a verbal description of the check that is performed by the alert. The check rule works in conjunction with the operator (see below). The field is "display only".
- Operator for Check Rule
  Here the operator used to check for an alert condition is shown. The field is "display only".
- Information Threshold Value
  This field is open for maintenance for all those alerts where threshold values can be defined. With the help of threshold values it is possible to influence the priority (or severity level) of the alert. Threshold values can be set for the levels "Information," "Warning," and "Error." If no threshold values are defined, the default SAP defined priority level as defined in the Standard Priority field is used.
- Warning Threshold Value
  See above explanation.
- Error Threshold Value

See above explanation.

In addition to the alert parameterization, other restrictions can be defined per alert type area.

- DP
  All entries explained below are optional.
  - InfoCube
    Restrict the validity of the DP alert profile to exactly one InfoCube.
  - InfoCube Characteristics
    Restrict the validity of the DP alert profile to one or multiple Characteristics Value Combinations. This is achieved with the help of selection ID's. The restriction can only be applied if an InfoCube restriction was defined.
  - Planning Books
    Restrict the validity of the DP alert profile to one or multiple planning books. This is achieved with the help of selection ID's. The restriction can only be applied if an InfoCube restriction was defined.
- SNP
  All entries explained below are optional.
  - Product Selection – Products
    Restrict the validity of the SNP alert profile to one or multiple products.
  - Product Selection – Locations
    Restrict the validity of the SNP alert profile to one or multiple product locations.
  - Product Selection – SNP Planner
    Restrict the validity of the SNP alert profile to one or multiple SNP planners.
  - Resource Selection – Resources
    Restrict the validity of the SNP alert profile to one or multiple resources.
  - Resource Selection – Locations
    Restrict the validity of the SNP alert profile to one or multiple resource locations.
  - Time Buckets Profile
    Restrict the creation of the SNP alerts in time according to a time bucket profile.

- TLB/Deployment
  All entries explained below are optional.
  - Product Selection – Products
    Restrict the validity of the Deployment alert profile to one or multiple products.
  - Product Selection – Transportation Planner
    Restrict the validity of the Deployment alert profile to one or multiple transportation planners.
  - Transportation Lane Selection – Source Location
    Restrict the validity of the TLB/Deployment alert profile to one or multiple source locations.
  - Transportation Lane Selection – Target Location
    Restrict the validity of the TLB/Deployment alert profile to one or multiple target locations.
  - Transportation Capacity Restriction – Transportation Method
    Restrict the validity of the TLB alert profile to one or multiple transportation methods.
- PP/DS
  All entries explained below are optional.
  - Days' Supply Type 1
    The PP/DS alert monitor can create an alert if the number of days' supply for a product is exceeded. The target days' of supply for all products is defined in a profile. In this profile all ATP categories are defined that need to be taken into consideration when calculating the total supply. The PP/DS alert monitor takes this default value if no other profile is defined here. The default days' supply profile is displayed automatically in the alert profile. Specify here another alternate days' supply profile if the default profile must not be used.
  - Days' Supply Type 2
    Additionally a second days' supply profile can be defined here. If this has been done, the alert will be related to the days' supply definition it relates to.
  - Days' Supply Type 3

Additionally a third days' supply profile can be defined here. If this has been done, the alert will be related to the days' supply definition it relates to.

- Planned Delivery Date
  Do not create alerts if the predicted component shortage is outside the lead-time.
- Product Selection – Products
  Restrict the validity of the PP/DS alert profile to one or multiple products.
- Product Selection – Locations
  Restrict the validity of the PP/DS alert profile to one or multiple product locations.
- Product Selection – Production Planner
  Restrict the validity of the PP/DS alert profile to one or multiple production planner.
- Resource Selection – Resources
  Restrict the validity of the PP/DS alert profile to one or multiple resources.
- Resource Selection – Locations
  Restrict the validity of the PP/DS alert profile to one or multiple resource locations.

- ATP
  All entries explained below are optional.
  - Product Selection – Products
    Restrict the validity of the ATP alert profile to one or multiple products.
  - Product Selection – Locations
    Restrict the validity of the ATP alert profile to one or multiple location products.
  - Allocation Selection – Product Allocation Group
    Restrict the validity of the ATP alert profile to one or multiple product allocation groups.

Please also refer to the SNP Guide "Alert Monitor Setup" for detailed information of activities to be carried out in order to receive alerts.

## 4.5.4 SNP Interactive Planning Screen

The SNP Interactive Planning screen is the hub of supply network planning. From there, all major tasks can be performed including master data maintenance, alert monitor, and obviously the planning as such. The SNP Interactive Planning screen is an "Integrated Production and Distribution Requirements Planning Application." It is similar in appearance to the DP Interactive Planning screen and can also be accessed either from the APO menu structure or from the Supply Chain Cockpit. The Interactive Planning screen can be started specifying a fixed time period (SAP delivered default is daily for the next three weeks), a fixed interval with start and end date, or according to a time buckets profile. The specified dates also determine the SNP planning time frame for the Heuristics, Optimizer and CTM runs.
On the left side is the tree structure with the three tabs for Products, Locations, and Transportation Lanes. Selection of data is supported by selection ID's. A header, which is suppressed initially (click on the hat to activate it), displays the selected model and planning version together with some selected profile entries. Although it takes some valuable space on the desktop, it is worthwhile displaying this header information. Like a lot of other APO screens, one has to be careful when selecting data in the tree structure. Double clicking on a symbol (such as the plant) in front of the object name (e.g. the plant name) does not give any results. It is required to double click on the text (the plant name)! The color of the object name turns from black to blue once selected.



The right hand side is table-like with five different tabs. On the Plan tab, together with some other data, the total of demand and receipts, the stock on hand and the backlog is displayed. The time roster is according to the initial specification and, if accepting the default, daily starting on the day after the APO system date. The time period used is specified on the initial screen either as a from-to date or according to a time bucket.

The second tab on this side, called the Capacity Check tab, shows for a given product the utilized resources. This screen gives a quick overview of all resources used by a certain product. In order to obtain information, a certain product and location has to be selected in the Products tree structure.

The Capacity Plan tab displays for a given resource the products using it. This information is specifically helpful when performing capacity leveling after a Heuristic run. It is required to select a location and resource in the tree structure to see the capacity plan. Once a resource has been selected in the Location tree structure tab, the display automatically switches over to the Capacity Plan tab. The Capacity Plan tab is the only tab from where SNP planned orders for production or transportation can be edited.

The Transportation Recommendations tab gives an overview of SNP planned transport orders (upper section, sorted by product) and transport recommendations as generated from the Deployment run (lower section, sorted by shipping date).

The Transport Order tab displays transport order header information in the upper section (sorted by transport order) and transport order item information (sorted by product) in the lower section.

Interactive planning is facilitated by the Alert Monitor, which can automatically point to problem areas. This enables an exception based planning activity. See also the chapter "Alert Monitor'.

Valuable information regarding the planning situation of a product can also be found in the PP/DS menu structure. Of special interest are the following transactions.

- Find Requirements
  This transaction offers a table display of all requirements for a product. After the DP plan was released to SNP, you will find here at least the independent requirements (forecasted demand). Other examples could be dependent demands or sales order demands.
- Find Orders
  The Find Order transaction display is the same as the one used for Find Requirements. It displays all orders for the product. Examples are SNP planned orders or PP/DS orders. This screen can be put into Edit mode, which allows editing and deleting of planned orders. To edit or delete an order switch over to Edit mode, double click on the order line, and select the Delete symbol on the upcoming screen.
- Planning Situation for a Product

This is a combination screen of the two above and combines data as well as features of the two. It also provides editing capability for planned orders. The Planning Situation for a Product transaction can also be called from the Goto menu of the Interactive Planning screen.

### 4.5.4.1 The Plan Tab

The plan tab displays the total demand and receipts per product. In order to obtain information, a certain product and location has to be selected in the Products tree structure first. The product tree structure, which is used with the plan tab, is shown in the table below.



| | | | |
|---|---|---|---|
| Product | | | |
| | → Location | | |
| | | → Sources | |
| | | | → Location |
| | | → Destinations | |
| | | | → Location |

**Table 70 – Plan Tab Tree Structure**

Sources and destinations are determined according to the transportation lanes defined in the Supply Chain Engineer. Double clicking on the location name below the sources or targets symbol switches the display over to the selected product in the location. Initially the totals for Demand and Receipts are displayed and can be broken down by double clicking on them to see individual elements of these two groups.

The Total Demand consists of the SNP key figures:

- Forecast — Remaining unconsumed forecasted quantity
- Sales Order — Total sales order quantity

| | |
|---|---|
| • Dependant Demand | Dependant demand from other orders |
| • Distribution Demand (planned) | SNP created planned orders for distribution |
| • Distribution Demand (confirmed) | Deployment created planned orders for distribution |
| • Distribution Demand (TLB confirmed) | TLB created planned orders for distribution |

The Total Receipts consists of the SNP key figures:

| | |
|---|---|
| ▪ Planned Production | Not yet firmed planned orders for production (SNP) |
| ▪ Joint Production | By product quantities of a planned order |
| ▪ Firmed Production | Firmed planned orders for production (PP/DS) |
| ▪ Distribution Receipt (planned) | SNP created planned orders for distribution |
| ▪ Distribution Receipt (confirmed) | Deployment created planned orders for distribution |
| ▪ Distribution Receipt (TLB confirmed) | TLB created planned orders for distribution |
| ▪ In Transit | Quantities shipped but not yet received |

The calculation of the SNP demand and receipt key figures is configurable. During customization each of these figures is linked to an ATP Group, which in turn is made up of several ATP Categories. The allocation of ATP Categories is time dependent and differs for the short, medium, and long-term horizon. The duration of these horizons is product specific as each product can have its own horizon definitions. To facilitate these definitions, products can be linked to the SNP Demand and Supply profiles that carry this information. It must be stressed again that although the key figure names are fixed, they only receive a meaning after the ATP Categories are linked to them. Therefore the description of the key figures above refers to which elements the key figures most likely represent.

The Demand, Supply, Stock, and Backlog figures from the upper section of the screen can also be shown optionally in a graph. The same applies to the details (see below).

Further details of the elements shown in the upper section of the screen can be seen at the bottom of the plan tab. Here the (daily) totals shown on top are broken down into single elements. It is activated by double clicking on a cell in the grid of the upper section. Double clicking on a planned production order cell for example would show all planned productions orders for this day.

The Plan tab is a tab from where SNP planned orders for production or transportation can be edited. To edit an order, drill down to the (production or transportation) resource for which you want to edit planned orders. As an optional step, double click on the product line in the upper grid to view in a new third window all orders of the selected product occupying the selected resource. Ensure that the Interactive Planning screen is in Change mode, and select in the middle grid a cell showing the planned order quantity. Change the quantity of the planned order and save. When changing the screen into the Change mode, all lines that allow editing, change their color from gray to off-white. Only after editing a cell, the Save option becomes available.



#### 4.5.4.2 The Capacity Check Tab

The Capacity Check tab shows for a given product all resources it is utilizing based on the current planned orders and the used PPM's. The layout of the upper section corresponds to that of the Plan tab described above. In the lower section that also appears in a table format the individual resources used by the product and their daily loads are listed. Activation of graphs is also possible. The product tree structure to be used in connection with the capacity check tab is shown below.

| | | | |
|---|---|---|---|
| Product | | | |
| | → Location | | |
| | | → Sources | |
| | | | → Location |
| | | → Destinations | |
| | | | → Location |

**Table 71 – Capacity Check Tab Tree Structure**



#### 4.5.4.3 The Capacity Plan Tab

The system switches to this tab automatically if a location together with a resource or a transportation lane has been selected in the Location or Transportation Lane tree structure. Note that in order to obtain information about a production capacity load, it is only required to select a resource. All products that utilize this resource will be displayed automatically. The tree structures are shown below.

| | | |
|---|---|---|
| Location | | |
| | → Resource | |
| | | → Product |

| | |
|---|---|
| Transportation Lane | |
| | → Resource |

**Table 72 – Capacity Plan Tab Tree Structures**

Resources have a capacity load indicator in the tree structure. A red point is shown in front of the resource name if the capacity is overloaded; otherwise the indicator is green. On this tab you see in the upper right section information in table form for the selected resource or for the combination of selected resource and the resource utilizing products. The information provided on this tab is based on planned orders created either manually or by one of the SNP planning runs. The capacity utilization is based on the PPM explosion.

The total available capacity, the total capacity consumption as well as the resulting load is displayed initially. By double clicking on the top capacity line, the Normal as well as the Maximum capacity of the resource are displayed. The capacity values are taken from the resource master. The Normal capacity is derived from the capacity variant 1, the Maximum capacity from the capacity variant 2. The Optimizer also uses these two capacity variants during the planning run. The relation of capacity variant 1 being the Normal capacity and capacity variant 2 being the Maximum capacity cannot be changed for display purposes in the Interactive Planning screen. This is although the Optimizer does not require this fixed link. The capacity load row displays the load of the individual resource as a percentage of the available capacity. When double clicking on this capacity load line, the average capacity load is displayed additionally. The average capacity load is the average load of all resources in the specified location.



Double clicking on the capacity consumption row displays in table form all products that contribute to the capacity consumption in the lower section of the screen. This information might also be visible immediately without activation. A red shaded cell is an alert sign that depicts a resource capacity overload on the specific day.

From this tab, the function "Alternative Resource" can be activated. First select a product by highlighting the appropriate line in the table, and then activate the function to get a list of possible alternative resources. Alternate resources are defined in the PPM that was also used when creating the planned order. On the PPM activity level several modes can be defined. Each mode is linked to a different set of alternative resources that can be used to process the required activity. Each mode has got at least one primary resource and one or multiple secondary resources. Please refer to the chapter "Production Process Model (PPM)" for more information.

The Capacity Plan tab is a tab from where SNP planned orders for production or transportation can be edited. To edit an order, drill down to the (production or transportation) resource for which you want to edit planned orders. As an optional step, double click on the product line in the lower grid to view in a new third window all orders of the selected product occupying the selected resource. Ensure that the Interactive Planning screen is in <u>Change</u> mode, and select in the middle grid a cell showing the planned order quantity. Change the quantity of the planned order and save. When changing the screen into the Change mode, all lines that allow editing, change their color from gray to off-white. Only after editing a cell, the Save option becomes available.

#### 4.5.4.4 The Transport Recommendations Tab



The Transport Recommendations tab displays the Transport Load Builder (TLB) generated multi-product shipments in the top grid and the single-product planned orders for transportation that were created by the Deployment run in the bottom grid. The Deployment run picks up SNP generated planned orders for transportation and compares them with the available supply. This is an intermediate step before the Transport Load Builder picks up the Deployment orders and generates multi-product shipments. TLB shipments are based on the recommended transport orders created by the Deployment run with the aim to use transport resources economically (e.g. full truckload). The Transport Recommendations tab is a real work screen from which several activities can be performed. The display of the transport recommendations tab is orientated towards transportation lane, which needs to be selected together with the transportation type when entering the screen.

| | | |
|---|---|---|
| Product | | |
| | → Source to Destination Location | |
| | | → Transportation Type |

**Table 73 –Transport Recommendations Tab Tree Structure**

The transport recommendations tab is the main screen for consolidating planned orders for transportation into transport orders or to check and change allocations done by the TLB run. We should see specifically in this area many new features coming up. SAP already announced the development of enhancements in the area of transportation planning, vehicle scheduling, optimization and route planning.

| Group | Field | Description |
|---|---|---|
| Product | Product | Product Number |
| | Quantity | Quantity of product in shipment |
| | Unit | Base unit of measure of product |
| Volume | Volume | Occupied volume of product |
| | Unit | Unit of measure for volume |
| | Cumulative Volume | Cumulated volume of all products this far |
| | Free Volume Capacity | Remaining volume capacity this far |
| | Unit | Unit of measure for cumulative and free volume |
| | % Load | Percentage volume load for this product |
| Weight | Weight | Occupied weight of product |
| | Unit | Unit of measure for weight |
| | Cumulative Weight | Cumulated weight of all products this far |
| | Free Weight Capacity | Remaining weight capacity this far |
| | Unit | Unit of measure for cumulative and free weight |
| | % Load | Percentage weight load for this product |
| Pallet | Pallets | Occupied number of pallets of product |
| | Cumulative Pallets | Cumulated number of pallets of all products this far |
| | Cumulative Floor Spots | Cumulated number of floor spots of products this far |
| | Free Floor Spot Capacity | Remaining floor spots this far |
| | % Load | Percentage floor spot load for this product |
| VMI | VMI Purchasing Group | Flag identifying VMI loads |

**Table 74 – Transport Recommendations Tab Fields - Top**

The upper grid displays information for exactly one TLB created transport order. In the header area, you can see the order number together with the transportation type and the source and destination location. The shipping and receipt date that are also displayed in the header can be changed. The upper grid shows for the selected transport order the products that it contains. The fields displayed in this grid are shown below.

The cumulative figures allow easy manual filling up of transport orders. The occupied floor spot is a function of the permitted number of stacking levels for a product. Which planned orders for transportation can be put into the transport order can be seen on the lower grid. Here all Deployment created planned orders are listed sorted by date, descending or ascending. Planned transportation orders can easily be selected and allocated to the transport order in the above grid. A reverse (de-allocation) function is also available. The fields displayed in the lower grid are listed below.



| Group | Field | Description |
|---|---|---|
| Order | Shipping Date | Shipping date of order |
| | Receipt Date | Receipt date of order |
| Product | Product | Product Number |
| | Quantity | Quantity of product in shipment |
| | Unit | Base unit of measure of product |
| | Rounding Value | Rounding value of product from product master Lot Size tab |
| | Stacking Factor | Stacking factor of product from product master Attributes tab |
| | Priority | Priority of product from product master SNP2 tab |
| VMI | VMI Purchasing Group | Flag identifying VMI loads |

**Table 75 – Transport Recommendations Tab Fields - Bottom**

#### 4.5.4.5 The Transport Orders Tab

The Transport Orders tab displays multi product shipments, which were generated by the Transport Load Builder (TLB) and/or manually edited in the transport recommendations tab. The display of the transport orders tab is oriented towards the transportation lane, which needs to be selected when entering the screen. The tree structure of the transport orders tab is shown below.

| | | |
|---|---|---|
| Product | | |
| | → Source to Destination Location | |
| | | → Transportation Type |

**Table 76 – Transport Orders Tab Tree Structure**

The grid on the upper right displays for the selected transportation lane and type the TLB generated shipments (transport orders). In the upper grid, the information as shown further down can be obtained per transport order.

| Group | Field | Description |
|---|---|---|
| Order | Transport Order | Number of TLB created transport order |
| | Shipping Date | Shipping date of order |
| | Receipt Date | Receipt date of order |
| Volume | Volume | Total volume in order |
| | Unit | Unit of volume |
| | % Load | Volume based load factor percentage for this order |
| Weight | Weight | Total weight of order |
| | Unit | Unit of weight |
| | % Load | Weight based load factor percentage for this order |
| Pallets | Pallets | Total number of pallets in order |
| | Floor Spots | Total number of floor spots used in order |
| | % Load | Floor spot based load factor percentage for this order |



**Table 77 – Transport Orders Tab Fields - Top**

The lower grid displays the products of the selected transport order. It is a breakdown of the order selected in the upper grid and provides the following information.

Line items of the transport order can be deleted, or new items can be added.

| Group | Field | Description |
|---|---|---|
| Product | Product | Product Number |
| | Quantity | Quantity of product in shipment |
| | Unit | Base unit of measure of product |
| Volume | Volume | Occupied volume of product |
| | Unit | Unit of measure for volume |
| | % Load | Percentage volume load for this product |
| Weight | Weight | Occupied weight of product |
| | Unit | Unit of measure for weight |
| | % Load | Percentage weight load for this product |
| Pallet | Pallets | Occupied number of pallets of product |
| | Floor Spots | Occupied number of floor spots of product |
| | % Load | Percentage floor spot load for this product |
| External | External Order | Reference to an externally created order (order number) |
| | Item | The item number of an externally created order |
| VMI | VMI Purchasing Group | Flag identifying VMI loads |

**Table 78 – Transport Orders Tab Fields - Bottom**

### 4.5.4.6 Capacity Leveling

An important task that has to be carried out after an SNP Heuristic run is capacity leveling. As said before, the SNP Heuristic run might not find a feasible solution to cope with all constraints. And even after an SNP optimization run, the planner might want to do adjustments before releasing the plan to PP/DS. This is done from the Interactive Planning screen. Capacity leveling offers four different options. Only option 1 is an automated rule based procedure. The options 2 through 4 are manual activities.



1. Time Based Capacity Leveling
   This is achieved by shifting of orders backward or forward to overcome peaks and use resource idling time. It is based on priority rules. Shifting is carried out as follows:
   - Backward
     With this capacity-leveling variant, the system tries to satisfy high priority demand by shifting it to an earlier date. This obviously does not constitute a due date violation.
   - Forward
     Low priority demand is shifted further into the future thus probably causing a due date violation.
   - Backward/Forward
     This is a combination of the two variants as described above.

   The definition of priorities is based on one of the following options:
   - Decreasing (Increasing) Order Quantity
     Level such demand-orders first that have the highest (lowest) order quantity.
   - Decreasing (Increasing) Target Days' Supply
     Level such demand-orders first that have the highest (lowest) target days' supply.
   - Decreasing (Increasing) Product Priority
     Level such demand-orders first that have the highest (lowest) product priority.

   If no priority rule is defined, the sequence is by random
2. Modification of resource capacity

Allocate additional shifts to temporarily overcome bottleneck problems.

3. Allocation of alternate resource
   This manual procedure entails a reallocation of products to resources with free available capacities. The capacity plan tab provides useful information to facilitate this process.
4. Adjust production or transportation orders
   Edit existing orders and shift quantities within orders. With this option, which is similar to the time based capacity leveling, orders might be changed or even deleted to overcome serious capacity problems.

Selecting the "Capacity Leveling" button activates options 1 and 2 as described above. In the pop up window, specify the method of the time-based capacity leveling. Should you select the "modification of resource capacity" option, the system switches over to the resource maintenance screen. Note that the maintenance is carried out in the planning version according to the Interactive Planning screen. When selecting one of the other options another pop up window is displayed. Here it is possible to define the priority in which the orders should be leveled. Finally the maximum load for the resource can be specified in form of a percentage. In situations where the resource consumption is fluctuating very much over time but mostly within the capacity limits, set the maximum load to lower than 100%. This will smooth the capacity usage. The cluster of pop windows is illustrated in the graphic below.

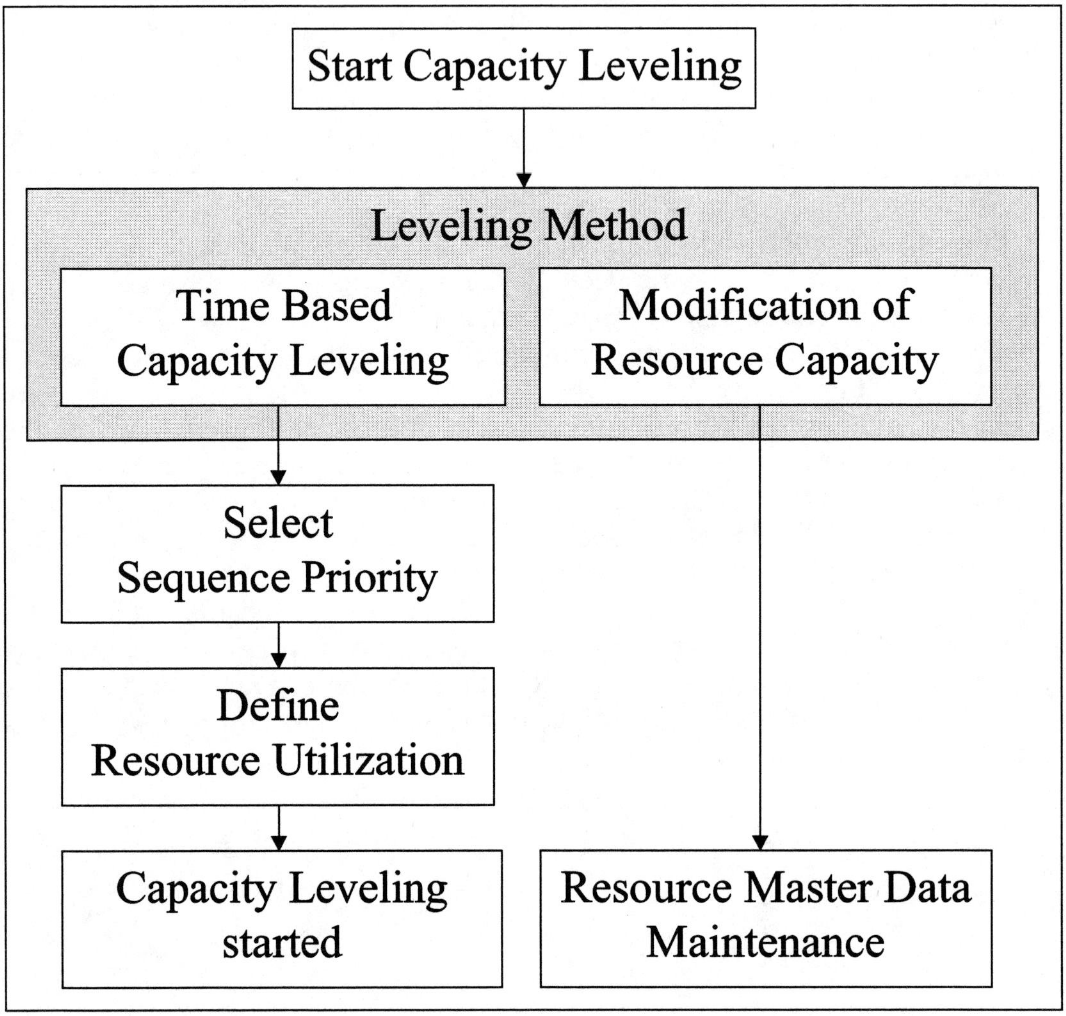


**Graphic 62 – Capacity Leveling Screens**

### 4.5.4.7 Planning Parameters

Planning Parameters are used in conjunction with the definition of the Target Stock Values for periods outside the time bucket profile. These Target Stock Values can be calculated in two ways.

- Define the Target Stock Values in the Interactive Planning Screen.
- Use safety stock and day's supply value in the product master, and calculate the Target Stock Values.

The definition of the target stock values must be carried out before the planning run is initiated. In order to update the planning table, it is necessary to save the data after the planning parameters have been applied. The following options exist:

- Safety Stock / Days Supply (Maintenance Period)
  After this option has been selected, it is possible to manually define the safety stock and the day's supply within the maintenance period. The maintenance period is the period as specified in the time bucket profile. In this case the values of the product master will not be used. Based on the new values the target stock values will be calculated.
- Target Stock Level (Maintenance Period)
  After this option has been selected, it is possible to manually define the target stock values within the maintenance period. The maintenance period is the period as specified in the time bucket profile.
- Safety Stock / Days Supply (additional)
  When this option has been selected, the safety stock and the day's supply as specified in the last column of the maintenance period are copied into the periods that fall outside the maintenance period. Based on these values the target stock values will be calculated.
- Target Stock Level (additional)
  When this option has been selected, the target stock value as specified in the last column of the maintenance period is copied into the periods that fall outside the maintenance period.
- Target Stock Level (Calculation from Lot Size Profile)
  This option will revert all target stock levels, which were manually defined to the value as defined in the product master.
- Reset all Profiles

This option will revert all safety stock and days' supply values, which were manually defined to the value as defined in the product master.

Note that the options 1 through to 4 are the equivalent to the options 1 through 4 of the "Calculation of TSL" field in the product master Lot Size tab.

#### 4.5.4.8 Forecast Allocation Display

Starting from the menu structure of the SNP Interactive Planning screen, a helpful tool can be accessed. It shows the up-to-date forecasted quantity (planned quantity), the consumed quantity (allocated), as well as the remaining forecasted quantity per product. The system provides this information irrespective of the product's requirements strategy, which means irrespective of whether forecast consumption is carried out or not.

# 4.6 Authorization Management

New with release 2.0 was the introduction of Authorization Management. Authorization objects allow the execution of specific functions in APO. Some of them are module dependent; other general ones are used throughout APO. The SNP related authorization objects are listed in the following table.

| Area | Authorization Object | Object Name | |
|---|---|---|---|
| | | | **Object Description** |
| SNP | | | |
| | C_APO_MOD | Supply Chain Model | |
| | | | This authorization is used to give access to specific supply network models. |
| | C_APO_VERS | Supply Network Planning Version | |
| | | | This authorization is used to give access to specific supply network planning versions. |
| | C_APO_CTM | CTM Profile | |
| | | | Permits access to the CTM profile definition screens. |

**Table 79 – SNP Authorization Objects**

The general authorization objects are included in the DP section in the chapter Authorization Management.

# 4.7 SNP Guides

## 4.7.1 Alert Monitor Setup

In order to see alerts the following activities must have been carried out:

- Alert Profile Allocation
  The definition of the alert profile can be carried out in a special transaction (use "Navigation – Supply Chain – Settings – Alert Monitor"). This calls the Alert Monitor Profile maintenance program. Select "Maintain Profile". The following settings are important:

| | |
|---|---|
| Alert Type | Activate alert types as required. |
| Object Selection | If the alert profile should only be used for a certain object types, specify it in the lower section of the respective profile definition screens. Examples of possible object types are locations or resource. These fields mostly contain a selection ID that in turn defines one or multiple object types with the corresponding values. |
| Priority Variants | Priority variants allow for some of the SNP alerts to define threshold values according to which the alert is classified as an Error, a Warning, or Information. The priority variant setting also influences the way the alert is displayed in the Control Panel of the Supply Chain Cockpit.<br>An example would be the SNP alert "Capacity overload on bucket resource". Any overload up to 5% is ignored, up to 10% leads to an informational message, up to 20% to a warning message, and everything above is an error. |

- Link of valid profiles to Alert Monitor settings
  This can be done after selecting the <Back> button. In this step the alert profiles are linked with the SNP planning versions. Also the time frame on which the alert creation is based on is defined there.
- Link of valid profiles to the Supply Chain Cockpit user settings

This can be done in the Supply Chain Cockpit by accessing the user profile. Note that without the user being linked to an alert profile, no alerts are displayed.

## 4.7.2 Maintenance of Transportation Lanes

Transportation lanes are the only master data objects that are model dependent. They can be created only in the Supply Chain Engineer. If the same transportation lane is required in two different models it has to be created twice. To access the Supply Chain Engineer, select starting from the SNP main menu Master Data > Supply Chain Engineer.

To create transportation lanes proceed as described below.

- Open the Supply Chain Engineer and select a model.
- Select the "Transportation Lanes" tab (optional).
- On top of the map change the display option from "Move Locations" to "Display Lanes".
- Select the location where the transportation lane starts.
- Hold down the left mouse button and drag the line to the destination location.
- Release the left mouse button once the destination location is selected.
- A pop up screen appears allowing the input of transportation lane specific data such as.
  - Description — Specify any name for the transportation lane.
  - Transportation Planner — In order to select the transportation planner in some of the SNP transactions define the responsible planner here.
  - Transportation Calendar — This is the calendar used for transport scheduling purposes.

  In some cases this pop up screen does not appear. In such a case simply select the transportation lane and choose "Change - Transportation Lane".
- Do not press the Okay (F5) button yet, as a time period must be assigned first.

- Select "New Time period" and specify the "Valid To" date and the "Mode of Transport". Modes of transport are defined in customizing and new values can be added.

The basic maintenance of the transportation lane is done now. The pop up screen can be closed and maintenance can be continued later. Note that data is only saved after pressing the "Save Model" button of the Supply Chain Engineer! The system automatically allocates an identifier to the transportation lane, which is made up of the source and destination location identifier separated by a dash.

For further maintenance continue without closing the pop up screen or select the newly created transportation lane. Selecting a transportation lane is possible either in the transportation lane tab in the tree structure section or on the map.

It is also possible to stipulate specific products that can be moved using this transportation lane and mode of transport. To do so it is necessary to position the cursor in the appropriate mode line and to select the "Product Allocation" button. This activates a new sub screen. On this screen select "New Product" to add a specific product or a multitude of products with their valid transport modes, costs (penalties), and lot size profiles. Only those transportation modes allowed for the transportation lane can be used for specific products. The "New Transportation Method" button allows adding additionally not already used transportation methods (modes) to the selected product.



### 4.7.3 Maintenance of Quota Arrangements

To maintain a quota arrangement, start the Supply Chain Engineer and select the locations tab. Note that quota arrangements can only be maintained if a transportation lane of the appropriate direction exists. From the location tab proceed as follows.

- Select the location for which the quota arrangement has to be created.
- Activate the context sensitive menu on the location, select "Quotations", and then "Change Incoming (or Outgoing) Quotas".
- On the upcoming screen select the "New Product" button.

- Select either "All Products" or a product as required and press <Enter>.
- On the upcoming screen select the "New Validity Period" button.
- Define the "Valid to" date and press <Enter>.
- You are now finally on the screen where the quota arrangement can be maintained. The following fields are open for maintenance.
- Flag — activates quota arrangement line
- Quota Arrangement — specify the quota percentage
- Priority — define a source priority used by CTM
- After all data has been maintained press <Enter> twice to return to the Supply Chain Engineer.

To update/delete a quota arrangement, proceed as follows.

- Select the location for which the quota arrangement has to be updated/deleted.
- Activate the context sensitive menu on the location, select "Quotations", and then "Change Incoming (or Outgoing) Quotas".
- On the upcoming screen select the product for which the quota arrangement must be updated/deleted.
- On the upcoming screen select the validity period for which the quota arrangement must be updated/deleted.
- On the upcoming screen change the quota as required or take the flag off to delete the quota arrangement.
- After the data has been updated as required press <Enter> twice to return to the Supply Chain Engineer.

# 5 Production Planning & Detailed Scheduling

## 5.1 Introduction

Production Planning and Detailed Scheduling within APO picks up the constrained mid-term plan generated in SNP. Unlike SNP, PP/DS is oriented towards a single plant and enables the user to carry out planning down to the second while considering not only component and capacity constraints, but also sequencing requirements. PP/DS focuses on single plant constraints whereby SNP plans the network. While saying that the focus is on the planning situation of a single plant, one must also see that the Scheduler can display and work simultaneously with resources across different plants. The result of Production Planning and Detailed Scheduling is a feasible plan. An optimizer can be used to optimize the sequence of production orders according to various rules, thus providing a feasible and optimized production plan. The medium term SNP plan can only provide a short term feasible plan if the CTM method is deployed. In such a case, the Production Planning and Detailed Scheduling module can be used to additionally optimize the production order sequence. CTM can also be seen as a PP/DS tool. There is no strict rule, and the usage decision depends on the business requirements. PP/DS functionality is also used to create production orders for such sales orders where no adequate supply elements can be found. This procedure referred to as Capable to Promise (CTP) is initiated by an ATP check that returns insufficient supplies.

PP/DS uses its own more detailed resource definitions (Single or Multi Activity Resources) as well as specific Production Process Models. In order for PP/DS to carry out the planning function, it is required to convert SNP planned orders to PP/DS planned orders. During this step the planned order is re-exploded using the PP/DS PPM's and consequently Single or Multi Activity Resources. PP/DS can also work with Single Mixed or Multi Mixed resources.

PP/DS is the logical next step after the rough cut planning performed in SNP has been carried out. Consequently, after the PP/DS planning, the transportation planning and vehicle scheduling (TP/VS) takes place. The PP/DS step is obviously applicable only to such sites that carry out production. In other cases the TP/VS step follows directly after SNP. The graphic below offers an overview of the APO planning steps.

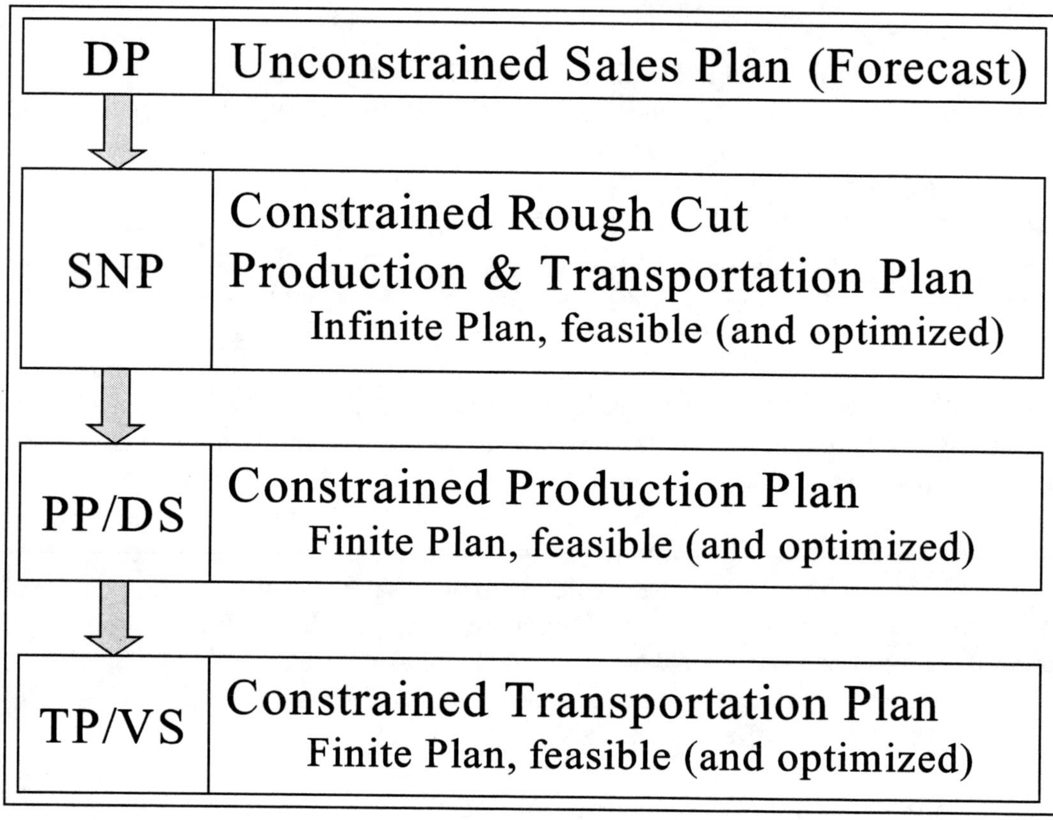


**Graphic 63 – Planning Steps**

# 5.2 Overview

PP/DS takes control of all PP/DS planned production orders. These planned orders originate from one of the following three activities:

- Conversion of SNP planned orders to PP/DS planned orders. This is a background function, which converts all SNP planned orders that start within the Production Horizon.
- Global ATP check that results in insufficient supplies with consequent creation of PP/DS planned order. Such orders can be created automatically if permitted in the product master.
- Manually created PP/DS planned order. The planner can create PP/DS planned orders anytime and within or outside the production horizon.

Unlike the other APO modules there are not too many different activities within PP/DS. APO offers the planner two main tools supporting the PP/DS panning activities.

- Product View
  Also referred to as the "Planning Situation" of the product, this transaction allows the display of demands (e.g. forecasts or sales orders) as well as display and maintenance of planned orders.
- Planning Board
  Also referred to as the "Planning Table," the planning board is a highly graphical tool used to (re-) schedule activities or entire orders. The scheduler is also the starting point for the PP/DS optimizer.

The fact that there are fewer transactions in the PP/DS environment does by no means imply that PP/DS is an easy to learn and configure module. Specifically the scheduler is extremely flexible and the customizing possibilities for the graphical appearance seem to be endless. All profiles that can be found for PP/DS deal with the scheduler. Scheduling is a time critical task, and it is mandatory to arrange the interaction between the APO planning system and the (R/3) OLTP system with the greatest care. Changes in planned orders need to be communicated immediately to the other system, and the difficulty is that both systems can theoretically update the same order at the same time.

Besides Global ATP, which is not really a functional module like DP or SNP, PP/DS is the module that has the tightest link to R/3 or any other OLTP system. It can handle planned orders for production, transportation, and for external procurement. Planned orders need to be transmitted to the OLTP system for further processing (execution). In cases where some components are not planned in APO, but only in the OLTP system, it is necessary to plan these components in the OLTP system as a separate step. In this case additional Master Production Schedule (MPS) or Material Requirements Planning (MRP) runs have to be carried out in the OLTP system.

In order to carry out Product Costing, it is mandatory to define BOM's and Routings in the OLTP system even if they are not needed for anything else. Within PP/DS, BOM's and Routings residing in R/3 can be used instead of the PPM, although it is still required to create PPM's for SNP purposes. The confirmation of a production order in the OLTP system is used to carry out variance control and to close the planned production order in APO.

## 5.3 The PP/DS Methodology

Production Planning and Detailed Scheduling, as the name indicates, consists of two main tasks. The production planning is a product-oriented planning activity and the detailed scheduling is resource-oriented. Traditionally production planning was focussed around the availability of the finished product and the components required for the production orders. Detailed scheduling, on the other hand, was orientated towards capacity planning of resources and assuring that enough capacity was available to fulfill the requirements of the production orders. This was often a two step process and while optimizing the one area, the other area was neglected. In practice various iterative planning steps were required to come to an acceptable solution. Optimized solutions considering both component and capacity requirements were nearly impossible.
In PP/DS, component and capacity requirements are always planned together, and thus the difference between production planning and detailed scheduling is not this stringent anymore. The two areas grew together as the system provides the tools to ensure feasible plans without a requirement to align plans. The following two definitions describe this relation.

**Production Planning is the product-oriented planning of production orders with detailed scheduling being performed in the background.**

**Detailed Scheduling is the resource-oriented planning of operations with production planning being performed in the background.**



It is immediately visible that in both activities, the same tasks are fulfilled; what is different is the direction in which the work is performed. The obvious question is then immediately why are both tasks performed if they achieve the same at the end? The difference is the focus of the two areas and their focus in the time line.

**Production Planning ensures that planned production orders are scheduled in time to balance demands and supplies at a certain point in time.**

**Detailed Scheduling ensures that operations and activities are scheduled in such a way that resources are used optimally over a period of time.**

We see that the focus of the two areas is different; product availability versus economical usage of resources. This must lead to conflicts, and that is why PP/DS offers optimizers that can be parameterized in such a way that the goals of both areas are weighted and influence the final result depending on requirements of the business.

By planning capacity and component requirements simultaneously, APO ensures that at any time the production plan is feasible down to the second of an activity. The optimizer, if applied, adds a new dimension, which is finite scheduling based on freely definable parameters. In the following chapters, we will go through all APO areas of Production Planning and Detailed Scheduling. This will provide a sound understanding of the functionality offered and the principles of the system. In the consequent chapters after that we will have a look at the main PP/DS transactions.

The following graphic depicts the direction of these planning steps and what they emphasize.

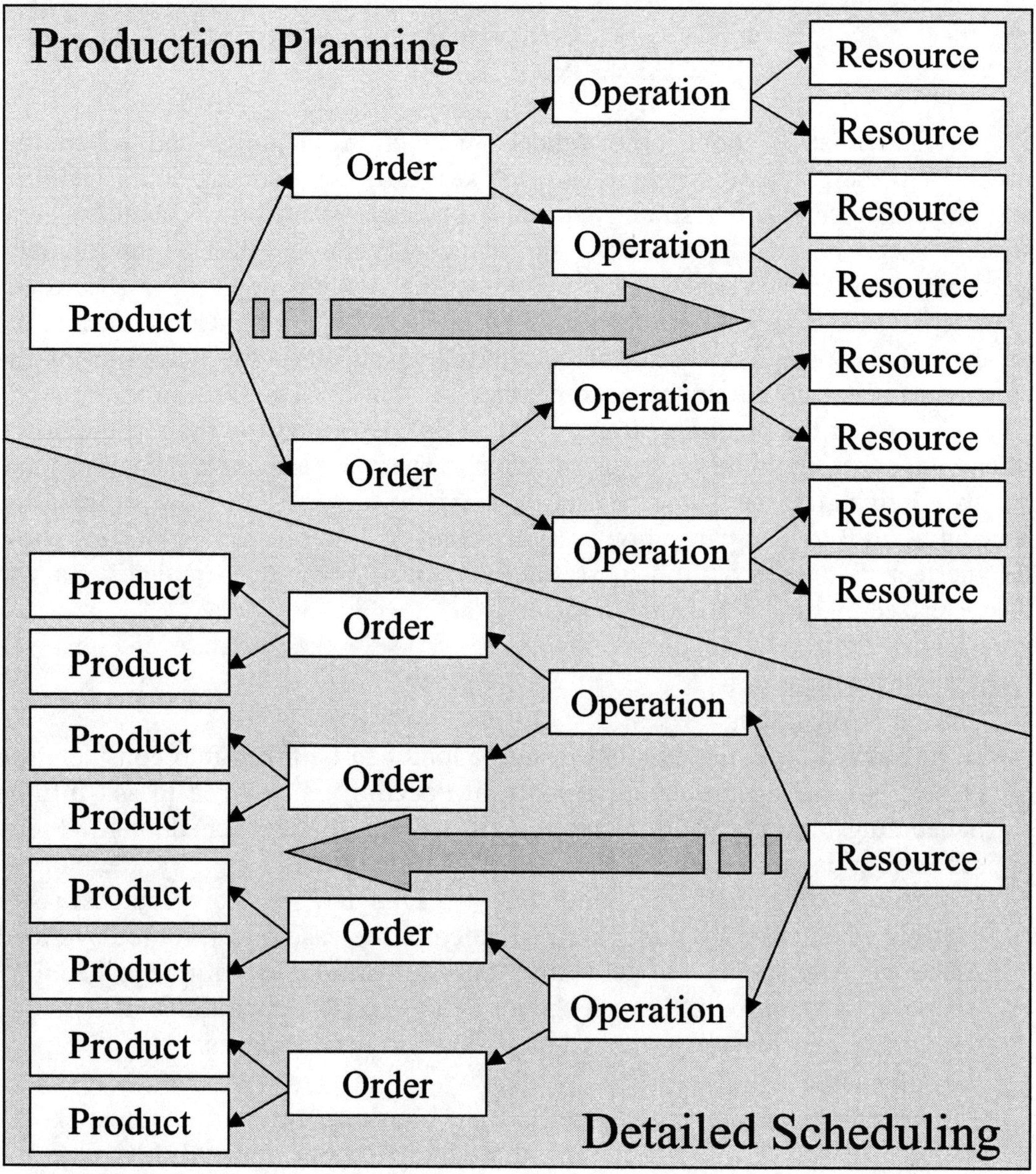


**Graphic 64 – PP/DS Planning Emphasis**

## 5.3.1 Planning Strategies

PP/DS is primarily about order-related production planning and scheduling orders, and the planning strategies are the key to these planning and scheduling activities. The scheduling strategy is not a product parameter. Several different strategies can be set up and used simultaneously in the PP/DS environment. Anytime the planner carries out scheduling, the default strategy profile of the planner is used. If another strategy is to be deployed, the planner can change the settings of the profile or use another alternative one. For the definition of the strategy profile, see the appropriate chapter in "The PP/DS Data Environment". The selection of the planning strategy is also not dependent on the resource used or any flags that might be set in the resource master. Nevertheless, some flags that can be defined in the resource master have an impact on how exactly the scheduling in PP/DS is carried out. Highly configurable planning strategies allow the perfect fit for most business requirements. Planning strategies can be characterized by the following parameters:

General Parameters:

- Capacity Constraints
  During scheduling, the existing resource load can be taken into consideration or not. Not taking the resource load into account is referred to as "Infinite Scheduling"; taking it into account is called "Finite Scheduling." Finite scheduling is activated by the planning strategy and not by the "Finite Scheduling" flag in the resource master. This flag in the resource master controls whether or not alerts are generated in the case of a resource overload situation. Alerts can be generated during finite and infinite scheduling whenever a resource overload occurs. The "Finite Scheduling" flag in the resource master must be switched on in order to receive alerts.
- Working Time
  The primary capacity constraints are the working times as defined in the resource master. Finite scheduling that is carried out automatically uses the available capacity only, as otherwise it would most probably find immediately available capacity in the non-working time that should not be used. Manually it is possible to schedule activities into non-working times. Infinite scheduling puts an activity where required irrespective of the available capacity and does

PP/DS

therefore not consider the available time. It does consider working and non-working time.

- Planning Direction
  Scheduling can be carried out in forward, forward with reverse, backward, and backward with reverse direction. With forward scheduling the order to be scheduled will be put at the first available date and time after the planning period's start date; backward scheduling finds the latest possible date. Forward (backward) and reverse scheduling first tries to find an available date and time in forward (backward) direction and, if this is not possible, a backward (forward) scheduling search is carried out.
- Time Slot Search
  During scheduling for each activity, a search takes place to find a free time slot. This free time slot can then be used for the activity. Alternatively a slot can be "made" by pushing other activities to the side on the time scale. This inserting of the new activity requires other activities to either be pushed backward (closer to today's date) or forward (further away from today's date). A third alternative is to exactly position the new activity where required. It is then squeezed in. Infinite scheduling puts an activity where required irrespective of the other already existing orders. It therefore does not require a time slot.

In addition to the general parameters described above, there are optional parameters that need to be decided upon when finite scheduling strategies are used. They are as follows:

<u>Optional Parameters</u>

- Order Internal Relationships
  An order internal relationship is the relation and sequence of operations and activities as defined in the PPM. Specific waiting times between activities are another type of order internal relationships that are also defined in the PPM. If the order internal relationship has to be considered, the system will reschedule all linked operations within the order at the same time. Order internal relationships can also be ignored completely.
- Pegging Network
  The pegging network links various orders. Based on this pegging network, the system can check the impact of the scheduling activity of a specific order on

other orders. These order external relationships can also be ignored completely or only outside the propagation range. It can happen that the scheduling activity of a certain resource or product has an impact on another resource or product that is not part of the propagation range. The propagation range defines the resources and products that can be rescheduled although not shown in the planning table. In environments where more than one planner is responsible for the scheduling of production orders, the propagation range is used to limit the individual planners' responsibility in terms of products and resources. Propagation ranges are defined in the Propagation Range Profile that is linked to the Overall Profile together with the Strategy Profile. Depending on the setting in the strategy profile, the other resources or products that are not part of the propagation range are then either planned as well or ignored.

- Scheduling Sequence (Priority)
  While performing a mass scheduling job, it is important to define a sequence for the objects (operations) to be scheduled. This could be for example by duration (long running operations first) or by product (strategic products first).

In the following chapters each of the PP/DS planning strategies will be discussed. Not all of the possible theoretically combinations of parameters explained above are feasible. In some cases there are restrictions in terms of mixing the various parameters as a (technically possible) combination might not make any business sense. The table below provides an overview of the PP/DS planning strategies and their general parameter settings. The "Schedule to Non Working Time" strategy is not included as it is not an automated strategy. Following abbreviations are used in the table:

F Forward Scheduling
B Backward Scheduling
SI Squeeze In

| Scheduling Group | Infinite | | Finite | | | | Insert Operation | | |
|---|---|---|---|---|---|---|---|---|---|
| Scheduling Direction | F | B | F | B | FR | BR | F | B | SI |
| Parameter: | | | | | | | | | |
| Capacity Constraints | | | | | | | | | |
| Finite Scheduling | | | X | X | X | X | X | X | X |
| Infinite Scheduling | X | X | | | | | | | |
| Working Time | n/a | n/a | | | | | | | |
| Only Working Time | | | X | X | X | X | X | X | X |
| Non Working Time | | | | | | | | | |
| Scheduling Direction | | | | | | | | | |
| Forward | X | | X | | | | X | | |
| Forward & Backward | | | | | X | | | | |
| Backward | | X | | X | | | | X | |
| Backward & Forward | | | | | | X | | | X |
| Time Slot Search | n/a | n/a | | | | | | | |
| Find Slot | | | X | X | X | X | | | |
| Make Slot | | | | | | | X | X | X |

**Table 80 – PP/DS Planning Strategies**

## 5.3.2 Planning and Optimization

Planning and Optimization in PP/DS can be carried out using various methods. The optimizer in PP/DS is a resource scheduling optimizer, the other planning tools are used for product planning. The options are:

- PP/DS Feasible Planning
  This method is similar to an MRP run in R/3 where products are planned according to the requirements date. During the planning and unlike the R/3 MRP, scheduling is carried out and resource capacity constraints are taken into account. With this mode, the system also automatically considers setup matrix definitions.
  PP/DS Feasible Planning is carried out when planning a product using the "Plan Product" button and no Heuristics method is defined in the product's master record.
- PP/DS Heuristics Planning
  This method is similar to an MRP run in R/3 where products are planned according to the requirements date without considering resource capacity constraints. Two methods are available, a "Standard Lot Size" and a "Periodic Lot Size" procedure. Because the heuristic method does not take capacity constraints into account, it is usually the case that the result leads to capacity overloads. It is the planner's task to adjust the heuristic plan in a separate step to achieve a feasible plan.
  PP/DS Heuristics Planning is carried out when planning a product using the "Plan Product" button and a specific Heuristics method is defined in the product's master record.
- Capable-To-Match
  Capable-To-Match (CTM) is a planning algorithm, which considers constraints and priorities in the search for a solution. The found solution is feasible but not necessarily optimal as it will stop searching after a feasible solution has been found.
  The main difference compared to the other planning options in PP/DS is that it is a network planning, rather than a single plant orientated tool. It can only be run as a mass processing job and is thus not adequate to plan single products. It can plan products irrespective of whether a Heuristics method was defined or not.

- PP/DS Optimization
  The PP/DS Optimizer offers two methods, the Constraint Propagation and the Genetic Algorithm. The optimization is based on "best solution" whereby the composition of the influencing constraints and their weight in the overall problem is user-definable. The optimum takes into account all defined constraints. Optimization can be carried out for single or multiple resources.

Each of these methods has got its distinct advantages and disadvantages, which will be explained in the next chapters. It is purely a business decision which method to use. With the exception of the Heuristic method, products are not flagged for a certain method; it purely depends on which program is started when performing the planning run. Products that need to be planned using a Heuristic method need to be flagged appropriately in the product master lot size tab.

#### 5.3.2.1 Automatic Planning

The PP/DS component within APO can plan products automatically every time a new requirement is detected or relevant master data is changed. This process is also referred to as "Incremental Finite Scheduling". Any new or changed requirements from an OLTP system, new or changed dependent requirements, the change of product master data, or the change of a PPM triggers this process. To allow automatic planning, the "Automatic Planning" flag in the product master PP/DS tab must be set. The automatic planning function can be seen as an automated "Plan Product" function as it is carried out in the "Product View" transactions, and indeed it uses the same calculation rules.



#### 5.3.2.2 Feasible Planning

Capacity requirements are checked based on the PPM, according to the strategy profile, and the parameters of the used resources. Product requirements are first checked against the stock. This netting procedure is the base for the next step, the procurement type selection. Based on the procurement type specified in the product master GR/GI field, a first decision is made whether the product is to be procured in-house or externally. External procurement in this context is either procurement from a supplier outside the supply chain model, from a supplier that is defined in the supply chain model, or transfer from another location such as an alternate plant or distribution center.

The selection of the source of supply is driven by the lowest cost principle. PP/DS selects the source (internal or external procurement) with the lowest cost. For internal procurement (production) this selection is not based on mode priorities defined in the PPM!

#### 5.3.2.3 PP/DS Heuristics

In the PP/DS area, various planning methods based on the Heuristics approach can be used. To enable the use of Heuristics in PP/DS it is required to define the type of the Heuristics in the product master PP/DS tab. If no Heuristics is specified there, the normal "Feasible Planning" approach is used. Possible Heuristics methods include the "Standard Lot Size" and the "Periodic Lot Size" planning method. Note that the Standard Lot Size method cannot be used in conjunction with the Automatic Planning option.

Own business specific planning algorithms can be developed and subsequently defined in the product master instead of an APO predefined method. This user exit will then be used automatically every time the "Plan Product" activity is carried out.



#### 5.3.2.4 Capable-To-Match

The Capable-to-Match (CTM) planning algorithm can be used to create either SNP planned orders or PP/DS orders. It is a business decision whether to use CTM and for which planning horizon. If used for the mid-term planning horizon, it can create SNP planned orders and act as an SNP planning tool. If used for the short-term planning horizon, it can create PP/DS orders. The principles and used algorithms are identical and are discussed in the SNP section of this book.

#### 5.3.2.5 PP/DS Optimization

The Optimizer is used to schedule operations in an optimum way. The definition of an "optimum" is depending on the business environment and requirements. Therefore the optimizer offers various criteria (also called parameters and abbreviated "P" in the optimizer screen) that define the optimum. These criteria, which can be freely selected and set by the planner, include:

P1 Total Lead Time
The total lead time is measured by adding up the time required from the start of the first operation to the end of the last operation for each order. The total lead time gives a good indication whether the production is streamlined in a way that products are not waiting too long between the various operations they have to go through in the production process.

P2 Setup Times
Minimizing the setup times is achieved by putting as many operations as possible of the same setup status behind each other. The setup status required for an order is defined in the PPM. Each operation of the PPM can have a different setup status. The required setup time for each transition is defined in the setup matrix that is linked to the resource.

P3 Setup Costs
Similar to the above, the setup costs are also defined in the setup matrix. Each transition is characterized by a setup time and the setup cost which do not necessarily change to the same degree or even in the same direction.

P4 Maximum Delay
The minimization of the maximum delay ensures that all operations have about the same delay. The aim is avoiding extraordinary individual delays for an operation. This might lead to an increased average delay.

P5 Average Delay
The average delay minimization tries to reduce the average delay encountered at all operations. In order to achieve this, some operations might have very long, others very low, individual delays.

P6 Total Costs

The total cost is the sum of all activity costs. This approach compares the costs when selecting alternative resources as defined in the PPM. The costs of the different modes are not defined in the PPM but in the Optimizer Cost Profile. In the PPM only the mode priorities, which are used when performing non-optimized scheduling, are defined. In the optimizer profile, the mode priorities "A" through to "O" are linked to fixed and variable costs. In order to distinguish the different mode costs, it is therefore always required to give modes different priorities, even if there is no priority.

All criteria are only measurable by comparing various results (for the same period) with each other. The relative best one is the optimum. No limit can be set that, if undercut, means that the solution is optimal. Total setup times of 300 hours in this period might identify the optimum although the total setup time last period was only 200 hours. Most often, the optimization criteria are conflicting with each other. As an example, the total lead time and setup time criteria in most cases move in a reciprocal fashion. The selection of the appropriate criteria is therefore just as important as the optimization process itself.

Interactive optimization can be run for a single resource, specified resources, or all resources. Select one or multiple resources before starting the optimizer or do not select any to use all resources. The PP/DS optimizer only optimizes operations on time continuous resources but not on bucket resources. Bucket resources are ignored if selected even if they appear in the list of selected resources. Only operations that lie entirely in the optimization period are considered and optimized. Fixed (firmed) operations or operations belonging to fixed orders are excluded from optimization. A fixed operation has an impact on other non-fixed operations of other orders as these other operations can only be moved according to their pegging parameters.

The PP/DS optimizer is a time constrained optimization engine that provides the best result it can find in the permitted time (the time setting parameter). This means that it does not necessarily provide the user with the overall best solution. Based on the maximum runtime setting, the optimizer can go through more or less iterations while improving the initial scheduling situation. A too short time defeats the purpose of finding an acceptable solution, allocating too long times does not really improve the planning situation anymore. The optimizer can be run using two different optimization algorithms. There is no general rule which algorithm produces the better result. This depends on the type of scheduling problem. The two algorithms are:

- Genetic Algorithm
  The genetic algorithm is primarily used when optimal solutions need to be developed, that is in cases where feasible solutions exist and need to be refined.
- Constraint Propagation
  The constraint propagation is used in situations where a feasible solution is required, that is that the non-optimized situation does not even provide a feasible solution.

Using the two algorithms does not necessarily provide different results. After the optimization run is finished, the results are copied into the planning board where they need to be saved to update the planning situation.

## 5.3.3 Supported Production Strategies

APO supports as of release 2.0 only Discrete Manufacturing. As an addition to the release 2.0 the support of Repetitive Manufacturing was announced. Process Orders are supported with the current release, but a Process Industry specific Process Flow Scheduler will be available at a later stage. The main areas that will be affected by this new functionality are the resources and (obviously) the scheduler in PP/DS. The current scheduler (abbreviated DS-SFS) is optimized for a discrete manufacturing environment. The scheduler for repetitive manufacturing will be abbreviated RS, and the one used for the process industry orientated orders DS-PFS. A new resource type, the line resource, will be introduced for repetitive manufacturing. It will allow the definition of rates and product specific rates for finite scheduling.

## 5.3.4 Pegging

Pegging is an essential function for any Supply Chain Planning software. The following chapters provide an introduction to the Pegging methodology and their realization in APO.

### 5.3.4.1 Introduction

In most planning systems, demand and supply elements are linked by a pegging relation. This pegging relation allows seeing exactly which demand and supply elements belong together. This works both ways, from a demand to the supply elements (top-down pegging) or vice versa (bottom- up pegging). Pegging has at least two levels. In this two level pegging, it is possible to relate a demand to the directly-linked supply element. A multi level pegging would also show all further subsequent levels. Theoretically pegging can be carried out in two different modes.

1. Pegging on Request
   This mode of pegging allows the user requesting a list of elements that belong to each other in a demand to supply (or vice versa) relation. This function allows the planner to view the pegging situation. An example for a top-down pegging is to see for a given sales order the production order with which the desired product will be manufactured (two level pegging) and possibly all the production order's dependent requirements (multi level pegging). A bottom-up pegging displays for a given component all production orders that it is used in (two level pegging) and possibly the sales order the product is manufactured for (multi level pegging). The emphasis in Pegging on Request is to provide the planner with background information. Every time the planner requests this information, the pegging situation is analyzed, and all data is processed for display. The pegging situation is not stored. Systems offering Pegging on Request usually do not use this information for any other purpose.
2. Permanent Pegging
   With Permanent Pegging, a system stores pegging relations. Each demand and supply element should be linked to at least one other element in what is called

the pegging network. Elements that do not have any pegging link are either demand orders that cannot be satisfied (at the moment) or supply elements that are not (yet) required. Even in a Make to Stock environment not too many unpegged elements should exist, as the stock manufactured according to a forecast is pegged against this forecast. As the pegging information is stored, all the display functionality of the Pegging on Request mode is also feasible. The response time is obviously much faster, as the pegging situation does not have to be evaluated prior to display. The pegging procedure can be fixed or dynamic.

- Fixed Pegging
  A Fixed Pegging relation links a demand and a supply element in a way that cannot be changed by the system. The system cannot change a fixed pegging relation; this can only be done manually by the planner. Fixed pegging relations may not be changed but all linked elements together can be moved on the time axis. The link between the elements is important and must not be altered. An obvious example is the relation between a sales order and a production order in a Make to Order environment.
- Dynamic Pegging
  A Dynamic Pegging relation links a demand and a supply element in a way that the system and planner can change it as and when required. The system and the planner can change dynamic pegging relations as required and as long as such a change does not lead to any due date violation. Dynamic pegging relations are changed when required. Typically, dynamic pegging is used in the relation between sales orders and stock (or stock replenishment orders) in a Make to Stock environment.

Over and above the display functionality, pegging can be used to efficiently determine supply elements that are affected by the change of the demand element. Changes can immediately be carried through to lower levels as and when required. Also, the effects on newly detected shortages on a lower level supply element can easily be carried through to the highest level.

It must be stressed that Pegging is not a method applied in a Make to Stock environment only. It can be used and has its advantages with any production strategy.

#### 5.3.4.2 Pegging in APO

The following table provides a quick overview about possible pegging levels and modes. APO, with its CTM and PP/DS functionality, support the dark gray shaded areas.

| | Pegging Mode | | |
|---|---|---|---|
| Levels | On Request | Permanent | |
| | | Fixed Procedure | Dynamic Procedure |
| Two Level | | | |
| Multi Level | | | |

**Table 81 – APO Supported Pegging**

In order to describe the pegging networks APO uses the elements Input Node, Output Node, and Pegging Edge. The pegging edge is the connection between two pegged elements and the link between an input node and an output node. It also has a quantity attached to it. The input node is the link of a demand generating order (e.g. a sales or planned production order). The output edge is the counterpart of the input node and is linked to a supply generating order (e.g. planned production or purchase order). In this context, stock is treated like any other supply element. Therefore, a demand element can be also linked with a stock supply element. Any input or output node has at least one related input or output node to which it is linked via a pegging edge. It is also possible that a node is the start or end for multiple pegging edges. An example is the situation where a planned production order is used to satisfy more than one demand. The quantity of the demand element does not have to be the same as the corresponding supply element. In such a case a residual shortage or excess quantity remains open. The following graphic provides an overview of a pegging network.

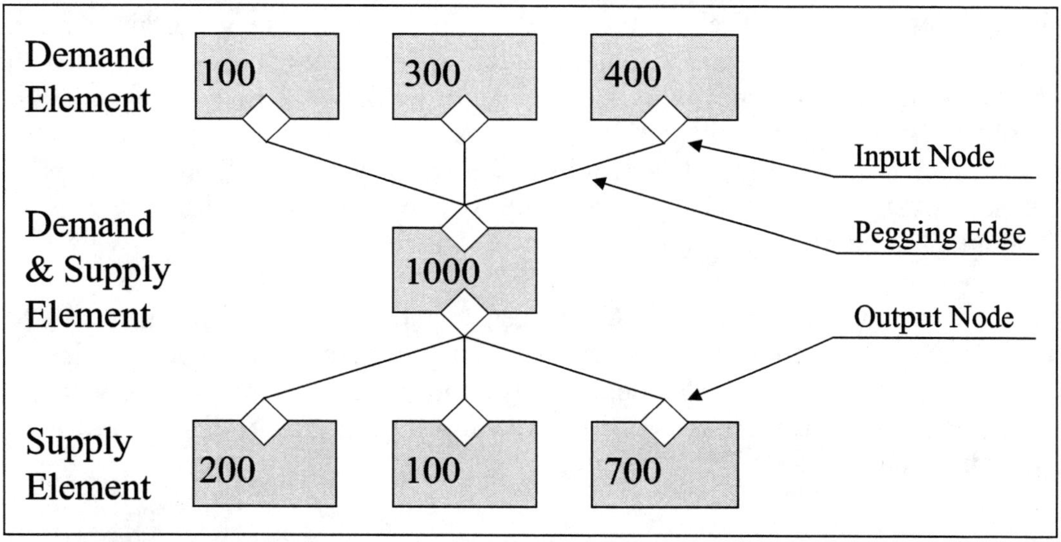


**Graphic 65 – Pegging Network**

Pegging can be carried out dynamically or fixed. With dynamic pegging, the pegging link can be changed and deleted as and when required. In order to carry out dynamic pegging, certain rules and restrictions need to be defined. They are described in the next chapter. Fixed pegging is used when the link between the demand and supply element, once it has been established, should not be changed anymore by the system. A classical example is the Make-to-Order production strategy where sales orders are linked to, for example, a production order. APO offers fixed pegging for this scenario. Additionally fixed pegging can also be used for any demand-supply relation, even in a Make-to-Stock environment. This opens totally new possibilities in industries, which do not use Make-to-Order, but want to link sales orders to specific production orders. Note that in such a situation the cost settlement in R/3 is still against stock and not against the sales order, as it is the case with Make-to-Order. Fixed pegging relations cannot be changed by the system during the PP/DS Scheduling. Fixed pegging is discussed further down in the book.

Is there any link between Production (Requirements) Strategies and Pegging Procedures in APO? Technically there is no need to use a certain pegging procedure with certain production strategies. What makes sense depends on the business. The planner can fix at any time an order that was pegged dynamically. Fixed pegging takes away the flexibility most companies want, and is therefore used only in cases where it is required. On the other hand, there are business scenarios that will greatly benefit from the fixed pegging possibilities, as they are not linked to a certain production strategy.

Can we peg against a forecast? A forecast, or independent requirement, in SNP and PP/DS is just another demand element and is pegged against a supply element just like, for example, a sales order. The dynamic pegging ensures that any change in the forecast, once it has been released from DP, leads to an update of the planning situation.

### 5.3.4.3 Dynamic Pegging

Demand and supply elements have individual due dates, and thus there is a potential time span between the input node requirement date and the output node supply date. In the product master demand tab, it is possible to define the maximum time that is allowed between those nodes when carrying out dynamic pegging. The following settings can be made:

- Maximum Duration Backward Pegging
  The time entered here defines the maximum time allowed between a demand and the corresponding supply element that covers the demand. It defines the maximum time the demand may be ahead of the supply element. Should a supply element be linked with a demand element within this time span, no alert will be generated although the supply lies after the demand.
- Maximum Duration Backward Pegging without Alert
  The time defined here works together with the above setting. It defines the maximum time the demand may be ahead of the supply without generating an alert. The time specified here should be less than the time specified above.
- Maximum Duration Forward Pegging

Defines the maximum time the supply element is allowed to be ahead of the demand. This ensures that supply elements that are far ahead of the demand are not used. By doing so the system ensures that demand and supply elements are close together.

The settings above do not have to be carried out per product individually. The demand profile carries the same settings and can be linked to the product. The lower the pegging duration values are set, the more difficult it will be for the system to match demand and supply elements during the pegging procedure. The following graphic gives an example for a typical setup of the Pegging parameters.

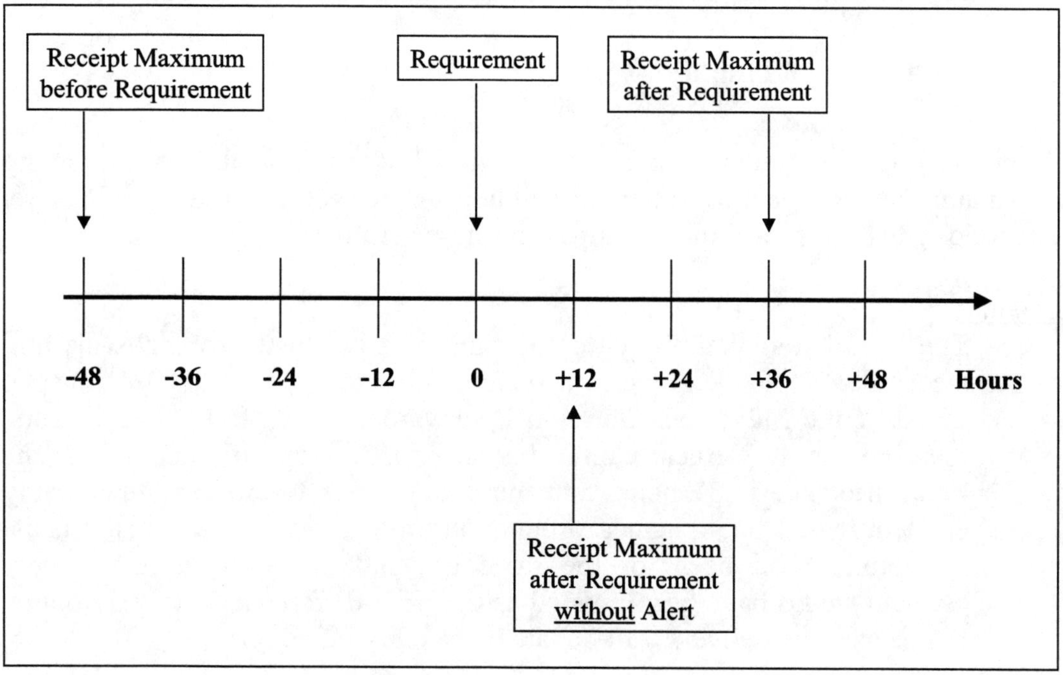


**Graphic 66 – Pegging Parameters**

Below are some examples based on the time line example in the graphic above.

| Receipt relative to Requirement (hours) | Dynamic Pegging Action | Example Number |
|---|---|---|
| +37 | No Pegging to Receipt Element | 1 |
| +35 | Carry out Pegging, generate alert | 2 |
| +8 | Carry out Pegging, no alert | |
| -46 | Carry out Pegging | 3 |
| -60 | No Pegging to Receipt Element | |

**Table 82 – Pegging Examples**

Specifically the Maximum Duration Backward Pegging and the corresponding Maximum Duration Backward Pegging without Alert need to be set up with care. The following examples show the impact of these settings.

Example 1

The expected availability date and time of a production order is the 06th December at 06.00. There is a requirement for the 04th of December at 17.00. If the Maximum Duration Backward Pegging is set to 36 hours, then the supply element cannot be used for this specific demand as the time difference is 37 hours and the system tries to create a new supply element (e.g. a new planned production order). On the other hand, if the requirement had been for the same day but at 19.00 no new supply element would have been created as the time difference is now 35 hours. In this case the delivery will be late by roughly one day.

Example 2

If we set the Maximum Duration Backward Pegging without Alert in the above example's scenario 2 to 12 hours and leave the Maximum Duration Backward Pegging at 36 hours, the system will again link the demand and supply elements. Additionally, an alert will be created to notify the planner about this situation.

The Maximum Duration Forward Pegging parameter is less of a problem. Its intention is to ensure that demands that are far in the future do not use up current supply elements, by doing so bringing more stability into the planning situation of a product.

<u>Example 3</u>

> There is a demand for the 10th of December at 15.00. The dynamic pegging procedure finds a supply element on the 8th of December at 17.00. The time difference is 46 hours and if the Maximum Duration Forward Pegging is set to 48 hours it will use this supply element. This as such is not a bad idea, but the problem starts if we receive another order for let's say the 9th of December at 16.00. No supply element is left,and the system would have to create a new supply element for the new demand, which might require a lot of "reshuffling". If we had not committed our supply element already we could easily use it for the new demand. It is also usually easier to create new supply elements that are further in the future.

The settings of the maximum pegging times are definitely business specific. A trade off has to be made between just in time delivery capability and thus customer satisfaction, and ease of planning.

Pegging ensures that the requested quantity from the demand element is exactly the same as or less than the provided quantity from the supply element. Specifically in a Make-to-Order environment it is not always feasible to deliver exactly the required quantity. In this case the two percentage settings "Under-delivery" and "Over-delivery" can be used to allow a close but not exact match between demand and supply elements. Another problem arises after the execution of a planning element (e.g. the planned production order) has been carried out. A production order output might not be exactly the planned quantity, but a fraction more or less. Strictly seen, any under-supply must result in the creation of a new planning object caring for the outstanding quantity. In the case of a production order over-supply, the excess quantity should be put in storage. Obviously this is not a practical solution and APO uses the over and under supply tolerances. Tolerances define the permitted over under-delivery percentages during the dynamic pegging process. Delivery in this context refers to the delivery of the supply element to the demand element. The demand element could also be for

example another planned production order, a purchase order, or a forecast requirement. The tolerances are defined in the product master demand tab. Values can also be taken over from the sales order. In this case the default product values defined in the product master are ignored.
The tolerance for under-supply defines the percentage by which the supply element quantity may be short in comparison the quantity requested by the demand element. The tolerance for over-supply is used to calculate the quantity by which the supply element may exceed the quantity requested by the demand element. In both cases the requested quantity represents the value 100%.
Two additional flags can be set that force dynamic pegging to use the entire supply element's quantity, or nothing. A second flag can be used to force dynamic pegging to take the entire stock if any is existing.

#### 5.3.4.4 Fixed Pegging

Fixed pegging uses the same logic as dynamic pegging. The only difference is that pegging relations, once they are fixed are not, or only under certain conditions, changed by the system. A fixed pegging relation makes it more difficult for the system to reschedule orders as orders with fixed pegging relations can only be moved together. Should any order of a fixed pegging relation cause availability violations, all orders in this pegging relation need to be moved together. Depending on the planning strategy defined in the planning strategy profile, it is possible to move an individual operation or the entire order nevertheless and create an alert regarding the other order in a fixed pegging relation that causes the violation. In such a case, the fixed pegging relation will not be broken! Fixed pegging relations cannot be changed by the system during the PP/DS Scheduling.



#### 5.3.4.5 Supply Chain Pegging

One of the important aspects of the APO pegging network is that it is not limited to a single production plant only. Pegging relationships change virtually permanently whenever there is a change of any demand or supply element with regards to availability time or quantities. As the pegging is carried out throughout the entire supply chain as defined in the supply chain model, any change of any element is planned immediately through the whole supply chain.

Let me give an example.

Data Environment

Our product is manufactured in house and requires a component from a supplier that is delivered just in time every day. Production takes exactly 8 hours, and the component is required at the start of the production process. The transport from the supplier to our manufacturing site takes 6 hours and is planned in our supply chain model via planned orders for transportation. We have defined dynamic pegging for this product with the pegging parameters as above.

Demand Situation

We have a sales order for such a product for the 10th of December at 14.00 and as no stock is available, the planned production order due at 12.00 will be used to satisfy the demand.

Supply Situation

We are now faced with the situation where the supplier has a machine breakdown and can only deliver with a delay of 13 hours. As soon as this information is made known to APO, the rescheduling of the purchase order causes the transportation order, the production order and the sales order to be re-planned. The re-planning is done using the pegging network. When APO reschedules the sales order for our product, it creates an alert. This is based on the fact that the receipt out of the production order is now 13 hours after the demand element's required date. The planner can now react and try to find alternate product sources, production modes and so on. It is also possible to change the transportation mode to a faster one, so that the receipt of the component can be done earlier.



Scenarios like this are the daily business of planners and the full supply chain pegging provides valuable help to detect these problems as fast as possible. Any change the planner makes to any element in the pegging network has an immediate impact on all other linked elements. Using the Collaborative Planning approach (see the Introduction section), the supplier could be the one that captures the information regarding the supply delay and the customer would immediately see an alert.

## 5.3.5 Characteristics Dependent Planning

### 5.3.5.1 Overview

Characteristics Dependent Planning is a planning methodology used to reduce the amount of master data kept on the system. It also allows a flexible adoption of new product requirements, as in order to sell and produce a new product variant, it is sufficient to create a new characteristic for an already existing product master. It also supports Block Planning and Campaign Planning activities (see below).

In Demand Planning we already used characteristics to describe the planning entity for which a forecast is created. The lowest planning level we used in Demand Planning for the dimension Product was the product number as such. We could have also broken this further down according to other characteristics. An example based on requirements in the textile industry would be the planning of shirts, which is on product number level, down to the level of sizes and colors. A product number exists for the generic item "Shirt." In demand planning we would then break this further down into shirts per size and color using additional characteristics and characteristic value combinations. Forecasting could then be done on the product level (the shirt) with consequent distribution of the requirements to the lower levels size and color. Alternatively, the forecasting is carried out on the lowest level (shirts per color and size) with consequent automatic aggregation of requirements to the product level (the shirt).

Supply Network Planning is presently (that is release 2.0) not supporting Characteristic Dependent Planning. Subsequently, any requirements that are existing in demand planning on a lower level that the product can not be transferred to SNP. The mid-term planning in SNP can only be based on products and does not consider characteristics.

Orders created in Production Planning & Detailed Scheduling use the characteristics definitions as required. Whenever a planned order is created, PP/DS checks for the appropriate PPM (or path within a PPM) based on the specified characteristics of the product. It also selects resources according to characteristics. Note that the classification and use of characteristics for products and resources are two different subjects and do not necessarily have to be used together. Orders in PP/DS are created when one of the following events occurs:

1. Requirement (sales order) from an OLTP system is transmitted.
2. Internally within PP/DS to satisfy a dependent demand.
3. Manual creation of orders.
4. Converting SNP planned orders.

While orders created under option 1 to 3 take characteristics into account, option 4 cannot, as the SNP order does not contain the required information (as of release 2.0).

Characteristics are propagated in the PPM from the output product to the various components. The characteristic values can be propagated directly, that means the value is copied to the component. Another option is the definition of macros, which interpret the characteristic values and set the new characteristics value for the component. The creation of macros is using program code that is basically the same as ABAP code.

### 5.3.5.2 Master Data

In order to attach a characteristic to a master data object, it must be allocated to a class. Within a class, various characteristics with their permitted values or value ranges can be defined (see also the chapter "Characteristics and Classes"). Following master data objects can be classified:

- Product
- Resource

Note that in order to support a multi-level propagation of characteristics, it is required that the requirement and receipt elements (products and components in the PPM) are assigned to the same class.

## Product Master

The characteristic values defined in the product master are used when reading the PPM during the planned order creation. Depending on the required characteristic values, the following components within the PPM are controlled (selected):

- Selection of PPM
- Selection of Input Products (Components)
- Definition of Output Products
- Selection of Operation
- Selection of Activities

Besides the selection of these entities, the characteristics can also be used to influence certain parameters of the PPM. The change of the parameter values can be carried out by means of:

- Replacing the basic value
- Adding values to the basic value
- Multiplying the basic value

The parameters that allow a value change depending on the characteristics are:

- Operation Sequence
- Activity Duration
- Activity Capacity Requirements
- Activity Component Requirements
- Activity Scrap Value
- Activity Mode Selection
- Setup Group and Key

## Resource Master

Resources can also be classified and given characteristics. The resource classification is used for the "Block Planning" functionality only (see below). Resource classification is not an integral part of Characteristics Dependent Planning.

### 5.3.5.3 Characteristics Propagation Screen

In order to enable Characteristics Dependent Planning, it is required to define various parameters in the PPM. As Characteristics Dependent Planning is a function of PP/DS, select a PPM of type "P." On the initial screen activate the option "Goto - Characteristics Propagation" to get to the characteristics propagation main screen. This screen is subdivided into three sections:

- Classifiable Component
  This section on the left-hand side of the screen displays all components of the PPM that can be classified. This section has 6 tabs with the initially displayed tab giving an overview of all components. Switching over to the other tabs allows seeing selectively only components of a certain type. To view default and detail values of a specific component, double-click on the appropriate line or press the "Propagation" button. In this screen section, only the field "Classification" is open for input.
- Component Defaults
  This section on the top right-hand side of the screen displays default values for the component that was selected on the left side of the screen. Depending on the selected component type, the functions "Standard Evaluation", "Rules", and "Standard Request" are enabled. Note that the word Standard means Default. The expression "standard evaluation" is misleading as this button deals with the "default values".
- Component Details
  This section on the bottom right-hand side of the screen displays details for the component that was selected on the left side of the screen. This section has 3 tabs displaying the "Evaluations", "Requirements", and "Parameters" of the selected component. The expression "evaluation" is misleading as this tab deals with the "values" of characteristics. Only some fields on these tabs are open for change. Which fields are open for change, depends on the selected component type. The Parameters tab remains blank if selected for a component where no class is defined.

## 5.3.6 Block Planning

Block Planning is a method to predefine resource capacity windows, which products with certain characteristics can utilize. This enables a more efficient usage of the resource, as it supports lower downtimes due to setup-related activities. A planning block is basically another constraint on the resource, as the operation cannot be scheduled freely at the next available slot but only at predefined time windows (planning block) of the resource. Block Planning is therefore a resource orientated planning method. In opposition to this, Campaign Planning is orientated towards a logical sequence of production orders. An order might have an operation within a planning block and others that are planned without the block planning functionality. Usually operations are allocated to a certain block according to characteristic values inherited from the product to be manufactured. Alternatively it is also possible using block planning without characteristics-dependent planning. The allocation of a section within a block depends then solely on the output product of the operation.

A block is characterized by rules that, in turn, are a collection of so-called requests. A request is the definition of allowed values for the characteristics of the class that is linked to the resource. The rule is therefore a collection of permitted characteristic values. The rule is then linked to a certain time period (the interval). During this time interval (the actual planning block) only operations that have a requirement as defined in the rule can be scheduled. Planning blocks can be manually added to the time axis, but no gaps are permitted. It is often required to repeat the same sequence of different blocks several times. This is facilitated by the definition of reference cycles. A reference cycle is a logical sequence of different rule definitions where each rule has a certain sequence number and time length. Sequences can easily be used to make up new planning blocks. A rule in APO can be used for one or multiple resources, thus facilitating easier data maintenance. Any change of a rule therefore potentially effects various resources. The following graphic gives an example of a planning block definition.

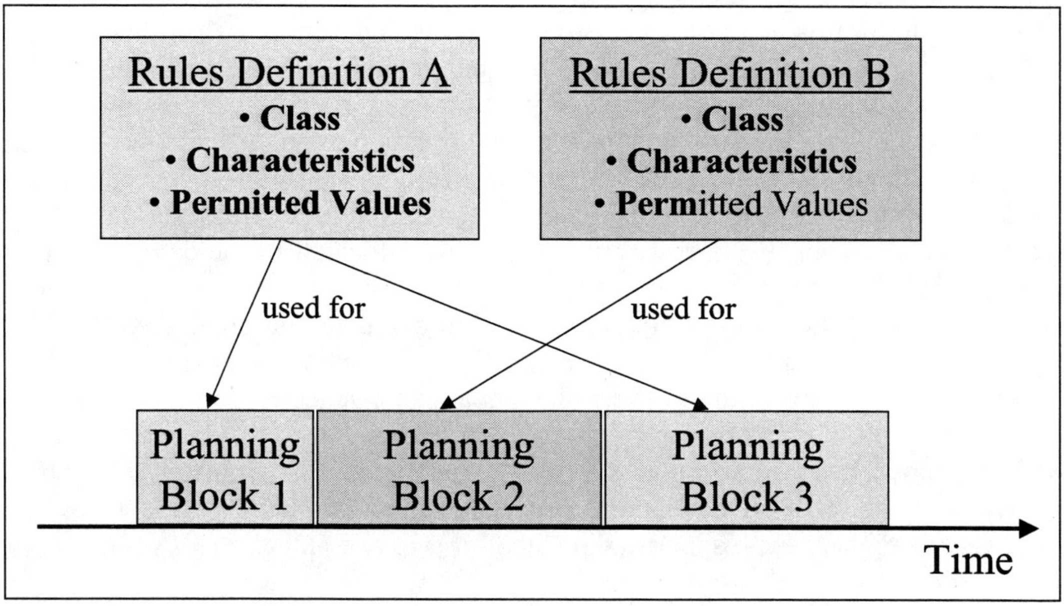


**Graphic 67 – Planning Block**

The maintenance of planning blocks is carried out in the transaction for resource master data maintenance. Rules, requests, and reference cycles are planning version independent, the actual planning blocks are planning version dependent. Once a planning block has been defined, it can be made visible in the PP/DS Planning Board by activating the option "Extras – Blocks – Display".

PP/DS

## 5.3.7 Campaign Planning

Production campaigns are used to combine several orders for one or multiple products into one planning unit, the campaign. This supports industries where a product cannot be processed

- just in one step, and/or

- without other products.

An example for this is a chemical process in which several finished products are produced in one process, but where the quantity relations between the several finished products is not fixed (no fixed joint production). Another example would be a production process that runs over several production orders and where certain time restrictions between these orders exist (orders must all be executed in a certain row, or even in a network type). The main benefit of using a production campaign is that, once the respective orders are allocated to the campaign, they are scheduled together with the campaign and no individual order or operation scheduling needs to be carried out anymore. Dragging and dropping any operation of the production campaign is all that needs to be done to carry out scheduling. All related operations in the production campaign are scheduled accordingly.

APO supports these requirements with the Campaign Planning function that is activated from the PP/DS Planning Board. Campaign Planning is a three-step process where there is no specific sequence for step one and two.

1. Create Production Orders
2. Create Campaign
3. Schedule Campaign

From a system point of view, production campaigns can be seen as a special order external relationship in addition to the standard pegging relations.



### 5.3.8 Push Production

Production is driven in most cases by the demand of a finished product. In this situation, planned production orders or purchase requisitions are typically created based on a sales order in a Make-to-Order environment or based on a forecast to replenish stocks in a Make-to-Stock environment. The finished product pulls the components as dependent requirements are created.

In a product-based push production a certain component is chosen to determine the production plan whereby the system checks which finished products could be manufactured with the component (according to the PPM) and which resources are required. Based on the available quantities of the component, other required components and the resource availability, the system suggests a production plan. Product-based push production is deployed if a certain component needs to be put into the production process. Another option is the resource based push production where the system tries to find finished products that could be manufactured on a resource that would otherwise be idle. APO supports product-based push production, but not resource-based push production.

In APO the alert monitor can be used to notify the planner about the necessity to invoke a push production planning run. This alert could be based for example on the current stockholding. The system selects finished products via the PPM's in which this component is used and creates a production plan proposal. This proposal needs to be confirmed by the planner before further processing is carried out. Push production functionality can be accessed from the PP/DS transaction "Product View."

Who needs push production? Product-based push production can be used in business environment where a certain component should be used up due to an overstock situation. The main user group for product based push production can be found in such industries where the supply of components (raw materials) cannot easily be planned for. The best example is the fishing industry. Only after each fishing trip, the exact quantity and combination of fish species can be determined. Also, time is at a premium as the fish cannot be stored easily. Deep freezing it usually goes hand in hand with a loss in value as a deep frozen product possibly loses in value. In general, any business with short shelf life expiration date products faces this problem.

Push production is a short term planning tool and is thus a feature in PP/DS only. Even if product-based push production is deployed in PP/DS, the long term forecast as well as the mid-term supply network plan are based on the finished product. A shortcoming with the current push production function is that only suggests all possible products that can be produced using the excess stock receipt element. It does not consider any cost or penalty settings that could reveal the cost optimum solution.

## 5.3.9 Convert SNP into PP/DS Orders

Planned orders for production, transportation, and purchase requisitions generated by SNP Heuristics, the SNP Optimizer, or CTM need to be converted into PP/DS planned orders before they can be used within PP/DS. The same applies to all otherwise-created SNP orders. During this process, orders are allocated a planned order number that allows an easy synchronization with the OLTP system. SNP planned orders are converted if any of their operations fall within the production horizon of the product. The production horizon is defined as a global APO parameter. It can also be defined additionally in the product master. In this case the product master value overrules the global APO setting. During the conversion of SNP-planned orders for production a PPM re-explosion takes place. PP/DS uses a more detailed PPM than SNP. The SNP Interactive Planning screen shows SNP planned orders for production under the SNP key figure "Planned Production." Directly after the conversion, these quantities can be seen under the SNP key figure "Firmed Production." PP/DS controlled planned orders can only be displayed within SNP but not changed.

The conversion of SNP to PP/DS orders can be carried out either in batch mode for all SNP orders as specified on the entry screen of the conversion transaction or individually per order in the "Product View" and "Process Requirements" transactions. Following parameters can be specified during the batch conversion:

- Receipt from In-house Production
  Select this option in order to convert SNP-planned production orders to PP/DS planned production orders.
- Receipt from Stock Transfer
  Select this option in order to convert SNP purchase requisitions for stock transfers to PP/DS purchase requisitions for stock transfers.
- Receipt from External Procurement
  Select this option in order to convert SNP purchase requisitions for external procurement to PP/DS purchase requisitions for external procurement.
- Firm Newly Created Orders
  Set this flag if the newly created orders should be firmed at the same time. Note that the expressions "fixing" and "firming" of orders are synonyms for the same activity.

- Product
  Specify a single product or a product range for conversion.
- Location
  The conversion can be carried out for single or multiple locations.
- Source Planning Version
  This is the planning version in which the SNP planned orders will be read.
- Target Planning Version
  Define the target planning version into which the PP/DS orders must be written. Source and target planning version can be (and are usually) identical.
- Delete Receipt Elements
  Once the PP/DS planned orders are created, the SNP planned orders should be deleted to avoid duplication of receipt elements. This is only true if the source and target planning versions are identical.
- Conversion Horizon
  This time offset allows increasing or decreasing the production horizon that the system reads from the global parameters or in the product master according to the value defined here. Enter the number of days in positive (negative) numbers to increase (decrease) the production horizon.

Finally select <Execute> to start the conversion. The conversion can also be scheduled as a mass process to run in the background. For the individual order based conversion, the following needs to be specified:

- Target Planning Version
  Define the target-planning version into which the PP/DS order must be written. This is most probably the planning version you are working in and is suggested as the default value.
- Delete Receipt Elements
  Once the PP/DS planned order is created, the SNP planned orders should be deleted to avoid duplication of receipt elements.
- Fix PP/DS Order
  Set this flag if the newly created orders should be fixed at the same time. Note that the expressions "fixing" and "firming" of orders are synonyms for the same activity.

## 5.3.10 Planning with SNP and PP/DS

SNP creates a mid-term plan based on simplified PPM's and bucket resources. In PP/DS, the short-term plan is based on more detailed PPM's and time continuous single or multi activity resources. The PP/DS planning horizon, called the production horizon marks the beginning of the mid-term SNP planning horizon. Any SNP order that enters the production horizon with at least one activity is not planned by SNP anymore. It needs to be converted to a PP/DS order and can be subsequently planned using PP/DS functionality. The conversion of SNP orders to PP/DS orders has to be carried out manually or via a batch job. It does not happen automatically! During this conversion, the order is re-exploded using the PP/DS PPM. At this time the bucket resource capacity load will be deleted, and the PP/DS time continuous resource will be loaded with the capacity requirements. The SNP order remains in the production horizon up to the moment where the conversion has been carried out and the SNP order is deleted.

SNP cannot create or change any orders (not even SNP orders) in the production horizon, although it displays the PP/DS orders in the production horizon on an aggregated basis per day. PP/DS orders are displayed as "firmed" production, SNP orders as "planned" production. Automated PP/DS processes, on the other hand, do not create or update any orders outside the production horizon. The planner can manually create orders inside and outside the production horizon. The PP/DS orders outside the production horizon are considered during the SNP planning runs, but cannot be changed or deleted. The total of SNP and PP/DS orders is displayed on an aggregated basis outside the production horizon. Should the SNP planning run detect a product shortage within the production horizon, it will create an SNP order directly after the end of the production horizon, which is the start of the SNP planning horizon. This is the same principle as with the R/3 MPS run.



For products that are planned automatically (see planning mode setting in the PP/DS product master tab), any new requirement that arises within the production horizon leads to an immediate planning activity in PP/DS (Incremental Finite Scheduling). If products are planned manually, the sequence of events is of importance. Let me give an example. A new sales order, for which no stock or other supply element exists, is created within the production horizon. As the product is not planned automatically, the demand remains unmatched, which means no supply element is pegged against it.

- Option 1:
  If the PP/DS planner now carries out a manual planning run for this product, the system will create a new supply element and pegging ensures that the two elements are linked. No further planning actions are required.
- Option 2:
  Before any PP/DS planning is carried out, an SNP planning run is started. SNP will detect the shortage caused by the sales order and create an SNP planned order. As the requirement is within the production horizon, the SNP planned order will be put not on the requirement date, but directly after the production horizon, which marks the beginning of the SNP planning period. The planned order will also be using the SNP PPM. Subsequently, this SNP planned order needs to be converted into a PP/DS order. But it will only be suggested for conversion the next working day as the newly created SNP order now falls within the production horizon. With the explosion of the PP/DS PPM, which is carried out during this conversion, the order will be scheduled according to the requirement date of the sales order and pegged to it. Certainly a more complex process than that of option 1.

The graphic below shows the sequence of events for both options.

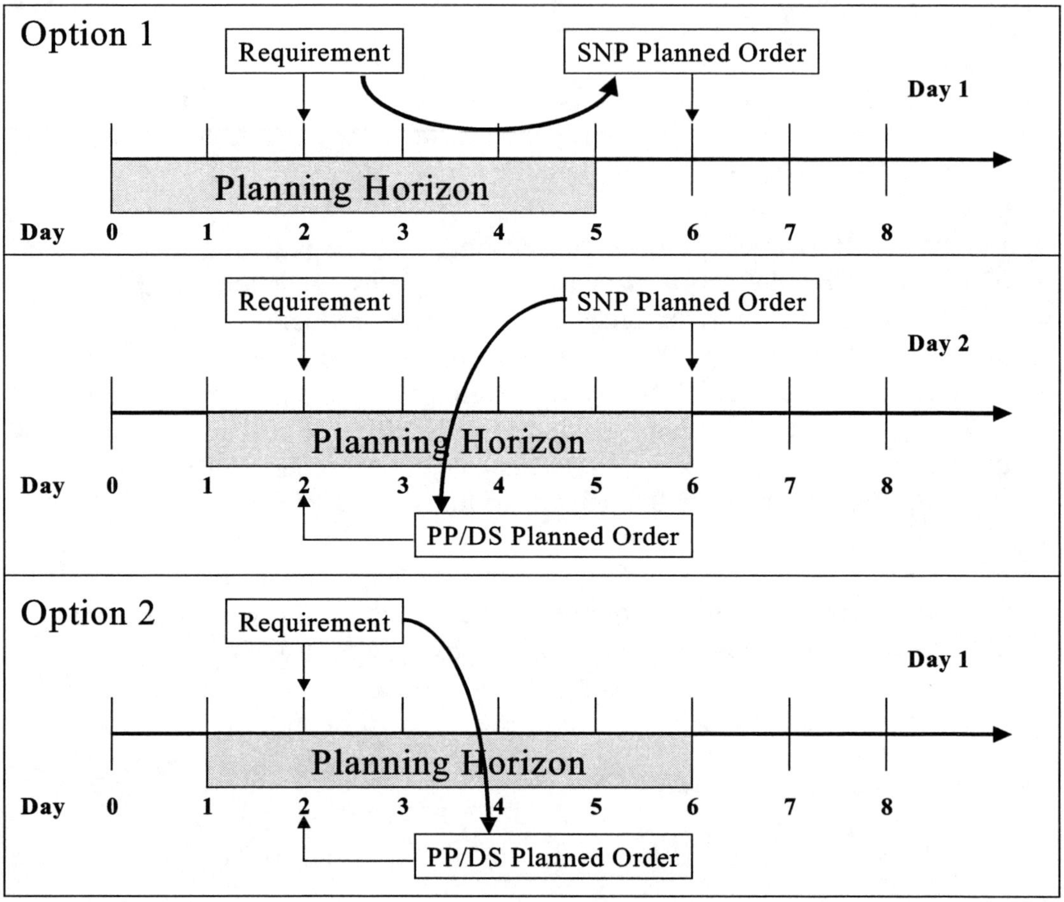


**Graphic 68 – Automatic Planning**

# 5.4 The PP/DS Data Environment

PP/DS shares most master data objects with SNP. In the case of location and product master, the same information is used for both modules. Resources and PPM's need to specifically set up for usage within PP/DS. For information regarding the product and location master, please refer to the SNP section. All profiles that can be maintained in the IMG are for the Planning Board. Besides these profiles, some other settings need to be carried out. The "Global Parameters and Defaults" define PP/DS specific settings and enable the co-existence of SNP and PP/DS.

## 5.4.1 Profiles and Definitions

Profiles and other profile-like definitions drive how the work is carried out within PP/DS. They are mostly used as a general source of information and are not linked to any master data object. They serve the same purpose just as any other customized entry. Understanding the profiles means understanding the functionality of PP/DS.

| Profile / Definition | Usage | IMG Chapter |
|---|---|---|
| Overall Profile | Master Profile linking other PP/DS sub-profiles used in the Planning Board | Supply Chain Planning – Production Planning and Detailed Scheduling – Profiles |
| Strategy Profile | Definition of Strategies used when Scheduling in the Planning Board | Supply Chain Planning – Production Planning and Detailed Scheduling – Profiles |
| Work Area | Defines Resources, Products and Orders to be used. | Supply Chain Planning – Production Planning and Detailed Scheduling – Profiles |

| Profile / Definition | Usage | IMG Chapter |
|---|---|---|
| Propagation Range | Defines the Resources and Products that may be automatically re-planned | Supply Chain Planning – Production Planning and Detailed Scheduling – Profiles |
| Time Profile | Defines the Evaluation and Planing Period | Supply Chain Planning – Production Planning and Detailed Scheduling – Profiles |
| Planning Board Profile | Defines the graphical layout of the Planning Board | Supply Chain Planning – Production Planning and Detailed Scheduling – Profiles |
| Optimization Profile | Defines the Parameters for the Optimization Run | Supply Chain Planning – Production Planning and Detailed Scheduling – Profiles |
| Global Parameters and Defaults | Basic PP/DS settings | Supply Chain Planning |
| Factory Calendar | Definition of Working Days and Times | Master Data – Calendar |
| Rounding Profile | Multiple Step Rounding Calculation that supports several Rounding Values | Master Data – Product |
| Setup Matrix | Minimize Transition Time and Cost when sequencing Planned Production Orders | Master Data - Resource |

**Table 83 – PP/DS Profiles**

Above is an overview of PP/DS related profiles and definitions. The following chapters deal with all available PP/DS profiles.

### 5.4.1.1 Overall Profile

One of the key profiles in PP/DS is the Overall Profile. It defines all aspects of the highly customizable PP/DS Planning Board. Various other sub-profiles are linked to the Overall Profile. This is similar to the Forecast Profile in Demand Planning. The key of the Overall Profile consists of the Profile Name and a Customizing ID. The Customizing ID should be the user's logon ID. When copying profiles, the system uses this method automatically.

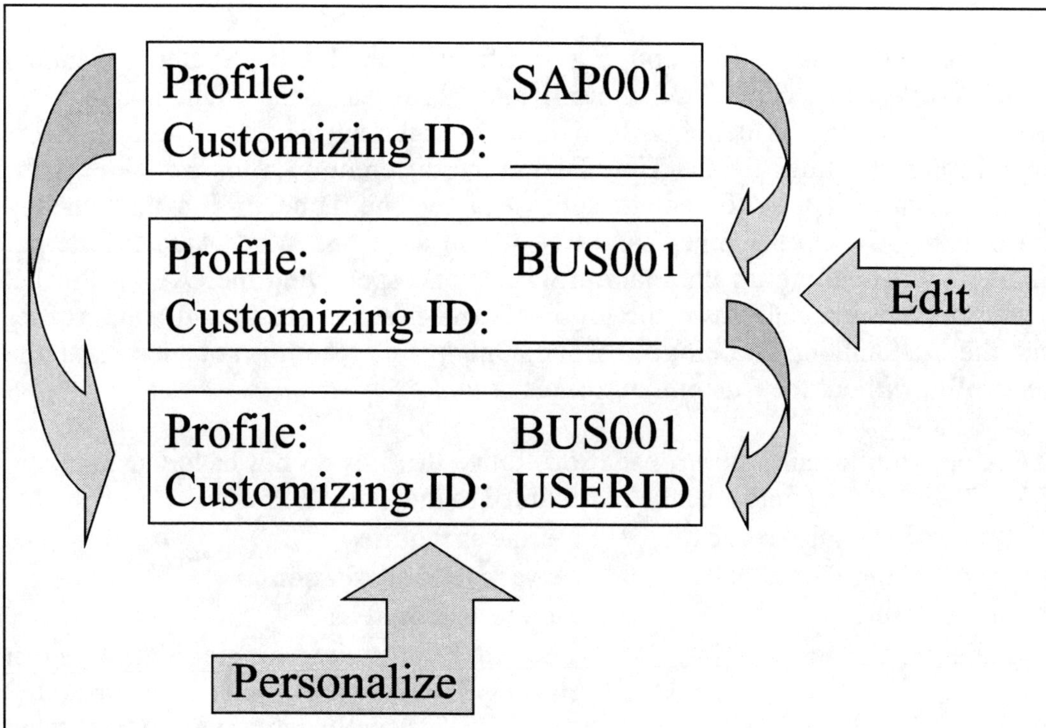


**Graphic 69 – Copying of Profiles**

The standard profiles delivered with the system cannot be edited, as they are mandatory with their specific name and setup for some transactions. In order to define profiles, they can be copied and modified from there. The usage of Customizing ID's allows maintaining user specific variants of a set of profiles. Every time an Overall Profile is copied, the possibilities as depicted in the graphic above exist. Option 1 (the left arrow) assumes that the standard delivered profile (e.g. the overall profile) should be used without changes for the business. Option 2 (the right arrow) shows the path to follow if the profile should first be changed according to business needs (no customizing ID) and then be personalized. It is good practice to copy the SAP delivered profile, even if it fits the business without change, and use a new version.

The same method as used for copying profiles is applied to the Strategy, Planning Table, Work Area, Time, and Optimization Profiles. This might sound a bit difficult, but it has its benefits. In a live environment usually several planners have the same settings for the Time Period but different ones for the Work Area. In such a case, it is sufficient to setup exactly one Time Profile without any Customizing ID. On the other hand, we would have one Work Area Profile per planner. When calling up the Planning Table and specifying the Overall Profile, the system automatically uses the logon ID and first tries to find all sub-profiles with the Customizing ID being specified. Only if this search is not successful, the sub-profile without the Customizing ID is used.

The Alert Monitor and the Propagation Range Profiles do not have Customizing ID's. The following fields can be maintained in the Overall Profile:

| | |
|---|---|
| • Name of Overall Profile | Define as required |
| • Customizing ID | See above for definition |
| • Short Description | Define as required |
| • Planning Version | The SNP planning version used when starting the Planning Table. Note that SNP and PP/DS usually work within the same planning version. |
| • Flag Skip Work Area | Disables so that the planner can change the work area as defined in the Work Area profile. |
| • Name of Strategy Profile | Link a Strategy Profile to the Overall Profile |

| | |
|---|---|
| • Name of Planning Table Profile | Link a Planning Table Profile to the Overall Profile |
| • Name of Work Area | Link a Work Area to the Overall Profile |
| • Name of Time Profile | Link a Time Profile to the Overall Profile |
| • Name of Optimizer Profile | Link an Optimizer Profile to the Overall Profile |
| • Name of Alert Monitor Profile | Link an Alert Monitor Profile to the Overall Profile |
| • Name of Propagation Range | Link a Propagation Range to the Overall Profile |

As one can see above, the Overall Profile is mainly a container for links to the other sub-profiles. It is possible to jump from the Overall Profile to any of the sub-profiles, or to access the sub-profiles individually from the Current Settings menu or the IMG.

#### 5.4.1.1.1 Strategy Profile

The strategy profile name consists of the profile name as such and a "customizing ID" (see above chapters). From the entry screen that provides an overview of all existing strategy profiles it is possible to drill down to a specific profile. For more information also see the chapter "Planning Strategies." It is used as the calculation rule when rescheduling tasks are performed in the "Interactive Planning Product View" screen and the "PP/DS Planning Board." From these transactions the strategy profile can be called up and changed if required or, alternatively, another strategy can be selected. The same or different strategy profiles can be used for the two transactions. It is also possible to schedule orders and operations according to different strategy profiles (e.g. depending on the product). The strategy profile contains five blocks with the fields as shown.

- Planning Direction
  The planning direction setting determines in which direction the scheduling is carried out. The planning period for scheduling in the PP/DS Planning Board is defined in the Time Profile. The end of the planning horizon is the end of

the planning period (PP/DS Planning Board) or the date 31.12.2099 (Interactive Planning Product View).

- Forwards + Reverse
  Instructs the system to start searching at the desired start date of the planned order. The earliest start date is the current date and time or the beginning of the planning period (whatever date and time is higher) into the future and then, if the search was not successful, into the past. Using the Offset Time, the start date of the search can be shifted forwards or backwards. This strategy is used primarily for the PP/DS Planning Board with a fixed planning period.
- Forwards
  This is the same as above but without reversing into the past if the forward search was not successful.
- Backwards + Reverse
  Instructs the system to start searching at the desired end date of the planned order. The earliest start date is the current date and time or the beginning of the planning period (whatever date and time is higher) into the past and then, if the search was not successful, into the future. Using the Offset Time, the start date of the search can be shifted forwards or backwards.
- Backwards
  This is the same as above but without reversing into the future if the backward search was not successful.

- Planning Mode
  The planning modes are dealt with in detail in the chapter "Planning Strategies".
  - Schedule Operation Infinitely
    Set this option together with the backward or forward direction if you want the system to schedule operations infinitely. This means the operation will be put exactly where required irrespective of a possible resource overload.
  - Find Slot
    The find slot strategy tries to find a slot not used by other operations. If found it will place the operation in this empty spot. This works with all planning directions.
  - Add Operation At End

This strategy is based on the "airline" principle and puts the operation after the last existing scheduled operation (forward scheduling only).

- Insert Operation
  With this strategy and backward (forward) scheduling, operations are put at the time where required or a bit earlier (later) if another operation is currently scheduled at this time.
- Squeeze In Operation
  Operations are put at exactly the time where required. Other operations that might be on this time spot are shifted forward and backward.

- Planning Parameters
  - Schedule To Non-Working Times
    With this flag set, scheduling into non-working time can be carried out. The system assumes that the resource capacity is available throughout non-working times with the same rate as during working times. Strategies with this flag set can only be used in manual scheduling using the drag and drop functionality in the PP/DS Planning Board.
  - Schedule As Early As Possible
    This option, which works only when using the PP/DS Planning Board and forward scheduling, will schedule the operation at the earliest possible date.
  - Offset In Minutes
    The offset time determines for how many minutes the start date of the search is shifted forwards into the future (positive numbers) or backwards into the past (negative numbers).
  - Lowest Mode Priority
    Each mode in a PPM resource definition can have a priority attached to it. If a mode priority was maintained, it is possible to restrict the scheduler to modes up to a certain priority. If for example the modes "A", "B", and "C" are defined in the PPM and the field "Lowest Mode Priority" is set to "B," the system will only consider the definitions in mode "A" and "B." This setting does not effect the capability to manually schedule to a resource as defined in mode "C".
  - Scheduling Sequence
    When performing mass scheduling, the system needs to be instructed in which sequence the operations have to be worked through. Using the "Scheduling Sequence" button, a pop window is displayed that allows the

definition of this sequence according to various parameters such as for example the quantity or the start and end date of an operation.

- Order-Internal Relationships
  Order-internal relationships are the relations between operations of a planned order. Scheduling and rescheduling activities of operations have a possible impact on other operations in the same planned order.
  - Do Not Consider
    With this option set, operations can be (re-) scheduled without considering the impact on other operations of the same order. As a result, a sequence violation might occur.
  - Always Consider
    When order-internal relationships are considered, the system ensures that during the (re-) scheduling activities no sequence violations occur at all.
  - Only Consider In Propagation Range
    If the order-internal relationships are considered within the propagation range only, the system ensures that during the (re-) scheduling activities no sequence violations occur within the propagation range as defined in the "Propagation Range Profile". Outside the propagation range sequence violations might occur.
- Product Availability (Pegging Relations)
  Pegging relations deal with the relations between planned orders. Usually orders are pegged to other orders in what is called the pegging network. When (re-) scheduling an order, most probably other orders need to be rescheduled as well to ensure that no sequence violations occur. A sequence violation might lead for example to the unavailability of components. In order to check the pegging relations, it is required to first check the order of internal relationships. It is therefore required to enable the check of order-internal relationships (see above) before pegging relationships can be checked as well. If set up accordingly, availability violations can be monitored by the Alert Monitor and brought to the planner's attention.
  - Do Not Consider Dynamic Pegging
    Set this flag if dynamic pegging relations between orders must not be checked and therefore be ignored. The system reschedules the order as required but leaves other orders to which probably a dynamic pegging relation exists untouched. An availability violation might occur.
    - Fixed Pegging – Do Not Consider

The system reschedules orders irrespective of whether fixed pegging relations exist to others or not. No attempt is made to reschedule other orders to which fixed pegging relations exist. Availability violations are possible.

- Fixed Pegging – Consider If Possible
  Set this flag if fixed pegging relations between orders should be considered. The system reschedules the order as required and tries to reschedule other orders to which probably a fixed pegging relation exists in accordance. If this is not possible, the possible availability violation remains.
- Fixed Pegging – Always Consider
  Orders will only be rescheduled if other orders, to which a fixed pegging relationship exists, can be rescheduled accordingly. If this is not possible, no order will be rescheduled. No availability violations can be created when using this option.

- Consider Dynamic Pegging If Possible
  Set this flag if dynamic pegging relations between orders should be considered. The system reschedules the order as required and tries to reschedule other orders to which probably a dynamic pegging relation exists in accordance. If this is not possible, it will create new dynamic pegging relations. If this is not possible, the possible availability violation remains.
  - Fixed Pegging – Consider If Possible
    Set this flag if fixed pegging relations between orders should be considered. The system reschedules the order as required and tries to reschedule other orders to which probably a fixed pegging relation exists in accordance. If this is not possible, the possible availability violation remains.
  - Fixed Pegging – Always Consider
    Orders will only be rescheduled if other orders, to which a fixed pegging relationship exists, can be rescheduled accordingly. If this is not possible, no order will be rescheduled. No availability violations can be created when using this option.

### 5.4.1.1.2 Work Area

When calling up the PP/DS Planning Board, the system needs to know which elements (operations) have to be displayed and thus are available for interactive scheduling. The more objects that have to be displayed, the longer the call up of the transaction will take. For this and other reasons, it makes sense to somehow restrict the number of objects in the PP/DS Planning Board. Depending on the business requirements, it might also be required to show a certain planner only a range of resources and/or products. This is particularly the case if more than one planner is performing the scheduling task, each for a certain range of resources. A separation according to products or product ranges is also viable but often difficult if various products or product ranges use the same resources. The definition of work areas in PP/DS therefore serves two purposes.

- Reduction of data according to planner groups.
  In this group we find the restriction according to specific resources or products.
- Reduction of data by deselecting specific objects.
  Irrelevant objects such as products or components that do not need to be visible in the PP/DS Planning Board can be either specifically deselected or the relevant objects specifically selected.

These definitions must be carried out with extreme care, as otherwise some objects that need to be visible are not displayed at all. In a multi planner environment it is also important to define rules in the case where the planning activities of a certain planner impact data objects controlled by another planner. This is dealt with in the "Propagation Area" profile.



APO allows restricting the data object display by resource, product, and order. The more restrictions are applied (defined), the faster the access to the requested data is. Furthermore, it is an advantage to restrict the data shown in the PP/DS Planning Board to the required minimum to support user friendliness. It is obvious that, the more stringent the restrictions are, the more care must be taken when setting up the work areas. The graphic below shows the impact of restrictions applied to the work area. A common restriction is per resource with the exclusion of some products.

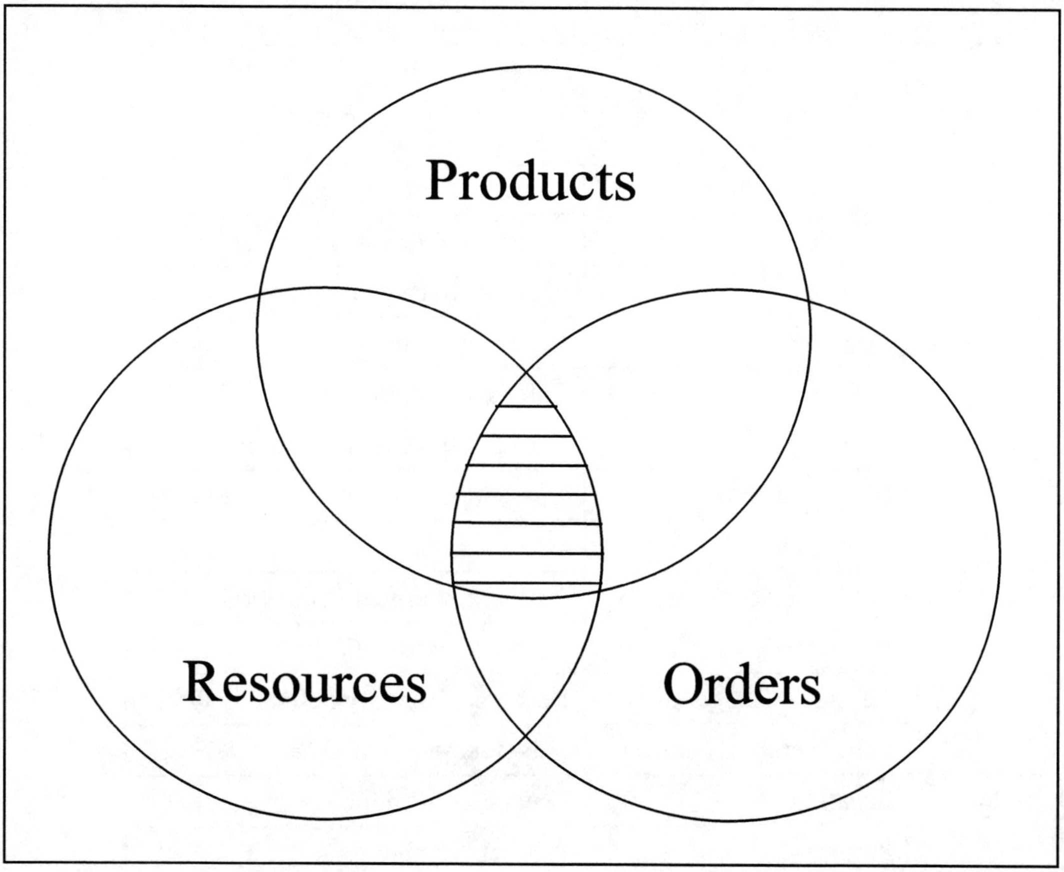


**Graphic 70 – Work Area Definition**

The restriction of data objects and the possible parameters for these restrictions is shown in the table below. Each restriction needs to be defined in the respective view and then be activated on the "Work Area Overview" screen. As with most other profiles in PP/DS, the work area profile name consists of the profile name as such and a "customizing ID."

PP/DS

| View | Available Selection Fields | Select according to |
|---|---|---|
| Resource | Bottleneck Resource | Bottleneck Flag |
| | Finite Scheduling | Finite Scheduling Flag |
| | Location | Location of Resource |
| | Planner | Planner allocated to Resource |
| | Resource | Resource Name |
| | Resource Category | Category of Resource |
| Order | Location | Location the Order is referring to |
| | Operation Number | Operation Number within the Order |
| | Order Number | Order Number |
| | Production Procedure | Procedure defined in the Order |
| | Resource | Resource used in Order |
| | Resource Category | Resource Category defined in Order |
| | Sub-Operation Number | Sub-Operation Number |
| Product | Location | Location of Product |
| | Product | Product Number |

**Table 84 – Work Area Selection Fields**

In order to maintain a specific view, select the profile name in the grid display and double-click on the view name in the tree structure. The upcoming screen shows various sets that can be maintained per view and thus per work area profile. Highlight one of the sets and select the "Set" button or create a new set. Depending on the selected view, a pop-up screen appears from which all parameters that can be used to restrict the data object selection are visible. Select the appropriate field(s) and transfer them to the left. When finishing this activity, define the restriction objects on the next pop-up screen that show all previously selected fields. All selection criteria specified within a set are linked by the logical "AND." A logical "OR" links various sets specified for a view.

If a planner has more than one possible work area to work with, and thus needs to make a decision when starting the PP/DS Planning Board, it is necessary to enable this choice by deselecting the "Skip Work Area" flag.

#### 5.4.1.1.3 Propagation Range

As we have seen above, in a multi planner environment the scheduling activity of one planner can influence data objects controlled by another planner. Let me give an example. Planner A controls the resources 1 to 10 and planner B the resources 11 to 20. Planner 1 carries out some scheduling activities and one of the operations that is scheduled affects resource 3. In the same order the next operation is carried out on resource 13, which planner 2 controls. APO offers 3 possibilities in this scenario. They are described in the strategy profile block "Order-Internal Relationships" (see above).

- Do Not Consider Order-Internal Relationships
  With this option set, operations can be (re-) scheduled without considering the impact on other operations of the same order. As a result, a sequence violation might occur.
- Always Consider Order-Internal Relationships
  When order-internal relationships are considered, the system ensures that during the (re-) scheduling activities no sequence violations occur at all. This takes place irrespective of whether the affected resource is in the propagation range or not.
- Only Consider Order-Internal Relationships In Propagation Range
  If the order-internal relationships are considered within the propagation range only, the system ensures that, during the (re-) scheduling activities, no sequence violations occur within the propagation range. Outside the propagation range sequence violations might occur.

In order for the last option to work, the propagation range must be defined in this profile. On the initial screen highlight, the propagation range is to be specified or a new one should be created. If the "From Work Area" flag is set, the propagation range is set to be the same as the work area that is used in the PP/DS Planning Board. In this case no further specifications are required. Otherwise select the two "Set" buttons to define the details.

- Resource Selection
  Click on this button to restrict the propagation range resources according to the following fields:
  - Bottleneck Resource
  - Finite Scheduling
  - Location
  - Planner
  - Resource
  - Resource Category
- Product Selection
  Click on this button to restrict the propagation range products according to the following fields:
  - Location
  - Product
  - Production Planner

Unlike most other profiles in PP/DS, the propagation area profile name consists of the profile name only; no "customizing ID" is added.

#### 5.4.1.1.4 Time Profile

The Time Profile defines the PP/DS display period as well as the planning period. The planning period defines the time span in which scheduling can be carried out. The display period defines the displayed period in the PP/DS Planning Board and must be the same as or greater than the planning period. Objects in the pre-evaluation and post-evaluation time period can be scheduled into the planning period but not the other way round. The following graphic depicts the functions of and the relation between the period settings.

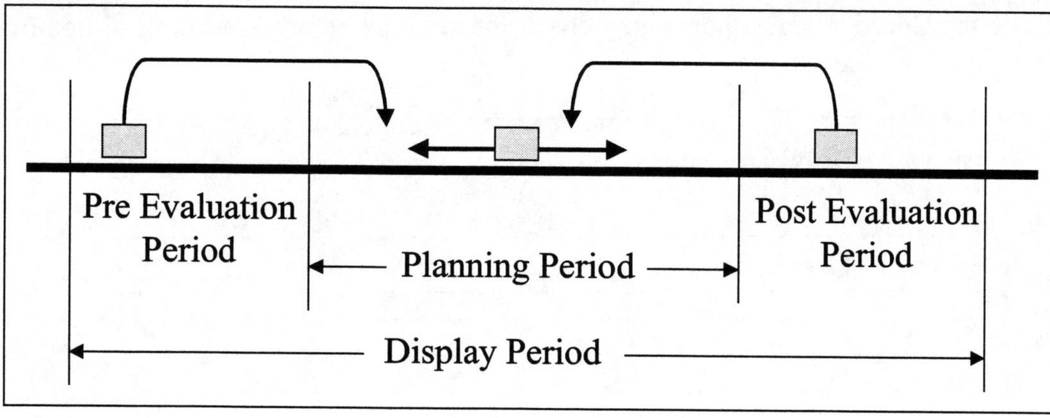


**Graphic 71 – Time Profile Periods**

Both, the evaluation as well as the planning period can be defined relative or absolute. A relative setting defines the number of periods (days, weeks, months, or years) when the period starts or ends. It is relative to the system date. This ensures that the period automatically slides with the changing date. It is also possible to define fixed start and end dates for both periods. As a third option, one can define one period with relative, the other with absolute dates. This is extremely dangerous and should not be done, as the one time frame slides and the other remains static. As with most other profiles in PP/DS, the time profile name consists of the profile name as such and a "customizing ID."

#### 5.4.1.1.5 Planning Board Profile

The Planning Board Profile is the tool to customize the appearance of the PP/DS Planning Board in terms of what is shown and how it appears. The standard APO system comes with a working profile that should satisfy most of the users' needs. If this is not the case, the planning board profile offers a multitude of possibilities to change the appearance of the PP/DS Planning Board. Nearly every display aspect can be changed. The only thing not possible (yet?) is to generate sounds based on predefined conditions. If a certain element cannot be seen on the PP/DS

Planning Board, always thoroughly check the settings before assuming something is wrong with the system.

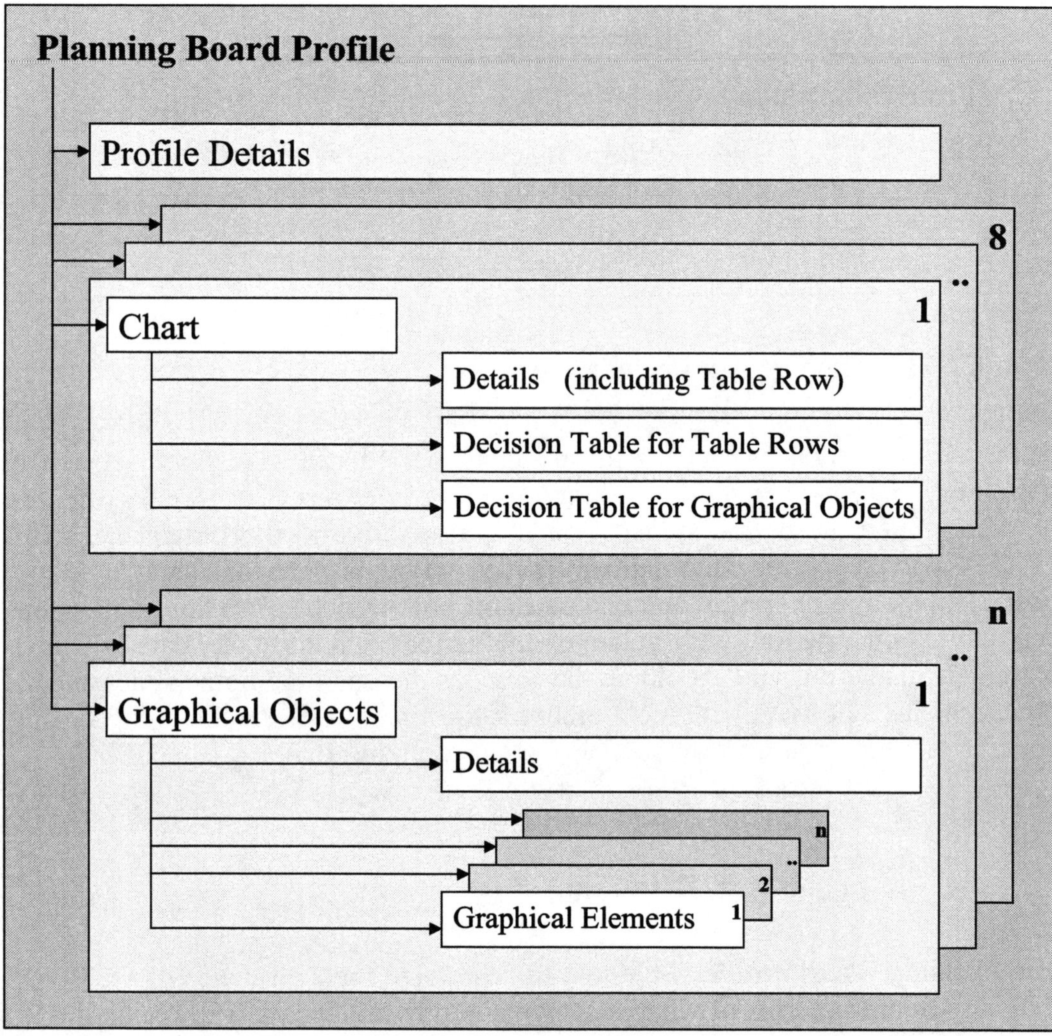


**Graphic 72 – Planning Board Profile Structure**

As with most other profiles in PP/DS, the planning board profile name consists of the profile name as such and a “customizing ID”. On the initial screen the flag “Copy Default Settings” can be activated per profile. If this flag is set the system uses the SAP default settings instead of the user defined parameters. The user-defined parameters remain as defined in the profile. Deselect this flag in order to see the changes carried out in customization. Per planning profile the “Chart” table and the “Graphical Objects” table need to be defined. The chart table contains all settings for the 8 (in release 2.0) SAP predefined charts. Each of these 8 charts has specific data details and one or multiple decision tables for table rows and graphical objects. The graphical objects table contains all settings for the 14 (in release 2.0) SAP predefined graphical objects. Each of these graphical objects has specific data details and details for several graphical elements. This is depicted in the graphic above.

The decision table for table rows defines display settings in the chart details view. Graphical elements, as defined in the graphical objects view, are used by the decision table for graphical objects.

Some detail data can be specified per planning profile. They mainly deal with color and other display settings. An important setting is the “Default Settings” flag that was explained above. Another setting deals with multiple loading (see the chapter PP/DS Planning Board”). If this flag is set, elements that overlap in time are displayed in different lines.

The following chapter deals with the fields that can be maintained in the chart and the graphical objects tables. The aim is to provide an overview of the maintenance possibilities for the PP/DS Planning Board and not a detailed description of each and every field. Once this overview understanding is gained, it is easy to drill down into the last detail of the customization in this area.



## Chart Table

The chart table contains detailed information for all 8 SAP predefined charts. When starting the PP/DS Planning Board transaction, only those charts are displayed that are marked “static”. Some of the views can be activated while in the PP/DS Planning Board transaction as and when required via the "Extra" menu command. They are marked in the "Extra" column in the table below. Charts that cannot be activated in this way and are not marked "static" cannot be displayed at all. The following table provides an overview. The "Displays" column indicates elements displayed in the charts as delivered by SAP.

| Chart Name | Displays | Chart Type | Extra |
|---|---|---|---|
| Resource Chart | Operations per Resource | Objects | No |
| Product Chart | Demand and Supply Orders for Product | Objects | No |
| Orders Chart | Products per Demand and Supply Order | Objects | No |
| Operations Chart | Operations per Order | Objects | No |
| Resource Load | Resource Load Percentage | Histogram | Yes |
| Product Stock | Product Stock Quantity | Histogram | Yes |
| Network View Operations | Operations Network within an Order | Network | Yes |
| Network View Orders | Order Network | Network | Yes |

**Table 85 – Planning Board Chart Overview**

On the detail view per chart, the following fields can be maintained (note that not all fields are discussed here in detail):

- Chart Object
  The chart object field defines the object displayed on the left side of the planning board. Possible entries are:
  - Resource
  - Product
  - Order
  - Operation
- Field Selection

Depending on the chart object some details are shown in the left column of the planning board. They can be selected here and reduced in terms of characters shown.

- Sort Sequence
  The sort sequence refers to the chart object. The displayed object (see below) is always shown in time sequence on the right side of the planning board.
- Displayed Object
  The displayed object is the object shown in the right side of the planning board. For example chart 2 (product chart) shows the orders for a product. The displayed object is therefore "Order." The displayed object depends on the chart object and can be:
  - Order
  - Operation
  - Activity
  - Order Network
  - Operation Network
  - Histogram
- Always Sort
  Displayed data is sorted automatically when starting up the planning board transaction. During the scheduling activities, no new sorting takes place if this flag is off. Switching it on forces the system to check the sorting with every scheduling activity. For performance reasons this should only be considered if absolutely required. The flag does <u>not</u> impact the accuracy of the data.
- Dynamic Chart
  Charts are static if this flag is set off and dynamic if the flag is on. Static charts are shown automatically when the planning board transaction is called. Dynamic charts can be displayed as and when required by selecting them in the menu structure "Extra" of the PP/DS Planning Board. Note that the Resource, Product, Order, and Operation chart cannot be called while in the transaction. If they are set to "dynamic", they cannot be displayed at all!
- Height
  Defines the row height (small, medium, large).

On the bottom of the details screen, various settings can be carried out that define the graphical appearance of the selected chart.

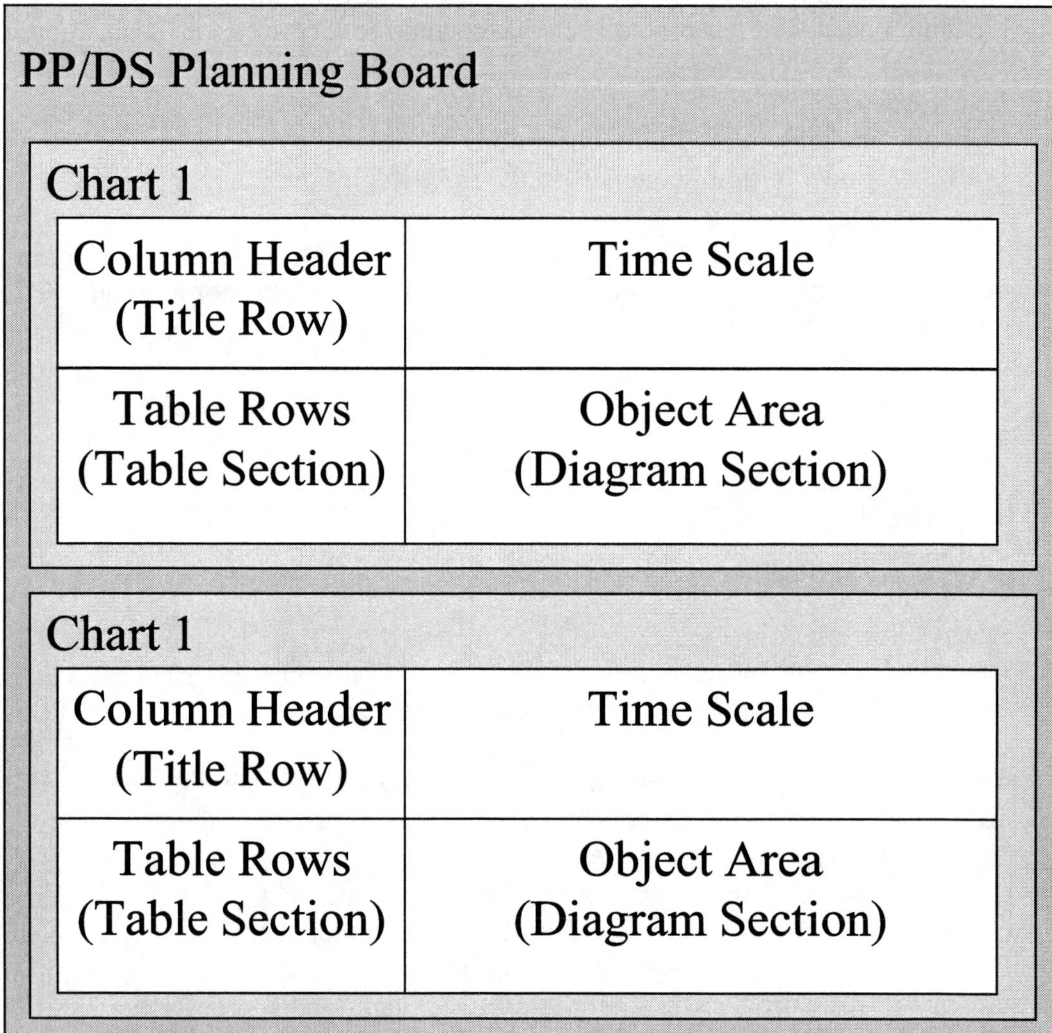


**Graphic 73 – PP/DS Planning Board Screen Layout**

Every chart is subdivided into the Table Area and the Chart Area. The table area consists of the column header and the rows, the chart area of the time scale and the object area. Various charts make up the PP/DS Planning Board screen. This is depicted in the graphic below. The definitions in brackets refer to expressions that are used alternatively in other areas of PP/DS.

All charts displayed in the Planning Board share the same time scale and time scale settings. The appearance of the column header can be changed in terms of background colors, fonts, and font alignment. To do so, select the “Column Header” tab. The short description on the tab defines the name of the tab and can be changed. The next tab “Standard Row” gives the display parameters for the table row section of the charts. The next 6 tabs are used to define the layout of the table rows depending on conditions that are defined in the “Decision Table for Table Rows” (see below). Again, the short descriptions on the tabs define the names of the tab and can be changed. The last tab “Histogram Data” is used to define the graphical display of the Object Area in the chart. Its layout and customizable fields depend on the displayed objects in the object area.

The “Decision Table for Table Rows” strictly spoken is some type of program code or macro that is used to determine the graphical appearance of the table rows depending on the value of selected fields of the object in the table row. The appearance of these rows can be changed in terms of background colors, fonts, and font alignment. Each decision table consists of decision groups and decision steps. In each decision group, you define the graphical appearance of the table rows (expressed as the row format) as a result of values (characteristics) of the displayed object. Per decision group, exactly one row format can be defined. Per decision step, exactly one condition can be defined. A condition can be the comparison of a field with a constant value or the comparison of two fields. Thus one or multiple decision steps make up a decision group. One or multiple decision groups can be defined per chart. Each decision step has one condition, but various decision steps can be linked to each other enabling logical <AND> conditions. The logical relationship of decision steps (if they are not linked to each other) is of type <OR>.

Example:

This example shows how all names of resources that are flagged in the resource master as “Bottleneck Resources” are displayed in red with a white background in the table row of the "Resources Chart". The normal display is black font on a white background.

- Select the details of the "Resource Chart"
- The Chart Object should be of type "1" (Resources) and the displayed object Operations
- Select the first tab "Column Header"
- Ensure the background color is white and the font color is black
- Select the third tab and change its description to "Highlight Bottleneck"
- Press <Enter>, which will change the tab description to "Highlight Bottleneck"
- Set the background color to white and the font color to red
- Go back one level (green arrow key on top), and then select the "Resource Chart"
- Double-click in the tree structure on "Decision Table for Table Rows"
- If an empty grid is displayed, select "New Entries"; otherwise continue
- Define the following data:
    - Decision Group 1
    - Decision Step 1
    - Table Name 1 (Resource)
    - Field Name Bottleneck Resource
    - Relational Operator EQ
    - Comparison Value X
    - Row Format 1

Save the profile and ensure that you have flagged at least one resource as bottleneck in the planning version you use. Start the PP/DS Planning Board and enjoy the altered appearance of bottleneck resources.

If you want to check various fields to use the <u>same</u> display parameters add more decision steps to the decision group and link the decision steps using the "Next Decision Group" field. If you want to check other fields to use <u>different</u> display parameters, add more decision groups. The system goes through all decision groups and steps until it finds a condition that is true.

The "Decision Table for Graphical Objects" works the same way as explained above. It is some type of program code or macro that is used to determine the graphical appearance of the objects in the object area depending on the type of displayed object in the object area. The appearance of these objects can be determined in terms of shape, color, and some other characteristics. The standard delivered APO system should contain all required graphical objects and their link to the respective charts. It is up to the user to check the graphical objects (see the chapter "Graphical Objects Table" below) and to change colors if required. Again, each decision table consists of decision groups and decision steps. In each decision group, you define the conditions under which certain graphical objects (expressed as the graphical object ID) are displayed. Per decision step exactly one condition can be defined. One or multiple decision steps make up a decision group. One or multiple decision groups can be defined per chart. The graphical objects that can be selected are defined in a separate step (see the chapter Graphical Objects Table below).

## Graphical Objects Table

The graphical objects table is a library of all objects that can be displayed in the object area of the chart. 14 of these SAP predefined objects exist in this library; new ones can be added. Each graphical object consists of one or multiple graphical elements. Each graphical element can be defined in terms of shape, color, and other characteristics. Even own custom shapes can be imported.

Following data can be maintained per graphical object:

- Field Selection
  The field selection of the graphical object determines which graphical elements can be used for the graphical object.
- Position of Text
  Align the text to left or right of the object or within it.
- Font
  Define the font together with color, size, and other parameters.

Following data can be maintained per graphical element:

- Shape

Use lines, rectangles, predefined symbols, or own graphical symbol files.

- Predefined Symbol
  Define the symbol to be used (if any).
- Graphical Symbol File
  Define the graphical symbol file to be used (if any).
- Color
  Define the color of the graphical element (not the font).
- Characteristic
  Set other characteristics of the element.
- Representation of Breaks
  Define how breaks are shown for such graphical elements that are relating to a time span (e.g. planned order for production).

#### 5.4.1.1.6 Optimization Profile

The Optimization Profile defines all required parameters for the PP/DS Optimizer. As with most other profiles in PP/DS, the time profile name consists of the profile name as such and a "customizing ID." The definitions are carried out in the detail view of the optimization profile and in the three subgroups Cost Mode Priorities, Capacity Change, and Extended Settings. The SAP delivered APO system comes with a configured profile. It should be renamed before adapting specific requirements.

The solid black dot in the listings below indicates that the setting can be changed interactively when starting the optimizer; the circle indicates that this setting can only be done in the profile directly using the profile maintenance transaction. Note that there is no possibility to save the profile values that were updated interactively.



**Detail View**

The optimization profile Detail View contains the fields as listed below.

- Optimization Procedure

Set the default optimization algorithm to be used (Genetic Algorithm or Constraint Propagation). Which one suits the situation better depends on the data environment.

- Maximum Runtime
  Based on the maximum runtime setting, the optimizer can go through more or less iterations while improving the current schedule. A too short time defeats the purpose of finding an acceptable solution, allocating too long of a time does not really improve the planning situation. The required time obviously also depends on the data environment. No recommendation for an appropriate time setting can therefore be made.
- Weighting of the Objective Functions
  The six single measurable (objective) functions (criteria) that make up the overall optimization goal need to be weighted. The weight of the six listed functions below can each be set between Zero and 100. All values together always make up 100% and while increasing (decreasing) the weight of one criterion, all others will reduce (increase) their relative weight.
  - Total Lead Time
  - Setup Times
  - Setup Costs
  - Maximum Delay
  - Average Delay
  - Total Costs

  Refer to the chapter "PP/DS Optimizer" for further explanation on the functions.

o Planning Parameters
  In the planning parameters group, only the backward pegging time can be defined. The backward pegging time is the maximum permitted time delay between a receipt element and the corresponding requirement. The optimizer pegs the receipt to the requirement as long as this time is not exceeded. This is strictly spoken a violation as the receipt is too late for the requirement. In a consequent step, the optimizer tries to reduce this time violation as far as possible.
  o Backward Pegging
    Define the maximum permitted lateness for the pegging relation. The default value is 24 hours.

o Follow Up Optimization

Once the optimization run has finished, a follow-up activity to reschedule operations that are too far away from the actual requirement date can be initiated. During this follow up procedure, the system deviates from the optimized solution, but, at the same time, reduces the work-in-process quantities. This follow up optimization is a backward scheduling activity.

- o Backward Scheduling
  Set this indicator to switch on the follow up optimization.
- o Resource Selection Unchanged
  Set this indicator to ensure that for operations that can run on various resources (based on different modes in the PPM) no resource selection is performed during the follow up optimization.
- o Resources Freely Selectable
  Set this indicator to allow resource selection based on the different modes as defined in the PPM during the follow up optimization.

- Time Settings
  When starting the optimizer, the time settings appear as a pop-up window prior to the optimization screen.
  - o Bypass Dialog
    Set this indicator to suppress the time setting pop-up window and thus disabling the possibility to change the time settings interactively.
  - Optimization Horizon
    The optimization horizon is the time period in which operations are considered for optimization.
    - o Indicator "Time - Relative Time"
      Set to Relative Time or Time depending on the type of time setting required in the Start field.
    - Start Date & Time
      Relative — Define the number of days, if any, the optimization horizon starts compared to the actual date and time of the system when starting the optimizer run. The number of days can be positive indicating the optimization horizon starts later then the system date or negative indicating an earlier start.
      Absolute — Set a fixed start date.
    - o Indicator "Time - Relative Time"
      Set to Relative Time or Time depending on the type of time setting required in the Finish field.

- Finish Date & Time
  Relative Define the number of days the optimization horizon.
  Absolute Set a fixed end date.
- Optimized Schedule
  The optimized schedule start date is the earliest date at which the optimizer puts the scheduled (optimized) operations. It has an open end.
  - Indicator "Time - Relative Time"
    Set to Relative Time or Time depending on the type of time setting required in the Start field.
  - Start Date & Time
    Relative Define the number of days, if any, the optimized schedule must start earlier or later than the start of the optimization horizon. The number of days can be positive indicating a later start than the optimization horizon or negative indicating an earlier start.
    Absolute Define the start date and time of the optimized schedule.

All operations that can be found in the optimization horizon and are not fixed are subject to optimization. The can be rescheduled to any date after the start date of the optimization schedule. The relation of the optimization horizon and optimization schedule is depicted in the following graphic.

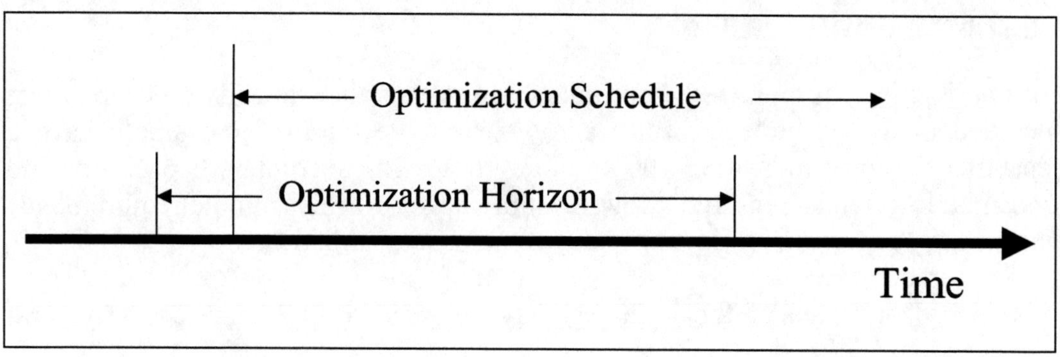


**Graphic 74 – Optimization Horizon**

## Subgroup Cost Mode Priorities

The subgroup screen for cost mode priorities links mode priorities as defined in the product's PPM to fixed and variable costs. These values are used for selecting the cost optimal solution. An empty screen can be easily filled with standard values by selecting the "Insert Standard Values" button. The "New Entries" button in this transaction has a different function compared to other transactions. When pressed, all current values are deleted and a new empty screen appears. The link of modes to costs permits that the same resource has different costs depending on the mode it is used in.

- Priority
  The priorities are predefined and only the first 20 from priority "A" through to "O" can be used.
- Fixed Costs
  Define the fixed cost when using a resource that is specified in any PPM with the mode of this line.
- Variable Costs
  Define the variable cost per unit processed when using a resource that is specified in any PPM with the mode of this line.

## Subgroup Capacity Change

For multi activity resources the optimizer can use a valid capacity other than that specified in the resource. A multi activity resource might for example have a capacity of 8 hours a day and 100 kg at any time. The secondary capacity of 100 kg can be lowered as required allowing some buffer for last minute requirements. The primary capacity of 8 hours per day remains unchanged.

- Resource
  Specify the name of the multi activity resource for which a capacity limit needs to be defined.
- Period Number
  Define all periods for which a reduced capacity should be used. The period number needs to be increasing and with no gaps. The first period starts at the beginning of the optimization period (not the optimization horizon).
- Period Duration

Define the period duration in hours.

- Capacity %
  Define the reduced capacity for the period.

**Subgroup Extended Settings**

- Fixing Orders
  - Fixed Order Overlaps Start of Horizon
    Set this flag if orders that have operations inside the optimization period and past it must be fixed initially and consequently not be considered by the optimization run.
  - Fixed Order Overlaps End of Horizon
    Set this flag if orders that have operations inside the optimization period and before it must be fixed initially and consequently not be considered by the optimization run.
- Started/Confirmed Orders
  The flags in this group apply to orders where all operations are inside the optimization period and some of the activities are fixed, started, partially confirmed, or finally confirmed.
  - Fix Order with Fixed/Started Activities
    If the flag is set, all activities of such an order are fixed and thus not considered by the optimization run. This fix is only valid throughout the optimization run and removed again afterwards.
  - Propagate Maximum Time Relationship as Hard Constraint
    If the flag is set, all internal order time relationships are fixed and cannot be changed by the optimization run. It therefore prevents a change of the time relationships for these orders.
- Data Input Processing
  - Without Data Consistency Check
    Set this flag to skip the data consistency check.
  - Without Infinite Pre-scheduling
    In order to derive an initial solution, the optimizer carries out scheduling based on an infinite scheduling strategy. By doing so, it determines a time frame for all activities, which is then used for the consequent optimization. This infinite scheduling step can be omitted for smaller environments (less

than 250 activities) but is carried out, even if switched off, for larger environments. Constraints taken into account are:
- Order Due Date
- Working Time of Resource
- Alternate Resources

Set this flag to not carry out an infinite scheduling initial solution.

- Without Finite Pre-scheduling

  In addition to an initial solution based on an infinite scheduling approach, the system can also use a finite scheduling approach. If doing so it will take the following constraints over and above those mentioned above into account:
  - Resource Capacity
  - Maximum Time Intervals

  Set this flag to not carry out a finite scheduling initial solution.

- Run Time Distribution

  The optimization is subdivided into the three blocks of finding an initial solution, improving it, and finally performing an optional backward scheduling. Define in the 3 parameters below, the relative distribution of time allocated to each of these tasks.
  - Initial Solution
  - Improvement to Initial Solution
  - Backward Scheduling
- Constraint Manipulation/Relaxation

  Relaxing constraints enables the optimizer to more easily find a solution, while at the same time the solution might not be feasible. Use these possibilities only if absolutely required (e.g. no result can be found otherwise).
  - Remove Maximum Time Constraints

    Set this indicator to ignore the maximum time constraints that might be defined in the PPM.
  - Set Utilization Rate of all Resources to 100%

    Set this indicator to set all resource capacities to 100% irrespective of the actual value in the resource master.
  - Remove Calendar

    Set this indicator to overwrite all resource calendar settings. In this case all resources are deemed to be available 24 hours per day.
  - Do not consider Setup Times/Setup Costs

PP/DS

Set this indicator to ignore the setup times and costs that might be defined in the setup matrix.

- Undo Fixing of Activities
  Set this indicator to allow the optimizer to move all activities including those that are fixed.

### 5.4.1.2 Factory Calendar

The factory calendar is used to determine the working days for master data objects like plants, resources, etc. The factory calendar defined on a lower level overrules the definition on a higher level. If for example the factory calendar allocated to a resource in a certain location is different to that allocated to the location, the resource definition applies. Factory calendars are made up of the Public Holiday definition and the Holiday Calendar.

Public Holidays are predefined in the delivered system. New ones can be added if required. Each public holiday has rules that define for example for moving holidays like Easter when they take place.

Holiday Calendars are also predefined and are made up of public holidays. Newly defined public holidays can be added or taken off. Each holiday calendar has an ID number and can be displayed in calendar form to give an overview. The exact amount of public holidays per year is also displayed. Holiday Calendars as well as the assigned Public Holidays have validity periods.

Factory Calendars combine the Holiday Calendar definition with individual per day definitions. Here each day of the week is marked as a working or a non-working day. This includes public holidays that can be set to working days as well. A Special Rules function can be used to define for example factory holidays or times of extended workdays.

#### 5.4.1.3 Rounding Profile

The Rounding Profile is used to round up or down the supply quantities' established demand. Each Rounding Profile has several levels. For each level a threshold value and a rounding value is defined. Rounding profiles are also used in SNP and are dealt with in detail in chapter "Rounding Profile" of the SNP section.

#### 5.4.1.4 Setup Matrix

When scheduling planned production orders for a resource, it is important to minimize the down time and transitional costs caused by set up and tear down time of the machine. The optimum is obviously to sequence production orders in a way that only minimal transitional downtimes and/or costs occur.

On the activity level of a PPM operation is a flag that, if set, ensures that setup time is calculated according to the setup matrix. If this flag is set, the system automatically suppresses the fixed duration field of the setup activity. The setup time is then calculated according to the setup matrix. Every single activity resource can have a setup matrix allocated to it. If the "use setup matrix" flag for an activity has been set, the system checks whether the resource defined in this activity is linked to a setup matrix. If this is the case, the setup time is determined according to the setup matrix. If no setup matrix is linked to the resource, the setup time is set to Zero! The "use setup matrix" flag can also be set for an activity with activity type "produce." In this case it is not required to specifically define an activity with the activity type "setup". The result is the same.

Each setup matrix is made up of multiple "setup groups". The setup group defines the technical condition of the machine required for the production order operation. It is purely an identifier and has no other information attached. Various setup groups are combined in the location specific setup matrix. Graphically displayed, both coordinates of the setup matrix carry the same setup groups. Within the matrix the transitional time and cost (penalty) attached to the change from one group to another is defined. An important aspect is that, for each transition, the duration and the cost can be specified independently. This allows in a time critical situation the choice of a more expensive transition that requires less time in order to achieve an overall (time) optimum. If time is not the main constraint, an optimization according to the penalty values can be performed. The PP/DS optimizer carries out the optimization.

Setup matrices are also stored in liveCache and constitute another constraint when scheduling is carried out. Due to performance reasons, SAP recommends to define as few setup matrices as possible. The same applies to the number of setup transitions within a given setup matrix.

The following table gives an example for a setup matrix. The data cells contain two sets of information, the transitional time before the "/" and the cost behind it.

| | | From Setup Group | | |
|---|---|---|---|---|
| | | <any> | G | H |
| To Setup Group | G | 30 / 150 | | 15 / 200 |
| | H | 20 / 300 | 10 / 100 | 2 / 0 |

**Table 86 – Setup Matrix Example**

An "*" can be used as a wildcard for the preceding or the subsequent setup group. Defining an "*" for both is the minimum to achieve a complete setup matrix. Each "single activity resource" can be allocated to a specific setup matrix in the resource master. Several resources can share the same setup matrix but any given resource can only be linked to exactly one setup matrix. For situations where the setup status is not determined (known in liveCache), entries are used where the "From" is not specified. Setup times can also be defined in cases where, although no transition takes place, a certain time is required.



The calculation of the setup time is an activity carried out with every scheduling task; it is not required to run the Optimizer to achieve this. During PP/DS optimization, the system will try scheduling planned production orders in such a way that the total transition times or penalties as defined in the table above are minimized. As part of the resource master data maintenance, a setup matrix is allocated to one or multiple resources. Please note that the use of a setup matrix works (as of release 2.0) with single activity resources only.

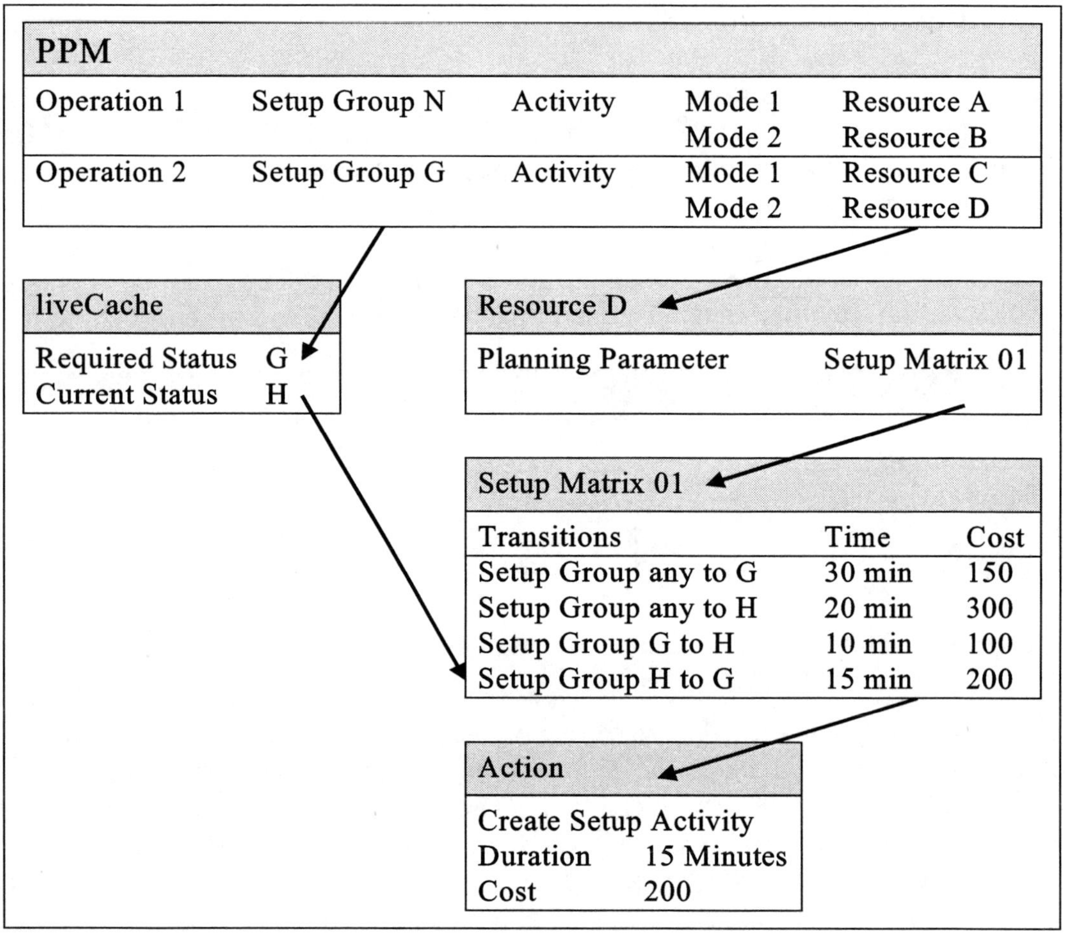


**Graphic 75 – Setup Matrix**

The above graphic illustrates the logical sequence of events during scheduling with regards to the setup time calculation.

## 5.4.2 Master Data Environment

Most of the master data required for PP/DS has already been discussed in the SNP section of this book. For the PPM's we will see in the following chapters that the additional data is required and where it has to be maintained. We will also look at the production calendar although this is not really master data. What is new is the maintenance of characteristics and classes. Following additions to already discussed master data need to be made:

- Location
  There are no PP/DS specific settings in the location master. Fields that influence PP/DS are the allocation of calendars to the location and the location's priority setting, which is used by CTM.

- Product
  Several fields in the product master are required for PP/DS or influence the calculations of PP/DS procedures. They can be mainly found on the PP/DS tab of the product master and on some other tabs. All the fields of the product master were discussed in the SNP section already. Please refer to this section for detailed information.

- Resource
  For PP/DS purposes, more detailed resources, the time-continuous resources, are required. It is also possible to use mixed resources instead of defining bucket resources (for SNP) and time-continuous resources (for PP/DS), The time-continuous and mixed resources were discussed already in the SNP section.

### 5.4.2.1 Production Process Model (PPM)

#### 5.4.2.1.1 PPM Overview

The structure and general features of PPM's are explained in the SNP section of this book. Please refer to the appropriate chapters. Specific features, only applicable to PP/DS PPM's are discussed in the following chapters.

**PPM Network**

A PPM consists of one or several operations, each in turn has one to several activities. The number of the operation as well as the activity has no impact on this network at all. One can define that operation or activity 10 follows operation or activity 20 and so on. Each activity has to be brought in relation to other activities. These relations can be defined very flexible supporting any possibility from simple sequences to highly complex networks. Each activity has at least one successor or predecessor. Supported relations between activities include:

- SS Start – Start
- SF Start – Finish
- FS Finish – Start
- FF Finish – Finish

Each of the relations can have a minimum and/or a maximum time constraint. Time constraints define the minimum or maximum time that is allowed to pass between the activities. These definitions are shown in the graphic below.

When using CTM functionality, it is mandatory (in release 2.0) to set the minimum and maximum time constraint indicators ($F_{MIN}$ and $F_{MAX}$) even if no time constraints need to be defined.

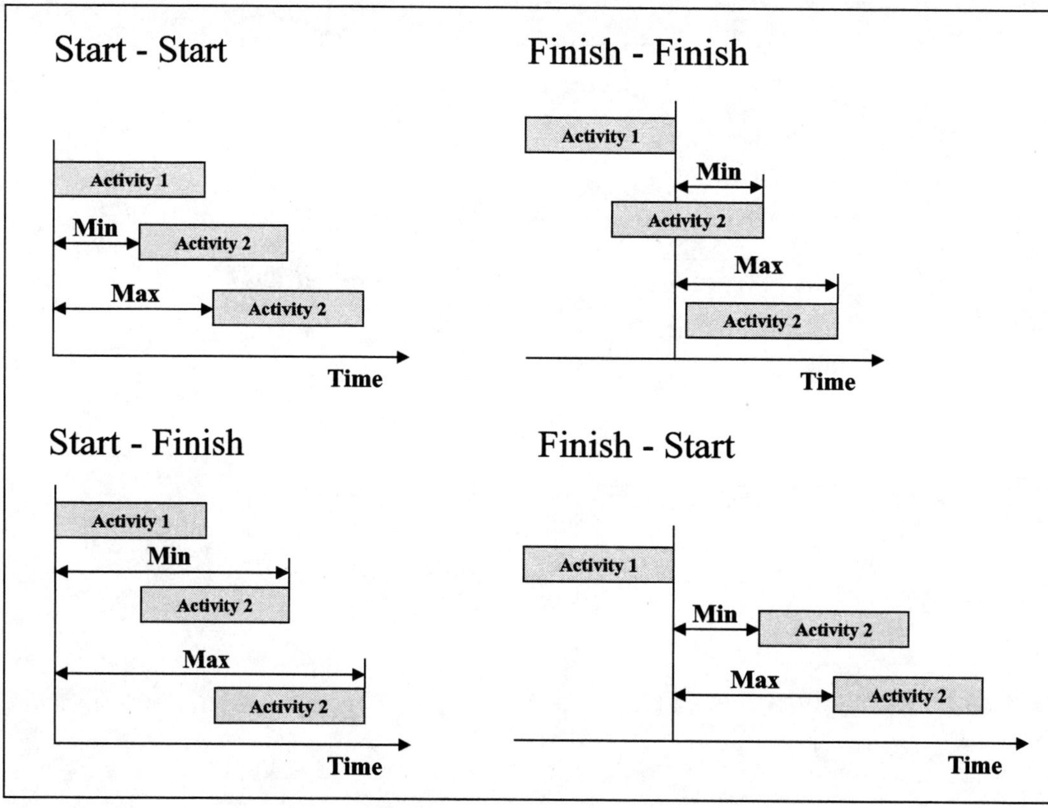


**Graphic 76 – PPM Activity Relations**

In a PPM the activities and not the operations are linked to each other. It is possible to link an activity to more than one other activity to build up complex activity networks. An example for such a network is shown in the graphic below.

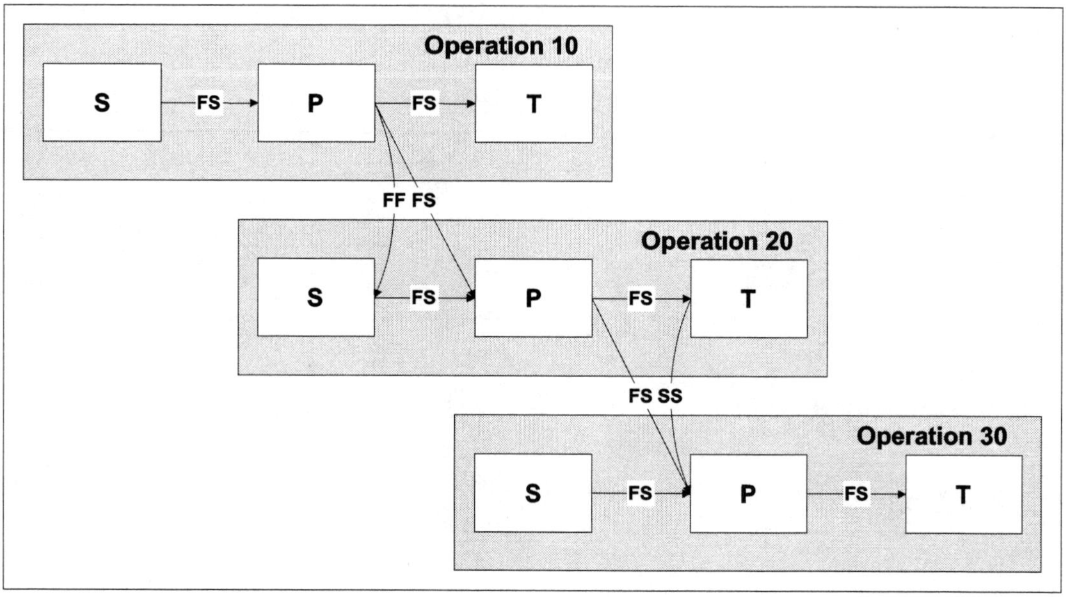


**Graphic 77 – Activity Network**



## Modes

To add some more flexibility but also more complexity, the (SNP & PP/DS) PPM allows defining various Modes per activity. A mode represents a possible set of one primary and one or multiple secondary resources that are used in order to process an activity. Each mode represents an alternative that can be selected in order to carry out the activity. Note that secondary resources are used in APO to fulfill a requirement together with the primary resource. They complement each other. In opposition to this, resources defined in the various modes define various possible alternatives to fulfill the same capacity requirement. In bucket resource-oriented PPM's, as used in SNP, there is usually only one activity per operation. For this reason, mode coupling, which will be discussed later, is not a stringent requirement. Scheduling is carried out according to exactly one resource (primary or secondary) as defined in the activity. The relation of various resource definitions is depicted in the graphic below.

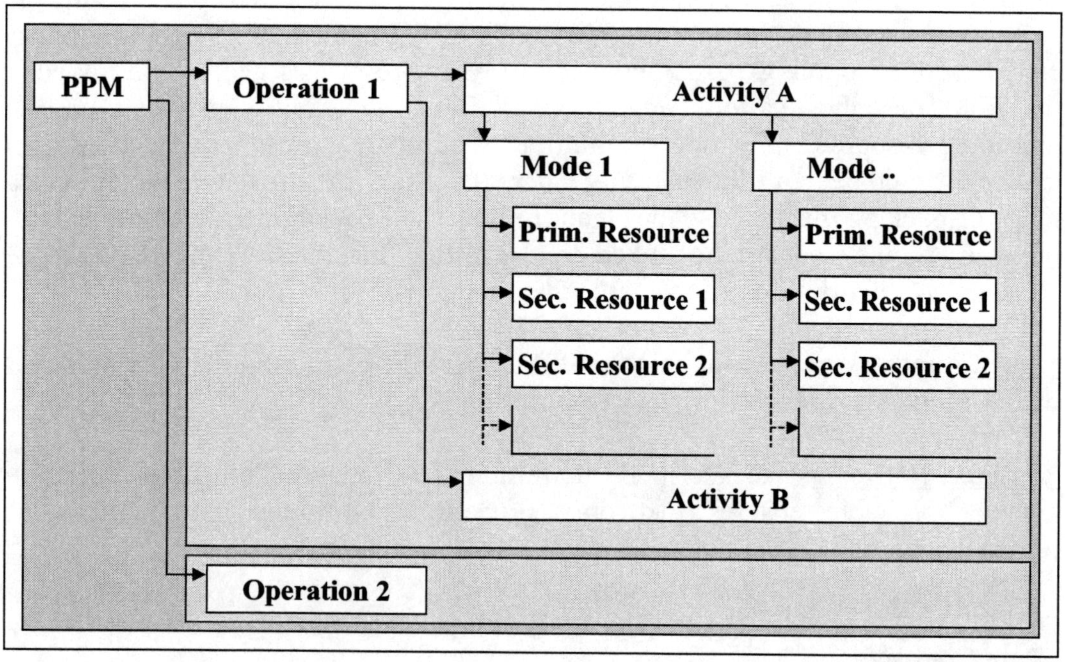


**Graphic 78 – PPM Modes**

Each activity has at least one mode. The resources with their individual consumption are specified per mode. Each mode has a user-defined priority that is used to select the modes.



## Resource Coupling

As we have seen above, it is possible to specify various alternative resources for each activity within an operation. The PP/DS scheduler and optimizer select the appropriate resource according to various parameters (see also optimization profiles definitions). In some cases it might be required to somehow limit the selection possibilities. Within an operation, it is quite often the case that the different activities describe the setup, production, and tear down for the operation. In this case it must be ensured that all the three activities take place using the same mode and thus the same resource. The PP/DS method to achieve this is called "Mode Coupling". Another scenario where resources need to be linked if the PPM describes various process possibilities is when, depending on the preceding resource, only one or multiple specific resources can be used. An example would be in a filling activity where the used filling machine determines a range of packing machines. Other than the specified packaging, machines cannot be used, as they cannot be linked to the filling machine. Within PP/DS the "Resource Network" is used to enable this functionality.

Mode Coupling is realized within the PPM where different modes are defined and linked by mode number or primary resource name.

Resource Networks also use mode definitions. During scheduling, the resource network principle ensures that only predefined permitted combinations of resources are used within an order.

## Mode Coupling



Mode coupling is an option that ensures that, throughout all activities of a specific operation or cross operations of the PPM, only modes with the same number or primary resource are used.

Type 2: Coupling by Primary Resource Name
With this type of coupling the system ensures that the same primary resource is used throughout an operation even if it was allocated to different modes. The mode number is irrelevant. Only modes with the same primary resource name are used (e.g. primary resource RES1 is used for all activities of all operations). Mode coupling of type "2" is switched on automatically if various activities are defined within an operation (e.g. setup and produce).

Type 3: Coupling by Mode Number

Only modes with the same mode number are used (e.g. mode 10 is used for all operations). This type of mode coupling is used mainly to ensure that a certain combination of resources is selected during scheduling. With this mode coupling type, it is required that all activities have the same amount of mode definitions.

Type 0: No Mode Coupling
With mode coupling switched off, modes with different primary resources or numbers can be used simultaneously (e.g. mode AB for activity 10 and mode CD for activity 20).

Mode coupling must be switched on if the activities of an operation must be all performed on exactly the same resource or on resources with the same mode number. An example where the system enforces mode coupling of type "2" is shown below where the activities within the operation describe the setup, production, and tear down activity, all of which must obviously be carried out on exactly the same resource. The mode number in this example is totally irrelevant, as the coupling is based on the primary resource name only.

Modes can be coupled according to the resource name as depicted in the graphic below. Alternatively, the mode number can be used as the determining factor for mode coupling. The mode number is also referred to as the mode name, as the mode field is alphanumeric.

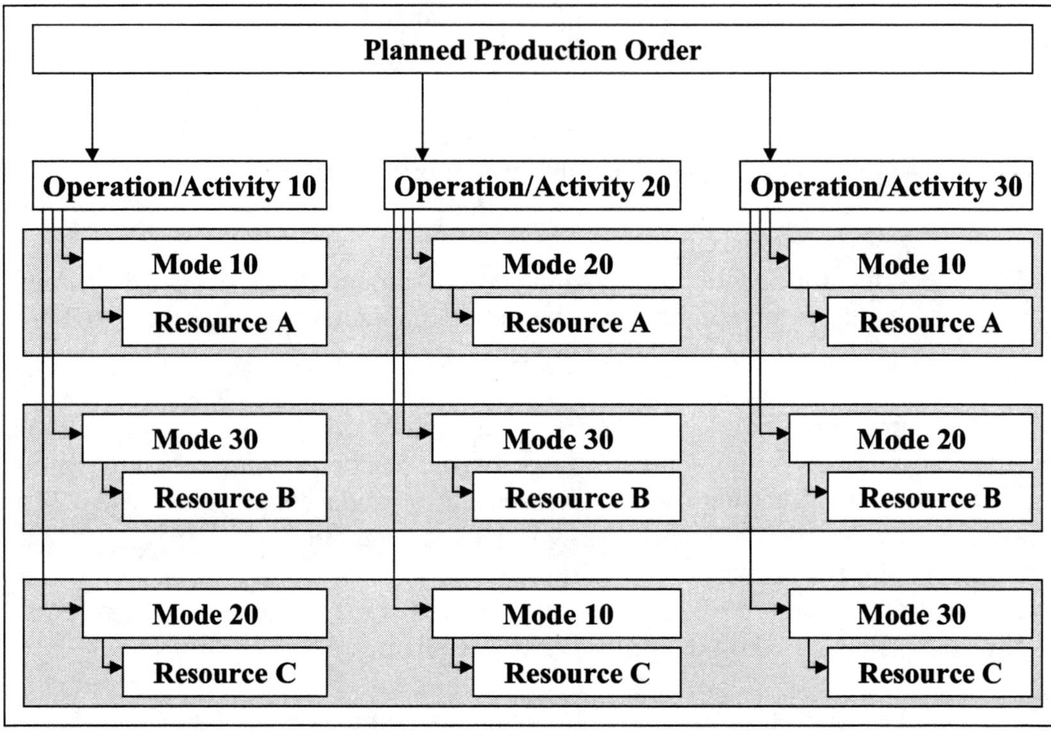


**Graphic 79 – Mode Coupling**



## Resource Network

A resource network is the definition of one or multiple possible sequences of used resources in an order. A resource network can be defined within one specific operation or across operations. The resource network definition is part of the PPM. In order to define a resource network, it is required to link various activities within one operation or across operations to the same mode and set the "Mode Connection" indicator to "3". The mode connection indicator is also used for mode coupling (see above). There are three possibilities for the relation of predecessor and successor in a resource network.

Option 1: One-to-One Relation
For each defined preceding resource exactly one succeeding resource exists. When changing from resource A to B in operation 10, the system will automatically change from resource C to D in operation 20.

Option 2: One-to-Many Relation
For each defined preceding resource one or multiple succeeding resources exist. When changing from resource A to B in operation 10, the system can select from a range of resources for operation 20, for example resource C or D in operation 20.

Option 3: Many-to-One Relation
For multiple preceding resources, exactly one succeeding resource exists. When changing from resource A to B in operation 10, the system does not need to change the resource of operation 20 at all. It remains C.

Option 2 and 3 can be seen the same way; it just depends whether the rescheduling is carried out for the predecessor and successor. The following graphic depicts the three options.

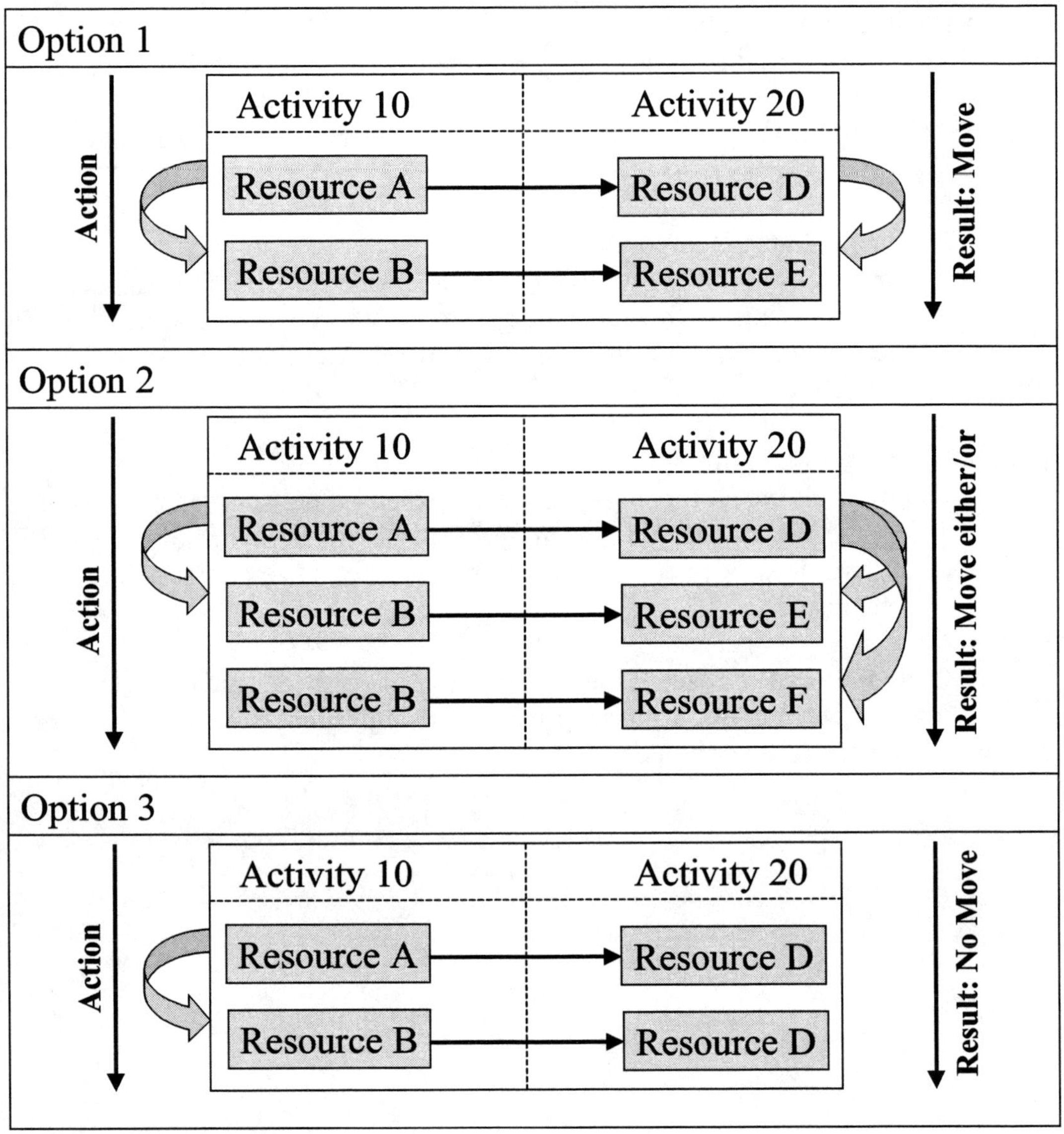


**Graphic 80 – Resource Network**

PP/DS

### 5.4.2.1.2 PPM Maintenance

In this chapter we will go through all fields required to set up a PPM for use in PP/DS.

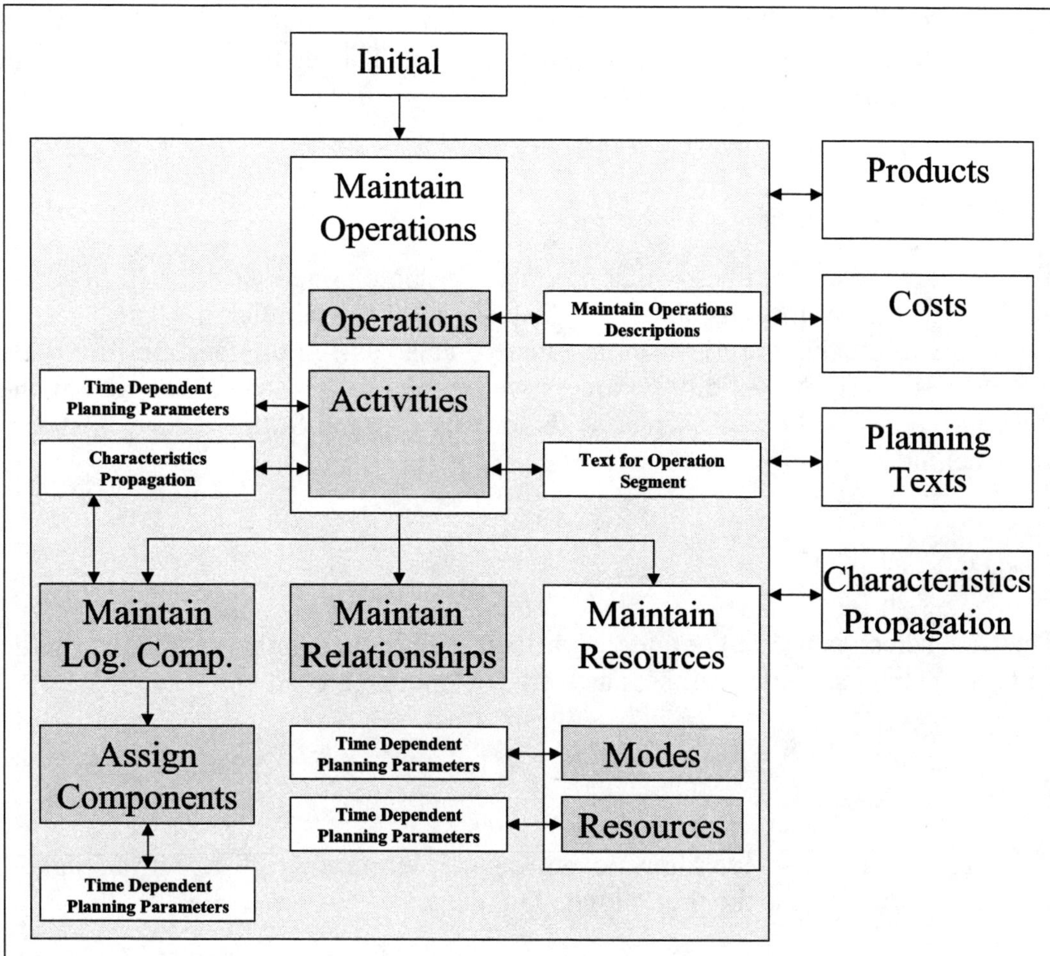


**Graphic 81 – PPM Screen Structure (PP/DS)**

For more information regarding PPM's used for SNP, please refer to the SNP section.

**Initial Screen**

In order to create a PPM, a plan number and a plan usage have to be defined followed by the plan name on the next screen. This leads to the "Maintain Operations" screen.

**Products Screen**

The Products screen defines which products can be planned with the PPM. Only products that are defined as output products in the "Maintain Components" screen can be planned using the PPM. In this step you also assign the location for which the PPM is valid, the validity period as well as the lot size range. Note that the PPM name assigned on this screen is the one used in the Supply Chain Engineer and Cockpit.

**Costs Screen**

The Cost screen is used to define the variable cost (penalty) that is utilized by the Optimizer. It must contain process as well as component cost.

**Planning Texts Screen**

The Planning Texts screen allows capturing of plan texts in different languages. The default language is the user's logon language.

**Characteristics Propagation Screen**

The Characteristics Propagation screen is used in conjunction with Characteristics Dependent Planning and can be maintained only for PP/DS PPM's.

## Screen Maintain Operations

- Header Level
  On this level the two fields PP/DS plan and Cost Function can be maintained. The PP/DS plan field serves as a reference showing for an SNP PPM what the corresponding PP/DS PPM name is. For this reason the usage of this field is not meaningful in a PP/DS PPM. The Cost Function field allows the definition of quantity dependent fixed and variable penalties, which are used by the Optimizer.

- Operations Level
  Following data can be maintained:
  - Operation — Name an operation as required. Multiple language descriptions can be captured by pressing the middle pushbutton next to the magnifying glass.
  - Description — Assign a name to the operation.
  - Setup Group / Key — Define the setup group required to start the operation. At the end of the operation, the used resource will also be set to the status of this setup group for consequent changeover calculations to another setup status. Note that the setup group that is allocated to an operation must also be part of the setup matrix that is linked to the resource that will be used in this operation and activity.
  - Location — Location of the setup group.

  Double click on the operations line or press the pushbutton with the magnifying glass to drill down one level to the activity. When creating a new PPM, the setup group specific fields will only be visible after this step. An operation can be deleted by selecting it and pressing the Delete Operation button.

- <u>Activity Level</u>
  Define the following data:
  - Activity Number — Specify any number as required.
  - Section — Give the activity a name in the field "Section." Pressing the pushbutton opposite the magnifying glass allows capturing multiple language descriptions.
  - Activity — Choose from Setup, Produce, Tear Down, and Wait (Queue) Time.
  - Activity Type — The activity description field is filled out automatically after pressing the <Enter> button.
  - Scrap (%) — Define a scrap percentage (if required). How scrap is calculated is dealt with in the chapter "Scrap Calculation".
  - Setup — Set this flag if the setup time must be calculated according to the setup matrix that is allocated to the resource.
  - Time Dependent — Time dependent parameters can be defined per activity by selecting the appropriate line and pressing the Time Dependent Planning Parameters button underneath the table.

  Double click on the activity line or press the pushbutton with the magnifying glass to get to the Maintain Components screen. Click on the Characteristics button to branch into the Characteristics Propagation screen. This button is gray-shaded as long as the Characteristics Propagation function is not active. Once activated, this button is colored. An activity can be deleted by selecting it and pressing the Delete Activity button.

- <u>Sub-Screen Time Dependent Process Parameters: Activity</u>
  The upper section of this screen shows the standard scrap value used if none of the time dependent parameters apply. On this sub-screen, define the following data as required:
  - Valid Until — Define the "valid until" date. If there are periods in-between where the default scrap value as

defined above should be used simply specify these periods here again and do not set the Scrap / Yield Indicator.

- Scrap / Yield Indicator — Set this indicator so that the defined scrap value in this time dependent parameter is applied.
- Scrap (%) — Define a scrap percentage. How scrap is calculated is dealt with in chapter "Scrap Calculation."

On the top of this screen is a "Scrap<->Yield" pushbutton. This is a toggle key and pressing it will change the display from scrap to yield or yield to scrap. Press the "Version" pushbutton to enable definition of this time dependent parameter per SNP planning version.

- <u>Sub-Screen Characteristics Propagation</u>
  The main Characteristics Propagation screen is called [?]. Data on this screen needs to be maintained only if Characteristics Dependent Planning is used.

**<u>Screen Maintain Components</u>**

This screen is a bit mixed up from a naming point of view. The screen name relates to components, the tab name to materials, the lines to logical components, and the consumption is called material consumption. For PP/DS PPM's, this screen only contains "logical components" that are further specified on a lower level screen. The logical name is a free form text field. One level down the actual products are allocated to the Logical Name. This allows linking several product numbers to the same Logical Name and thereby specifying product alternatives. The selection of alternative products is based on time validity. Note that even if no product alternatives need to be defined, it is still required to define a logical product first and then drill down to specify the precise number of the product.

The following fields can be maintained per activity on the Components screen:

- Logical Component — Name the logical component. This field is not validated against any master record and therefore accepts any name.

- I/O — Specify whether the logical component is an input (I) or output (O) in this PPM.
- Consumption Mode — Select one of the consumption modes S, E, or C (for consumption being at the start, the end, or continuously).

Double click on the activity line or press the pushbutton with the magnifying glass to get to the Maintain Logical Components screen. Click on the Characteristics button to branch into the Characteristics Propagation screen. This button is gray-shaded as long as the Characteristics Propagation function is not active. Once activated, this button is colored. A component can be deleted by selecting it and pressing the Delete Component button.

- Sub-Screen Maintain Logical Components
  On this sub-screen define the following data as required:
  - Product — Define the product number.
  - Short text — The product description is a display only field.
  - Valid from — The validity start date and time (in the next field).
  - Valid to — The validity end date (in the next field).
  - Material Consumption (v) — Define the variable consumption or output quantity of the product. This is measured in the product's base unit of measure.
  - Material Consumption (f) — Define the fixed consumption or output quantity of the product. This is measured in the product's base unit of measure.
  - Base Unit — The base unit is a display only field.
  - Time Dependent — Time dependent parameters can be defined per product by selecting the appropriate line and pressing the Time Dependent Planning Parameters button underneath the table. Time Dependent parameters refer to time dependent definitions of consumption values, not to the product selection.

  A product allocation can be deleted by selecting it and pressing the Delete Component button. Various products can be defined per logical product. The selection of the product used during the PPM explosion depends on the validity dates. Various products with the same validity ranges can be specified. In this case the selection of the product during the PPM explosion is random!

- Sub-Screen Time Dependent Process Parameters: Component Alternative
  The upper section of this screen shows the standard fixed and variable product consumption values as well as the variable penalty used if none of the time-dependent parameters apply. On this sub-screen define the following data as required:
  - Valid Until — Define the valid until date. If there are periods in-between where the default consumption values as defined above should be used, simply specify these periods here again and do not set the Variable Parameter and/or Cost Indicator.
  - Variable Parameter — Set this indicator so that the defined variable product consumption value in this time dependent parameter is applied.
  - Material Consump. (v) — Define the variable material consumption in the base unit of measure.
  - Fixed Parameter — Set this indicator so that the defined fixed product consumption value in this time dependent parameter is applied.
  - Material Consump. (f) — Define the fixed material consumption in the base unit of measure.
  - Penalty Indicator — Set this indicator so that the defined variable penalty value in this time dependent parameter is applied.
  - Penalty Variable — Define the variable penalty.

  Press the "Version" pushbutton to enable definition of this time dependent parameter per planning version.

**Screen Maintain Relationships**

The following fields can be maintained per activity on the Relationships screen:

- Operation — Select an operation for which a time relation should be defined.
- Activity Number — Select the activity within the operation as defined above.
- P/S — Select one of the two relation parameters V or N (for predecessor or successor).
- Reference Type for Cons. — Define the time relationship between this activity and others. Options are "start-start," "start-finish," "finish-start," and "finish-finish."
- Unit of Measure — Define the unit of measure used when specifying the time lags below.
- Flag Min Time Difference — Set this indicator so that the system considers the minimum time difference defined below. If this flag is not set, the system can schedule the selected activity even before the one selected in the header. A minimum time difference of Zero is used if the flag is set and no time difference is stipulated.
- Minimum Time Difference — Define the minimum time difference between the activity seen in the header of the screen and the activity shown in this line.
- Flag Max Time Difference — Set this indicator so that the system considers the maximum time difference defined below.
- Maximum Time Difference — Define the maximum time difference between the activity seen in the header of the screen and the activity shown in this line.
- Mode Connection — In order to enable mode coupling between all activities of an operation, it is required to set this field to "2" (mode coupling driven by resource name) or "3"(mode coupling driven by mode number).
- Cover Flag — This flag is set to ensure that the optimizer run does not squeeze in another operation between two activities that need to be carried out consecutively.

- Material Flow — Used to determine the scrap calculation for consecutively running activities.
- Activity Category — The activity category is a display only field showing the selected activity's category.
- Description — The description is a display only field showing the selected operations name.

Relationships need to be defined only in one direction. The system adds the counterpart automatically. Relationships can be deleted by selecting it and pressing the Delete Activity Relation button.

## Screen Maintain Resources

On the Resources Screen, the primary resource can be maintained. Double click on the resource line or press the pushbutton with the magnifying glass to drill one level down to the secondary resources level.

- Primary Resource Level
  The following fields can be maintained per activity on the Primary Resources level:
  - Mode — Define a mode number.
  - Unit — Define the unit of measure used to specify the variable and fixed resource consumption (duration).
  - Duration variable — Define the variable time consumption of the resource for the quantity structure defined in the "logical components" screen. This field is not displayed if the "setup" flag for the activity is set.
  - Duration fix — Define the fixed time consumption of the resource for the quantity structure defined in the "logical components" screen. This field is not displayed if the "setup" flag for the activity is set.

- Increment — For step function resource consumption, define here the width of the step. Leave the field blank if no step functionality is required.
- Primary Resource — Select the primary resource for this activity.
- Location — Specify the location of the resource used above.
- Break Duration — Define the maximum permitted break time within an activity.
- Break not allowed — Switch this flag on if activities must not be interrupted by breaks.
- Produce within a shift — Set this flag to ensure that the activity is carried out entirely in one shift. Be careful with this flag because, if the activity is too long for a shift, it cannot be scheduled at all.
- Activity Start Control — Set this flag to force the activity start to be at the shift start.
- Mode Priority — Define a mode priority. Priority "A" is the highest and the scheduler tries to use this mode first.
- Time Dependent — Time dependent parameters can be defined per product by selecting the appropriate line and pressing the Time Dependent Planning Parameters button underneath the table.

The maintenance of the primary resource needs to be continued on the same screen where the secondary resources are defined (see below). A mode definition with its primary resource allocation can be deleted by selecting it and pressing the Delete Mode button.

- <u>Sub-Screen Time Dependent Process Parameters: Mode</u>

  The upper section of this screen shows the standard fixed and variable resource consumption values as well as the variable penalty used if none of the time dependent parameters apply. On this sub-screen, define the following data as required:

  - Valid Until — Define the "valid until" date. If there are periods in-between where the default consumption values as defined above should be used simply

| | |
|---|---|
| | specify these periods here again and do not set the Variable Parameter and/or Cost Indicator. |
| • Fixed Parameter | Set this indicator so that the defined material consumption value in this time dependent parameter is applied. |
| • Duration Fix | Define the variable time resource consumption in the duration time unit of measure. |
| • Duration Time Unit | Define the unit of measure used above for specifying the resource consumption. |
| • Cost Indicator | Set this indicator so that the defined variable penalty value in this time dependent parameter is applied. |
| • Penalty Variable | Define the variable penalty. |

Press the "Version" pushbutton to enable definition of this time dependent parameter per SNP planning version.

- Secondary Resources Level

  When switching to this screen, the primary resource is shown on the top line with some fields as display only. The following fields can be maintained per activity on the Secondary Resources level:

| | |
|---|---|
| • Resource | Define a secondary resource. The first line automatically shows the primary resource. |
| • Location | Specify the location of the secondary resource. The first line automatically shows the location of the primary resource. |
| • Multi Activity | The Multi Activity flag is a display only field and if switched on showing that the selected resource is a Multi-Activity resource. |
| • Calendar | Mark exactly one resource per activity (primary or secondary) as a calendar resource. The marked resource with the defined resource consumption is used for scheduling purposes. |
| • Unit | Define the unit of measure used when specifying the resource consumption (see below). |

- Resource Consump. (v) — Specify the variable resource consumption in the unit of measure as defined above.
- Resource Consump. (f) — Specify the fixed resource consumption in the unit of measure as defined above.
- Time Dependent — Time dependent parameters can be defined per resource by selecting the appropriate line and pressing the Time Dependent Planning Parameters button underneath the table.

A secondary resource allocation can be deleted by selecting it and pressing the Delete Resource button.

- <u>Sub-Screen Time Dependent Process Parameters: Resource Consumption</u>
  The upper section of this screen shows the standard fixed and variable resource consumption values used if none of the time dependent parameters apply. On this sub-screen define the following data as required:
  - Valid Until — Define the "valid until" date. If there are periods in-between where the default consumption values as defined above should be used, simply specify these periods here again and do not set the Variable Parameter Indicator.
  - Variable Parameter — Set this indicator so that the defined resource consumption value in this time dependent parameter is applied.
  - Resource Consump. (v) — Define the variable resource consumption in the unit of measure as defined below. For further explanation regarding the calculation of the resource consumption, refer to the chapter "Resource Consumption Calculation" further above.
  - Unit of Measure — Define the unit of measure used when specifying the resource consumption.

  Press the "Version" pushbutton to enable definition of this time dependent parameter per SNP planning version.

### 5.4.2.2 Characteristics and Classes

The definition of classes and characteristics is required in order to use the "Characteristic Dependent Planning" functionality in APO. Classes and their corresponding characteristics are allocated to products and resources. The setup and definition of classes and characteristics is similar to that in R/3. The definition of classes and characteristics cannot be taken over from an R/3 system. A class can be any grouping terminology. Depending on the master data object it will be allocated to, it could be for example "Textiles" for products or "Bottling Equipment" for resources. A class has one or multiple characteristics attached to it. For the class textiles, the characteristics could be "Size" and "Color." If we now create a product master for a shirt, we need exactly <u>one</u> product master but with the help of the characteristics of the class "Textiles" that we allocate to the product, we can further define the shirt according to the characteristics sizes and colors. The benefit is a reduced number of product masters. Later, in Characteristics Dependent Planning, the appropriate PPM definitions and possibly the selection of a resource have to be carried out according to the characteristics of the shirt that is defined in the planned order. Note that with the current release 2.0 only PP/DS uses the classification data in planning.

In order to use this functionality, first create the characteristics and then the classes. In a consequent step, the characteristics need to be given possible values. They are then linked to classes.

### 5.4.2.3 Number Ranges

PP/DS is the only APO module that creates orders for which a number range has to be set up. One or several number ranges can be defined, of which exactly one is then used as the number range for PP/DS created orders. The number range maintenance is part of the "Current Settings" of PP/DS. There are no system restrictions in terms of possible ranges. It is absolutely sufficient to create just one number range spanning from 1 to 99999999.

## 5.5 The PP/DS Transactions

Besides the master data maintenance transactions that were touched already when discussing the master data required by PP/DS, there are two groups of user transactions in PP/DS. Group 1 supports primarily the production planning tasks, and group 2 the detailed scheduling tasks. The production planning related tasks can be found in the PP/DS menu structure under "Interactive Planning" and the detailed scheduling tasks under "Detailed Scheduling". The graphic below provides a first overview of the transactions in these areas.

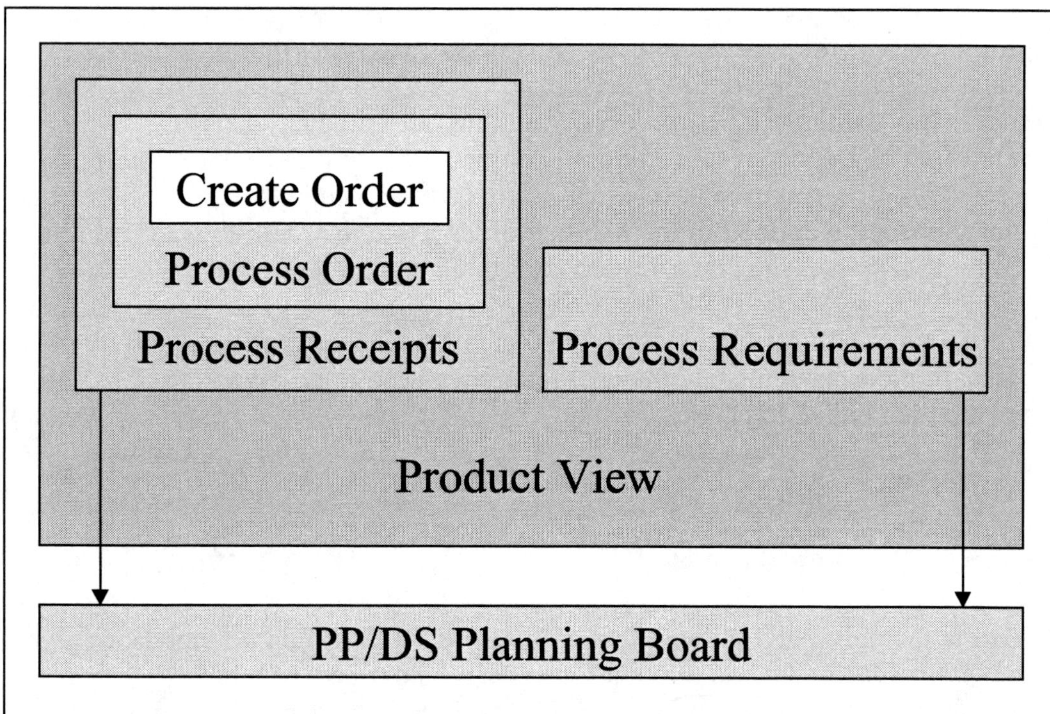


**Graphic 82 – PP/DS Transactions**

Nothing is black and white and, while working with the system, the user will quickly learn to appreciate the usage of Interactive Planning transactions while performing detailed scheduling and vice versa. And even within the transactions, as we will see, there is no strict distinction between these two areas.

The "Create Order" transaction is part of the "Process Order" transaction, which in turn are both incorporated in the "Process Receipts" transaction. The "Process Receipts" as well as the "Process Requirements" transaction have a possibility to jump to the "PP/DS Planning Board" and are both part of the "Product View" transaction. As production planning is usually carried out initially, we will start with this topic.

## 5.5.1 Production Planning Transactions

### 5.5.1.1 Create Order

The "Create Order" transaction can be used to create planned production orders. While these orders are created, a full PPM explosion is carried out in the background and alternate PPM's can be selected. The field "Yield" on the initial screen refers to the planned order quantity. The "Start Date" field is not necessarily the start date of the planned order, but rather the start date for the scheduling activity. The system starts scheduling at the date specified in this field and uses the predefined scheduling strategy. The used strategy profile amongst other settings is stored per user. Once the planned order has been created, the system switches to a planned order detail screen. This is the same screen that can be seen in the "Product View" transactions when selecting planned order details for a receipt element from the Elements tab. It therefore offers the same functionality. See the appropriate chapter for more information.

### 5.5.1.2 Process Order

The "Process Order" transaction allows the display and/or editing of various order types from an OLTP system and of APO originating planned orders. In order to see an external order from an OLTP system, it is necessary to stipulate the Business System Group. When specifying an APO order, the Business System Group is not required but therefore the planning version and the APO order number with leading Zeroes. When processing an APO order, the system switches to a planned order detail screen. This is the same screen that can be seen in the "Product View" transactions when selecting planned order details for a receipt element from the Elements tab. It therefore offers the same functionality. See the appropriate chapter for more information.

### 5.5.1.3 Process Receipts

The "Process Receipts" transaction allows the displaying and/or editing of all receipt elements of the product specified on the initial screen. It is not location specific. Additionally new orders can be easily created. In order to edit or create an order, the screen must be switched over into the Change mode. This opens the fields for date, time, quantity, and location. Any of these fields can then be changed and new lines (orders) can be created. This is a very simple and fast way of creating orders. Orders can also be deleted directly out of the overview screen. Select the appropriate line and press the "Delete" icon on the bottom of the screen. Note that, while the orders are changed, created, or deleted, the scheduling is carried out in the background simultaneously. The scheduling changes can be seen immediately after the new and/or edited orders were saved. Double-click on any order line in the main overview screen (while in Display or Change mode) to switch to a planned order detail screen. This is the same screen that can be seen in the "Product View" transactions when selecting planned order details for a receipt element from the Elements tab. It therefore offers the same functionality, which includes the possibility to delete orders. See the appropriate chapter for more information.

### 5.5.1.4 Process Requirements

The "Process Requirements" transaction allows the displaying of all requirements elements of the product specified on the initial screen. It is not location specific. Although the screen can be put into Change mode, it is obviously not possible to edit and/or delete any requirements (e.g. sales orders or product forecasts). Double-click on any order line in the main overview screen to switch to a planned order detail screen. This is the same screen that can be seen in the "Product View" transactions when selecting planned order details for a requirement element from the Elements tab. It therefore offers the same functionality. See the appropriate chapter for more information.

### 5.5.1.5 Product View

The "Product View" transaction can be called the hub of production planning. All functionality with the exception of the quick creation of planned orders as described in the "Process Receipts" chapter can be performed from here. It is location specific. The initial screen allows the specification of the "Special Stock" assignment. The special stock indicator, or account assignment as it is also called, allows viewing specific customer- or project-dedicated receipts and requirements only. If not specified, all account assignments including those special ones are displayed. Various functions can be initiated from the main screen. Amongst them are the Alert Monitor, the definition of the used strategy profile, and the switch over to the Edit mode. Once the screen is in Change mode, two other functions "Create Order" and "Plan Product" are accessible.



The initial screen offers four tabs dedicated to different areas of information and tasks.

## The Elements Tab

The Elements tab joins the information shown in the Process Requirements and Process Receipts transactions. With some exceptions it offers the same functionality as these two transactions. In this context the word requirements is a synonym for planned order. The functions are:

- Display Requirements
- Drill down on Requirements
- Display Receipts
- Drill down on Receipts
- Edit Receipts
- Delete Receipts
- Create Receipts

It furthermore provides an excellent overview of the planning situation of the product. Per line, which refers to either a requirement or a receipt, the following information can be obtained:

- Requirements / Availability Date and Time
  These two fields indicate the exact time of a requirement or the final receipt time for a planned order.
- Element Category
  This is the ATP category of the displayed order. Stock is handled within APO as another type of order and is also linked to an ATP category.
- Element Number
  This field displays the order number.
- Confirmed Quantity / Yield
- Quantity Alert
  The interpretation of the quantity alert depends on the element type (requirement or receipt) it refers to.
  - Requirement Element
    Green light indicates that one or multiple receipt elements are allocated (pegged) against this requirement. No shortfall exists.
    Amber light is not possible for requirement elements.
    Red light indicates that the total quantity of the planned orders allocated (pegged) to the requirement is not sufficient and, as a result, a shortfall exists. This also applies to situations where no receipt

element at all was pegged to the requirement. An entry exists in the Surplus / Shortfall field.

- Receipt Element

  Green light indicates that the total quantity of the planned order is allocated (pegged) against a requirement. No surplus exists.

  Amber light indicates that part or the whole quantity planned for receipt is not allocated (pegged) against a requirement and, as a result, a surplus exists. An entry exists in the Surplus / Shortfall field.

  Red light is not possible for receipt elements.

- Date Alert

  The interpretation of the date alert also depends on the element type (requirement or receipt) it refers to.

  - Requirement Element

    Green light indicates that no date violation exists. The product requirement is covered in time by an allocated (pegged) receipt.

    Amber light is not possible for requirement elements.

    Red light indicates a date violation. The product receipt allocated (pegged) to the requirement takes place too late for the requirement or no receipt at all is allocated (pegged) to the requirement.

  - Receipt Element

    Green light indicates that no date violation exists. The product receipt is planned to be in time for the requirement it is allocated (pegged) to.

    Amber light indicates that no requirements date can be found. This is the case if no requirement is allocated (pegged) to the receipt.

    Red light indicates a date violation. The product receipt is planned to take place too late for the requirement.

  Note that, while reading the date alerts, it is easy to misinterpret the color settings. The expressions "in time" and "too late" are not a result of the direct comparison of dates and times. If for example a receipt is 10 minutes after the requirement, it is, strictly spoken, too late. If, at the same time, the product master allows in the demand tab receipts to occur up to 60 minutes after the requirement, the system displays "in time" and the green light!

- Requested Quantity

  The requested quantity is shown only in the case of a requirement.

- Surplus / Shortfall

In the case of a requirement, this field shows the shortfall, which is the difference of the requirement quantity and the total of all receipts (if any) allocated (pegged) to the requirement. If the element refers to a receipt, the surplus shows any unallocated (not pegged) quantity of the order. It indicates that this quantity to be received is not required.

- Available Quantity
  The available quantity is a cumulative figure that starting from the initial stock adds receipts and subtracts requirements as defined in the Confirmed Quantity / Yield field. It cannot be derived from the Requested Quantity or Surplus / Shortfall field.
- Unit of Measure
  This is the product's unit of measure.
- Target / Source
  The Target / Source fields indicates the location that is the target or the source of the element. It can be blank for various reasons. One example is that the receipt is from an external supplier that is not part of the supply chain model.
- Resource
  The Resource field depicts in case of a planned production order, the resource from which the final product receipt is to be made. This column can be hidden.



**The Periods Tab**

The Periods tab provides per period the Available Quantity together with the total of Requirements and Receipts. Additionally the Actual Days Supply and the Original Forecast are displayed per period. Periods without planned product movements (Zero Columns) can be hidden.

**The Stock Tab**

The Stock tab displays all stocks of the selected product at all locations. In order to carry stocks at a location, it is required to create the product in the respective location and to link the location product to the supply chain model. This tab contains "display only" information.

**The Product Master Tab**

This tab allows the display of all views (tabs) of the selected product. Note that even if the Product View transaction was set to Change mode, the product master can only be displayed.

Various functions can be initiated from the main screen. Some of them have dedicated buttons, others must be selected via the <Goto> menu point. Note that some of the functions can only be accessed once the product view was switched over to the Change mode. Once the main screen is in Change mode, it cannot be set back to Display mode anymore.

**Plan Product Function**

Once the screen has been put into Change mode, an additional button "Plan Product" appears. The Plan Product function can be compared to a single product single location MRP run. The difference to an MRP run is that the Plan Product function plans both, product and capacity availability simultaneously. The scheduling is carried out according to the parameters specified in the strategy profile. The scheduling changes can be seen immediately after the planning run was carried out and saved. This planning run is carried out in the background automatically for any products that are flagged for "Automatic Planning" in the product master PP/DS tab.

**Push Production Function**

Push production functionality is used in cases where excess receipts of a component were identified by the alert monitor. Excess receipts in this case refer to excess stock and/or planned receipts that cause the alert. In the following explanation we shall use the expression "excess stock" as a synonym for the physical stock and planned receipts. To enable the Push Production function the product view screen must be in Change mode. From there simply select "Goto > Push Production" on the menu bar to start the push production screen. This opens another screen that provides information in four different blocks.

- The Tree Structure on the left side shows all PPM's where the product with the identified excess stock is used as an input product. The PPM's are shown independent of the locations they can be used in. The tree structure can be expanded to show per PPM all product requirements and receipts.

- The Grid Structure on the top right screen displays all receipt elements of the selected product (the product with the excess stock). The excess quantity can be seen in the field "Surplus/Shortfall."
- The List Structure on the middle right screen displays again all PPM's that contain the excess product as an input product and can be used for push production. It also contains the two fields "Desired Quantity" and "Possible Quantity" that will be updated during the Push Production calculation. The Possible Quantity field displays the quantity of the finished product that could be manufactured using the excess stock component element selected in the grid structure on top, taking into consideration all production constraints.
- The Grid Structure on the bottom right screen displays the planning situation of the finished product referring to the PPM that is highlighted in the middle section (just above). This grid is initially empty. To display information, select a product in the tree structure. This screen area is for information purposes only.

To start the Push Production functionality, perform the following steps:

1. Select in the top right grid structure a receipt element that causes the excess stock.
2. Activate the "Copy" button, which will update the "Desired Quantity" and "Possible Quantity" fields in the list structure.
3. In order to change a Desired Quantity, select any line in the list structure. Then activate the "Change Quantity" function. Type in the new Desired Quantity.
4. Select any PPM in the list structure and activate the "Create Order" function. This creates a planned production order for the quantity as defined in the Desired Quantity field. This reduces the surplus quantity shown in the top grid structure and a corresponding new planned order for the finished product is shown in the tree structure.
5. Depending on the required next activity, return to step 1 or 3 for further Push Production activities.
6. Return to the Product View screen and save all created planned orders.



## Drill Down Function on Requirements

This function can be initiated from the Elements tab by double clicking on an element that represents a requirement. The system switches over to the

"Process Order" screen for the selected order. In the tree structure on the left, the system displays information depending on the type of selected requirement element. Further context sensitive drill-down paths are available from there.

- Drill Down on Planned Product
  When drilling down on the planned product, the system opens some kind of a new "Plan Product" window. In this window an additional tab called "Pegging Structure" is displayed. On this tab is a function that allows fixing (unfixing) of a dynamic or fixed pegging relation between the selected requirement and a planned order receipt element. On the same tab, a function "Pegging Alternatives" provides an overview of all possible replenishment elements for the planned product order together with their pegging status (none, dynamic, or fixed). Any of them could be used for pegging to the planned product order. This function is pegging downwards from requirement to receipt element.

From the Process Order screen, a new function button labeled "Context" is visible. When activated, the system switches over to a new screen that displays on the top in table form the requirement element started with on the initial screen. The lower section of the screen provides information in the three tabs "Structure", "Planning Board 1", and "Planning Board 2." The Structure screen shows detailed information related to the requirement element. When selecting the Planning Board 1 screen, the system activates the PP/DS Planning Board transaction and displays the "Network View Orders" chart. The Planning Board 2 screen shows, using the PP/DS Planning Board transaction, the Resource, Product, and Product Stock charts. In both cases the full PP/DS Planning Board functionality, including the Optimizer, is available, and the system can be switched over to full screen mode, hiding the top table like area.

<u>**Drill Down Function on Receipts**</u>

This function can be initiated from the Elements tab by double clicking on an element that represents a receipt. The system switches over to the "Process Order" screen for the selected order. In the tree structure on the left, the system displays information depending on the type of selected receipt element. For a planned production order, information such as the receipt product, the required components, and the operations are shown. Further context sensitive drill-down paths are available from there.

- Drill Down on Planned Product
  When drilling down on the planned product, the system opens again some kind of a "Plan Product" window. In this window two additional tabs are displayed, the Pegging Structure and Alternatives tab. In the Pegging Structure tab, all requirements that are pegged to the planned order are displayed. It allows from there fixing (unfixing) of a dynamic or fixed pegging relation between the planned order and the selected requirement. On the same tab, a function "Pegging Alternatives" provides an overview of all requirement elements of the planned product and their pegging status (none, dynamic, or fixed). Any of them could be used for pegging to the planned order. This function is pegging upwards from receipt to requirement element.
  The "Alternatives" tab provides information about alternate sources for the planned product. This enables the planner to see alternate sources with availability for the same product anywhere in the supply chain model. Any alternate product source is listed with availability date, time, quantity, and cost. Of specific interest is the transportation duration information, which allows a real network view for requirements.
- Drill Down on Component
  When drilling down on a component, the system opens some kind of a new "Plan Product" window. In this window on the Pegging Structure tab is a function that allows fixing (unfixing) of a dynamic (fixed) pegging relation between the planned order (output product) and the selected receipt (component). On the same tab, a function "Pegging Alternatives" provides an overview of all replenishment elements of the component and their pegging status (none, dynamic, or fixed). Any of them could be used for pegging to the planned order. This function is pegging downwards from requirement to receipt element.
- Drill Down on Operations
  The drill down on an operation displays operation specific data such as the used resources and their relationships. The information is display only.
  From the Process Order screen, a new function button labeled "Context" is visible. When activated, the system switches over to a new screen that displays on the top in table form all pegged requirements for the selected receipt element started with on the initial screen. The lower section of the screen provides information in the three tabs "Structure", "Planning Board

1", and "Planning Board 2." The Structure screen shows detailed information related to the planned order (receipt element) of the requirement shown in the upper section. When selecting the Planning Board 1 screen, the system activates the PP/DS Planning Board transaction and displays the "Network View Orders" chart. The Planning Board 2 screen shows, using the PP/DS Planning Board transaction, the Resource, Product, and Product Stock charts. In both cases the full PP/DS Planning Board functionality, including the Optimizer, is available, and the system can be switched over to full screen mode, hiding the top table-like area.

When drilling down on an SNP order, another function named "Convert SNP Order" with a button labeled "Order" is displayed. Activating this button allows an order specific SNP to PP/DS conversion of the selected order. For more information see the chapter "Convert SNP into PP/DS Orders".

## 5.5.2 Detailed Scheduling Transactions

Within the Detailed Scheduling environment, four transactions can be found. They are the "Planning Board Variable View" and the "Planning Board View 1", "-2", and "-3". In all cases the same program, the PP/DS Planning Board, is called. The Planning Board Variable View uses an overall profile, as specified in the transaction itself. When starting the transactions Planning Board View 1, 2, and 3, the program is started with an overall profile as defined in the Own Data of the User Profile. In the user profile, only the profile name is stipulated. When starting any of the Planning Board Views 1, 2, or 3, the system tries to find the profile with the customizing ID that is the logon ID of the user. If no such combination of profile name and customizing ID can be found, the profile without customizing ID is used. If not or the wrong overall profile is linked to the Planning Board View 1, 2, or 3, proceed as follows.

1. Select "System – User Profile – Own Data"
2. Switch over to the Parameters tab
3. Type in the first parameter "/SAPAPO/CDPS_VIEW_1" and select an existing overall profile in the Value field. This can be any fully maintained overall profile.

4. Repeat this step two times for the parameters /SAPAPO/CDPS_VIEW_2 and /SAPAPO/CDPS_VIEW_3 by again specifying the appropriate overall profile.
5. Save the parameters and return to the menu structure.

Note that the parameters cannot be found using the F4 functionality on the parameter field. While in the user parameter maintenance screen, you might also want to set another parameter. The parameter /SAPAPO/CDPS_APPLI determines whether only SNP or PP/DS elements are displayed in the PP/DS Planning Board. Set this parameter to "SNP" to view only SNP-related objects, or to "CDPS" for PP/DS objects. To view both, do not set this parameter at all.

The following chapter refers to the PP/DS Planning Board, and as we have just seen, there is no difference in terms of functionality between the different views of it.

#### 5.5.2.1 PP/DS Planning Board

The PP/DS Planning Board is a graphical, highly configurable screen that displays orders, operations, activities, resources, products, and their relationships. It also offers various interactive functions such as scheduling and optimization. Although it can be found as part of the PP/DS environment, it can display not only PP/DS related objects and transactions but also those of SNP. The PP/DS Planning Board is also referred to as the "Planning Situation for Product".

PP/DS and SNP orders can be displayed. This is defined in the user profile. Depending on the settings in the work area and/or the user profile, all or only selected resources are displayed. Resources that can be made available are:

- Time Continuous Resources
    - Single Activity and Single Mixed Activity
    - Multi Activity and Multi Mixed Activity
- Bucket Resources
    - Single Mixed Activity
    - Multi Mixed Activity
    - Production, Storage, and Handling

- Transport

We were already dealing with the possibilities for changing the graphical appearance of the PP/DS Planning Board in the chapter "Planning Board Profile." Please refer to this chapter for further information. The functions offered in the PP/DS Planning Board enable the user to view the scheduling situation and to change it manually or automatically. Furthermore, the PP/DS optimizer can be started interactively.

The functions in the planning board can be grouped into the four areas of:

- Scheduling Support
- Scheduling Information
- Display Options
- Evaluations

In this chapter we will go through the main functionality offered and through some graphical settings that can be carried out and are not part of the planning board profile. The aim is not to provide a full coverage of all functions, but to rather provide an overview of the multitude of functions offered in the planning board.

## Scheduling Support

Scheduling Support offers various tools that help to resolve scheduling problems due to reasons such as resource overload or internal order as well as pegging relationship violations. All scheduling activities need to be saved before leaving the planning board to become active.

- Manual Functions
  Calling up the strategy window sets the strategy used for manual scheduling activities.
  - Scheduling using Drag and Drop
    Any operation that is displayed in the planning board can be easily rescheduled to another time on the same resource or alternatively to another resource. Rescheduling to alternate resources is only possible if the PPM that was used when creating the order to which the operation belongs has more than one mode defined. In this case the system displays

all possible resources (as defined in the modes) when dragging an operation. The system also automatically updates required setup times in the case where two operations in a sequence have the same setup status. In order for this to work, the PPM's of the two operations must have the setup group (or key) defined and the resource must be linked to a setup matrix that describes the transitions. Operations in the pre- or post-evaluation period can be scheduled into the planning period, but not the other way round.

- Schedule to Non-Working Time
  Operations can be manually scheduled into and out of non-working times. During these non-working times, the scheduler assumes that the resource has the same capacity and restrictions as during normal working times. Operations that are shifted to non-working times are fixed automatically.
- Fix and unfix
  Operations or orders can be manually fixed (firmed) and unfixed. This ensures that no other automatic scheduling activity changes the order or operation anymore. Fixing and unfixing of orders or operations can be done per object or for all objects in a range.
- De-allocate Operations
  De-allocation of operations breaks the link between an operation and the resource it was allocated to. The capacity is then released and can be used by other operations. The de-allocated operation can later again be allocated to this or other resources according to the modes in the PPM. This too, is helpful if some more important operations need to be scheduled first without any other operations being "in the way". Once the important operations have been scheduled, the de-allocated operation can be allocated to a resource again. De-allocated operations can be displayed in a special chart, the so-called "Pool Chart". The pool chart is a special resource chart that needs to be defined in the planning board profile. To allocate an operation again, just drag and drop it onto the resource as required or use other scheduling tools (e.g. the rescheduling function).
- Campaign Planning
  With Campaign Planning, selected orders are bundled together. This functionality is mainly used in process-oriented production environments where the processes potentially run over longer periods. For more information please refer to the chapter "Campaign Planning".

- Master Data Display and Update
  The following master data objects can be maintained starting from the planning board:
  - Product — Display only
  - Resource — Display and Change
  - Order — Display, Change, Create, and Delete
  - Operation — Display only

  Note that any update is carried out in the planning version that was specified when starting the planning board.
- Automated Functions
  The automated functions allow an interactive controlled mass scheduling according to defined rules. Within this group we find the Heuristics methods and the Optimizer.
  - Heuristics
    The PP/DS Heuristics methods, unlike the SNP Heuristics, consider component and capacity constraints at the same time. They are called Heuristics, as they do not optimize the sequence of operations. They merely bring them in a predefined sequence.
    - Remove Backlog
      Often not all orders scheduled for a certain day are actually carried out or finished in time. This creates a backlog of operations in the past that need to be planned for again. Orders in the past can obviously be deleted, but they can also be pushed on the time line further into the future. The remove backlog scheduler uses the strategy settings and pushes operations after the defined earliest start date.
    - Schedule Sequence
      The schedule sequence function allows scheduling operations in a defined sequence (e.g. by order size or requirements date). The definition of this sequence can be found in the strategy profile.

    Both Heuristics methods do not use the standard strategy profiles. It is required to define the parameters for these methods in the PP/DS Planning Board directly using the path "Settings – Heuristics". The settings can be saved selecting "Settings – Save Current Settings".
  - Optimizer

The optimizer allows rescheduling of operations according to various parameters. The overall optimum can be based on more than one parameter. Each parameter is given a weight with which it influences the search for the optimum. The optimizer is explained in detail in the chapter "PP/DS Optimizer".

## Scheduling Information

In order to evaluate the planning situation, various reports and auxiliary functions provide valuable input. The needed information includes:

- Scheduling Log
  Any messages generated by the system during the scheduling activities can be seen in the scheduling log.
- Scheduling Quality
  To view the quality of the current scheduling situation the Scheduling Quality window can be displayed. It offers useful information such as, for example, the total of all setup times or the average resource load.
- Alert Monitor
  The alert monitor can be called for viewing all relevant alerts according to the displayed objects in the planning board. For more information regarding the alert monitor, refer to the appropriate chapter.

## Display Options

To facilitate the work with the planning board, some display options can be set. Note that the display options described here are over and above the functionality described in the planning board profile. They comprise:

- SAP Defined Display Options
  - Dynamic Chart Display
    Charts are defined in the planning board profile as either static or dynamic. A static chart is displayed in the planning board automatically. Dynamic charts need to be activated. Note that of the 8 available charts only the Resource Load, Product Stock, Network View – Orders, and Network View – Operations chart can be activated. Should any of the other charts be defined as "dynamic," then it cannot be displayed at all.

- Multiple Loading
  In some of the charts so-called multiple loading can occur. An example is the product chart where, at a certain point in time, more than one order is scheduled. In this case a red line (predefined by SAP) is displayed under the element (e.g. the order). To break open this line and view all elements, a function called "Edit – Multiple Loading – Expand" can be used.
- Planning Block Display
  Planning blocks are time segments of a resource where only operations with certain defined characteristics can be scheduled (see the chapter "Block Planning"). These blocks can be indicated using the "Extras – Blocks – Display" option.

- Display Settings
  - Time Segment
    The displayed time scale (or visible time segment) can be set to start either with the current date or at a specific date. After selecting a row (for example a resource), the visible time segment can be set to start with either the first or the last graphical element (for example an operation) in the selected row. Zooming in and out can also change the visible time segment.
  - Legend
    The legend provides an overview of all symbols used in the planning board. Once brought up, it displays per chart that is used in the planning board two sections. The upper one provides information about the table section, the lower about the diagram section of the planning board. Double-clicking on a table row or the table row header allows customization of the row display. Graphical elements can also be edited by selecting (double-clicking) them. These activities update the used planning board profile directly.



**Evaluations**

The various evaluations offered by the system are all shown in list format and allow amongst other functions user specific sorting, printing, downloading, and mailing.

- Operation List

This list displays all operations that relate to one or multiple resources, planners, or locations.

- Production Overview
  The production overview provides production quantity information per product based on a multitude of different selection parameters.
- Resource Load
  The resource load displays accumulated per freely-definable period the available and used capacity as well as the percentage load.
- WIP List
  The Work-In-Process (WIP) list displays stocks of components that are waiting for further processing. The waiting stocks can be evaluated within an order (WIP list) or between orders (WIP network list).

## 5.6 Authorization Management

New with release 2.0 was the introduction of Authorization Management. Authorization objects allow the execution of specific functions in APO. Some of them are module dependent; other general ones are used throughout APO. The PP/DS related authorization objects listed in the following table.

| Area | Authorization Object | Object Name | Object Description |
|---|---|---|---|
| PP/DS | | | |
| | C_APO_RELO | PP/DS, Resource Reservations | |
| | | | Allows to display or change the resource reservation in the scheduling table |
| | C_APO_MALO | PP/DS, Requirements/Stock Situation | |
| | | | Allows to display or change particular products in the stock situation |
| | C_APO_PPDS | PP/DS, Propagation Area | |
| | | | Allows the display or update of the propagation area |

**Table 87 – PP/DS Authorization Objects**

The general authorization objects are included in the DP section in the chapter Authorization Management.

# 5.7 PP/DS Guides

When setting up APO as a stand-alone system for development purposes, it is of hindrance that no transactions such as sales orders can be transferred from the OLTP system. This can be overcome by using a non-documented utility program capable of creating orders of various order types. Furthermore, it is possible to delete orders of any order type with another non-documented utility program. In both cases data is only created or deleted in liveCache. The usage of both utilities must be strictly avoided in an environment where APO is linked to an OLTP system as otherwise the systems get out of sync.

To create sales orders start transaction "SE38", specify the program name "/SAPAPO/SJKTST01" and select <Execute>. On the upcoming screen, the following data can be captured:

- Version
  This is the SNP version in which the sales order will be created.
- Location
  Select the location in which the sales order will be created.
- Category
  Each order has an ATP category. Define here the ATP category of the sales order that needs to be created. "BM" is for sales orders.
- Product
  Specify the product number of the sales order. Note that only single product sales orders can be created with this program.
- Date
  This is the date of the sales order transaction.
- Horizon
  Be careful with this field! It stipulates the number of identical sales orders that this program creates when executed.
- Quantity
  Stipulate the sales order quantity.

Select the radio button "CUST (Cat: BM)" to create a sales order and leave all other fields blank. Finally select <Execute> to create the sales order.

To delete orders of any order type start the transaction “SE38”, specify the program name “/SAPAPO/RLCDELETE” and select <Execute>. On the upcoming screen following data can be captured:

- Version
  This is the SNP version in which the orders have to be deleted. The version is the only mandatory field. If all other fields are left blank <u>all</u> orders in the planning version will be deleted.
- Category
  Each order has an ATP category. Select here, if required, only a certain category or category range.
- Product
  Specify selected products for which orders have to be deleted.
- Location
  Select locations in which orders have to be deleted.
- Period
  Stipulate a time period in which orders have to be deleted.

Make sure all parameters are defined correctly and select <Execute>.

# 6 APO Implementation

APO is specifically of advantage for companies that face one of the following environments:

- Multiple plants
  APO provides the tools required for balancing production over various plants, thereby coordinating the single plant activities. This is achieved mainly in SNP.
- Distribution Network
  Optimal sourcing decisions as well as planning of transportation activities is supported by APO in a much better way than for example in R/3. Flexible definitions and integration of suppliers and customers in the supply network support this task.
- Customer and Consumer
  APO supports Vendor Managed Inventory, which becomes more and more common in the Consumer Packaged Goods (CPG) environment. It therefore allows streamlining the entire supply chain process from supplier over manufacturer through to customer and consumer.
- Distributed Systems
  Often various stand-alone systems need to be linked to allow a global view on stocks and other supply elements. This is the domain of Global ATP. It allows an efficient check with rapid response.

What are the options when implementing APO; install all or nothing? Or are there are other possible reasonable scenarios?

<u>Start with Demand Planning (DP)</u>

Demand Planning is the first step in Supply Chain Management. It can be carried out in R/3 using the "Flexible Planning" functionality. This task could also be carried out in APO and results then can be transferred back to R/3. As of release 2.0, the forecast generated in APO Demand Planning can be given back to R/3 where Independent Requirements will be created based on the forecast. This is a feasible option, as not too much master data needs to be set up in APO to use

Demand Planning functionality. It allows using the advanced functionality in APO, but leaves all other functionality on R/3. This should only be an interim step, as APO provides the user, specifically in the SNP and PP/DS area, much more and sophisticated functionality compared to that offered in R/3. As only standard interfaces are used, this option is a viable option for a phased implementation of APO.

Start with Global Available-to-Promise (G-ATP)

Global ATP is partially interwoven with SNP and requires PP/DS when using the CTP (Capable-to-Promise) functionality. DP has no link to Global ATP, although Global ATP uses InfoCubes to store Product Allocation data. Global ATP could be implemented without using the SNP module. The usage of PP/DS is only really feasible if the SNP module is used. Based on that, CTP functionality cannot be deployed in such a scenario. Depending on whether Demand Planning is used or not at the same time, Product Allocations can be used or not. In an environment where the emphasis is on introducing product availability checks based on existing supplies, it is sensitive to introduce Global ATP on its own.

Start with Supply Network Planning (SNP)

Supply Network Planning is the logical follow up of the Demand Planning step. In Demand Planning an unconstrained long-term forecast is generated, which is then followed up by SNP to create a constrained mid term plan. As such, SNP could run without having DP implemented. The hand-over of data between these two modules is not too complicated. Nevertheless, there are no standard interfaces from an external system into SNP, which would transfer the forecast data and generate independent requirements in SNP. Starting with SNP as a transition, therefore, does not make too much sense and might become a difficult scenario. If the decision is made to use SNP, DP should go in at the same time (if not earlier). PP/DS is sort of a follow up function on SNP that might, but does not have to, be implemented at the same time. The mid-term SNP planning results can be transmitted back the OLTP system for further processing.

Start with Production Planning/Detailed Scheduling (PP/DS)

At a first glance, PP/DS seems to be highly interwoven with SNP and should therefore not be considered to be the first step in an APO implementation. But when investigating the situation further it becomes clear that PP/DS could also work on its own. This is particularly the case for business scenarios where the main emphasis is not on the network planning and optimization, but rather on the single plant production planning. PP/DS requires a tight link with the OLTP system as planned production orders are scheduled in APO, but also accessed by the OLTP system during the production process. SAP provides standard interfaces to accomplish this task.

Conclusion

From a practical point of view I see only two possible scenarios for a phased or partial implementation of APO.

Option 1 for multi plant and distributed systems
1. Start with DP
2. Add SNP and possibly PP/DS
3. Add PP/DS if it was not part of step 2

Global ATP can be introduced together with DP or with PP/DS.

Option 2 for single plant (no distribution network) systems
1. Start with DP
2. Add PP/DS

Global ATP should not be of major importance in this environment, but can be introduced together with DP or with PP/DS.

# 7 Outlook into the APO Future

As APO is a rather new product on the market, lots of new functions are added virtually every month. Specifically with release 3.0, if not earlier, a whole lot of new functions will be available. There seems to be still some discussion about the numbering of the upcoming release, but it appears that a new release 3.0 will be launched in about July '00. The difference between release 1.1 to 2.0 was primarily the quality of the system; from 2.0 to 3.0 we will see a real transformation in terms of offered functionality. Besides a more stable system, release 2.0 also offered for the first time a Graphical User Interface (GUI) based on the "SAP Enjoy" initiative. This GUI is based on the same principles as the R/3 release 4.6. On top of this, another initiative was started to further enhance the user friendliness of APO. This initiative is referred to as the "Cooper" design.

The following chapters provide an overview of current developments that will be incorporated into release 3.0 or maybe even earlier as an addition to release 2.0.

## 7.1 Network Design

The supply network consists of locations that represent manufacturing plants, distribution centers, vendors, or suppliers as well as the transportation lanes connecting these locations. The network is built up using the Supply Chain Engineer. There also the master data, which consists of locations, products, resources, and production process models, are allocated to the locations. This is all a manual task and based on decisions outside of APO. Currently APO can only be used to build a model of what has been decided somewhere else.

Network Design will change this and provide the user with strategic help by providing not only useful information (which APO does partially already today) but also by optimizing supply network parameters based on user defined criteria.

## 7.1.1 Planning Methods

In order to efficiently plan and optimize the supply network, two different planning methods are offered. The first method of Network Design will offer the following analytical tools:

- Assignment of Products to Locations
- Demand Supply Comparison per Location
- Evaluation of Capacity Requirements
- Total Cost of the Supply Network

All this information is based on a currently defined supply network, which could be the active or a simulation model. It provides valuable data to understand the network and as well for optimizing it. Based on this information, the system provides different planning methods. They are Assignment of Products based on:

- Geographical Distance
- Minimal Cost considering Capacities
- Minimal Cost not considering Capacities

Optimization of locations is the other area of Network Design that provides suggestions and decision support for the following tasks.

- Geographical Placement of new Locations
- Optimum Number of Locations in the Supply Network
- Closure of existing Locations

The aim of this part of Network Design is to establish the best-fit supply network. Unlike the first planning method, the system works out recommendations for closing or adding locations as required. The location network can be optimized based on:

- Preset Number of Locations and Geographical Distance
- Minimal Cost Placement of new Locations
- Minimal Cost Usage of existing Locations

## 7.1.2 Data Input

In both planning modes the optimization is based on data stored in APO. This data is the live data used for the ongoing processing or data of potential locations and transportation lanes. Network Design deals solely with the supply network and is <u>not</u> a tool to optimize the product mix. Therefore the data used for optimization is the following.

- Planning Horizon and Demand
  Optimization is based on the demand in the planning horizon for a given range of products. Products as such are not a variable in Network Design. The demand is taken from Demand Planning. Either the active version or any planning version can be used.
- Supply Chain Network
  The supply chain network comprises existing and potential locations and transportation lanes as well as products. Locations include manufacturing plants, distribution centers, vendors, and suppliers.
- Capacities
  These are the existing and potential production, transportation, storage, and handling capacities.
- Costs
  The production, transportation, handling and inventory costs are the costs that can be normally found in APO. In addition to these costs, it is possible to define per location:
  - Fixed Periodical Costs
  - Once off Closing Down Costs
  - Once off Opening Up Costs
  - Obtainable Subsidies

## <u>7.1.3 Data Output</u>

The output of the planning depends on the selected-planning method and comprises the following information:

- Selected and Obsolete Locations
  Here all locations that are required in the supply network are shown alongside with those that can be closed.
- New Locations with Geographical Positioning

If new locations are required, the system will suggest so while specifying their optimal geographical position.

- Product/Location Assignment
  Not all products might be required at all locations. The optimal allocation will show what needs to be manufactured and/or stored in which location.
- Product/Transportation Lane Assignment and Usage
  Used transportation lanes are shown with their respective product assignments.
- Product Quantity Load of Supply Network
  This output delivers a quantitative view on the supply network.
- Capacity Usage in Supply Network
  The capacity usage reveals the anticipated utilization of resources and might provide useful information for further streamlining.
- Total Cost of Proposed Supply Network
  The total cost of the entire supply network is calculated and displayed. This is helpful to compare various network designs when performing a What-If analysis. Costs are broken down into several components (e.g. production and transportation costs).

Over and above the current planning for Network Design, some further possible enhancements are the inclusion of the maximum transportation duration, consideration of different transportation modes, and the adoption of capacity constraints.

## 7.2 Transportation Planning & Vehicle Scheduling

In the area of Transportation Planning and Vehicle Scheduling (TP/VS), important new functionality was announced by SAP already in mid-July 1999. Extended Transportation Planning and Vehicle Scheduling functionality will be available for the first pilot customers in February ’00 with general availability planned for July ’00. This is overdue, as Transportation Scheduling is core functionality within the Supply Chain Management. APO then not only offers planning but also an extended set of optimization tools in this area. The TP/VS component is utilizing the ILOG Dispatcher software. It will allow simultaneous planning of inbound and outbound shipments as well as intra-company movements. Transportation Planning is long-term oriented, and Vehicle Scheduling is short-term oriented. TP/VS will be tightly integrated with the R/3 Logistics Execution System (LES). LES consists primarily of the well-known Warehouse Management (WM), the shipping functionality of the R/3 Sales and Distribution (SD) module as well as the relatively new Shipment Costing module in R/3. Shipment Costing will include Freight Procurement thus enabling accurate measurement of actual shipment costs. Tracking of shipments is another new functionality of LES. New APO functionality can be found in the following areas:

- Shipment Planning and Freight Consolidation
  Plan and consolidate freights across business boundaries.
- Selection of Transport Mode and Carrier
  These two tasks go hand in hand as for each required transport a comparison of feasible transport modes (e.g. truck or courier) needs to be performed taking into account the different cost and duration. Even for the same transport mode, costs can be different which requires carrier selection as an integrated task.
- Negotiation of contracts, volumes, quotas, schedules and features of the supply network
  Base contracts on estimated volumes based on APO simulation runs.
- Static or Dynamic Organization of Routes
  Apply routes in a dynamic way taking advantage of the best route at a time instead of a fixed route definition.
- Multi-pick and Multi-drop Capabilities
  Specifically for the Consumer Packaged Goods industry, picking and dropping products at various points is a requirement as shipped quantities to or from a specific point can be rather small. In this scenario not only the consolidation of small quantities but also the sequencing are of utmost importance.
- Round-trip Capabilities
  Planning for Round-trips is a key function to reduce transportation cost, as carriers are confronted with high costs for empty return trips and usually charge a substantially lower price per trip if both directions are used productively. Applications are the coordination of inbound and outbound

transport activities as well as the optimization of intra-company transport activities.

- Fleet Sizing and Management
  Estimate fleet sizes and their usage, thus managing it better and more efficient.

Unlike some other transportation planning software packages available on the market, the APO TP/VS module not only plans the short-term activities, but also is an integrated function through all planning steps. TP/VS offers transportation planning focused on forecasts and orders. Based on the long-term Demand Plan, an initial transportation forecast can be carried out determining carrier and transportation mode requirements. Together with the mid-term SNP plan, specific capacity constraints can be taken into consideration exceeding the basic transportation capacity planning offered with APO release 2.0. The short-term deployment plan will benefit through an enhanced integration of inbound and outbound processes as well as the planning of round trips. Required transportation capacities can be offered via the Internet (Carrier Tendering) and carrier rates and offers can be accessed via the Internet. All transactions in TP/VS will be Internet-enabled to allow for easy remote usage of this module.

## 7.3 Collaborative Planning

As the first real Internet enabled component, Collaborative Planning will have its General Availability (GA) in February 2000. Collaborative Planning is the functional name of a whole lot of Internet enabled planning tools used in Demand Planning. Collaborative Planning is not a function that can be used also via the Internet; it actually requires it. The functionality of Collaborative Planning is identical with that of the Demand Planning function, which is forecasting. The difference is that this planning is carried out involving various partners that could be within the company or external. Specifically for the external partners, the planning tools were simplified and web enabled. As a result of this effort, easier to handle screens (HTML pages) are provided to the user who only needs an Internet browser and not the SAP APO GUI on his or her PC.

Collaborative Planning is a joined planning effort of anticipated sales or, in other words, the sales forecast. The forecast data is stored in the InfoCube and can be accessed using the normal non web-enabled transactions or the new web-enabled tools. It is important to understand that collaborative planning is a planning approach and not an alternative forecast. Any data can be maintained using the web-enabled or the non web-enabled tools. The Collaboration Engine, which consists of the specific web-enabled functionality to support the Collaborative Planning, consists of the following elements.

- Planning Book Designer
  The planning book designer is used to create the planning book used in the collaborative planning process. At the end of the planning book definition, it generates the HTML pages that can be accessed via the Internet.
- Planning Book
  The planning book used in Collaborative Planning is a streamlined version of the normal planning book, concentrating on those tasks that need to be performed by an exterior planning partner. Its appearance is similar to that of the normal planning book. The selection of data is improved and only such selection ID's that are relevant to the specific planner are displayed. The selection ID can also be used to predefine a certain set of activities with the sequences in which they have to be carried out. As each activity has a status precondition, even the inexperienced user cannot miss a single step.
- Alert Monitor
  The alert monitor provides the user with alerts related only to the data that is available for planning. Alerts are grouped and can be filtered according to different parameters.
- Enhanced Macros
  Specific macro functions are added for the use in Collaborative Planning. Macros can either be run automatically (e.g. after every update), or manually.
- Administration Component
  The administration component is used to define the data access rights (who can see what) as well as how the data is presented. It is also possible to define a collaboration flow. In this flow certain sequences for the planning steps can be predefined. This is helpful if for example a forecast has to be checked and possibly updated by various partners in a given sequence. Creating activity profiles that are then linked to collaboration partners is part of the administration maintenance. In this way the same profile can be linked to

several partners and a given partner can be attached to several activity profiles. The principle used here is similar to that of authorization management.

# 7.4 Optimization Extension Workbench

A new development in the SNP area is the Optimization Extension Workbench (APX). It will be available in May '00 with a first set of BAPI's. In order to optimize the production or distribution of products, APO offers various optimizers that are based on commonly accepted standards and on common requirements. These optimizers are usually sourced from a company called ILOG that is specialized in the optimization and visualization of data. They are seamlessly plugged into APO. Optimizers are mostly written in C++ and not in ABAP. Compared to applications written in ABAP, these C++ programs are less customizable. At the same time, it is more expensive to write C++ than ABAP programs.

Quite often, optimizing is dependent on very specific business requirements. The APO optimizers do not meet these specific business requirements as they are written to cope with standard problems. In such cases it will be possible in the future to plug in special optimizers that were either developed by the client or by another software vendor (e.g. ILOG). This functionality is also referred to as "Plug and Plan". Possible users for APX will be clients with already existing optimizers that will be adapted to run in an APO environment and clients that require specific optimizers to suit their needs.

Usually one can find situations where a multi-level optimization is carried out. An example would be that in step one the standard APO SNP optimizer is used to plan the overall distribution plan and to make "buy or produce" decisions. Once this is done, the APO PP/DS optimizer is used to schedule operations across all resources, maintaining the order of internal relations. This is the Initial PP/DS Optimization. In a third step, it might then be required to optimize a specific resource, as the standard optimizer cannot use some constraints, the custom optimizer uses. This is the PP/DS Repair Optimization. When using more than one optimizer for the same problem (on different levels of detail) it is necessary to firm some of the created planned orders that were created by the first optimization run. The second optimization can then run within this framework of planned orders and optimize further, but without changing the framework. Otherwise a competition of optimizers may start that can easily result in a never-ending loop.

The approach of sequential optimizing does most probably not lead to the overall optimum. But it might be the best solution, as an overall optimum cannot be found due to the complexity of the problem. Optimizing is always a balance between what is theoretically possible and practically feasible.

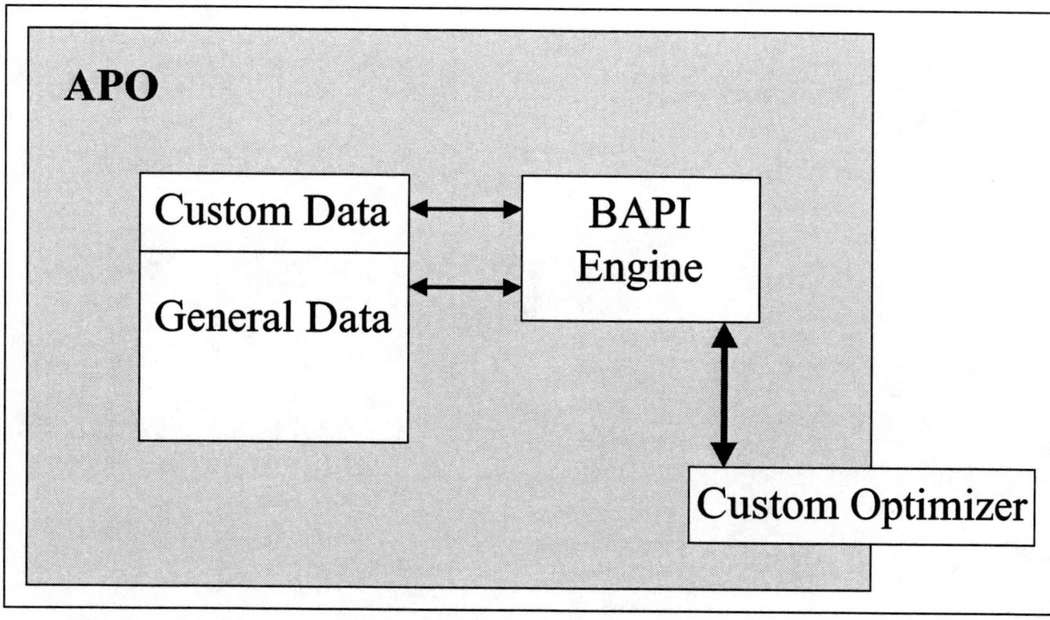


**Graphic 83 – Optimization Extension Workbench**

From a system point of view, APX provides an interface between the APO database and the external optimizer. APX makes available all data required by the external optimizer. It will also take back any changed master data and/or transaction data to update APO. Data can be from any source such as table-based, time series or liveCache data. In cases where a custom optimizer requires additional master data, the APO database will be extended and the above-described principle applied. Communication between APO and the custom optimizer is via BAPI's. It is intended to start the custom optimizers from the standard APO screens (e.g. the PP/DS Planning Table). The graphic above gives an overview.

In a consequent step, ILOG plans to market their development environment called ODF to clients who wish to develop their own APO Extension Modules (optimizers). Interested clients will then be in a position to develop their own programs.

# 8 Indices

## 8.1 Index of Graphics

# 8.2 Index of Tables